THE AMERICAN SHORT STORY IN THE TWENTIES

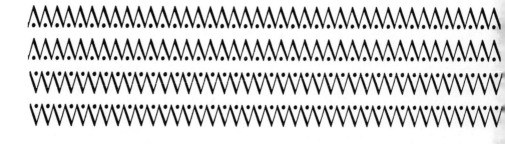

THE AMERICAN SHORT STORY

Austin McGiffert Wright

IN THE TWENTIES

THE UNIVERSITY OF CHICAGO PRESS

The University of Chicago Press, Chicago 37
The University of Toronto Press, Toronto 5, Canada
© 1961 by The University of Chicago. Published 1961
Composed and printed in the U.S.A.

To K. M. W. and J. K. W.

ACKNOWLEDGMENTS

My first debt is to the writers of those short stories that have given me pleasure and provided me with my subject. Without them there could have been no book. The same might also be said, however, of many individuals — especially former teachers of mine at the University of Chicago — my indebtedness to whom is not so obvious in the text. I owe much to Dean Napier Wilt, who, besides steering my curiosity about the inner workings of the art of fiction, was most directly responsible for putting me on the track of the particular problem that grew into this book. I owe much also to Professor Ronald S. Crane, whose teaching has helped me to find and understand the principles of criticism and analysis that I employ in this book. I do not mean to suggest that this book is simply an application of Crane's principles of criticism, but what he has taught, both formally and informally, has helped me to solve many difficult problems of analysis.

Professor Walter Blair has been familiar with this project from the time of its conception. By asking me questions and by making positive suggestions, he did much to open my eyes to the ways in which my problem must be limited, to the kind of inquiry that would be most fruitful, to the kind of evidence that would be most valuable, to the kind of presentation that would be most clear. An adequate expression of my indebtedness to him is impossible, as it is also to Professor Richard G. Stern, whose critical comments on the text have been extremely useful and who has helped me in other pertinent ways with a warmth and generosity that neither footnotes nor a note under Acknowledgments can do justice to.

Many friends in conversations and discussions — at lunch, while driving to work, in department offices — have given me insights that, developing most casually, have turned out to be useful. They cannot all be named, but four of my former colleagues at Wright Junior College — James Schroeter, Sumner Scott, Kenneth Telford, and Donald G. Thompson — have helped to sharpen my understanding of critical problems in ways that this book reflects, and a fifth, Walter Blinstrub, has in addition given me detailed criticism of the Introduction.

I am most grateful to those who read the manuscript critically in its various stages of imperfection. These include Mr. Blair and Mr. Stern, both of whom have endured several revisions, and Mr. John K. Wright, formerly of the American Geographical Society, who volunteered, when I was about to send the book to the publisher, to go through the entire manuscript with his skilled editorial pencil, doing much to make it more lucid and stylistically more pleasant. I mention him with a special pleasure because he is my father.

I am grateful to the publishers and individuals listed below for permission to quote from the following copyrighted works: Evelyn May Albright, *The Short Story: Its Principles and Structure*, by permission of The Macmillan Company. Copyright, 1931, by The Macmillan Company.

John W. Aldridge, *In Search of Heresy: American Literature in an Age of Conformity*, published by McGraw-Hill Book Company, by permission of the author. Copyright, 1956, by John W. Aldridge.

Sherwood Anderson, *The Triumph of the Egg*, published by B. W. Huebsch, Inc., by permission of Harold Ober Associates, Inc. Copyright, 1921, by Eleanor Anderson. *Winesburg, Ohio*, by permission of The Viking Press. Copyright, 1919.

Henry Seidel Canby, *The Short Story in English*, by permission of Holt, Rinehart and Winston, Inc. Copyright, 1902, by Henry Holt and Company.

Willa Cather, *Youth and the Bright Medusa*, by permission of Alfred A. Knopf. Copyright, 1920, by Alfred A. Knopf.

Malcolm Cowley, *Writers at Work: The Paris Review Interviews*, by permission of The Viking Press, Inc. Copyright, 1958, by the *Paris Review*, Inc. *The Portable Hemingway*, edited and with an introduction by Malcolm Cowley, by permission of The Viking Press, Inc. Copyright, 1944, The Viking Press.

Stephen Crane, *Stephen Crane: An Omnibus*, edited by Robert W. Stallman, by permission of Alfred A. Knopf. Copyright, 1952, by Alfred A. Knopf.

William Faulkner, *Collected Stories of William Faulkner*, by permission of Random House. Copyright, 1950, Random House.

F. Scott Fitzgerald, "Winter Dreams" (copyright, 1922, by Frances Scott Fitzgerald Lanahan; renewal copyright, 1950), "Absolution" (copyright, 1924, *American Mercury*, Inc.; renewal copyright, 1952, by Frances Scott Fitzgerald Lanahan), "The 'Sensible Thing'" (copyright, 1924, Colorato Corporation; renewal copyright, 1952, by Frances Scott Fitzgerald Lanahan), "The Rich Boy" (copyright, 1925, by Consolidated Magazine Corporation; renewal copyright, 1953, 1954, by Frances Scott Fitzgerald Lanahan), from *All the Sad Young Men*, by permission of Charles Scribner's Sons. "The Rough Crossing" (copyright, 1929, by Curtis Publishing Company; renewal copyright, © 1957, by Curtis Publishing Company and Frances Scott Fitzgerald Lanahan), from *The Stories of F. Scott Fitzgerald*, edited by Malcolm Cowley, by permission of Charles Scribner's Sons.

Hamlin Garland, *Main-Travelled Roads*, published by Harper and Brothers, by permission of Constance Garland Doyle and Isabel Garland Lord. Copyright, 1899, by Harper and Brothers.

Katharine Fullerton Gerould, *The Great Tradition and Other Stories*, by permission of Charles Scribner's Sons. Copyright, 1915, by Charles Scribner's Sons.

Carl H. Grabo, *The Art of the Short Story*, by permission of Charles Scribner's Sons. Copyright, 1913, by Charles Scribner's Sons.

Ernest Hemingway, "Big Two-Hearted River," "Cross-Country Snow," "The Doctor and the Doctor's Wife," "The End of Something," "Indian Camp," "My Old Man," "Soldier's Home," "The Three-Day Blow," from *In Our Time*, by permission of Charles Scribner's Sons. Copyright, 1925, by Charles Scribner's Sons; renewal copyright, 1953, by Ernest Hemingway. Introduction by Edmund Wilson to *In Our Time*, by permission of Charles Scribner's Sons. Copyright, 1930, by Charles Scribner's Sons; renewal copyright, © 1958, by Ernest Hemingway. "An Alpine Idyll," "Hills Like White Elephants," "In Another Country," "The Killers," "Now I Lay Me," "A Simple Enquiry," "Ten Indians," "The Undefeated," from *Men Without Women*, by permission of Charles Scribner's Sons. Copyright, 1927, by Charles Scribner's Sons; renewal copyright, © 1955, by Ernest Hemingway. *Death in the Afternoon*, by permission of Charles Scribner's Sons. Copyright, 1932, by Charles Scribner's Sons; renewal copyright, © 1960, by Ernest Hemingway.

Frederick J. Hoffman, *Freudianism and the Literary Mind*, by permission of Louisiana State University Press. Copyright, 1945, by Louisiana State University Press.

Henry James, "The Tree of Knowledge," "Brooksmith," "Greville Fane," from *The Novels and Tales of Henry James* (New York Edition), published by Charles Scribner's Sons, by permission of Paul R. Reynolds and Son. Copyright, 1907–9, by Charles Scribner's Sons. *The Middle Years*, by permission of Charles Scribner's Sons. Copyright, 1917, by Charles Scribner's Sons; renewal copyright, 1945. "Flickerbridge" and "The Beldonald Holbein" from *The Better Sort*, by permission of Charles Scribner's Sons. Copyright, 1903, Charles Scribner's Sons. *The Art of the Novel*, by permission of Charles Scribner's Sons. Copyright, 1934, by Charles Scribner's Sons.

Edward O'Brien, *The Advance of the American Short Story*, reprinted by permission of Dodd, Mead & Company. Copyright, 1923, by Dodd, Mead & Company, Inc.

Séan O'Faoláin, *The Short Story*, published by William Collins Sons & Company, by permission of Séan O'Faoláin. Copyright, 1948, by Séan O'Faoláin.

Katherine Anne Porter, *Flowering Judas and Other Stories*, by permission of Harcourt, Brace & World, Inc. Copyright, 1935, by Harcourt, Brace & Co., Inc. *The Days Before*, by permission of Harcourt, Brace & World, Inc. Copyright, 1952, by Harcourt, Brace & Co., Inc.

C. Alphonso Smith, *The American Short Story*, by permission of Ginn and Company. Copyright, 1912, by Ginn and Company.

Ray B. West, Jr., *The Short Story in America: 1900–1950*, by permission of Henry Regnery Company. Copyright, 1952, by Henry Regnery Company.

Edith Wharton, *Xingu and Other Stories*, published by Charles Scribner's Sons, by permission of A. Watkins, Inc. © 1916, by Edith Wharton. *The Descent of Man and Other Stories*, by permission of Charles Scribner's Sons. Copyright, 1905, by Charles Scribner's Sons.

TABLE OF CONTENTS

◇◇

INTRODUCTION

◇◇◇

The most a critic can ever do is pay tribute to the work of writers. He can do this directly and positively with praise of those he admires or negatively by disparaging their inferior rivals. Or he may do it simply by describing, as dispassionately and exactly as he can, what it is that he thinks writers have done.

Since this book is a critical-historical examination of what certain writers appear to have done, it constitutes a tribute of the latter kind. It springs from an original curiosity about the kind of short story commonly called "modern" — the kind one finds in the collections of Hemingway and Faulkner, in Katherine Mansfield's *The Garden Party* and Katherine Anne Porter's *Flowering Judas* — that branch of the art whose ancestry is traced by most literary genealogists to Joyce and Chekhov. But since such writers, known to everybody, hardly need the tribute

1

of direct praise in 1961 — since I prefer to give them the quieter tribute of analytical study, this study will have to be limited to the work of just a few of them, some few standing in a prominent position near the center of the group, at a point in time when the "modern movement" achieved full maturity and covered itself with glory. The specific tribute which this study consti- tutes is directed to five American writers of the 1920's — to Sher- wood Anderson, F. Scott Fitzgerald, Hemingway, Faulkner, and Miss Porter — five who perfected the forms of the modern short story in America, who stand at the top of the list in what has been called the American short story's "most brilliant period."

The tribute which, in the following pages, I have tried to pay to these writers is the determination and description of what happened to the art of the American short story in their hands. That they did something to this art, that it was not quite the same art when they used it that it had been in the hands of others, is obvious to every reader familiar with the history of the American short story. That what they did is important and worth studying is also evident, for several reasons. It is worth studying, in the first place, because the stories they wrote are masterpieces, and masterpieces are always worth studying. Con- fronted by a masterpiece, the critic of inquiring mind always feels a challenge, just as the scientist does when confronted by the mysteries of nature. Knowing that he cannot "explain" the masterpiece, but believing that the ideal, the perfect human mind could, he wants to go as far as he can in pursuit of the aesthetic laws which the writer has intuitively perceived and employed and to which we have all responded.

What these writers do with short-story art is worth studying, in the second place, because it is so close to what the other major artists in the modern tradition are doing. This is something that all of us recognize through our feelings when we read these stories and the stories of others, and we acknowledge it when- ever we remark, for example, that a perfectly good American story of 1907 or 1910 seems "somewhat dated," whereas another, published in 1919, does not. Why is it that the stories of *Wines- burg, Ohio*, published over forty years ago, still do not seem dated in the manner of the stories of Garland's *Main-Travelled*

Roads? Why is it that *Dubliners*, written during the first decade of this century, still seems to us in 1961 contemporary, whereas stories written by Edith Wharton in the same period do not? What is the family kinship that we recognize between the stories of Joyce, Miss Mansfield, Hemingway, Anderson, Miss Porter, and the writers of the present age, enabling us to say at once, whenever we read a story by Mary Wilkins Freeman, Katharine Fullerton Gerould, or Wilbur Daniel Steele, "This is of a different family"? Although studying the five major writers of the twenties will not enable us to describe the features of the whole modern family in all its branches, it may illuminate some of them.

Third, what they do is worth studying because of what such a study can contribute to our appreciation and enjoyment of all short stories. It is not that the modern stories are so much better than earlier stories — they have, I believe, sacrificed some kinds of things that were good in the art of the earlier stories, as will be seen. It is, rather, that as they employ a different art they imply a different conception as to what a short story is or can be. Such differences in conception are of concern to us because our response to a story depends so much on what we know of the tradition of which the story is a part — and from which it deviates in its own original way.

Yet such benefits, such "broader implications," were never expected to be more than by-products, incidental fruits and rewards, of the study that I originally planned to undertake. The object was not intended to be the modern short story in general or even the American short story of the twenties in general but, rather, one significant turning point in the history of the American short story, a point at which one tradition of short-story art (perhaps one should say a complex of traditions), a tradition that had been dominant for many years, attracting the best writers and the applause of critics, yielded its dominance to a new tradition which attracted in its turn the best writers of a new generation and won the applause of a new generation of critics.

The short story as a major literary genre was still young when the new generation of the twenties burst upon the scene and reshaped it to their ends. Growing throughout the nine-teenth century, it did not reach the maturity of serious critical recognition in its own right until almost the end of the century, by which time it was flourishing in magazines, appearing in col-lections, and offering itself to major writers, many of whom had long since given it the stamp of their genius. Now, in the first decade of the twentieth century, critics began to insist that the short story was not simply a piece of short fiction but had devel-oped an identity and principles of its own that should be dis-tinguished from other kinds of short prose fiction such as the "tale" or "sketch." Trying to indicate its special nature by calling it the "short-story" or the "Short Story," they wrote textbooks about its techniques and treatises on its philosophy and prin-ciples, and they worked out its history. They acknowledged Poe and Hawthorne as its most significant ancestors, gave credit to Washington Irving, and traced its remoter ancestry to the begin-nings of English literature, without finding in the earliest fore-bears the artistic respectability of the latest descendants. Among these latest descendants they singled out for honors in England and America (with, of course, some disagreements as to their relative merits) such writers as Kipling, Stevenson, Garland, O. Henry, and sometimes James.

Even in the midst of this critical enthusiasm, however, there were signs of stagnation. As early as 1909, complaints were heard about the growing artificiality in the genre (see below, p. 22). These complaints continued and grew louder, even as popular enthusiasm reached a point where not one but two annual collections of "best" stories could be inaugurated.[1] Later critics have seen in the first two decades of this century a quies-cent period in the development of the short story, in which production was inferior to that of the nineties.

The beginning of the new development of the twenties is commonly associated with the publication of Anderson's *Wines-*

---

[1] Edward J. O'Brien (ed.), *The Best Short Stories of 1915 and the Yearbook of the American Short Story* (Boston: Small, Maynard & Co., 1916).

Society of Arts and Sciences (eds.), *O. Henry Memorial Award Prize Stories: 1919*, introduction by Blanche Colton Williams (Garden City, N. Y.: Double-day, Page & Co., 1920).

Each of these volumes initiated a series of annual anthologies of selected short stories written during the previous year.

burg, Ohio in 1919. It was acclaimed immediately and was followed swiftly by the eruption upon the scene of a whole cluster of brilliant writers writing brilliant stories: there was F. Scott Fitzgerald, whose first collection (not up to later ones) came out in 1920, to be followed by *Tales of the Jazz Age* in 1922 and *All the Sad Young Men* in 1926; Ernest Hemingway, with *In Our Time* in 1925 and *Men Without Women* in 1927; and a host of excellent lesser writers, such as Ring Lardner, James Branch Cabell, Floyd Dell, Ruth Suckow, Manuel Komroff, Dorothy Parker, Katherine Brush, William Carlos Williams, and Conrad Aiken. Toward the end of the period, William Faulkner and Katherine Anne Porter began to appear as short-story writers; Miss Porter's *Flowering Judas* was published in 1930 and Faulkner's *These 13* in 1931. "On its short stories alone," say the editors of a recent anthology, "the Twenties would have been notable." In their view, although modern developments were anticipated in the 1890's by Stephen Crane, there was an "interruption caused by the resurgence of sentimental romance in the early 1900's," but "when the long drouth ended, and the promises of the 1890's were fulfilled, everything came with a rush and the American short story, together with all the other arts, exploded into what history may very well call its most brilliant period."[2]

The intellectual history and general character of this period have been extensively studied, both seriously and nostalgically. Among journalists and historians, indeed, it is the most popular decade of this century. There is no need to remind the reader of what was happening then — the postwar boom, the attitude of moral revolt, the bohemianism and expatriation, the stress on youth, the jazz, the strenuous and carefree experimentation in all the arts. One feels in all the arts, as in the short story, that there has been no period in recent history when the discontinuity between the older and younger generations was so marked. The success of this younger generation is suggested in the short story by, among other things, the way in which critics and historians of the genre have changed their ideas as to who and what were important in the history of the short story. Contem-

[2] Wallace and Mary Stegner (eds.), *Great American Short Stories* (Laurel Edition; New York: Dell Publishing Co., 1957), pp. 22–23, 25.

porary critics tend to accept with little question a new version of the family tree of the short story's aristocrats, in the light (or shade) of which many older reputations have been lost and many branches have turned out to be sterile. Chekhov and Joyce, as we have noted, hold the places of honor. James is fitted into the ancestry somewhere; among earlier writers, Hawthorne has retained more respectability than Poe, and previously unrecognized ancestors, such as Melville, have been rediscovered. Former favorites, such as Maupassant and Kipling, have had to struggle against disparagement, and still others, such as O. Henry, have died. The earlier critics would be astonished at what has happened to some of their favorites: although Hamlin Garland's stories, for example, still appear in anthologies, the compilers of the recent *Short Fiction Checklist*, which attempts to list all significant short-story criticism since 1925, have found not one analysis of his work important enough to be included.

The changes which the writers of the twenties made in short-story art are easier to see and feel than to define or describe accurately. There is no lack of efforts to define them, to be sure — or at any rate to define the changes made by modern writers in general or by this or that individual writer. There have been a few — not many — histories, such as Ray B. West's history of the American short story between 1900 and 1950. There have been many books on the technique of the short story — most commonly in the form of an anthology with detailed commentary on specific stories: the volumes by Séan O'Faoláin, by Brooks and Warren, by West and Stallman, are celebrated examples. From them we can glean many insights into what distinguishes modern stories in general from old-fashioned ones. We know, for example, that the modern short story is strongly influenced by Joyce's concept of the "epiphany" as manifested in *Dubliners*; that it is less "plotted" than earlier stories; it has less action; its techniques are subtler; its effects are more delicate and less optimistic, by and large; it is full of symbolism, full of irony, full of paradox; it has come to resemble more and more the lyric poem. On the basis of his own direct experience with stories, the general reader is likely to second these observations with little question.

Yet there is a question about them. The question arises less from doubt of their general truth than from doubt as to what they actually mean when applied to particular stories, and from doubt as to whether these are necessarily the most significant differences. If we consider three or four famous modern stories — say, Anderson's "The Egg," Faulkner's "A Rose for Emily," Miss Porter's "Flowering Judas" and "Maria Concepcion," and Hemingway's "The Killers" and "In Another Country" — we may see so many differences between them that we find it hopeless to try to specify what makes them all "modern."

The critics and historians of the short story are at a disadvantage when they try to make such distinctions in artistry as we would like them to make. They are hampered by the large body of material — the large number of excellent and important stories — that faces them. It is easier to collect short stories than to write about them, easier to make generalizations about them (however sound) than to support the generalizations by analysis, and easier to analyze individual stories than to analyze stories in large groups. Most of the histories that have been written, though they are useful for orientation in the field, for summing up prevailing critical judgments, and for making broad distinctions between leading schools and tendencies, are likely to be concerned more with authors, with their attitudes and ideas, than with individual stories. In such studies the historian is obliged, when he turns to the question of artistry, to rely on generalizations which he can support, at best, only by the occasional detailed analysis of a few prominent stories that must be accepted as "typical." On the other hand, studies primarily critical and analytical tend to lack authority as history; if, like O'Faoláin's study, they try to make contrasts between types, they too must base these contrasts upon the evidence of a minimum of particular stories, selected as representative. Whether they are representative cannot be demonstrated.

To some extent this problem faces the historian and critic in any art: he is always obliged to choose representative works for particular consideration, and we are obliged to accept his word for the choice on the basis of the authority we grant to him. Even so, it seems to me that the art of the modern short story —

or the art of the modern short story in the American twenties —
needs a more precise and systematic description than it has thus
far been given. There is need for a study the objective of which
is not necessarily to discover new things, but simply to consoli-
date, to put in order, with some kind of assessment of their
relative importance, the discernible characteristics of this art,
whether they have been observed before or not. It should be a
critical-historical study using principles of inquiry as objectively
as possible.

When I first thought of attempting such a study, I had little
conception of the extent to which I would have to narrow its
scope, nor did I anticipate the rather unusual method that my
objectives were committing me to, both in investigation and in
presentation to the reader. These limitations, this method, and
the plan of this book can best be explained by a brief recapitulation of the major decisions that had to be made at the outset
in response to the problems that presented themselves.

First, of course, this was to be a study of *art* as displayed in
the short stories of the twenties. This decision could lead in
various directions, depending upon what conception of art was
used to direct the inquiry. I preferred as most suitable to my
objectives that conception that regards each work as a discrete
whole with its own integrity. I accepted the view that the work
of art was first of all an object of intrinsic beauty whose nature
could be studied analytically, and that to study its nature meant
not to regard it as a projection of the author's personality or of his
times or of some eternal truth but to examine it for its own sake
as an effective combination of parts. According to such a view
of art, the critic's primary concern in analyzing a work is to
discover what particular complex principle unites the parts and
to determine how the parts themselves function with respect to
that principle. Such an approach seemed to me more satisfactory for the investigation of changes and developments in the
art of the short story than that which is used today by so many
of our most excellent critics who happen to be concerned with
the specific nature of art in a work but whose intensive analyses
are directed to the discovery not of differences between works

of art but of likenesses: the discovery of elements — paradox, ambiguity, irony, and the like — which in their view distinguish art from science or good art from bad art. My purpose, on the other hand, is not to show that the art in the stories of the twenties is necessarily good art but to determine what distinguishes one good story from another.

A further assumption (perhaps implicit in those already described) is that the organizing principles in works of art can be distinguished according to whether they have a rhetorical, didactic purpose — to advance an idea or thesis — or, instead, what Aristotelian critics would call an "imitative" purpose — to arouse specific emotions through the display of particular characters involved in particular actions. The consequences and meaning of this will be explained in the text, but it has significance at the start of my inquiry since most of the significant stories I have chosen to study are, according to this distinction, imitative. This is not to say that these stories have no didactic significance but that such significance must here be subordinated and the analysis limited to such problems as face the writer in his attempt to tell a story as story.

It was clear from these decisions that the study would have to be based upon the comparative analysis of individual stories. The next decision concerned the application of such a method — what stories were to be compared? In just what way could the specific analysis of individual stories be made to reveal most clearly and accurately the distinctive characteristics of the new art of the twenties? It was this problem which led to what is the most severe limitation on the scope of this study and probably the most unusual feature in the plan and method of this book.

It became clear that the only way in which the distinctive characteristics of the new art could be determined was through a contrast between this new art and other short-story art that was not new. Since the study was to be based upon the analysis of individual stories, this decision had major consequences. It meant that I had to set up a large, well-defined body of specific stories — what I shall call hereafter a "canon" of stories — to represent the art of the twenties, and that I had to set up another body of stories, another sample, another canon, to provide a standard of comparison. Since what mattered was the contrast, all these stories would have to be analyzed according to the same principles: the same questions must be asked and answered about each one.

The advantages of such an approach are apparent. Only in this way could I achieve some measure of precision and accuracy in determining the relative importance of the various artistic habits of the new movement. Through use of a canon one can see (within the canon) just how widespread or universal particular artistic features are, just which will differentiate the new movement from the old and which will not, which appear regularly and which only occasionally. Of course I knew that such a statistical approach could only be a beginning, not an end, of my inquiry, since the statistics would concern works of art that are not only complex and various but also different in quality, in merit, in "weight," in a host of incalculables. It was perfectly obvious that such statistics would be a final answer to nothing, that they must be weighed carefully and critically with respect to the individual stories, and that a feature that appeared, for example, only rarely but in stories that were masterpieces might be much more significant than a feature that appeared more frequently but only in stories that were mediocre. Yet, carefully judged with due regard for these complexities, the force of numbers might provide some very useful hints — and more than hints — as to the relative importance of various artistic devices.

Two major questions remained to be answered before the study could proceed. The first concerned the choice of my canons, and most especially the nature of the canon to be used in contrast with that of the twenties. I decided that I was not concerned with the absolute originality of the new movement any more than with the matter of influences or causes. Nor was I concerned with the period as such or with proving that the art of all important writers of the twenties was different. My concern was with the new tradition that appeared, even though the old tradition continued to be practiced by such writers as Edith Wharton and Katharine Fullerton Gerould throughout the decade. The distinctive thing about this new tradition is its deviation from the tradition which it displaced, the tradition that had been dominant just before. The contrast to be studied, therefore, was the contrast between these traditions, the contrast between the stories of the new generation of the twenties and the stories of those writers (from a period preceding the twenties) who were *most comparable* to them in stature, seriousness, and critical repute.

The more particular principles that governed the selection of the canon are summed up in Appendix A. The chief determinants were that the stories be limited to those of serious artistic intent and high repute within what may be loosely called the "realistic tradition" (this being the tradition in which the new movement was strongest), that they be imitative rather than didactic, and that, after such exclusions have been made, they be chosen according to methods that would reduce to a minimum the possibility that prior notions as to what to expect would influence my discoveries.

As a result of these considerations, a total canon of 220 stories was selected, more or less evenly divided between the two periods. The decade of the twenties is represented, as I have said, by the work of Anderson, Fitzgerald, Hemingway, Faulkner, and Miss Porter in the period 1919–31. The older tradition — hereafter to be called the "early period" — is represented by stories by Ambrose Bierce, Henry James, Mary E. Wilkins Freeman, Hamlin Garland, Edith Wharton, Stephen Crane, Theodore Dreiser, Willa Cather, and Katharine Fullerton Gerould written in the period 1890–1919.

The final major problem that had to be solved concerned the specific kinds of analytical questions to ask about each of these stories. According to the assumption about art that I had accepted, the most central questions would be those pertaining to the principles of *form* that unify and organize these stories. In order to clarify these principles, however, it would be necessary to compare the stories with regard to their *subject matter*, not for its own sake but as material of which the forms are composed. In addition, a study of the art of these stories could not afford to neglect the kinds of *techniques* by which the forms are executed and made vivid to the reader. There are of course many other kinds of questions that could also be asked, but these seemed to be of most promise when applied to this particular subject. (What these distinctions mean and how they are related to each other are explained in the text.)

The most exact way to describe the purpose of this book, then, would be to call it a study of contrasts in art between two groups of short stories, 220 in all, one group representing the given eight writers of the early period, 1890–1919, and the other representing the given five of the twenties, 1919–31. It is organized according to the three major variables of artistic invention that are examined, the first part of the book being concerned with contrasts in subject matter, the second with contrasts in form, and the third with contrasts in technique.

In presenting the results of this study to the reader, I have concluded that the most interesting findings would be lost if I did not give at least a skeleton key to the particular evidence upon which my conclusions are based. I have included the canon, which is listed in full in Appendix A, and I have made an effort at every point where it is not obvious to list the stories I consider significant.[3]

I am much aware, of course, of the dependence of the whole structure — despite all safeguards — upon subjective interpretation of the evidence. This has been particularly present to me in the chapters on form, in which I have been obliged to present as if they were absolute fact what are, after all, only hypotheses as to the organizing principles of nearly all the 220 stories of the canon. I have no doubt that even the friendliest reader will disagree with me on some interpretations, finding pathetic what I find comic and comic what I find pathetic, or noting things important to him which I have ignored in his favorite stories. To him I must admit that I expect to change my own mind someday about some of the interpretations; it is inevitable in dealing with something as complex and subtle as literary form, and I think there must be something wrong with a critic who cannot change his mind. Granting this and admitting also the

[3] To incorporate as much of the evidence as possible, I have resorted to abbreviated titles in the notes and to a number of appendixes. The index also contains, in codified form, a summary of certain kinds of salient points that have been made about the form of each story.

loss I have felt in having to telescope almost everywhere the arguments and evidence that I would like to use, I can assert that I have made an effort to confine my points about particular stories only to those that I felt might be readily confirmed by any reader who accepts my basic premises and methods. I have tried to rest my conclusions only upon points that, once made clear, will be self-evident to such a reader. I cannot claim that these conclusions are facts. They are theories which at present "command my belief." They also command my conviction that these writers built a new art that is one of the finest achievements of twentieth-century American literature, and that it deserves the tribute of close analytical study, however imperfect.

I: THE WORLD OF A STORY

The village of Winesburg, Ohio, created by Sherwood Anderson on the model of Clyde, Ohio, is very different from the New England villages depicted by Mary Wilkins Freeman in stories written thirty years before. The rich people invented by F. Scott Fitzgerald face problems different from those faced by the upper-class people in stories by Henry James and Edith Wharton. The soldiers in the stories of Stephen Crane and Ambrose Bierce are unlike those in the stories of Ernest Hemingway and William Faulkner. They differ in their objectives, their ways of pursuing those objectives, and in the kinds of difficulties that confront them. They live in different worlds, dominated by different problems.

The reader who is aware that the short stories of the twenties are different from earlier short stories is likely to think first of

14

such differences in the people and human problems treated by these stories — that is, differences in their subject matter. These are perhaps more obvious than other differences between the stories of the two periods. Here we can detect significant changes in social, psychological, and moral ideas. They reveal much about what the writers thought of the world in which they lived, and they contribute to our understanding of the intellectual history of the time — a history explored at length by such scholars as Curti, Randall, and Commager and, in its particularly literary manifestations, by Alfred Kazin and Frederick J. Hoffman. Of themselves, however, such changes do not tell us much about the art of the short story, or of how it developed. Nevertheless, they cannot be ignored in a study such as this. A plot cannot be conceived independently of its subject matter. An artistic technique must be appropriate to the particular human problem represented. If we wish to discover how Anderson's art differs from that of Mrs. Freeman, we can do little until we have distinguished how Anderson's subjects differ from those of Mrs. Freeman.

Much of the first enthusiasm for the new writers of the twenties concerned the subjects of their stories more than the new art which they displayed. The new art was described as a "revolt" against earlier artistic practices, but for many critics this was identified with a moral revolt, an attack upon the supposedly stifling moral conventionality of the earlier society and the earlier literature. Thus four years after the publication of *Winesburg*, Edward O'Brien, editor of the recently initiated annual collection of best American short stories, said of Sherwood Anderson that

[The technical revolt is only a] sign of a much more profound revolt in him . . . against a dull conformity which custom has staled, a conformity based upon the principles of leveling down rather than leveling up, a conformity of negation rather than of healthy growth.[1]

Anderson, whom he ranked with Hawthorne, Poe, James, Balzac, Maupassant, and Chekhov,[2]

[1] O'Brien, *The Advance of the American Short Story* (New York: Dodd, Mead & Co., 1923), p. 247.
[2] *Ibid.*, p. 260.

is uncovering the soul of America reverently, and liberating it and curing it by giving it knowledge of itself. And so he would heal America, as he healed himself, by faithful discovery and impersonal compassion.[3]

Another critic, in an introduction to a reprint of *Winesburg,* characterized the movement to which it belonged as

a resolute insistence upon the fundamentals of life, upon facts so strenuously denied, or ignored, by the conventional imitators of British orthodoxy. It is essentially a literature of revolt against the great illusion of American civilization, with all its childish evasion of harsh facts, its puerile cheerfulness, whose inevitable culmination is the school of "glad" books, which have reduced American literature to the lowest terms of sentimentality.[4]

What was good about the new short stories, everybody seemed to agree, was that they told the truth, the real truth about society, people, and life, in a way more satisfying than their forebears had done. Look, for example, at the criticism that O'Brien leveled at Mrs. Freeman, using Anderson as his standard of comparison:

[Her work is] stark and bitter naturalism, limited, to be sure, by the prudish conventions of the time, yet by no means hesitant or flattering to New England. . . . [Her stories] form as complete a study of suppressed desires as Sherwood Anderson's stories, but somehow they fail in their desperate reality to offer a solution, or even to plumb the essential depths of knowledge, the first step necessary to spiritual liberation. Perhaps it is because they came too soon. America had not begun to question.[5]

More detached critics recognized, of course, the absurdity of saying that "America had not begun to question" until Anderson came along. Even so, the admirer of the short story of the twenties, or the modern short story in general, is still likely to explain his admiration, at least in part, by the assertion that it is more "sincere," that it tells more of the truth than earlier writings in the genre, and its truthfulness arises from a more questioning or "pessimistic" view of life. And this, he will tell us, is in

---

[3] *Ibid.,* p. 259.
[4] Ernest Boyd, introduction to Sherwood Anderson, *Winesburg, Ohio; A Group of Tales of Ohio Small Town Life* (New York: Modern Library, [n. d.]).
[5] O'Brien, *Advance,* p. 165.

the most important American tradition. As Ray B. West in his history of the short story in this century put it:

[Hawthorne, Melville, and Mark Twain all] came finally to recognize intuitively what James saw more clearly — that the American story was a story of initiation, a recognition of the significance of evil, a pessimistic rather than an optimistic view of man.

[The years from the Civil War to the end of World War I] were essentially years of optimism in America. . . . Such writings as the novels of Howells and Stephen Crane, Hamlin Garland's tales of the settling of the prairies, Frank Norris's novels of California farmers and Chicago businessmen were all dreary enough in tone and subject matter but filled with the optimism of social progress. . . . During and following the war, however, a generation of writers appeared to challenge such a view, to challenge it both in theory and in a practical evaluation of the works themselves.[6]

The striking point in all this commentary is not, of course, simply the idea that these writers were telling the truth — most writers and their admirers insist on that — but that telling the truth involved clearing away falsehoods, that telling the truth was difficult, that telling the truth was not the same thing as presenting an affirmative view of life or defending certain moral principles. The writers themselves thought of themselves as truth-tellers in this sense. The most famous comment Hemingway ever made about his own writing was probably the remark that he inserted as a subordinate phrase in the following statement of purpose:

I was trying to write then and I found the greatest difficulty, aside from knowing what you really felt, rather than what you were supposed to feel, and had been taught to feel, was to put down what really happened in action.[7]

It was the truth of his own feelings that Hemingway wanted to write about, and he conceived as the most difficult of all a writer's problems the task of distinguishing these feelings from conventional ideas. Similarly, in "The Book of the Grotesque," which serves as a kind of thematic introduction to *Winesburg*,

[6] Ray B. West, Jr., *The Short Story in America: 1900–1950* ("Twentieth-Century Literature in America"; Henry Regnery Co., 1952), p. 18.
[7] Ernest Hemingway, *Death in the Afternoon* (New York: Charles Scribner's Sons, 1954, first published, 1932), p. 2.

Anderson attributes to an old writer a theory about the nature of truth and falsehood which serves as a key to the stories that follow:

That in the beginning when the world was young there were a great many thoughts but no such thing as a truth. Man made the truths himself and each truth was a composite of a great many vague thoughts. All about in the world were the truths and they were all beautiful.

The old man had listed hundreds of the truths in his book. I will not try to tell you of all of them. There was the truth of virginity and the truth of passion, the truth of wealth and of poverty, of thrift and of profligacy, of carelessness and abandon. Hundreds and hundreds were the truths and they were all beautiful.

And then the people came along. Each as he appeared snatched up one of the truths and some who were quite strong snatched up a dozen of them.

It was the truths that made the people grotesques. The old man had quite an elaborate theory concerning the matter. It was his notion that the moment one of the people took one of the truths to himself, called it his truth, and tried to live his life by it, he became a grotesque and the truth he embraced became a falsehood.

One can see the same preoccupation in Faulkner, too, when he says,

If the writer concentrates on what he does need to be interested in, which is the truth and the human heart, he won't have much time left for anything else, such as ideas and facts like the shape of noses or blood relationships, since in my opinion ideas and facts have very little connection with truth. . . . Life is not interested in good and evil. Don Quixote . . . entered reality only when he was so busy trying to cope with people that he had no time to distinguish between good and evil. . . . [Man's] moral conscience is the curse he had to accept from the gods in order to gain from them the right to dream.[8]

And Katherine Anne Porter puts herself in the same family when she stresses the dishonesty of technical tricks, insisting that as a writer you should tell your story "with all the truth and tender-

[8] William Faulkner, quoted in Malcolm Cowley (ed.), *Writers at Work: The Paris Review Interviews* (Compass Books edition; New York: Viking Press, 1959), pp. 135, 138–39.

ness and severity you are capable of; and if you have any character of your own, you will have a style of your own." [9]

Such an emphasis upon the truth of the subject matter of the twenties makes one wonder if there had been an actual change in theory as to the kinds of truth a story should tell. One cannot answer such a question simply by comparing what critics have to say. The term "truthfulness," applied to a writer, is always a term of approbation, regardless of what the critic who uses it means by truth. No earlier writer would admit that he did not care about telling the truth; the difference must be that the writers of the twenties were not satisfied with what the earlier writers regarded as truth.

One does find in some of the critical writings of the earlier period—writings from viewpoints that were sympathetic to some or all of the earlier writers—statements that suggest the possibility of a subtle difference in theory as to the kinds of truth that literature should tell. Most important is perhaps the position of James when he defended his invention of such "supersubtle fry" as the protagonists of "The Death of the Lion," "The Next Time," and "The Figure in the Carpet":

. . . I was able to plead that my postulates, my animating presences, were all, to their great enrichment, their intensification of value, ironic; the strength of applied irony being surely in the sincerities, the lucidities, the utilities that stand behind it. When it's not a campaign, of a sort, on behalf of the something better (better than the obnoxious, the provoking object) that blessedly, as is assumed, *might* be, it's not worth speaking of. . . . "If the life about us for the last thirty years refuses warrant for these examples, then so much the worse for that life." [10]

For James the presentation of a world "better than ours" had a critical intent whose irony was perhaps lost upon some of his contemporaries. It shared, however, with these contemporaries the notion that telling the truth involved an affirmation of the

[9] Katherine Anne Porter, *The Days Before* (New York: Harcourt Brace & Co., 1952), p. 136.
[10] Henry James, *The Art of the Novel: Critical Prefaces*, with an introduction by Richard P. Blackmur (New York: Charles Scribner's Sons, 1947), p. 222.

good — a view quite distinct from the notion of the truth that the writers of the twenties had. The idea was a critical commonplace of the time, though it was asserted more baldly and naïvely by the short-story critics of the period than by the writers themselves. Garland saw his purpose, for example, as a profoundly motivated effort to evoke sympathy and understanding for the hard-working, suffering farmers of the West.[11] The critics took such ideas and made them into a general justification for regionalism and local-color stories of a strictly utilitarian kind:

Has [the local color story] been worth while? Immensely so. . . . If the service rendered to the art by the local color story has not always been of the highest, the service of curiosity, and the broadening of human sympathies, has been immense.[12]

Our short-story writers . . . have . . . helped to bridge the chasm made by the Civil War. They have enabled the different sections to know each other, and with wider knowledge there has come a better understanding and a more intelligent sympathy.[13]

The extreme of the attitude which the writers of the twenties apparently wished to reject may be represented by the following comments made in 1907 by the author of a textbook on the short story. Notice that the tendency of "the growing realism" is viewed not as a moral movement but as a technical development:

This growing realism in characterization is not so much in opposition to idealism as to romance. The ideal in human character will always be admired and sought after so long as there are worthy writers. . . . We have come to realize that a very good man may have small weaknesses; in fact, most of the very good men we know

[11] See his dedication to *Main-Travelled Roads*: "To my father and mother whose half-century pilgrimage on the main-travelled road of life has brought them only toil and deprivation, this book of stories is dedicated by a son to whom every day brings a deepening sense of his parents' silent heroism."
See also the conclusion of his foreword to the same collection: "Mainly [the main-travelled road in the West] is long and wearyful and has a dull little town at one end, and a home of toil at the other. Like the main-travelled road of life it is traversed by many classes of people, but the poor and the weary predominate."
[12] Henry Seidel Canby, *The Short Story in English* (New York: Henry Holt & Co., 1909), p. 321.
[13] C. Alphonso Smith, *The American Short Story*, (Boston: Ginn & Co., 1912), pp. 40–41.

are open to criticism on at least one point. The eminently natural way to picture such a man includes this flaw.[14]
For this critic, the moral test is not truthfulness alone but moral serviceability:

> Horror and evil lend themselves readily to tragic treatment. How shall the author view them? We say at once that a story which presents horror and evil with any touch of cynicism or pessimism is a story with a bad aim. . . .
> The chance for making deep and vivid imaginative impressions will probably keep the stories of horror and sin in favor with the greater writers and with many readers. But a story cannot receive universal or lasting appreciation if it leaves the bad taste of cynicism, pessimism, or despair. It is not high art to relax morally, to disgust with life, to dishearten, to render hopeless. This does not mean that art cannot portray the darker emotions: it means that they can and must be presented in a wholesome or at least unharmful way.[15]

One must be careful not to exaggerate this contrast in critical views. One infers from the attitude displayed in the passage just quoted that its author would probably have condemned many of the greatest stories of the twenties; yet the passage could be construed in a sufficiently broad way — depending on what one means by "despair," "harm," "cynicism," and the like — to make even the bitterest stories of the twenties acceptable. Nor must one forget that the writers and critics of the twenties themselves sometimes sounded not too different from this. Anderson, for example, was constantly stressing his desire to evoke sympathy for people's sufferings, and O'Brien saw Anderson as "reverently . . . curing" America's soul. Faulkner said that man has no time to distinguish between good and evil, yet his affirmations of the nobility and heroism of the human spirit are celebrated, so that even that mouthpiece of popular conservatism, the magazine *Life*, took him to its bosom after his Nobel Prize speech.

In fact, if one examines the critical studies of the short story that flourished just after the turn of the century, one is much more likely to be struck with their emphasis upon points of

[14] Evelyn May Albright, *The Short Story: Its Principles and Structure* (New York: Macmillan Co., 1931, first published, 1907), pp. 120–21.
[15] *Ibid.*, p. 214.

technical construction than upon moral prescriptions or subject-matter prescriptions of any kind. The subject was to be subordinated to the particular artistic problem. James himself makes this point again and again in *The Art of the Novel* — we see it in the kinds of germinal ideas (characters, situations) that usually occurred to him, in his distinction between two kinds of stories — the little anecdote and the little picture — and in his assertions that no subject was intrinsically moral or immoral, that what counted rather was the amount of "felt life" that the writer put into his story.

Similarly, the same critic whose distaste for the unwholesome story has just been cited, chose to reject the stories of James and Howells as of "a pale and intellectual sort, because there is little stirring action and almost no attempt at climax." [16] For these early critics, the primary intention of the short story was to produce the "single impression" or the "single effect," and more than anything else they were concerned with the technical logic that might produce such an effect. What this logic involved will be touched on in later chapters; [17] what it meant for the short story was felt by some critics as early as 1909:

[The effect in the modern short story is often] merely technical. The specific word, the rapid introduction, the stressed climax, the careful focus, and the studied tone, are too often the masters, not the servants, of the story. Facility is widespread, artificiality rampant. . . . [18]

Such a passage, with its complaint about artifice that calls attention to itself — thereby distracting attention from something more important — is close to the attitude observed in the twenties. When one speaks of artificiality, one has in mind as its opposite a more effective art, an art that veils its artifices. But one also has in mind that which is natural — that which is "true."

There is little question that for the writers and their critics in the twenties the quest for truth and the quest for a finer art were the same. Quite possibly they would regard a distinction between art and subject matter as unnatural. Yet this attitude makes it all the more important that we consider subject matter

[16] *Ibid.*, p. 50.
[17] See chaps. xi–xvi.
[18] Canby, *The Short Story in English*, p. 349.

in our study of changes between the two periods and that we separate subject matter from more purely artistic and technical problems.

One can manage the otherwise vague term "subject matter" by identifying it with the world or universe which a writer treats, and by dividing this into its components of people and the problems they face. Other elements of a world — its geography, its astronomy, its scenery — usually exist in a story only in relation to these people as parts of their problems. More technically, one can describe this world as the complex of ground rules which the author has laid down to control the action in which his hero is involved. It is all that might happen to the hero — all that is "given" at the beginning of the plot to predetermine what happens. It is thus nothing less than the entire material of which the plot is composed. But the material is conceived independently of the shaping principle which welds it into a unity. It is whatever the story depicts, considered prior to or independently of the author's choice of a particular hero and action from that world.

Ultimately the world of each story is unique. Nevertheless, it will share much with the worlds of other stories, especially stories by the same author. One can speak, for instance, of the world of Winesburg, Ohio, and predict fairly accurately what may or may not happen in any *Winesburg* story. These stories share with each other a certain common ground of "probabilities" established by the author — forces present in the story that tend to lead the action in some particular direction. So, too, Anderson's stories share with Hemingway's and those of the other writers of the twenties a certain common ground, and of course all the stories of the twenties share much with their predecessors. They all depict a world which is, to some extent, the same.

Our first problem, then, is to determine how much subject matter the stories of the twenties share with each other which they do not share with the earlier stories. To what extent is their common world different? We can expect to discover few absolute differences — elements common to *all* stories of one period, but missing in those of the other. What we can look for are "tendencies." We can, quite arbitrarily, lump all the varied, diverse, unique little worlds of the different stories of the twenties into one great "collective world" and define the character of this world by the kinds of things that happen frequently and the kinds of things that happen infrequently. Then we can distinguish the character of this collective world from that of a similarly assembled world in the earlier period.

A study of the differences between these two collective worlds is not in any sense, of course, a sociological history. The two worlds so accumulated are no more than a composite invention of the authors in question. The actual world of the twenties probably differed from that of the early period far less than does the invented world, as one can see readily enough if one realizes that Anderson's Winesburg, belonging to the time of Anderson's boyhood, was roughly contemporary with Mrs. Freeman's New England and probably earlier than much of Mrs. Wharton's world. What the contrast between the two collective worlds can show, more than anything else, is a difference between the preoccupations and interests of the two sets of writers as they constructed the materials for their stories.

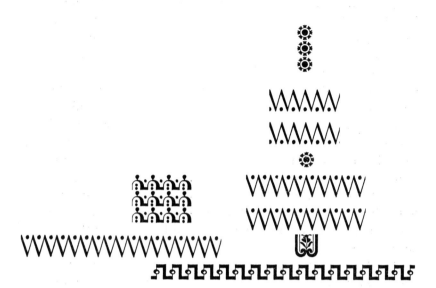

II: PEOPLE AND PLACES

The world of a short story gets its character primarily from the problems it contains, but these problems may depend to some extent upon the purely accidental circumstances of the physical or material environment. What people does a story deal with? what society? what country or what part of the country? Simply because they are American villagers, Anderson's villagers may face different problems from those faced by James's cultured English people. If Anderson has, as he tells us, transplanted to Winesburg some characters whose real-life models he met in Chicago, there must be something about a village environment that he thought would illuminate their problems. Certainly, the geographical and social differences should be considered carefully.

Such consideration, however, may be brief. A geographical, economical, and occupational census of characters in the two

25

periods would reveal few significant differences. Of course there are great differences between individual authors. The worlds of Hamlin Garland and Henry James are about as far apart as one can imagine for writers of the same period dealing with Americans; a similar diversity can be observed within the collective world of the twenties. Perhaps in the twenties the divisions between geographical and economic segments of this world are not drawn quite as rigidly as they were earlier by the differences between particular authors: the tendency of a writer to be a regionalist, to carve out one particular section of America and call it his own, was not so marked among the five important new writers. Nevertheless, broad diversity is as notable in the world of the twenties as in the earlier world, and when the various individual fragmentary worlds are joined, the material composition of the later world is not so very different from that of the earlier one.

Most stories in both periods are placed in America, with American characters.[1] The depicted time is usually contemporary; except for Crane's Civil War stories and two or three of Faulkner's Yoknapatawpha stories, they do not go back before the lifetime of the author and his readers. This contemporaneity means, of course, that the stories of the twenties tend to deal with a time more recent than those of the early period: one sees the evidence of this in the fashions, the technological details, and occasional historical allusions of some of the deliberately "modern" stories by Fitzgerald and Hemingway. But the periods embraced by the two worlds may also overlap, as when Anderson, Faulkner, and Hemingway go back to their boyhoods.

For the most part, the same general social groups are prominent in both worlds. These include country people and villagers — the chief subject of Mrs. Freeman and Garland, as well as of Anderson, Faulkner, and sometimes Miss Porter — although the actual working farmer, hero of many Garland stories, declines in importance. Soldiers are also important in both periods — in Bierce and Crane, in Hemingway and Faulkner. Middle-class Americans from the small town or small city are prominent in

[1] The stories of James, most of which are set in England or on the continent, and many of which have no American characters, are exceptions to this statement.

Dreiser, Miss Cather, Mrs. Gerould, Crane, and all the writers of the twenties.

The so-called "upper class" declines somewhat in the stories of the twenties. Earlier, it was important in Miss Cather's and Mrs. Gerould's stories and formed almost the entire subject matter of stories by Mrs. Wharton and James. In these writers, this class combined wealth and status with high cultural and intellectual development; there was an easy interchange between those who had great fortunes, either inherited or achieved in business, and those who made artistic or academic careers. In the twenties, the wealthy class is prominent only in Fitzgerald; it is not intellectual in its interests, it measures status more exclusively by the outward displays of wealth, and, although an occasional story such as "The Rich Boy" deals with inherited social position, is composed mostly of successful recent invaders from the middle class. Intellectuals, on the other hand, not common in the twenties, usually have no connection with the upper classes and tend to be divorced from society in general, as can be seen in Miss Porter's "Theft," "That Tree," and "Flowering Judas," or Hemingway's satirical "Mr. and Mrs. Elliot."

If a solidly entrenched upper class with deep traditional roots disappears in the stories of the twenties, so do some other groups at the opposite end of the scale. The frontiersmen, prominent in Crane, and the pioneer settler, prominent in Garland, are gone, though Miss Porter's Granny Weatherall remembers pioneering days, and Faulkner occasionally looks back to Indian days in Yoknapatawpha. More significantly, the writers of the twenties show little interest in the bottom level of society — the downtrodden slum-dwellers, derelicts, laborers, and immigrants who figured, for example, in Crane's "Maggie: A Girl of the Streets" and "An Experiment in Misery," or Dreiser's "The Cruise of the 'Idlewild'" or "Old Rogaum and His Theresa." Poverty in stories of the twenties not only is rare but is usually the result not of class inheritance but of personal problems, such as the impossible ambition of the hero in Faulkner's "Victory."[2]

[2] Two possible exceptions (stories of poverty caused by class inheritance) appear in Miss Porter: "Magic," dealing with a prostitute in New Orleans, and "He," dealing with a struggling farm family in the South.

This lack of interest was of course remedied by the depression stories of the thirties, and even in the twenties certain other writers dealt with the subject. But it had little place in the five writers who best represent the new artistic movement.

On the other hand, the world of the twenties contains some kinds of people considerably more prominent than they were earlier. Among these are the popular entertainers, associated with the movies, night clubs, and, especially, sports. Although public performers, artists, musicians, and writers appeared earlier in the work of James and Miss Cather, these were "serious" artists, in quite a different category from the prize fighters, bull-fighters, jazz musicians, and racing hands in the stories by Hemingway, Fitzgerald, and Anderson.[3]

More difficult to explain are the characteristics that distinguish the travelers, adventurers, and expatriates of the twenties from those of the early period. Our impression is that such people are more significant in the twenties than they used to be — that there is more restless moving about, more emigration, that the world of the twenties is rootless.

Even so, such people are prominent in the early world: James's stories are peopled with Americans traveling or settled in Europe: they commute back and forth with ease, and such easy access to Europe is also implicit in many stories by Miss Cather, Mrs. Wharton, and Mrs. Gerould. Crane's West is populated by adventurers and nomads, and some of Garland's farmers have recently settled. Moreover, even though characters such as the farmer in "Up the Coolly" or the farm wives in "Mrs Ripley's Trip" or "A Day's Pleasure," all by Garland, seem firmly and unhappily trapped in their lives, and though the protagonists of Miss Cather's "Paul's Case" and "A Wagner Matinee" cannot escape from their bleak environments into the worlds they long for, it is not impossible for an exceptional person to move from the farm or village to the cosmopolitan city, as in Garland's "God's Ravens," or Miss Cather's "The Sculptor's Funeral" or

[3] The world of popular entertainment is seen in the twenties in, for example, Anderson, "I Want to Know Why," "I'm a Fool," "Man Who Became a Woman"; Fitzgerald, "Magnetism," "Offshore Pirate," "Rough Crossing"; Hemingway, "Pursuit Race," "My Old Man," "Undefeated." (Abbreviated titles in this and following notes correspond to alphabetical listing of stories in the index.)

"A Death in the Desert." The heroine of Dreiser's "The Second Choice" is trapped in a lower middle-class urban world which she hates, but the heroine of Dreiser's "Married" does succeed in moving from a standard middle-class American community into New York society, though she never becomes adjusted to the move.

The new travelers and migrants of the twenties give an impression of much greater rootlessness. If the earlier travelers are not busy establishing firm roots in the new society to which they have moved, their travels indicate no severance of their old roots at all. Even Crane's nomads show a marked tendency to settle down and establish stable communities (see, for instance, "The Bride Comes to Yellow Sky" or "The Blue Hotel"). As for the Jamesian travelers, if they are not transplants to English society, like the skilful social "agent" in "Mrs. Medwin," their easy commuting, like that of the narrator in "Europe," suggests what is really a pertinent point — that in the Jamesian world there is, at the top, an "international society" whose base is in England but to which fortunate Americans can aspire, since it bridges the two countries. Hence, it is natural that many of James's short stories deal entirely with English society, with no visible connection to Americans at all. English society, despite the marked differences that James stresses, is merely the top stratum of the same society to which cultured Americans belong and to which they aspire in such stories as "Europe," "Miss Gunton of Poughkeepsie," "Fordham Castle," and "Mrs. Medwin," however little they may understand it.

In the twenties, on the other hand, the migrant generally has no such roots. The expatriates in Europe (and, in stories by Miss Porter, in Mexico) have usually unspecified origins and unspecified purposes; if they have anything to do with the society of the place they are visiting, which is rare, it tends to be a casual relation with the kinds of people the earlier travelers would have disregarded as the "common people" or "the natives." The hero of Miss Porter's "That Tree" makes friends with impoverished artists and Mexican peasant girls; the heroine of "Flowering Judas" joins a revolutionary movement. Others, such as the couple in Hemingway's "Mr. and Mrs. Elliot," live in little clusters with other expatriates; others, notably the people in Hemingway's "Hills Like White Elephants," "Cat in the Rain," "Cross-Country Snow," or "An Alpine Idyll," seem more or less completely cut off from any society but that of a few intimate friends; they travel, apparently, more for sport than for culture, and one can infer from "Hills Like White Elephants," for example, that what they most desire in travel is anonymity, escape from all society. One detects similar motives in the wanderings of young people within America itself, as seen chiefly in Hemingway and Anderson: Nick Adams riding the freights, Krebs going off to lose himself in Kansas City, Seth Richmond planning to leave Winesburg for the city, young horse swipes traveling about the country to county fairs.

This is the most striking kind of migration that is new in the twenties, but there is another kind — that which reflects the great American "success drive" — that also seems more prominent than earlier. This is the ambition for a career that leads George Willard to leave Winesburg, or Fitzgerald's Dexter, a grocer's son, to become a great business figure in "Winter Dreams," or Katherine Anne Porter's unnamed young heroine in "Theft" to go to New York and struggle to become a good playwright, or other young men, especially in Fitzgerald, to work so hard to climb the ladder to success.[4] This point, however, must be carefully qualified, partly because it is subject to possible accidents in the choice of our canon of stories, and partly because social climbing is evident among the earlier writers, in the work of James and, to some extent, Miss Cather, as are frequent allusions to self-made men who have made fabulous fortunes through business. But self-made men are only on the periphery of James's world; only for the women is the upward social migration dramatized directly, and for them it is strictly a matter of winning acceptance in an exclusive high society. Thus, within the canon of the early period, at any rate, one can say that there are no equivalents to the direct treatment of the career-ambition of the twenties.[5]

[4] See Fitzgerald, " 'Sensible Thing,' " "Gretchen's Forty Winks," "Hot and Cold Blood," "Head and Shoulders," "May Day," "Magnetism," "Four Fists."
[5] Several early stories deal with problems faced by a wife in connection

One other physical change is detectable between the two worlds, although it is difficult to demonstrate its full scope: the increased importance of youth. Distinctly youthful protagonists — children, adolescents, and young adults — are more common than before,[6] but the change may be broader than this. One notices in Fitzgerald's world, for example, how important youthful values have become as criteria for membership in the fashionable classes.[7] Sports, so important in Hemingway's world, suggest the dominance of youth in that society, even though the jockey in "My Old Man" is no longer young. But he, like the aging bullfighter in Hemingway's "The Undefeated," faces, in part, problems that also reflect the importance of youth in the new world: problems caused by the continued attention to youthful needs and objectives. These supplement the more distinctively youthful problems — of naïveté or innocence and of sex — that haunt so many other characters in the period.

with her husband's pursuit of a career in business or politics: James, "Abasement"; Gerould, "Wesendonck"; Wharton, "Quicksand." James's "Flickerbridge" deals in part with the problems of a young man whose fiancée is pursuing a career. Two stories, Wharton, "Long Run," and Gerould, "Bird in Bush," deal more directly with a character's pursuit of such a career. In both cases the hero's ambitions are frustrated; in regard to these, however, see below p. 61.

[6] In the early period, children, adolescents, or conspicuously young adults are protagonists in some ten stories: Bierce, "Chickamauga"; Freeman, "Gentle Ghost," "Amanda," "Calla-lilies," "Up Primrose Hill"; Crane, "Maggie"; Cather, "Paul's Case"; James, "Marriages"; Dreiser, "Old Rogaum," "Second Choice."

In the twenties, children are protagonists in some twenty-two stories: Anderson, "Nobody Knows," "Awakening," "Thinker," "Drink," "Sophistication," "Ohio Pagan," "I Want to Know Why," "I'm a Fool," "Man Who Became a Woman," "Chicago Hamlet," " 'Unused,' " "Unlighted Lamps"; Fitzgerald, "Absolution," "Winter Dreams," "Bernice," "Ice Palace"; Hemingway, "Indian Camp," "End of Something," "Three-Day Blow," "Ten Indians," "Battler," "My Old Man."

In the twenties there are also many secondary characters who are very young: George Willard in most *Winesburg* stories, Nick Adams in Hemingway's stories of Michigan, and the children in Faulkner's "That Evening Sun" and "A Justice."

[7] Notice the importance of knowledge of the latest songs and dances in such stories as "Bernice," "Offshore Pirate," and others. Notice the importance of youthful parties (although the older generation may also participate) in such stories as "The Rich Boy" and "Winter Dreams." Notice in "Winter Dreams" the importance of such activities as motor boating and swimming (in addition to golf) as social criteria. Notice also in this story the importance of one's choice of college as a gauge of social standing: "They [Dexter's "winter dreams"] persuaded Dexter several years later to pass up a business course at the State university . . . for the precarious advantage of attending an older and more famous university in the East . . . ."

All the same, such circumstances of geographical and social distribution are relatively trivial and perhaps questionable. They do little to account for the new look of the subject matter of the twenties. More noteworthy are the differences in the problems that dominate the lives of the characters, and in the motives and values that lead these people into these problems.

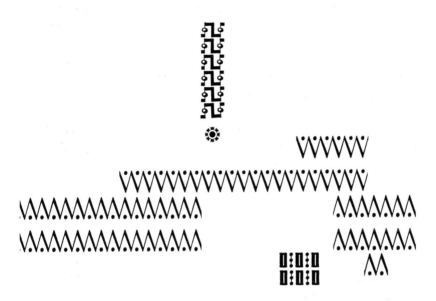

III: SOCIAL PROBLEMS

In Hemingway's "The Killers," Ole Anderson, slated for execution by a Chicago gang, turns his head to the wall in his rooming house and awaits his fate, declining Nick Adams' offer to help him. He says that nothing can be done; it will do no good to call the police. Earlier in the story we had seen Nick himself tied up by the killers, who showed their indifference to society's power of law enforcement by boasting of what they were going to do and then, later, letting him and his friends go free.

Though Ole's own attitude to his fate is an important "problem" in the story, contributing to its power, his predicament obviously depends also in a major way upon his relation to his society. He has, in the past, shown a sufficient disregard of social taboos to involve himself with gangsters, and he has done something ("double-crossed somebody" is George's guess) to make

33

these gangsters eager to kill him. More to the point, he is now in a spot where law enforcement cannot protect him; he is in part the victim of something wrong in his society, the victim of a problem belonging to the community as a whole that makes it impossible to protect him from murder.

The fate of many heroes of short stories in both periods is influenced because the society in which they live wields or fails to wield some power over them. The protagonist gains or suffers because he is a member of such a society; he profits or loses because he is involved in problems which face that society. Such problems are significant subject matter whenever they influence the lives of the protagonists in any important way.

PROTECTION

A primary function of any society is to protect the lives of its members and insure their well-being in an equitable manner. Sometimes the society in a story has difficulty performing this function, and this difficulty is reflected in the life of the individual protagonists, just as Ole in "The Killers" suffers from the inability of society to enforce its laws.

Some of these difficulties appear in the stories of both periods. For one thing, neither collective world can provide security against certain natural misfortunes: the problems of aging, bereavement, and natural death. This point is not quite as obvious at it seems. What it means is that writers of both periods sometimes prefer to confront their characters with such problems — problems universal to all members of the community and completely beyond the power of any community to solve — even though a writer is by no means obliged to include them in the world he depicts. As will be seen later, in most cases the natural misfortune, when it appears, is merely the means of bringing about some other development: illness and approaching death in Mrs. Freeman's "A Village Singer," for example, bring the heroine to an important discovery about graceful retirement from her post as church soprano. Sometimes, as in Dreiser's "The Lost Phoebe" or Hemingway's "In Another Country," the issue is central; the protagonist is face to face with biological fatality, a universal fact which no social organization can alter, and the story deals specifically with his reaction to this fatality.

Both worlds, furthermore, share one great man-made social problem that threatens the well-being of the members of the society. This, of course, is war, threatening or taking lives in the stories by Bierce, Crane, Mrs. Wharton,[1] Hemingway, Faulkner, and Miss Porter. If death by war is actually represented a little more frequently in the earlier stories, this does not mean that it is less threatening in the later ones, but only that the later writers have chosen to look at the battlefield from somewhat different angles.[2] Besides death, a number of stories in both periods show a psychological crack-up brought about by war. Many of the stories by Bierce provide a further horror of war not seen in the twenties: the local nature of the Civil War enables Bierce to exploit the misfortune of families divided, their members enlisted on opposite sides, often meeting by terrible accident at the scene of combat.[3]

One important community problem in the early period is almost always missing in stories of the twenties. Much of the misery in many earlier stories is economic, the consequence, direct or indirect, of the inequity, inefficiency, or other economic malfunctioning of society. Although the victims themselves are not usually aware of the source of their trouble, it is clear what this source is meant to be. In Crane's "Maggie: A Girl of the Streets," we infer from the extended description of Maggie's slum background that her own mistakes are made in innocence

---

[1] "Coming Home" was written during World War I and deals with the war. Below Mrs. Wharton's usual standards, it differs from other war stories in the two canons in its effort to portray the "enemy," in this case the Germans, as vicious.

[2] Even in the early period, however, Bierce is the only writer whose protagonists die in war.

[3] Such Civil War mischances occur in Bierce, "Horseman in the Sky," "Affair at Coulter's Notch," "Mocking-Bird." Other war stories in the two canons are Bierce, "Affair of Outposts," "Chickamauga," "Killed at Resaca," "Occurrence at Owl Creek Bridge," "One Kind of Officer," "One Officer, One Man," "One of the Missing," "Parker Adderson," "Son of the Gods," "Story of a Conscience"; Crane, "Death and the Child," "Episode of War," "Gray Sleeve," "Little Regiment," "Mystery of Heroism," "Three Miraculous Soldiers"; Wharton, "Coming Home"; Hemingway, "In Another Country," "Now I Lay Me," "Soldier's Home," "Very Short Story"; Faulkner, "Ad Astra," "All the Dead Pilots," "Crevasse," "Victory." In Porter, revolutionary war is in the background in "Flowering Judas," "Maria Concepcion," and "That Tree."

and that her environment is the villain. The laborers in Dreiser's "The Cruise of the 'Idlewild'" are the victims of an economic system which prevents them from finding a better living and numbs their minds so that they scarcely desire one.

Extreme poverty is not the most usual sign of the economic shortcomings of the early society. It is, indeed, rather rare in these stories. More significant is the daily hardship of making a living, as experienced by people who do not consider themselves poor — especially Garland's farmers and Mrs. Freeman's village housewives. Most of the suffering in Garland's world is a result of the community's struggle with the "land" — the struggle, shared by all, to keep the farms going and to support the families who live on them. The painfulness of unremitting hard labor, endured by all, wives and children as well as men, and the heavy anxiety caused by uncertainties of crops and weakening of bodies — a kind of suffering strongly underscored in Garland's treatment — are the direct result of this society's economic problem. This struggle embitters the farmer in "Up the Coolly"; it haunts and worries the returned soldier-farmer facing his future in "The Return of a Private"; it makes dreary and burdensome the lives of the women in "A Day's Pleasure," "Among the Corn Rows," and "The Creamery Man"; in "Under the Lion's Paw" it has defeated Haskins and his family, throwing them upon the mercy of the town, and when he has somewhat regained his feet, his prosperity exacts the most strenuous continuing and ceaseless physical labor.

Such suffering is not necessarily the primary issue in these stories. Indeed, some of these people have chosen this existence with obvious pride. Nevertheless, the suffering is usually there, and an element of economic victimization cannot be denied. Just as the slum dwellers and laborers in "Maggie" and "The Cruise of the 'Idlewild'" are trapped in their communities by the inequities of the economic system, so are the people in "A Day's Pleasure" and "Up the Coolly" trapped in theirs. If the spring of the trap is sometimes pride, the trapper himself is still society as a whole, as this speech by the young farmer in "Among the Corn Rows" shows:

"I consider myself a sight better 'n any man who lives on some-body else's hard work. I've never had a cent I didn't earn with them hands. . . . Well, so I come West, just like a thousand other fellers, to get a start where the cussed European aristocracy hadn't got a holt on the people. . . . I'm my own boss, as I say, and I'm going to *stay* my own boss if I have to live on crackers an' wheat coffee to do it. . . ." This working farmer had voiced the modern idea. It was an absolute overturn of all the ideas of nobility and special privilege born of the feudal past. . . . Seagraves felt that it was a wild, grand upstirring of the modern democrat against the aristocrat, against the idea of caste and the privilege of living on the labor of others. . . . He had declared rebellion against laws that were survivals of hate and prejudice. He had exposed also the native spring of the emigrant by uttering the feeling that it is better to be an equal among peasants than a servant before nobles.

Though this particular farmer's optimism makes us less aware of suffering than we are in other stories by Garland, the fact is perfectly clear: the farmer moves West because the East can-not accommodate him. The hardship of his labors is the price that the American economy exacts for independence.

In the stories of the twenties, the economic problem is less evident. In such rural communities as Winesburg, it is not the struggle for subsistence that causes the people to suffer. Though some of Fitzgerald's young couples must economize stringently in order to achieve their goals, they are seeking more than in-dependent subsistence; their purpose is competitive, their labors necessary to their movement upward on the social ladder. Though economic inequality still exists, though some people, especially Fitzgerald's, find this galling, it no longer threatens the livelihood, health, or leisure of those at the bottom — the bottom, at least, of the world that those writers have chosen to write about.

Nevertheless, the world of the twenties is scarcely a more secure place in which to live than was the earlier world. The threat to man's physical well-being now comes not from eco-nomic malfunctioning but from the internal violence in society. The world of the twenties is more dangerous.

Violence in the early period is largely confined to war. Otherwise, we can find in the whole canon only four killings (one a lynching, and one a murder in the "background," the protagonist a bystander) and four thwarted murders. A majority of these occur in stories by Crane, making still more striking the absence of violence in more representative writers. Even mild physical violence is rare: mob action briefly threatens the embezzler in Garland's "A 'Good Fellow's' Wife," and there are brutalities in "Maggie," but otherwise the early world is physically peaceful.[4]

The canon of the twenties has twice as many murders, which may be represented or may be left implicit (as in "The Killers"), and several instances of lesser violence: a mob expelling the hero of Anderson's "Hands" from a Pennsylvania town, cruel and vicious beatings in Faulkner's "All the Dead Pilots" and Miss Porter's "Magic." Other stories show milder beatings, and in others there are threats of violence which, like poverty in Garland, do not materialize.[5] In a later chapter subtler kinds of violence will be noticed: the internal violence of character, for instance, threatening to erupt in irrational acts and producing such bloody consequences as the suicide in Hemingway's "Indian Camp"; the covert violence in the exploitation of one character by another, verging sometimes upon the physical, as in the virtual rape of Liz in Hemingway's "Up in Michigan." In Hemingway, also, there is a hint that nature itself is violent; Edmund Wilson finds this in "Big Two-Hearted River," ostensibly a fishing story;[6] perhaps the unexpected premature death

[4] The four killings take place in Dreiser, "Nigger Jeff"; Freeman, "Life-Everlasting"; Crane, "Blue Hotel"; Wharton, "Coming Home." The thwarted killings are in Wharton, "The Choice"; Crane, "Five White Mice," "Horses — One Dash!" and "Bride Comes to Yellow Sky."

[5] Murder in the twenties appears in Hemingway, "Killers"; Porter, "Maria Concepcion"; Faulkner, "That Evening Sun," "Rose for Emily," "Justice," "Victory," "Mistral." In "The Killers" and "That Evening Sun" the narrative ends before the murder is committed, although the reader infers it will take place.

[6] Edmund Wilson, introduction to Ernest Hemingway, *In Our Time* (New York: Charles Scribner's Sons, 1930), p. xi: "But the brutality of life is always there, and it is somehow bound up with the enjoyment. . . . Even Nick's fishing-trip, when he is away by himself happy and free in the woods, has aspects which must make it unique among the fishing-trips of literature — for through all Nick's tranquil exhilaration we are made conscious in a curious way of the cruelty involved for the fish — and not only this, but even of the martyrdom of the grasshoppers used for bait. The condition of life is still pain — and every calm or contented surface still vibrates with its pangs."

of the major's young wife in "In Another Country" suggests the same point.[7]

Most of the violence in the early period took place on the borderlands of society and was far more common in Crane's frontier world than anywhere else. In the twenties it appears in the heart of the American community. It seems to increase as the period progresses: Anderson's and Fitzgerald's worlds are peaceful compared with Hemingway's and Miss Porter's, and these are peaceful compared with Faulkner's, in whose collection of thirteen stories no less than five involve murder.

LAW

Just as a society tries to protect the well-being of its members, so it also tries to impose its laws, its customs, and its institutions upon them. One obvious reason for the increase of violence in the twenties is the greater weakness of the society in performing this function.

The early society is usually powerful in enforcing its will. Its severity is exemplified by the military executions in no less than four stories by Bierce. Except in Mrs. Gerould's "Pearls," no one gets away with theft; even in Mrs. Freeman's "Calla-lilies and Hannah" and "A Stolen Christmas," where the thefts are extremely petty, the pangs of conscience felt by the gentle heroines show the respect for and fear of the law that prevailed in the period.

In Mrs. Freeman's "Christmas Jenny" the community organizes an inquiry into the heroine's life, which the author calls a "witch-hunt," undertaken because they cannot understand her "eccentricity, her possible uncanny deviation from the ordinary ways of life," a hunt fortunately averted at the last moment. The early community can also punish effectively by extra-legal means. In "Paul's Case," the Pittsburgh community makes a scandal out of Paul's escape from the city and in the person of his father tries to force his return, which he avoids only by suicide. In Mrs. Freeman's "Calla-lilies and Hannah," Crane's "The Monster" and "Maggie," and Mrs. Wharton's "Autres

[7] One story in the early period directly treats the violence of nature: Crane's "Open Boat," in which the sea manifests this violence.

Temps," the community ostracizes its victim, doing so with power and unity of purpose and causing great suffering thereby. The ostracizing community, whose injustice is always established by the author, may be a New England village, a small town, a New York slum, the New York elite. In some stories by James, the English elite guards its integrity very carefully: great cleverness, effort, and a surprising turn of unforeseen luck are needed for Mamie Cutter to carry out the task, which everyone thought impossible, of getting the ostracized Mrs. Medwin restored to society.[8]

The society of the twenties seldom shows such power. Peaceful ostracism is seldom attempted.[9] The mob action of Anderson's "Hands" and Faulkner's "Dry September" indicates a breakdown of law and order, and hence weakness rather than strength in the community structure. In "The Killers" and one or two other stories — Hemingway's "My Old Man" and perhaps Miss Porter's "Magic" — underworld communities show, indeed, a power to enforce their laws and punish transgressions far more effective than that displayed by the law-abiding community.

Indeed, in all eight of the murders that occur in stories of the twenties, the killers apparently escape punishment, despite the fact that in five cases (including "The Killers") the intent to murder or the identity of the murderer is known to the community. Of the two thieves depicted in the canon of the twenties, one is sent to Congress by a hoodwinked community and the other challenges her victim's right to object to her thievery.

---

[8] Mamie, to be sure, exploits a foible of this society which superficially seems to be a contradiction to this statement: the fondness of the British society for entertaining itself with people of another class, mostly Americans and artists. This is also seen in such stories as "Death of the Lion," "Coxon Fund," "Lesson of the Master." Such "outsiders" are brought in for the novelty, however; since their very eccentricity is what is sought and since this serves to emphasize the essential class barriers, this foible cannot be regarded as a real breakdown of class barriers.

[9] Exceptions: Anderson, " 'Unused' "; Porter, "Cracked Looking-Glass." In " 'Unused' " the attempt of some members of the community to ostracize the heroine as a prostitute (a mistake they make because her sisters are prostitutes) is successful largely because of the heroine's own emotional vulnerability; she aggravates the situation by ostracizing herself. In "Cracked Looking-Glass" some of the heroine's Connecticut neighbors attempt to ostracize her, but she is less dependent upon their acceptance than are the earlier victims; her primary problem has to do with her relations with her aged husband.

Many lesser crimes also go unpunished, such as the appropria-
tion of company property, the violation of game laws, the fixing
of sports events, and abortion.[10] The prohibition amendment is,
of course, widely ignored.

Although actual crimes and other overt breakdowns of community law and order occur only occasionally, even in the twenties, it is already clear that the earlier society is, collectively, a
stronger one than that of the twenties — though not always good
to its members, by any means. Often it imposes cruel and unjust
sufferings. But these sufferings are imposed by its strength; the
individual trapped in the slum or on the farm, or banished from
society, is powerless not because of his own failings but because
of the power of the collective will or the rigidity of the structure
surrounding him. In the twenties, the individual seldom has this
to contend with; he may even commit murder and get away
with it. Nor does he have to struggle for his livelihood. On the
other hand, he may suffer from the very weakness of society.
Like Ole, he may be endangered by the incipient violence, or he
may find, even in his freedom, new problems and new kinds of
suffering opened up by that freedom.

[10] Stories cited: Hemingway, "Killers"; Porter, "Maria Concepcion"; Faulk-
ner, "That Evening Sun," "Justice," "Mistral"; Fitzgerald, "Dalyrimple Goes
Wrong"; Porter, "Theft"; Hemingway, "Doctor and Doctor's Wife," "Out of
Season," "My Old Man," "Hills Like White Elephants."

IV: THE INDIVIDUAL IN HIS SOCIETY

One of the murders of the twenties is that committed by the heroine of Faukner's "A Rose for Emily." Last descendant of an old aristocratic Southern family, Emily has always held herself aloof from the people of the town. After the death of her father, she is seen frequently in company with a Yankee laborer, and the people gossip about her and say "Poor Emily." The laborer disappears and Emily thereupon retires into her house, where she becomes a recluse. Upon her death, many years later, it is discovered that she has murdered her lover, has kept his body in a room decorated as for a bridal, and (from the evidence of the strand of iron-gray hair found upon the pillow) has slept for years with his rotting corpse.

This story has the violence of which we have spoken and reflects, also, the weakness of the society in enforcing its laws and principles: for even if they might be excused for failing to track down the disappearance of the lover, the members of the community show great timidity toward Emily, remitting her taxes when she refuses to pay, and sprinkling lime around her house at night when the body begins to smell, because one cannot "accuse a lady to her face of smelling bad." Yet the violence and weakness of society are the smallest parts of Emily's case. Her fundamental problem is personal — a question of her attitudes toward love and toward her emotions — but even the social problem turns more significantly upon her attitudes toward society than upon society's treatment of her. The murder and the perversion are grotesque manifestations of her total rejection of society: her withdrawal from others and her attack upon society's laws and taboos. Yet it is not a simple rejection. We can also infer from the murder and the bridal decoration of her lover's room a contrary yearning, not merely for love but for marriage, which is a social institution. We can infer a deep loneliness.

The most striking social differences between the worlds depicted in the two periods concern the attitudes of individuals toward the society to which they belong. In her grotesque way Emily is characteristic of many of the protagonists in the twenties. She differs sharply from the majority of those of the early period.

EARLY PERIOD: INTEGRATION

A prominent feature of the world of Garland is the co-operative community spirit, solidarity that is highly effective and beneficial to all. All are engaged, as has been seen, in a painful struggle with the "land," and all unite to help each other in every possible way. The co-operation begins at home, within the family unit, the wives laboring as hard in the kitchens as their husbands do in the fields, while the children are enlisted as soon as they are able to lend a hand. Neighbors share in doing each other's heavy work; the farmers band together (as, for instance, in "A Branch Road") to bring in a neighbor's crop, and the wives and daughters go along to get the common meals; the indebted neighbor repays his obligation by helping at the other farms. If a person has trouble, his neighbors co-operate to help him out. If he is a newcomer, they lend him what he needs to get back on his feet. If he is ill, they help to nurse him back to health. If a woman's husband has gone to war, the other wives provide companionship and consolation.[1]

Though this co-operative spirit is most marked in Garland's world, it also prevails in many other parts of the early world. In Mrs. Freeman's New England, spinsters make a virtual career of helping people (and animals) in need. One devotes herself to comforting the bereaved, others to the care of some particular helpless individual — an orphan, a lonely wanderer, an elderly relative. In such stories as "Life-Everlasting" and "Christmas Jenny" the community shows its respect for the virtue of charity by honoring charitable people. It institutionalizes charity in its almshouses.[2]

Upper-class characters also show a spirit of service in stories by Mrs. Wharton and Mrs. Gerould, though not notably in stories by James. The protagonists of Mrs. Wharton's "The Long Run" and "The Quicksand" and Mrs. Gerould's "The Bird in the Bush" feel a strong duty to devote their lives to the public good, although they are thwarted in this aim for various reasons. Their careers, in a sense political, are directed toward making existing institutions function well and toward alleviating injustice under the present system.[3]

[1] The labor of women is stressed in "Day's Pleasure," "Branch Road," "Return of a Private," "Mrs. Ripley's Trip." Other particular situations cited in this paragraph appear in "Under the Lion's Paw," "God's Ravens."

[2] See especially Freeman, "Stolen Christmas," "Poetess," "Gentle Ghost," "A Solitary," "Innocent Gamester," "Calla-lilies," "Louisa," "Sister Liddy."

[3] In "Bird in the Bush," the hero has the offer of a diplomatic post. In "Quicksand," the heroine's liberal principles are directed to reform by persuasive journalism; the mistake that she regrets is having married the publisher of a reactionary journal. In "The Long Run," the nature of the hero's projected but frustrated career is suggested by this summary of its beginnings: "After leaving Harvard he had spent two years at Oxford; then he had accepted a private secretaryship to our Ambassador in England, and had come back from this adventure with a fresh curiosity about public affairs at home, and the conviction that men of his kind should play a larger part in them. This led, first, to his running for a State Senatorship which he failed to get, and ultimately to a few months of intelligent activity in a municipal office. Soon after being deprived of this post by a change of party he had published a small volume of delicate verse, and, a year later, an odd uneven brilliant book on Municipal Government."

The spirit of service is also manifest in the extreme patriotism depicted in the war stories by Bierce, most of which show this spirit triumphant over some other pressing claim. Sometimes the issue is simply the soldier's courage in performance of his duty; here — as in "A Son of the Gods" — he usually shows enough or more than enough courage, which may lead him to an unnecessary death.[4] Sometimes the issue goes well beyond mere courage; the hero may be placed by chance in a spot where he must choose between duty and the main emotional values of his life. Such situations display the military solidarity of the early period at its most extreme: a sentry knowingly kills his own father, an artillery officer obeys his general's order to shell and destroy his own house and family, an officer executes the man who had earlier saved his life (and then commits suicide to square his personal debt).[5] Military discipline may triumph over patriotism: an officer knowingly bombards his own troops because his commander, in ignorance of the battle situation, has ordered it; a Southern sympathizer who has enlisted on the Northern side for personal reasons gives his life gallantly for the Northern cause even though his original reasons for enlisting have been removed.[6] Each of these men has placed adherence to the letter of military law above all other values — even, in "One Kind of Officer," above good military judgment.

The spirit of community co-operation is epitomized in miniature in Crane's "The Open Boat." The little group stranded in a lifeboat work together; though they raise questions about the justice of the fates, they think and feel as one, without friction or conflicting interests.

Other kinds of community spirit can be seen in stories by Dreiser — the banding together of the laborers in "The Cruise

[4] Exceptional courage is displayed in "Killed at Resaca" and "George Thurston," as well as in Crane's "Mystery of Heroism," "Little Regiment," "Episode of War" (with emphasis on stoical acceptance in the latter two). Most of these stories stress the needlessness of the courage displayed; a few are interested in the mystery of the origins of such courage. Courage fails in Bierce's "One Officer, One Man," "One of the Missing," "Parker Adderson," and Crane's "Death and the Child." In the first two, the protagonist goes mad and kills himself; the last two deal with cowards, ashamed and astonished by exposure of their own cowardice.

[5] Bierce, "Horseman in the Sky," "Affair at Coulter's Notch," "Story of a Conscience."

[6] Bierce, "One Kind of Officer," "Affair of Outposts."

of the 'Idlewild'" to make their lives more tolerable, or the social conscience of the reporter in "Nigger Jeff," who is unable to prevent a lynching yet tries to make a constructive report of it. Even in stories by James, although few characters show such a social conscience as has been described, many do believe in serving or assisting other individuals, even when this means sacrifice to themselves: Ruth Anvoy in "The Coxon Fund" gives up a personal fortune in order to endow an "earnest and loyal' seeker"; Dencombe in "The Middle Years" sacrifices himself in his effort to get the devoted young doctor to claim the fortune due him; the narrator of "The Tree of Knowledge" stifles the great temptation to express his contempt for the art of Morgan Mallow and keeps to himself his love for Mallow's wife; the heroine of "The Abasement of the Northmores" renounces her plan to humiliate publicly the family of her dead husband's rival; the hero of "Fordham Castle" submits to the complete self-effacement that his wife desires of him.

Such behavior contrasts sharply with that displayed in stories of the twenties. This is not to say that the individuals in the twenties are notably antisocial or unco-operative. The point of contrast is, rather, that a belief in service is seldom manifested effectually; it seldom motivates significant action.[7] There are some cases — like that of Nick Adams in "The Killers" — in which people try to help others in need, or at least feel that they should. Such efforts usually fail because of the inadequacy of the person who wants to help or the failure of society to support him.[8]

The contrast also appears in the war stories by Hemingway and Faulkner. Patriotism and the spirit of military duty tend to break down as the primary incentive for action. This does not mean that heroism and courage under fire have disappeared; there are no significant cases of cowardice or dereliction of duty,

[7] Exceptions are the sacrifices of the heroine in Anderson's "Death in the Woods"; the generous behavior of the hero in Fitzgerald's "Hot and Cold Blood"; and the lessons in altruism learned by the hero in Fitzgerald's "Four Fists."

[8] Conspicuous failures of one character to help another are seen in most of the *Winesburg* stories in which George Willard is a helpless onlooker, in Hemingway's "Pursuit Race," "Now I Lay Me," "Three-Day Blow," and Faulkner's "That Evening Sun," although in each case the onlooker would like to help.

and one can assume that the soldiers in the stories of the twenties have done what they were supposed to do at crucial moments; a few have apparently done more than was needed.[9] But the typical emphasis of the twenties is on the psychological damage done to a character who is exposed to war, rather than on his choice of doing or not doing his duty. Wartime trauma tends to make even the most heroic characters withdraw from life: the brave young Italian heroes of Hemingway's "In Another Country," compared by the narrator (no hero) to hunting hawks, are transformed by their experiences into an elite, "a little detached," cut off from intimacy with others. The more sophisticated major in the same story "did not believe in bravery"; with quiet contempt for the heroics of the younger men, he attempts to make his life outside the military community, and expresses great doubt about the validity of the war effort: "What will you do when the war is over if it is over?"

Sometimes military discipline breaks down. An officer in one of Faulkner's stories feuds with his superior officer over a prostitute. American soldiers defy regulations and antagonize their French allies by making friends with a German prisoner and showing him off in a cafe. A young Mexican deserts his army and comes home when he is tired of the adventure. An enlisted man, ambitious for promotion, murders his sergeant in the heat of battle.[10]

A few characters — mostly teachers and priests — are fired by pedagogical zeal. They want to teach important lessons about life to certain promising youngsters.[11] But the resemblance to the earlier ideal of service stops here, since the lessons they teach differ radically from the common social attitudes of the early period. Two characters in stories of the twenties are driven by political zeal.[12] But here, too, as will be seen, the nature of

[9] In Faulkner's "Crevasse," a stalwart officer leads his men successfully through an accident in a cave. Sartoris, in Faulkner's "All the Dead Pilots," gives his life in reckless battle in the air. In Hemingway's "In Another Country," the young Italian officers are admired for their heroism.

[10] Stories cited: Faulkner's "All the Dead Pilots," "Ad Astra"; Porter, "Maria Concepcion"; Faulkner, "Victory."

[11] See pp. 124–25.

[12] In Hemingway's "The Revolutionist," and Porter's "Flowering Judas." See pp. 54–55.

the intended political contribution is not to be compared with that of the earlier characters. The spirit of community service or service to others in the early period — significant at least occasionally in the work of all the early writers except perhaps Miss Cather — reflects a highly affirmative attitude toward society in general. This is in sharp contrast to the attitudes that dominate in the twenties, attitudes which must be examined separately.

THE TWENTIES: ISOLATION

Unlike most of the characters in earlier stories, Faulkner's Emily is isolated from her society. In the twenties perhaps all characters who have any claim to being typical are isolated, although seldom in as extreme a way as she. Usually this isolation is a subjective phenomenon: the character feels it, but the community in general may be quite unaware of it. Occasionally a different kind of isolation exists: the character considers himself an integrated member of the community, unaware that the community in general regards him as odd or peculiar (e.g., the hero of Anderson's "A Man of Ideas"). In either case the isolation is primarily emotional — a matter of the individual's attitudes; a separation is felt, some failure of communication, understanding, or sympathy between him and those around him.

Withdrawal

Certain characters in the twenties isolate themselves deliberately. One takes up the life of a hobo, though he has money; two different boys plan to bury themselves in anonymity in the city; at least three people in small towns are virtual or actual recluses.[13] The rootless wanderers in Mexico and Europe are doing essentially the same thing: the traveling couples in Hemingway's "Cat in the Rain," "Out of Season," and "Hills Like White Elephants," whose only visible human relationships are with guides and waiters, are losing themselves, cutting themselves off from society. Sometimes the flight is less drastic: a common practice of Hemingway's characters is to take to the woods or the hills, a temporary, therapeutic escape into fishing, hunting, or

[13] See Hemingway's "The Battler," "Soldier's Home"; Anderson's "Thinker," "Hands," "Loneliness"; Faulkner's "Rose for Emily."

skiing.[14] It is, nevertheless, a self-isolation, reflecting some fundamental dissatisfaction with one's relationship to society.

More common than the character who withdraws physically is the one who, although he maintains a working relationship with society, withdraws from intimate or emotional involvement in its activities. In *Winesburg*, the misanthropic Doctor Parcival, the frightened Wing Biddlebaum, the dirty, woman-hating Wash Williams, all of whom confide their secrets only to George Willard, are typical. They reject love, they draw back from threatened intimacy, they guard themselves, they hold themselves detached. Most of the *Winesburg* characters whom Anderson calls "grotesques" are like this, since the same moral or emotional bias that makes them grotesque also isolates them. So are the psychologically wounded characters in the war stories by Hemingway and Faulkner: the "detached" heroes (as well as the grief-stricken major) in "In Another Country," for example, or the reckless lone wolf, Sartoris, in "All the Dead Pilots." A common experience for Hemingway's young hero, Nick Adams, in many stories, is to see the detachment, the emotional withdrawal, caused by the suffering of someone else: he sees Ole turn to the wall in "The Killers," the Indian husband in "Indian Camp" commit suicide. The heroine of Anderson's "Seeds" reveals another common pattern, that of the girl who repels the advances she has invited. Such varied patterns of withdrawal and rejection are very common in the stories of the twenties, appearing in almost half of the total canon.[15]

Reasons for such withdrawals vary, and are discussed in a

[14] See Hemingway's "Big Two-Hearted River," "Cross-Country Snow," "Doctor and Doctor's Wife," "Now I Lay Me."

[15] See Anderson's "Adventure," "Chicago Hamlet," "Door of the Trap," "Drink," "Hands," "Loneliness," "Mother," "New Englander," "Out of Nowhere into Nothing," "Paper Pills," "Philosopher," "Respectability," "Seeds," "Surrender," "Tandy," "Teacher," "Thinker," "Unlighted Lamps," " 'Unused' "; Fitzgerald, "Benediction," "Dalyrimple Goes Wrong," "Ice Palace," "Offshore Pirate," "Rags Martin-Jones," "Rich Boy"; Hemingway, "Alpine Idyll," "Battler," "Big Two-Hearted River," "Cat in the Rain," "Cross-Country Snow," "Doctor and Doctor's Wife," "End of Something," "Fifty Grand," "Hills Like White Elephants," "In Another Country," "Indian Camp," "Killers," "My Old Man," "Now I Lay Me," "Out of Season," "Pursuit Race," "Soldier's Home," "Three Day-Blow"; Porter, "Flowering Judas," "Maria Concepcion," "That Tree," "Theft"; Faulkner, "Carcassonne," "Hair," "Rose for Emily."

later chapter. What matters here is that they are rejections of society, reflecting discontent with what it can give or dread of what it may demand.

Few of the earlier stories show comparable behavior. Characters in the early period who move or travel are, as has been suggested, less concerned with cutting their roots than with enriching their lives (like the aging daughters who want to go to Europe in James's "Europe") or with setting down new roots (like the frontiersmen in Crane's "The Bride Comes to Yellow Sky" or the social-climbing girl from Peoria who enters high English society in James's "Fordham Castle"). The Western movement depicted in Garland's stories has been described as an attempt to build a new, more equitable society. As social criticism these various activities are more moderate than Nick's flight in Hemingway's "Big Two-Hearted River" or Wash Williams' rejection of all women in Anderson's "Respectability."

In James's stories a few artists wish to withdraw from the demands of a social existence: Paul Overt, in "The Lesson of the Master," is persuaded to give up his desire for wife and child, which would, he fears, be a hindrance to his pursuit of artistic perfection; Neil Paraday, in "The Death of the Lion," is destroyed by his exposure to publicity and the resultant social whirl. In these stories society is inimical to artistic production. Yet in spite of this, artists are seen at all times as on perfectly good terms with society people, attending their dinners, going to their weekend parties, paying social calls, and the like.

Though there are some recluses in Mrs. Freeman's world, these also differ significantly from the later ones. If a character's attitude is initially antisocial, as in "A Solitary," it will be overcome before the end of the story. Otherwise, the most striking thing about most of the recluses and spinsters is their social good will; the acts of charity and kindness with which they fill their lives testify to essential satisfaction with their place in society. What other voluntary withdrawal occurs, such as the self-effacement of the heroes of James's "Fordham Castle" and Mrs. Freeman's "Kitchen Colonel," is a deliberate sacrifice for altruistic principles in a particular situation and reflects no hostility to or dread of society as such. The only rejections of society as such in the early period are in the suicides of Miss Cather's Paul and Crane's Maggie, the senile insanity of the bereaved old man in Dreiser's "The Lost Phoebe," the flight to the South Seas for the sake of art by the hero of Mrs. Gerould's "Pearls." It should be noted that three of these writers (Miss Cather, Crane, and Dreiser) are included in the canon as "forerunners." Yet even these withdrawals tend to differ from those of the twenties, not merely by their more melodramatic expression (which is not, of course, relevant to the point), but by their affirmation of more positive social values (art, marriage, the sanctity of love) that the fleeing character thinks have been violated in his life.

Disregard of Social Institutions

Emotional isolation from society is also seen in many characters in stories of the twenties who disregard or defy certain of the established institutions of society that were accepted or supported by those in earlier stories. A character need not withdraw from society to be isolated in this way; the isolation exists in the discrepancy between his interests and those of society, as reflected by the institutions that he ignores.

The contrast between the two periods is seen in two ways. In the case of certain institutions, virtually all characters in stories of the twenties are indifferent to what many characters in earlier stories actively supported. In the case of others, those of the twenties more or less actively repudiate institutions that earlier were almost universally accepted.

In the twenties the writers concern themselves with those who tend to be indifferent to the class structure of their society. In the early period two contrasting attitudes may be seen: support of this structure and the desire to revise or reform it. Miss Cather's and James's social climbers desire not to break down the barriers but to slip into the circle of elite. Mamie Cutter, in James's "Mrs. Medwin," makes it her business to get people into English "society," and the greatest source of suffering for Mrs. Lidcote, in Mrs. Wharton's "Autres Temps," is that she is banished from New York "society." [16]

[16] Other stories in which Society with a capital S is valued and sought after are Gerould, "Great Tradition"; James, "Broken Wings," "Abasement," "Miss Gunton," "Fordham Castle," "Real Thing," "Brooksmith," "Beldonald Holbein."

On the other hand, Garland's farmers, as represented by the speech quoted from "Among the Corn Rows," on page 37, have moved West because they cannot tolerate the traditional class system. Yet this speech is "social" in its values and in keeping with tradition: the American tradition of democracy, "a wild, grand upstirring of the modern democrat against the aristocrat." The farmer is building a new society based on old ideals — and we have already seen the co-operative social spirit that prevails in his society. In a sense he is a reformer, pruning the social system of its inequities to make it work better.

A few of the protagonists in stories of the twenties attempt to cling to old class prerogatives: Faulkner's Emily tries to preserve her aristocratic heritage, yet she takes a Yankee laborer as a lover; Fitzgerald's Anson Hunter, in "The Rich Boy," clings to his traditions as a member of the very wealthy class, yet he is lonely and makes feeble efforts to find friends and love outside of his class. There is the hero of Faulkner's "Victory," a Scot from the laboring classes with ambitions to raise himself to the ranks of the aristocrats in England. Yet even the most strenuous pursuers of success and status in Fitzgerald's stories, as well as in those by Anderson and Miss Porter, are generally less interested in class membership as such than in their own eminence. George Willard wants to be a "big man, the biggest that ever lived here in Winesburg." Even Dexter Green, in Fitzgerald's "Winter Dreams," who more than most desires social success, is described as wanting "not association with glittering things and glittering people — he wanted the glittering things themselves. Often he reached out for the best without knowing why he wanted it."

An interesting light is thrown on the decline of interest in the class system by the change in the social position of artists as characters in the stories of the twenties. Artists — that is, painters, sculptors, musicians, and writers — are prominent in many stories by Miss Cather and James, and what is most striking about them is their intimate relationship with the elite, the wealthy and cultured and aristocratic groups. This intimacy is suggested with varying degrees of directness in a large number of stories, including Mrs. Gerould's "Leda and the Swan," Mrs. Wharton's "The Long Run," Miss Cather's "Flavia and Her

Artists," "The Garden Lodge," "The Marriage of Phaedra," and perhaps "The Sculptor's Funeral," and James's "The Middle Years," "Greville Fane," "Broken Wings," "The Tree of Knowledge," "The Real Thing," "The Beldonald Holbein," "The Story In It," "The Lesson of the Master," "The Death of the Lion," "The Figure in the Carpet," and "The Coxon Fund." [17] It may be that the upper class supports, entertains, or woos the artist, or that the artist paints or portrays the aristocrat, thereby mingling with him socially, or that the artist himself has an income or lives in a sufficiently comfortable and gracious way to put him on a footing with the leisured class, or that the aristocrat envisions not merely a social or political contribution to society but also an artistic one such as "a small volume of delicate verse," [18] or even that the artist or his children marry aristocrats, as in "The Marriage of Phaedra" and "Greville Fane." The impoverished or struggling artist is not unheard of, but he is usually, like the heroine's father in "The Garden Lodge," a failure artistically as well as socially.[19] The artist sharply detached from, conspicuously indifferent to, good society is indeed rare; only Mrs. Gerould's "Pearls" shows an artist who has such an attitude. All the same, it is true that some of these stories draw a fairly sharp line between the artist and the aristocrat.

It is clear that the artists depicted in the early period by and large accepted or even supported the class system as willingly as did any other characters of the period. Similarly, the upper classes supported the artist, for to love art was, at least ostensibly, a mark of class distinction, an aspect of their refinement or cultivation.

In the twenties the artist as a character is much rarer. When he does appear, he is almost completely dissociated from the upper classes or from the class system. He may be merely a

[17] In James's "Coxon Fund," note how the important question about Frank Saltram, the brilliant intellectual, for the narrator's friend George Gravener (if not for the narrator himself) is whether or not Saltram is a "gentleman."

[18] See above, p. 44, n. 3.

[19] This is not so in James's "The Next Time," which stresses the unpopularity of the true artist. Other James stories also make this point, but it is noteworthy that, even so, the artist, if financially unsuccessful, nearly always has enough income to live fairly comfortably. The case of Frank Saltram, in "The Coxon Fund," who does not have money, differs also in that Saltram is not a productive artist.

potential artist — George Willard wanting to write in "The
Teacher" and "Sophistication," but without notions of class distinction — or he may be poor and struggling — the writers in Miss
Porter's "Theft" and "That Tree" in New York or Mexico, associated with other artists in the same position and otherwise either
friendless or befriended by ordinary people of lower or undif-
ferentiated class. The successful artist in the twenties, such as
the writer-hero of Fitzgerald's "The Rough Crossing," has become a popular celebrity and is thus also dissociated from class;
his artistry is likely to be expressed in fields of popular entertainment which earlier characters would not have considered
art: prize fighting, bullfighting, burlesque, the movies, all directed to a mass audience without class distinction.

Politics and the economic system do not interest most characters in either period, but where they are significant a similar
contrast between the two periods appears. The man in the early
period who lends his brilliance to foreign diplomacy, who believes that "men of his kind" should take a greater part in
domestic affairs, who writes a brilliant book on municipal government, and the woman who believes in a liberal newspaper
advocating peaceful reforms leading to a more equitable society,
are, as has been suggested, supporting the political and economic institutions of their day by lending their talents to their
improved functioning.[20] In the twenties, however, of those few
who show any interest whatever in politics, two show only
enough to deplore (implicitly) Italian fascism, and one merely
uses politics as his material for his jump to fame as a journalist.[21]
Only in two stories are characters sufficiently interested to make
a career of politics, but their political commitments are a far
cry indeed from those of the early characters. They are revolu-
tionaries; the most extreme is Braggioni, in Miss Porter's "Flowering Judas," who describes his political objectives thus:

Some day this world, now seemingly so composed and eternal, to the
edges of every sea shall be merely a tangle of gaping trenches, of
crushing walls and broken bodies. Everything must be torn from its

[20] Wharton, "The Long Run," "Quicksand." See p. 44, n. 3.
[21] Hemingway, "Che Dice"; Faulkner, "Mistral"; Porter, "That Tree."

accustomed place where it has rotted for centuries, hurled skyward and distributed, cast down again clean as rain, without separate identity. Nothing shall survive that the stiffened hands of poverty have created for the rich and no one shall be left alive except the elect spirits destined to procreate a new world cleansed of cruelty and injustice, ruled by benevolent anarchy.

If the characters of the twenties tend to be indifferent to the political and class institutions that earlier characters either support or try to reform, many characters in stories of the twenties disregard or attack through more positive action the domestic traditions of society that characters in earlier stories almost invariably accepted. They disregard, especially, the tradition of marriage as the only legitimate outlet for sexual activity.

The primary social functions of marriage are, of course, to channel sexual energies and provide for the raising of children. In the worlds depicted in both periods (as well as the actual world of today), society as a whole acknowledges only those sexual relations that it has institutionalized by marriage; anything else is, from the point of view of society, "illicit," no matter how many individuals may privately ignore the taboo or tolerate violations in others. Even though some stories of free sexual behavior, such as Hemingway's "A Very Short Story" or "Hills Like White Elephants," may not explicitly indicate the existence of such a taboo, its existence must be assumed if the reader is to appreciate the story.

In the early period, illicit sexual relations (usually delicately veiled) are implied in some five stories by Henry James, but in most of these they are engaged in only by secondary characters and are seldom a part of the central action.[22] Elsewhere in the early period, the only significant violation of the institution of marriage is divorce, which is accepted sometimes in the upper-class worlds of Mrs. Wharton and Mrs. Gerould (and in one story by Garland). Divorce may be regarded as a modification

---

[22] Frank Saltram, in "The Coxon Fund," is the most active in this regard: the narrator tells us explicitly that he has fathered three "natural children." The son in "Greville Fane" has various unspecified liaisons; the possibility of bigamy is raised by the wife in "Fordham Castle"; the son in "Marriages" was probably forced into marriage by sexual imprudence; the heroine's friends in "The Story In It" are engaged in an affair. "Mrs. Medwin" may also belong in the same category, although the lady's offense against society is not specified.

of the institution of marriage, a legitimate device to enable the institution to function more satisfactorily. Hence the character who accepts divorce in the early stories is analogous to the reformer whose object is to improve the functioning of economic and political institutions. Even so, most of those who consider divorce usually end by rejecting it. The heroine of Mrs. Gerould's "The Great Tradition" refrains from divorce as a matter of social principle: she refrains lest she influence society to relax its "great tradition" of the permanence of marriage. And society may sometimes punish the divorcee by ostracism, as in Mrs. Wharton's "Autres Temps." [23] Otherwise, except for the affairs of Crane's prostitute and one adultery suggested by Garland (of all people), there are no evident sexual relationships unblessed by marriage in stories of the early period,[24] although there are a handful of characters (in James, Mrs. Wharton and Dreiser) who restrain a desire for them.

Curiously, such disregard of the sexual taboos, rare enough in the early period, is limited almost wholly to the upper-class worlds of Mrs. Wharton and James (Crane's slum-dwelling Maggie being an exception). In stories of the twenties, on the other hand, it becames general, occurring with a frequency in truly radical contrast to that of the early period. One-third of the stories of the twenties involve illicit relations — occasionally frustrated but usually consummated — and occur in the works of all five authors. These relations include both adulteries, often very casual, and unmarried relationships.[25] They include occasional instances of prostitution and also of undesired pregnancy which may force marriage or (in Hemingway's "Hills Like White Elephants") lead to abortion. They reflect a determined if not always bland disregard of the institution of marriage; the

---

[23] Divorce is a given event prior to the beginning of Wharton's "Autres Temps," "Reckoning," and "The Other Two"; it is implicit at the end of Garland's "Branch Road"; it is considered but rejected by the protagonists in Gerould's "Great Tradition" and "Weaker Vessel" and Wharton's "The Choice." Social censure of divorce is indicated only in "Autres Temps."

[24] The stories cited are Crane's "Maggie" and Garland's "Branch Road." Dreiser's "Old Rogaum" contains a threat of prostitution for the heroine.

[25] Homosexuality is an issue in only four stories: "Hands," "Man Who Became a Woman," "Simple Enquiry," and "Divorce in Naples," in all of which the homosexual tendency is repressed. Other perversions which more recent writers treat are not represented.

usual absence of punishment is another instance, to be added to those already cited, of society's inability or unwillingness to enforce its laws and customs.[26] In view of this, it may seem odd that divorce in stories of the twenties is as rare as it is. Only one protagonist actually gets a divorce (and he takes his wife back),[27] and divorce is contemplated or appears in the background of only a handful of other stories.[28] This may be taken as a further sign of the low regard in which people in the stories of the twenties hold the institutions of society, so little do they care, even when miserable in their marriages, to avail themselves of a socially approved solution.

It is going too far to suggest that most, or even a few, of these characters are attempting through their behavior to bring about a social revolution or revision of society's sexual customs. Their motives are private and personal; even the intention to be "rebellious," as such, is seldom in evidence. What their disregard of the social taboos suggests is simply their emotional alienation from society. Even if those who disregard the taboos are so numerous as to make contempt for the taboos a dominant attitude in a large segment of the society, as appears to be the case in many stories, yet what this would seem to indicate is a discrepancy between the ostensible principles of society and the actual principles and motives of those individuals who compose society.

Loneliness

The withdrawals and rejections so far considered indicate alienation brought about through a character's own attitudes and behavior, whether wilful or compulsive. The obverse of this

[26] Stories of the twenties in which illicit sexual relationships are significant include Anderson's "Death," "Death in the Woods," "I Want to Know Why," "Nobody Knows," "Other Woman," "Out of Nowhere into Nothing," "Paper Pills," "Respectability," "Untold Lie," " 'Unused' "; Fitzgerald, "Four Fists," "Rich Boy," "Benediction," "Winter Dreams" (implicit); Faulkner, "That Evening Sun," "Mistral," "Divorce in Naples," "Hair," "All the Dead Pilots." An explicit desire for some such relationship also appears, to be frustrated, in Anderson's "Strength of God," "Door of the Trap," "Seeds," "Awakening"; Fitzgerald, "Rough Crossing," "Rich Boy"; Porter, "Maria Concepcion," "That Tree," "Magic."

[27] Porter, "That Tree."

[28] Fitzgerald, "The Adjuster," "Rough Crossing," "Rich Boy"; Hemingway, "A Canary for One."

situation, often visible in the same characters, is the painful suffering that many feel in their isolation — their yearning for acceptance, their suffering from loneliness. For reasons to be discussed later, they suffer from a real or imagined need for sympathy or understanding. In a sense, all the isolated characters of the twenties are lonely, although some are not conscious of it, and others have twisted their discontent to make their rejection of society more prominent than their longing for it. The most conspicuously and consciously lonely characters are in *Winesburg* — one story has as title "Loneliness" — although there are conspicuous examples in the stories of the other writers, too.

Elmer Cowley, in Anderson's "Queer," shows the desperate yearning for acceptance at its most extreme when he tries frantically to prove to George Willard that he is not queer, that he is a normal member of the community. Like others among Anderson's characters, he suffers from a nearly complete lack of social relationships of any kind.[29] More common is the kind of loneliness seen in Anderson's "Drink"; a boy has social relationships, yet these do not include women. The story concludes as he goes off to drink alone for the first (and, he insists, the last) time, and has fantasies of loving a girl named Helen White. This act and fantasy show his loneliness, which he does not fully understand and cannot explain to others. Many stories show similar loneliness implicit in an inability to communicate a particular fear or yearning that the individual would like to share.[30] Some characters express their loneliness through a quest for love, whose peculiar characteristics will be described later. Loneliness may also be inferred in many supposedly intimate relationships — love affairs or marriages — in which there is no real intimacy, but only suffering because the lonely person is misunderstood or unappreciated by his partner.

The opposite situation — a character clearly content in his

[29] See also Anderson's "Loneliness," "Adventure," "Hands," " 'Unused,' " "Thinker."
[30] Evident in Anderson's "Teacher," "Philosopher," "Mother," "Strength of God," "Unlighted Lamps," "Death in the Woods," "I Want to Know Why"; Fitzgerald, "Absolution" (the priest); Hemingway, "End of Something," "Ten Indians," "In Another Country," "Alpine Idyll," "Now I Lay Me," "Soldier's Home"; Porter, "Flowering Judas," "Theft," "He."

relations with others — is unusual. One sees occasional instances in the lighter stories by Fitzgerald,[31] but elsewhere a triumph of communication or a fully satisfactory relation with others is rare: in Anderson's "Sophistication," perhaps, and Faulkner's "Crevasse."[32]

Loneliness exists in stories of the early period, but there are usually some important differences. Some of Garland's and Mrs. Freeman's rural people — especially spinsters and farmers' wives — suffer to some extent from loneliness.[33] They differ in that they succeed, for the most part, in reconciling themselves to it, in ways to be examined later.[34] They do not allow themselves to suffer long. Their loneliness is usually the result of a specific sequence of happenings, a final misfortune in an action that has moved from happiness to misery. Such loneliness, whether due to ostracism as in Mrs. Wharton's "Autres Temps" or to a fatal circumstance as in Bierce's "Chickamauga," differs from that in stories of the twenties in that it represents the *loss* of some happiness, some companionship the character once had. In stories of the twenties, the typical loneliness is assumed to be present, a given condition more or less inherent in the character's social relations.[35]

Loneliness "given" and not appreciably overcome — like that noted so often in stories of the twenties — is common subject matter only for those earlier writers who now are acclaimed as

[31] For example, "Hot and Cold Blood," "Offshore Pirate," "Gretchen," "Four Fists," "Head and Shoulders," "Rags Martin-Jones," " 'Sensible Thing,' " "Ice Palace." In several of these, of course, the contentment is not achieved until the end of the story.

[32] In leading his men through danger, the officer in "Crevasse" is able and willing to accept social responsibilities; he is stronger than the rest of his company and employs his strength for their benefit. This is a most unusual pattern in stories of the twenties.

[33] Notably, Garland, "Day's Pleasure"; Freeman, "Poetess," "Stolen Christmas," "Innocent Gamester," "Scent of Roses."

[34] See below, pp. 110–11.

[35] Examples of terminal loneliness in stories of the early period are found in Freeman, "Village Lear"; Dreiser, "Lost Phoebe"; Wharton, "Bunner Sisters," "The Choice," "The Reckoning," "The Long Run"; Bierce, "Affair at Coulter's Notch"; Gerould, "Leda"; James, "Fordham Castle." Note that in stories of the early period where loneliness exists at the beginning it tends to be relieved by the end, as in Freeman, "Gala Dress," "A Solitary," "Poetess," "Village Singer," "Innocent Gamester," "Gentle Ghost"; Garland, "Day's Pleasure," "Branch Road"; James, "Abasement."

forerunners of the twenties: Dreiser and Miss Cather.[36] It may
also be inferred occasionally in stories by James: the case of
Greville Fane, the inept novelist who does not understand why
she is scorned, and the case of the mother-ridden aging daughters in "Europe," whose dream of travel is thwarted.[37]

The contrast between the success drive of characters in
stories of the twenties and the social climbing of the earlier
period may also be taken as a sign of the greater loneliness in
the later period. The quest for individual eminence in the twenties is competitive, a desire not to join but to stand out from a
group, such as George Willard's wish to be the "biggest man"
from the village of Winesburg. This can be described as a desire
to impress oneself upon society — to make oneself noticed, respected, or honored for one's contributions or one's prowess or
effectuality. Looked at this way, the success drive resembles
closely the drive of other characters to communicate with
others; it mirrors a similar kind of loneliness — that of non-
recognition — which it is thought may be overcome by conspicuous success. Many of Fitzgerald's young men so motivated
succeed, and their loneliness is thus to an extent conquered; but
the loneliness behind such a drive is most apparent in characters
whose ambition is frustrated, such as the unfortunate hero of
Anderson's "The Egg," whose attempts to become the jolly host
of a successful restaurant end in humiliation and tears that can
scarcely be comforted by his wife.

Miss Cather's and James's social climbers — the ambitious
middle-class American girls who seek a place in English society
or who marry well and make themselves hostesses for brilliant gatherings of artists — appear to be far less interested in
individual eminence than in the advantages of the societies that
they have joined. Even though they may, as in James's "Fordham Castle," ruthlessly reject those they think will hinder their
quest, they nevertheless seem more interested in the way of life
they hope to achieve — the relations with artists or with aristo-

[36] See Cather, "Paul's Case," "Wagner Matinee," "Sculptor's Funeral,"
"Death in the Desert," "Garden Lodge"; Dreiser, "Free," "Second Choice,"
"Married," "Old Rogaum."

[37] In James's "Story In It," the heroine's secret passion, which might make her
lonely, seems to be mastered by the use she makes of it.

crats — than in personal distinction. It is less to impress themselves upon others than to receive what they suppose to be the
best things of life that these people try to climb the social ladder
— a feat, incidentally, which they almost always manage successfully.[38]

Elsewhere in the world of the earlier stories, status is far
less important than it is to the careerists of the twenties. The
Garland farmer, such as Haskins in "Under the Lion's Paw," pas-
sionately eager to be the owner of his own farm, desires not superior but equal status in the community. The gossipy rivalry
(reflecting jealousy of status) seen in some of Mrs. Freeman's
stories is intended more to protect status than to elevate it; invariably it disintegrates as people learn more about each other
and the threat is removed.[39] Even Mrs. Wharton's and Mrs. Gerould's careerists show relatively little interest in raising their
status: because of the expectations that their brilliance has
aroused, one may describe their efforts as attempts to live up to
the status already reserved for them by society. Their failures,
then, are in a sense not frustrations of attempts to reach higher
status, as in "The Egg," but losses of a status already held in
trust.[40]

SOCIAL INTEGRATION AND DISINTEGRATION

As has been shown, the final social attitude of the typical character in the earlier stories — we must stress "final" since in some

[38] The serious artists in such stories as James's "Lesson of the Master," "Middle Years," "Death of the Lion," and "The Next Time" are not really an exception
to this point about the pursuit of eminence. Their passion, as made most explicit
in "Lesson of the Master," is for the mastery of perfection in their art; public
eminence, although desirable, is secondary to this. The attitude of Hugh Vereker
in "Figure in the Carpet," keeping his artistic intention a secret from the public,
is typical of this indifference to fame as such. Even Ray Limbert, in "The Next
Time," who tries so hard to write a popular success, is prevented from doing so
by his inborn desire for perfection and subtlety — a stronger motive, which sub-
verts every effort he makes to lower his standards.

[39] In "Gala Dress," the neighbors' desire to humiliate the heroine turns to
pity; in "Amanda," the haughty neighbor is moved to pity by a direct appeal;
hostile attitudes are softened by understanding in "Stolen Christmas," "Pot of
Gold," and "Up Primrose Hill."

[40] Those men in Mrs. Freeman's stories who return to the village after having
gone off to seek their fortunes (in "New England Nun," "Scent of Roses," and
"Discovered Pearl") also seem sublimely indifferent to status, as indicated by
their resumption upon their return of virtually the same status that they had
before they left.

cases the character learns this attitude in the course of the story — involves three variable elements: (1) the service that he gives to the community as a whole or to individuals who need help within the community, (2) the support that he gives, fully or in a reforming spirit, to social institutions and traditions, and (3) his acceptance of his place in the community structure or, at least, his satisfaction with the places that can be reached by him. These are the attitudes of a kind of character who is well-integrated in his society, even on those relatively uncommon occasions when he is victimized by it. The earlier society is distinguished from that of the twenties in that its members feel bound together emotionally, are agreed as to the fundamental purposes and values of community life, and are enabled thus to make the community a strong one. The early community, in other words, is coherent and stable.

This coherence, stability, and spirit of sharing are evident at various levels of the social scale: they express themselves strikingly in the co-operativeness that dominates the rural worlds of Garland and Mrs. Freeman, the respect for discipline and duty that dominates the military world of Bierce, the attitude of *noblesse oblige* apparent in the upper-class worlds of Mrs. Wharton and Mrs. Gerould, the pride in belonging to an exclusive society that motivates many characters (for good or ill) in stories by James. In these worlds especially, the only social evil of which most characters are aware is an occasional malfunctioning of the system: the kind of thing that a Wharton careerist would like to reform. Other evils are individual, not social, matters — the villainy, for example, of the usurer in Garland's "Under the Lion's Paw," an individual whose morality is in direct conflict with that of the community as a whole.

The malfunctioning is seen sometimes in the excessive power that the community acquires over individuals, as when it engages in unjust ostracism. The most usual malfunctioning is the imbalance that develops between different groups, whereby some are denied the social advantages that others have. Dreiser's laborers, Crane's slum dwellers, Garland's farmers are all victims of such an imbalance. It can give rise in some characters to attitudes of strong social criticism which need not, in the more forward-looking writers, be confined merely to the operation of the system itself. Thus, in Miss Cather's "The Sculptor's Funeral," the narrow and vicious attitudes of a small town are bitterly attacked by a sensitive citizen, and the attack is implicitly seconded by an outsider from Boston. The point for us is that "Boston" exists; there is, in the story, a good, cultivated society in which the arts and humanity flourish (a kind of society seen more directly in such stories as "The Garden Lodge" and "Flavia and Her Artists"). The evil of the community of "The Sculptor's Funeral" is measured against the good of a better community where ignorance and prejudice hold less sway. Society itself, in other words, provides the measure by which the more critical characters judge the shortcomings of certain communities or classes.

The social attitudes of most characters in stories of the twenties — marked sometimes by a tendency to withdraw from human society, by an indifference to social institutions, traditions, and ostensible principles, and by a painful feeling of loneliness — are in direct contrast to the attitudes in earlier stories. Society in stories of the twenties is composed of individuals who, in their most important relations with it, are emotionally isolated or alienated. No doubt it is this conception of the nature of society — apparent in all five writers, most completely in Anderson and Hemingway, least consistently in Fitzgerald — that accounts for the portrayed weakness of society in enforcing its laws and customs and protecting its members. Society in the stories of the twenties is disintegrated by the personal alienation of most of its members. It matters to the individual in a story primarily for this reason. He suffers from this feeling of alienation, and society consistently fails to relieve this suffering or to offer resistance if he attacks it, violates its law, rejects its institutions, or cuts his roots in the community.

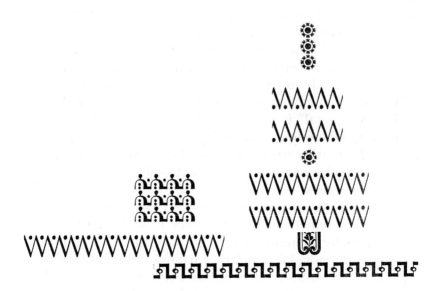

V: PROBLEMS IN LOVE

In Fitzgerald's "Winter Dreams," Dexter Green, a grocer's son in a Midwestern city, turns himself into a fabulously successful man of business. His ambition is the epitome of the success drive shown by many characters in stories of the twenties; stimulated by envy and by the desire to possess things and impress people, this ambition is typical of social attitudes common in the period. Most of the story, however, is more directly concerned with Dexter's relationship to a rich girl, Judy Jones. She, more than anything else, is the source and focus of his ambition. His "winter dreams" of success center in her; she is the embodiment of the glittering things that he would like to possess. But his relationship with her is stormy. His feeling is a mixture of attraction and resentment. He wins her with ease, but she throws him over as easily. When he tries to break away by becoming engaged to another girl, she intervenes and wins him back. Yet she will not have him permanently. At the end of the story, several years later, he hears that she is married to another man; the revelation that she has lost her beauty and her hold over men is shocking to him and makes him realize for the first time the loss of his youth.

As in most stories of both periods, Dexter's social attitudes are less important than his personal relationship with Judy Jones. Most of the stories I discuss deal primarily with such personal relationships, occurring within a framework of social relations, but of interest for their own sake. Dexter's problems with Judy, typical of the stories of the twenties, are seldom if ever anticipated in the earlier stories.

Some personal relations are chiefly expressions of an individual's relations with society, as, for example, a teacher's relations with his students or those between a servant and his master. Relationships of these kinds in these stories reflect points made in other chapters.[1] For example, relationships between servants and masters in the early period show a kind of mutual devotion; in the twenties, on the other hand, they tend to be tense and hostile, manifesting again the distance between the individual and his society.[2]

Personal relations pursued for their own sake are another matter. We can examine them by considering them as revealing either personal love or a perversion or distortion of love. This may be sexual, but it can also include family love and the emotions in personal friendships. Family relationships (chiefly between parent and child) and personal friendships are not uncommon in the stories of either period, but a distinctive contrast between these periods does not appear often enough to add anything very significant to what has already been observed. If there is a tendency for such relationships to change in stories of the twenties, this may appear chiefly in conflicts between a parent and a child. In an earlier story, such as Dreiser's "Old Rogaum and His Theresa," the conflict is likely to turn on the

---

[1] See chaps. iii–iv.

[2] See, for example, Hemingway's "Doctor and Doctor's Wife," "Out of Season," "Simple Enquiry."

question of parental authority: the father tries to restrict his daughter's freedom and force her to conform to certain conventional norms, and the child rebels. In a story of the twenties, such as Hemingway's "My Old Man" or Anderson's "Mother," this issue is swallowed up in the issue of understanding and sympathy between parent and child. The parent's authority is likely to be ineffectual; the child tends to reject such a parent, with whom he becomes disillusioned or of whom he is ashamed, for a variety of reasons: thus in "My Old Man," the boy, after he has become fully aware of his father's crookedness, says: "Seems like when they get started they don't leave a guy nothing." Or it may be the parent who yearns to express feeling for the child, as in "Mother," when Elizabeth "wanted to cry out with joy because of the words that had come from the lips of her son, but the expression of joy had become impossible to her."

The implications of such a contrast become clear in the light of more extensive contrasts in the relationship between the sexes. This is by far the most common kind of personal relationship in both sets of stories. Contrasts are seen both in the love situations the stories show and in motives — let us say concepts of love, explicit or implicit — that drive characters into these situations.

THE PURSUIT OF LOVE

Many love situations spring from a character's interest in the pursuit of love — they present him with a variety of questions, such as whether or not to pursue love, how to choose a beloved, how to win her, and so on. These questions, which beset many characters in both periods, appear in different guises and may mean many different things.

Early Period: Choosing and Winning a Mate

In stories of the early period, problems involving the pursuit of love are almost entirely one or the other of two kinds: those of choosing a mate and those of winning her. In both cases the object is marriage; we may call the situations in which they occur "courtships," even though in some cases a character may decide against marrying a certain person. In rare cases — Mrs. Wharton's "The Long Run" or "Garland's "A Branch Road" —

the character's beloved may be already married; the issue, however, is still the question of a permanent alliance, the equivalent of marriage. Courtship stories, always important in popular literature, were common in the early period in the work of Mrs. Freeman and Garland.

The simplest courtship stories are those in which the lover's problem is the winning of his mate. In these the chief obstacle to success is usually his own behavior. In Mrs. Freeman's stories the impediment is an excess of timidity or self-disparagement which is misunderstood by the beloved: thus the girl named Love, in "Amanda and Love," scares away her suitor by her cold, aloof manner, a manner caused by shyness and insecurity but one which he takes for a rebuff. In stories by other writers, pride or selfishness interferes with the lover's quest. The hero of Garland's "A Branch Road" loses his girl through a misunderstanding that results from a fit of adolescent petulance and self-pity.

To win the beloved, the lover has to change his behavior — overcome the timidity, swallow the pride, show his love in some sort of self-transcending manner. Love's sister Amanda, a proud girl, humbles herself before the man's mother on Love's behalf.[3] Garland's young man returns, years after the girl has married his rival, and wins her back by showing that he does care for her, and far more than does her cruel husband. In other stories love triumphs when a pair of professional artists clear up a misunderstanding based on envy and pride by revealing to each other the humiliating failures they have both suffered in their careers; when a girl takes the blame for a theft she did not commit; when a shy couple break through their mutual timidity to confess their love.[4] Sometimes a lover fails to overcome his egotism and discovers his error too late. The promising young careerist, in Mrs. Wharton's "The Long Run," finds out that his talents and imagination have shriveled because he failed to give himself boldly to the woman who loved him; another Wharton

[3] She is really the protagonist in the story, the reversal in her behavior being more important than that in Love's. The point is still valid, however; she makes herself Love's deputy, and Love's interests and problems become her own.

[4] Stories cited: James, "Broken Wings"; Freeman, "Calla-lilies," "Scent of Roses."

hero learns how cruel his fastidious chastity has been to the woman who loved him. In variations of this problem, a pair of lovers decide to marry after seeing the wreckage of a couple who, through pride and caution, gave up their love, and a Northern soldier wins a Southern girl by his display of understanding and sympathy.[5]

The other major courtship problem in stories of the early period — that of choosing a suitable mate — nearly aways involves a weighing of love against practical and moral considerations. In a few stories the lover makes the discovery that someone deserves his love and decides therefore to marry her.[6] Revelation of the beloved's character decides the issue; her unselfishness, her capacity for devotion and hard work make him conscious of what a good helpmeet she would be. The decision is notable for its practicality: when the lover recognizes the girl's suitability to be his wife, love follows as a matter of course.[7] In a variation on this, a woman who has failed to win her man justifies her love, nevertheless, on the grounds that he was a good man. Satisfying herself as to his questioned honesty, she feels great relief: "'. . . but it seems to me as if bein' sure that anybody was all right an' honest was the completest kind of bein' married that anybody could have.'"[8]

In other stories, the lover decides that he does not love sufficiently and therefore rejects the candidate. One of Mrs. Freeman's heroines wins a long battle with her mother on this issue; another discovers that she prefers the "placid serenity" of single life to marriage. Rather than reject the daughter who has fought his plan to remarry, the father in James's "The Marriages" gives up his plan. James's impulsive Miss Gunton from Poughkeepsie prefers to break her engagement to a great Italian prince rather than surrender her demand that his mother, the haughty old princess, shatter the aristocratic tradition and write to her first. In James's "The Lesson of the Master," Paul Overt, persuaded

[5] Stories cited: Wharton, "Dilettante"; Freeman, "Up Primrose Hill"; Crane, "Gray Sleeve."

[6] Freeman, "Discovered Pearl"; Garland, "Creamery Man," "Among the Corn Rows."

[7] In Garland's "Creamery Man," the hero chooses the suitable girl in preference to the unsuitable, unattainable flirt whom he originally loved.

[8] Freeman, "Pot of Gold."

to relinquish a girl for the sake of his art, is never sure whether he did the right thing or whether the artist who so persuaded him (and who afterward married the girl) may not have swindled him by cashing in on his artistic egoism.[9]

In some cases the lover chooses unwisely and comes to regret it: this is implicit in all early stories of divorce. Two Wharton stories, especially, stress discovery of the unwise choice: "The Quicksand," in which the heroine recognizes the error of marrying a man whose political principles conflict with her own, and "Bunner Sisters," in which tragedy develops because the heroine's sister did not know that the man she married was a drug addict.

All these stories demonstrate the lover's ultimate belief that his feelings should be ruled by practical considerations of what in the long run is best for him. Marriage should not be undertaken without love,[10] and love should be governed by the lover's awareness of his social needs and moral responsibilities. It should be given only to the candidate whose virtues deserve to be loved and whose situation makes love socially or morally legitimate. Under these conditions, it should be given unstintingly.

Remarkably enough, in stories of the twenties there are no comparable courtship situations except a few in lighter vein by Scott Fitzgerald. The problem of how to win a beloved seems to be totally absent, although that of the choice of a mate does, it is true, appear occasionally. But except in a rare case such as Faulkner's "Hair," it is subordinated to the more general question of whether or not to marry at all: the specific identity of the mate is, as far as the story is concerned, not the issue. Although the heroine of Miss Porter's "Theft," for example, has rejected a suitor, we infer that she did this not because of who he was but

[9] Besides these, the hero of James's "Flickerbridge" breaks his engagement to a too enterprising young American journalist because he fears what her fondness for publicity will do to a fine old English home and its inhabitant, who have hitherto escaped all modern influences and represent to him the uncorrupted past. The heroine of James's "Story In It" keeps her love for a married man secret from her beloved for the sake of her virtue, though she uses her own case to support her argument that an interesting story can be written about a perfectly virtuous woman.

[10] Stressed in Freeman, "Louisa."

because she would have rejected any suitor. In "Hair," when Hawkshaw, the barber, selects a small child to be his future wife and ultimately marries her, though she has "gone bad" in the meanwhile, we infer that his particular choice is less important than the motive that makes him stick to any choice he has made, regardless of how circumstances may change.

To be sure, unhappy marriages imply, in stories of the twenties as before, mistakes in courtships. Yet these mistakes are not emphasized. In most cases, as will be seen, such unhappiness results more from general attitudes toward love than from particular misjudgments of individuals.

The Twenties: Need and Fear of Love

The typical character in the earlier stories usually conceives of love only in connection with a specific person; he displays no desire for love until such a person evokes it in him. His problem in choosing a mate involves determining whether a particular person has evoked sufficient love for marriage and whether this is enough to justify disregard of other principles. His problem in winning her assumes such love: given the beloved, how can he win her?

For the typical character in stories of the twenties, on the other hand, the pursuit of love in a sense precedes the discovery of any love-worthy object. The character shows a strong need for love which exists independently of any specific person. For him the question is not how to win her or whether to pursue her, but where to find her? Elizabeth Willard, in Anderson's "Death," is a good example. Married to a man she despises, she spends a lifetime of transitory affairs with the traveling men who come through Winesburg; nothing satisfies her yearning for love until, near the end of her life, Doctor Reefy exclaims to her, "'You dear! You lovely dear!'" The promise in this (a real feeling, a real love for her) is interrupted; soon after, she falls ill and on her deathbed turns to the only thing that can now satisfy her: her new lover, Death.

In stories of the early period the pursuit of love for love's sake is seen only in those few by Dreiser [11] which anticipate

[11] Dreiser, "Free," "Old Rogaum," "Second Choice." In Crane's "Maggie"

rather closely stories of the twenties. In the twenties it takes a variety of forms. It is most active in people who, like Elizabeth Willard, engage in brief or casual sexual affairs.[12] The brevity or casualness itself is the evidence that love, or its sexual expression, is more important than the identity of the beloved. The outcome of such affairs varies. The protagonist may be nearly satisfied, at least for the time being; he may claim to be satisfied while actually betraying great anxiety, as in Anderson's "Nobody Knows"; he may be dissatisfied, as is Elizabeth Willard; or he may be defeated by others before he can achieve consummation, as in Anderson's "An Awakening."

More commonly, the character in search of love is impeded by inner problems and makes only a half-hearted effort to find it. This is the pattern anticipated by the earlier Dreiser stories. Sometimes a character may make a tentative, timorous, perhaps almost involuntary advance or appeal to a potential lover. In at least two stories dealing with married people, a character's need for love is revealed primarily in his attempt to conceal that need: a husband orders one of his students out of his life after kissing her, and a wife tries hard to repress her apparent desire for a lover younger than her husband. In some highly characteristic stories the suppressed need for love suddenly erupts into action that is more or less out of the character's control. The eruption is a perverted expression of need: one heroine accosts a stranger naked, another writhes among the cornstalks, a minister is overcome by a compulsion to peep, a priest goes mad.[13] Like Faulkner's Emily, who murders her lover and sleeps with his corpse, all are victims of powerful desires which, frustrated, explode in bizarre forms.

Except in stories by Fitzgerald, this need for love seldom motivates a courtship and is satisfied still more rarely. The hero

and Garland's "Among the Corn Rows," the protagonist's quest for love, which here precedes the discovery of the beloved, is motivated by desires other than a desire for love as such: Maggie wants relief from her slum environment; the hero of "Among the Corn Rows" needs someone to help him on the farm.

[12] Such casual affairs occur or are sought in Anderson's "Nobody Knows," "Awakening," "Death," "Other Woman"; Faulkner, "Divorce in Naples," "All the Dead Pilots."

[13] Stories cited: Anderson, "Door of the Trap"; Porter, "Cracked Looking-Glass"; Anderson, "Adventure," "New Englander," "Strength of God"; Fitzgerald, "Absolution."

of Fitzgerald's "The 'Sensible Thing'" is unusually lucky in winning his girl to marriage, yet when she is won he feels that he
has lost something; it is not the love that he most wanted.[14] In
other writers, the closest approaches to success in the pursuit
of love are probably the moments of understanding reached by
Elizabeth and Doctor Reefy in Anderson's "Death" and George
and Helen in "Sophistication." But these are moments: Elizabeth turns from Reefy to her "lover, Death"; George, in a sequel
to "Sophistication," has already forgotten Helen in the excitement of his departure from Winesburg.

The inner forces that usually interfere with the quest for
love in stories of the twenties give rise to another situation that
also sharply distinguishes these stories from stories of the early
period: the situation of a character running away from love.
Few early stories show anything comparable. We have suggested that when the typical character in the earlier stories
makes a choice against love, his decision is determined by the
particular circumstances of the case and by the character of
the rejected individual. When the heroine of Mrs. Freeman's
"Louisa" refuses to marry a certain man because she does not
love him, there is no hint that she is incapable of love; it is simply that this particular man is not sufficiently worthy or attractive. Although a few characters show a temporary fear of
expressing love, through shyness or fastidiousness, possibly the
only character in the entire early canon who rejects a lover as
a result of an enduring fear of the emotion of love itself is the
heroine of Mrs. Freeman's "A New England Nun," also named
Louisa. She has become so accustomed to a placid spinster's life
during fifteen years of waiting that when her fiancé finally returns after making his fortune, she discovers that she no longer
wants to marry.

Flight from love in stories of the twenties occurs most commonly in combination with the yearning for love, as in the stories
of ambivalence that have just been described. In a few cases the
avoidance of love is much stronger than the yearning. The protagonist feels a pressure or a demand from others for a love that
he is unable to give. The young Nick Adams, in Hemingway's

[14] See p. 87.

"The End of Something," suffers the mysterious death of his love for the girl Marge; Krebs, in Hemingway's "Soldier's Home," does not want to become involved with others;[15] Laura, in "Flowering Judas," guards herself against emotional commitments, and so does the heroine of Miss Porter's "Theft." This fear of love makes the character uncomfortable, especially if, as in "Theft," she realizes that she is depriving herself by it: "I was right not to be afraid of any thief but myself, who will end by leaving me nothing." Yet there is no sign that she will be any more capable or desirous of love hereafter.

In stories of the twenties the character who fears love resembles the one who pursues it for its own sake, in that for him, too, the experience is more important than the identity of any particular beloved. For him it is an experience to be avoided rather than pursued. The reasons are deep and irrational.

CONFLICT IN LOVE

Most of the remaining stories dealing with love — stories in which the issue is other than its pursuit — are concerned with conflict between lovers. The problem is not whether to pursue — a question presumably already decided — but what to do about the differences that arise. In stories of the early period this problem, when distinguished from the courtship problems already discussed, appears almost exclusively in marriages. In stories of the twenties, where unmarried love is no longer necessarily a courtship, it concerns both married and unmarried couples.

The Early Period

In some marriages in stories of the early period, there is no conflict between the couple. This fact itself may be a major point in the story. In James's "The Tree of Knowledge" and Miss Cather's "Flavia and Her Artists," it emerges in the course of the action to confound the skeptics who thought the couple were ill-matched or ignorant of each other's faults. In both stories it turns out that the more sensitive partner is indeed per-

---

[15] Traumatized by his war experiences, he tries to shun any kind of a relationship involving his emotions. This includes relationships with girls, which he regards as too complicated for his present state of mind.

fectly aware of the other's faults and that it makes no difference: love is stronger. More commonly, the harmonious love is seen in action, fortifying the couple against the outside world. Thus a devoted widow in one of James's stories struggles to find a way to perpetuate her husband's memory. Similarly, in stories by Garland and Mrs. Freeman, wives and husbands, faced with the external hardships of the world, tighten their bond — like citizens of the community in general — to face these hardships.[16] Here are materialized the values of love sought by characters in most courtship stories. Love is devotion to the beloved, more important than one's personal pride or idiosyncrasies; love — especially in the rural communities — is a source of strength and courage. If, as in Dreiser's "The Lost Phoebe," a weak man's wife dies, his own life and mind may disintegrate.

Other marital stories in the early period involve a conflict between a couple who are, fundamentally, in love. Here, as the dispute comes to a head, love triumphs. As in the stories of successful courtship, love is revealed by some concession that one character makes to the other, a yielding that restores harmony to the marriage. The conflict may range from a mere crotchety coolness of manner, as in Garland's Ripley stories, to a headlong clash of moral values, as in his "A 'Good Fellow's' Wife." The concessions which resolve it affirm the unselfish nature of love; the individual rises above his pride, his greed, or his weakness. Uncle Ethan Ripley paints out the sign on the barn which his wife does not like, and she, touched, comes out to keep him company in the middle of the night; an embezzler saves his marriage by agreeing to work for years to repay those he has wronged, and his wife helps him; a farmer allows his wife to keep his new barn which, in his absence, she has converted into the new house he has always denied her; a weak and henpecked husband voluntarily gives up his long-awaited vacation to help his daughter's chances for a good marriage, thus winning his wife's gratitude; a wife acknowledges that she must perform her household duties for her husband's sake even when they seem "intolerable."[17]

[16] James, "Abasement"; Freeman, "Wayfaring Couple"; Garland, "Return of a Private," "Under the Lion's Paw."
[17] Stories cited: Garland, "Uncle Ethan," " 'Good Fellow's' Wife"; Freeman,

Occasionally the resolution of conflict between a married couple in love is less complete. One character defeats the other. Waythorn, in Mrs. Wharton's "The Other Two," ruefully, yet with good humor, swallows the objections he has felt to his thrice-married wife's easy notions of propriety, love, and marriage. The husband in Dreiser's "Married" reconciles himself to a future in which he will have constantly to reassure his insecure wife. The painter's wife in Miss Cather's "The Marriage of Phaedra" wins her victory after her husband's death by sending out of the country the masterpiece that she has never understood and always resented. The wife in Miss Cather's "The Garden Lodge" determines to kill the romantic and emotional impulses that she thinks threaten the security of her comfortable marriage, even though her husband himself would like her to be a little less practical. Yet even these compromises (with the possible exception of that in "The Marriage of Phaedra") reveal a strength of saving love, a good grace and good humor that can minimize the unhappiness of the conflict.

Although most marital conflict in stories of the early period is thus resolved by concessions, Mrs. Wharton, Mrs. Gerould, and James portray certain more stringent conflicts in which love has more or less died. The reason for its death is seldom a major issue; it may be spontaneous, as in Mrs. Wharton's "The Reckoning," or the spouse may have shown himself to be a morally inferior person, such as the husband in Mrs. Wharton's "The Choice," who is dishonest and wasteful of his wife's money. The real issue in such stories is the question of what to do with the marriage. Should it be ended or not? These are the stories that most directly treat the question of divorce. Although Abel Taker, in James's "Fordham Castle," has agreed to drop out of his wife's life and even obliterate his identity (without divorce) so that she can pursue her social objectives unhampered, the more typical conclusion is against breaking up the marriage.[18] The

---

"Revolt of 'Mother,'" "Kitchen Colonel"; Gerould, "Wesendonck."

[18] Again, the case of Frank Saltram, in "Coxon Fund," who has easily chucked his wife and family before the story begins, is an exception. This action, of course, is but one of many intended to show his disregard for social custom and personal obligation. It is comparable to the behavior of the hero of Mrs. Gerould's "Pearls," who chucks his family in order to pursue an artist's life in the South Seas. In both cases this behavior is viewed by society in general as extraordinary

heroine of Mrs. Wharton's "The Reckoning" has divorced one husband because of the death of love; faced now with divorce by her second husband, she decides that her first divorce was based on false principles. The protagonists of two stories by Mrs. Gerould both give up their plans for divorce, and another Wharton heroine, who has contemplated the murder of her husband, changes her mind and rescues him instead of her lover in the accident that was intended to kill him. In no case does love prevent the break-up of the marriage. If love alone were the basis of marriage, indeed, none of these people would hesitate to end it. What these stories show, rather, is the triumph of other principles over the principle of love.

The Twenties

The typical love conflicts in stories of the twenties are anticipated in the early canon only in Dreiser's "Free" and, to an extent, in his "The Second Choice," Bierce's "Killed at Resaca," and Miss Cather's "A Death in the Desert." "Free" is the story of a bullied husband who longs for love and romance and freedom, only to find, after his wife's death, that he is too old to make any use of his freedom. "A Death in the Desert" deals with a man's love for a woman who loves only the man's brilliant brother; though he tends her all through her last illness, on her deathbed she confuses him with his brother. Even these suffering, however, have compensations: Dreiser's hero is granted a termination to his marital misery, and Miss Cather's hero has at least the satisfaction that the woman recognizes his goodness and devotion.

"Free" foreshadows a common marital situation in stories of the twenties: although love between a couple has either died or become mixed with strong hostility, they remain chained to their antagonism or restlessness, which persists as a cause of suffering. Unable to love sufficiently to mitigate their misery, they are equally unable to free themselves. In some cases the unhappy partner shows his misery, like the hero of "Free," in his still unsatisfied desire to pursue love outside of his marriage. As we have shown, this desire may lead to a series of adulteries, as with

---

and eccentric. The very surprise engendered is a measure of the strength of the prevalent standard of conduct here noted.

Anderson's Elizabeth Willard, or it may be stalwartly suppressed, as when Rosaleen O'Toole, in Miss Porter's "The Cracked Looking-Glass," suppresses her desire for a younger lover and forlornly turns to her old husband for emotional support.

Occasionally, hostility between the couple is open and bitter and largely unrelieved.[19] In most cases, the character tries to cover up his discontent. As a result, in some stories, the antagonism manifests itself either in a low-keyed persistent tension, such as that which prevails between the doctor and the doctor's wife in Hemingway's story of that title, or in an explosive eruption of violent quarrels with little rational cause, as in Miss Porter's "Rope" or Fitzgerald's "The Rough Crossing."[20] In the latter cases a reconciliation and even an "affirmation" of love follow the quarrel, but bring no resolution, for they fail to reach the mysterious origins of the quarrel. Though the couple denies it, we can infer from this that the underlying hostility has simply been buried again as it had been before the outbreak. Notice how the couple tries to dismiss their quarrel in "The Rough Crossing:"

. . . "Who do you suppose those Adrian Smiths on the boat were?" he demanded. "It certainly wasn't me."

"Nor me."

"It was two other people," he said, nodding to himself. "There are so many Smiths in this world."

And in "Rope":

He was a love, she firmly believed, and if she had had her coffee in the morning, she wouldn't have behaved so funny. . . . He knew how she was, didn't he?

Sure, he knew how she was.

"A Death in the Desert" foreshadows, albeit in a very mild way, a still more characteristic sort of love conflict in stories of the twenties: the situation of a character who is made to suffer because he needs another's love more strongly than the other needs his. Generally speaking, if the character in an early story

[19] Notably, Anderson's "Surrender" and "Untold Lie," although in the latter story the hero finds some quality in his marriage to mitigate the misery.

[20] See also the subdued but unrelieved conflicts in Hemingway's "Out of Season" and "Mr. and Mrs. Elliot."

should give his love in this fashion (which he would regard as an unwise thing to do), he would be able, once he perceived his error, to renounce his love and thus free himself emotionally, if not circumstantially, from his bond.[21] A similar character in a story of the twenties, however, although he may see his error clearly, cannot free himself; he goes on loving in spite of his injuries.

Two situations are common. In one, the lover is jilted or betrayed; because he depends more on the relationship than does the beloved, he suffers. His reaction varies: Granny Weatherall, in Miss Porter's story, buries her hurt in her subconscious and lives a happy life until memory of suffering emerges into consciousness on her deathbed. The boy Nick also suffers only mildly and has to remind himself that he is "heartbroken"; another Hemingway hero turns bitterly to a cheap shopgirl from whom he contracts a venereal disease; Anderson's Wash Williams turns against all women; and two jealous lovers commit murder.[22]

More commonly, the beloved will selfishly exploit the lover's dependency. Usually the exploitation is sexual; in no less than five stories a man uses the girl's love for his sexual advantage without giving to her any of the things — child, home, married respectability — that she wants.[23] This may occur in either married or unmarried relationships. Sometimes the girl exploits the man, as in Dexter's relationship with Judy Jones, discussed at the beginning of this chapter. Judy is fickle, alternately jilting and reclaiming Dexter; on the other hand, the woman may be a conventional prude, such as Miriam in Miss Porter's "That Tree," using the hero's love to satisfy her own ambitions and ideas of respectability, even though he detests them. In all cases, the exploited lover knows perfectly well that he is being ex-

[21] In such stories as Crane's "Maggie," Mrs. Wharton's "Bunner Sisters," Garland's "Creamery Man," and all the divorce stories, the character ceases to love when his error is apparent, even if he remains trapped in the situation caused by his mistake.

[22] Stories cited: Porter, "Jilting of Granny Weatherall"; Hemingway, "Ten Indians," "Very Short Story"; Anderson, "Respectability"; Porter, "Maria Concepcion"; Faulkner, "Mistral."

[23] Anderson, "Out of Nowhere into Nothing" (implicit in the future); Fitzgerald, "Benediction"; Hemingway, "Up in Michigan," "Hills Like White Elephants," "Cat in the Rain."

ploited, yet he is quite incapable of resisting it. His yielding cannot be compared to the loving concessions seen so frequently in the early period. He is motivated, not by an appreciative response to the beloved's virtues or needs, but by a desperate fear of loneliness or by other similar uncontrollable emotions which make him a victim. His love needs remain unsatisfied, as is true for those who engage in a quest for love. The exploited character has allowed the same need to enslave him to someone who does not deserve his love.

What the foregoing contrasts in love situations show most clearly is that love in the stories of the twenties is far more consistently a source of misery than it is shown to be in stories of the early period. If a character in the early stories can learn to control love by reason, to solve the problems that it raises, and often to draw strength and courage from it, in stories of the twenties he is almost always frustrated in his need for love. He may be driven into miserable situations from which he sees no escape; he may be made vulnerable to exploitation by unscrupulous characters; he may find his need raising insuperable barriers between him and others. The enjoyments he gets from love are transitory; he seldom seems to benefit appreciably from marriage. Worst of all, his needs and his fears alike defy his reason and his control. Dexter Green knows that Judy Jones is no good for him, but this knowledge cannot help him. He is in the grip of deep and irrational forces within.

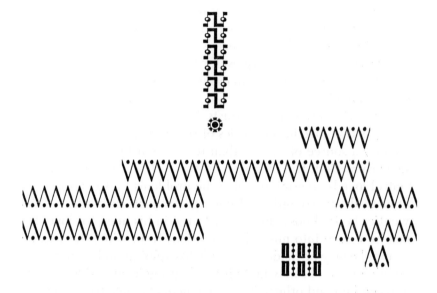

VI: THE IDEA OF LOVE

In Garland's "The Creamery Man," Claude Williams, after being rebuffed by the flirtatious and snobbish Lucindy Smith, recognizes the goodness and devotion of another girl, Nina Haldeman. The story ends with his abrupt proposal. He asks her to go for a ride with him:

"With you?"

"With me. Get your best hat. We may turn up at the minister's and get married — if a Sunday marriage is legal."

As she hurried up the walk he said to himself,

"I'll bet it gives Lucindy a shock!"

And the thought pleased him mightily.

Obviously, when Claude chooses Nina over Lucindy, he is acting according to a somewhat different conception of love from that which causes Fitzgerald's Dexter Green to abandon his reliable sweetheart for the fickle and unreliable Judy Jones. In a sense, the two situations could be described as tests, devised by their authors, of two different ideas of love. The contrast between the love problems of the two periods is not complete, therefore, until we have examined and compared these conceptions — the ideas of love that motivate lovers.

These ideas of love are not necessarily explicitly stated. Claude's and Dexter's conceptions are indicated in the choices they make. The kind of happiness a character seeks in love, the misery he tries to avoid, his manner of pursuing — these are the primary signs of the idea of love he holds.

EARLY PERIOD: PRACTICAL UNSELFISHNESS
The typical character in the early stories is motivated by a two-fold idea of love as (1) an outgoing, self-transcending emotion, based on a genuine, clear-sighted admiration of the true merits of another individual, and (2) a socially desirable emotion, subject to reason and obedient to one's sense of social needs and moral responsibilities. The early situations involve these beliefs; if the characters have other ideas about love they cause no problems in the stories and thus in a sense do not exist.

The unselfish aspect of love is the primary issue in two typical love situations in early stories: the courtships that succeed through the lover's conquest of his timidity, pride, or selfishness, and the marital conflicts that are resolved in the same way. Because love is unselfish, it resolves conflicts stemming from egotism or selfishness.[1]

The social and moral suitability of love is manifest especially in the other situations: courtships in which the problem is to evaluate the potential mate, and marital stories in which one must decide what to do when love is dead. In the courtship group, the individual learns either to give love to the person who, from a practical viewpoint, deserves it, or not to give it where not deserved. In the marital group, as well as in some of

[1] Stories treating this issue are Freeman, "Calla-lilies," "Amanda," "Scent of Roses," "Revolt of 'Mother,'" "Kitchen Colonel"; Garland, "Branch Road," "'Good Fellows' Wife," "Uncle Ethan," "Mrs. Ripley"; Wharton, "Long Run," "Dilettante"; Gerould, "Wesendonck." Unselfish love is given prominence also in Freeman, "Wayfaring Couple"; Cather, "Death in the Desert," "Flavia"; James, "Tree of Knowledge."

the courtship stories, the individual must measure against larger responsibilities the demands of his emotions of love and hate. Even his consideration of divorce points up another aspect of the social suitability of love — the intimate association between love and the social institutions provided for it — and his usual rejection of divorce subordinates his emotions to social and moral demands.[2]

As a consequence of both the clear-sightedness of love (as admiration of true virtues) and its subjection to the character's feelings of responsibility, the protagonist in early stories invariably regards true love as a lasting emotion whose only proper outlet is the establishment of a permanent domestic partnership, serene and tranquil in nature. Thus all unmarried relationships are courtships, and unhappy marriages must either be restored to tranquillity or be scrutinized as to the justifiability of divorce.

Love in stories of the early period thus clearly conforms to the prevalent attitude by which the individual feels integrated in his society. In its unselfishness, its practicality, its respect for social institutions and moral considerations, the idea of love in stories of the early period tends simply to repeat on the most personal level the ideas that govern the social relationships of most of the characters portrayed.

THE TWENTIES: SATISFACTION OF NEEDS

Such ideas about the nature of love are largely rejected in stories of the twenties. Although some people may cling to them in part, they do so without conviction in an unsympathetic world. In the first place, except in certain "old-fashioned" stories by Fitzgerald,[3] love is seldom depicted as an unselfish emotion. One sees this in the failure of lovers to make such concessions to the beloved as were common earlier, and in the cruel behavior of those who exploit their lover's vulnerability. One sees it also

[2] These aspects of love are most evident in Freeman, "Discovered Pearl," "Pot of Gold," "Louisa," "New England Nun," "Up Primrose Hill"; Garland, "Creamery Man," "Among the Corn Rows"; Wharton, "Quicksand," "The Choice," "The Reckoning," "Bunner Sisters"; Gerould, "Great Tradition," "Weaker Vessel"; James, "Miss Gunton," "Story In It," "Flickerbridge," "Lesson of the Master."

[3] Chiefly "Offshore Pirate," "Rags Martin-Jones," "Hot and Cold Blood," "Head and Shoulders," "Four Fists," "Adjuster."

in those who would like to be loving and generous but who, because love has failed, find themselves unable to be.[4]

Second, love in stories of the twenties is seldom a spontaneous admiration of another's virtues. This is obvious in those who
are in search of love but have not found it; something other than
an admiration of character must be involved here. It is equally
obvious in all stories of jiltings, exploitations, and marital ten-
sions. Lovers are not loving according to merit if they love and
continue to love those who exploit them or hurt them or fight
them.

Third, love in stories of the twenties is usually independent
of an individual's social conscience or feelings of social responsibility. This is evident in the typical lover's dissociation of love
and marriage, which is visible not only in the violations of sexual
taboos but also in the disappearance of courtships,[5] of solvable
marital problems, and in divorce questions. Instead, love is conceived as the satisfaction of certain pressing emotional needs.
Although these vary in intensity and in the degree to which
the lover is conscious of them, they are compulsive in nature,
rooted at a level deeper than consciousness. Obviously an attempt to satisfy such needs is selfish rather than unselfish, and
for this reason love in stories of the twenties must be described
as self-centered, asocial, and perhaps amoral.

It might of course be said that love as a psychological phenomenon has always involved the satisfaction of just such needs.
One can assume that the individual in early stories who fell in
love and married found, or hoped to find, satisfaction for these
needs. The difference between the two periods is this: in the
early period, this satisfaction either is taken for granted or is not
admitted to exist as an element of love. The love problems in
stories of the time are simply not concerned with them. Stories

[4] Compare Nick's uncomfortable conviction (in Hemingway's "End of Something") that he must break off with Marge and his unintentionally cruel way of
doing so, with Louisa's attitude (in Freeman's "New England Nun") upon her
discovery that she does not want to marry Joe. It does not enter either her head
or his that they might break their engagement until each is quite satisfied that
this is what the other wants.

[5] Of course, the existence of marriage means that courtships must be taking
place somewhere in the world of the stories of the twenties, although they do
not take place "on stage."

of the twenties, however, are concerned with them directly and primarily: the motivation to love, its conduct, and its sufferings are associated with these needs rather than with other matters.

Sexual Needs

One great need of lovers in the twenties is for sexual satisfaction. Obviously, it is also a component of love in stories of the early period, but it is comparable there to other natural human needs with which we are not directly concerned. In stories of the twenties it becomes an issue — an important part of the idea of love there displayed — whenever it shows itself independently of other elements of love.

The sexual need, as such, is revealed on at least two levels in the stories of the twenties. On the simplest level, the individual wants to satisfy his physical desires, a significant motive in its own right in any story in which the question of a physical relationship becomes an issue: any of the numerous stories, for example, in which violations of the sexual taboos occur, as well as those in which they are attempted or desired. This level of sexual need is seen most clearly in such stories of casual or crude seduction as Anderson's "Nobody Knows" and Hemingway's "Up in Michigan," both of which deal with an abrupt sexual encounter between a couple who have otherwise virtually no relationship at all.

The physical need usually appears only as an aspect of a somewhat more complex sexual need — that of playing the masculine or feminine role. Implicit wherever a physicial relationship appears, this becomes significant as an issue chiefly when it is frustrated in some way. The women in Hemingway's "Cat in the Rain" and "Hills Like White Elephants," for instance, suffer because their husbands or lovers will not allow them to play the feminine role of wife and mother. George Willard, in Anderson's "Nobody Knows," suffers (although he tries to deny it) from doubt that his sexual initiation has made him a man. The same thing appears in the discontent of the married person who seeks or suppresses a desire for extramarital relations, a desire unquestionably based in part upon dissatisfaction with the role he is allowed to play in his marriage. Such frustration is evident in those who suffer from being jilted, for such betrayals are obvious affronts to a person's sexuality. It is clear in the sufferings of many of the characters who are engaged in the quest for love and, still more, in those who are exploited by their lovers, since the exploitation in a majority of cases consists primarily of a denial by the selfish beloved of the victim's need to play his sexual role. Some of the fiercest hatreds to be seen in these stories — such as that of the narrator for his wife in Miss Porter's "That Tree" or the bitter misogyny of Wash Williams in Anderson's "Respectability" — are based upon insults done the masculine ego.[6]

Need for Appreciation

The lover's sexual need in stories of the twenties is often supplemented or overshadowed by a personal need of another sort. We are told, for example, concerning the heroine of Anderson's "Seeds," that even though she expresses her needs in a sexual fashion, "The need for a lover was, after all, a quite secondary thing. She needed to be loved, to be long and quietly and patiently loved. . . ."

This sort of need is especially clear in the case of Anderson's Elizabeth Willard (see p. 70). In all her lifetime of sexual affairs, the closest she comes to a true satisfaction of her love needs is in the moment when Doctor Reefy utters a few sincere words: "'You dear! You lovely dear!'" This, then, is what love must mean to her: not a sexual union, primarily, but to be recognized and appreciated as a "lovely dear." She wants to be valued as she would like to value herself. This need to be appreciated on one's own terms is one of the most powerful motives driving lovers in stories of the twenties.[7] Its egocentricity is apparent; such char-

---

[6] Stories showing such frustrations of the sexual role include Anderson's "Awakening," "Door of the Trap," "Nobody Knows," "Death," "Strength of God," "Out of Nowhere into Nothing," "Respectability"; Fitzgerald, "Benediction," "Winter Dreams"; Hemingway, "Up in Michigan," "Hills Like White Elephants," "Cat in the Rain," "Very Short Story," "End of Something," "Ten Indians," "Doctor and Doctor's Wife"; Porter, "Jilting of Granny Weatherall," "Maria Concepcion," "That Tree," "Cracked Looking-Glass"; Faulkner, "Mistral," "Rose for Emily."

[7] From the viewpoint of Freudian psychology, these needs might all be described as aspects of the same need — all varieties of the sex drive at different levels of rationalization or sublimation. Our analysis here is concerned not with

acters want to be the recipients of the kind of love that individuals in earlier stories were happy to give. In the early period this idea of love was as rare as the direct expression of sexual need.[8]

Such a need — which also accounts largely for the general loneliness cited in Chapter IV — underlies much of the sexual behavior just described, most notably that of those men and boys who want their masculinity to be bolstered. It is, indeed, the primary motive for many of the characters who are looking for love, and in many cases the primary source of vulnerability of exploited lovers. The heroine of Hemingway's "Hills Like White Elephants," for example, is trapped because her need is so great that she would rather hear her lover's protestations of love, shallow and hypocritical though they be, than be left alone. Thus she permits the frustration of her need to be a mother, this other need being so much greater. Obviously, the chief problem arising from such a conception of love is that it is almost universally frustrated. When it leads, as in "Hills Like White Elephants," to the frustration of other desires as well, the result is an agonizing intensification of suffering.[9]

The Aesthetic Need

Dexter Green's attraction to Judy Jones, in Fitzgerald's "Winter Dreams" (see p. 64), is not wholly a matter of either of the needs we have discussed. Why, otherwise, would he reject for her sake the attractive girl who really loves him? He is drawn to her as to the "glittering things and glittering people" that he would like to possess for himself: "No disillusion as to the world in which she had grown up could cure his illusion as to her desira-

a clinical interpretation of motives but with the distinctions between the ways in which motives are expressed in action. For convenience and clarity we are regarding what Freudians would regard as different kinds of "sublimations" as different kinds of motives.

[8] Exceptions in the stories of the early period: Dreiser, "Free," "Married," "Old Rogaum."

[9] The need for appreciation is especially evident, also, in such characters as Seth in Anderson's "Thinker," who tries to make Helen see the value he puts on himself; Enoch in Anderson's "Loneliness"; Alice in Anderson's "Adventure"; Kate in Anderson's "Teacher." It can be inferred as the primary cause for a character's vulnerability to exploitation in Anderson's "Out of Nowhere into Nothing," Fitzgerald's "Benediction," and Hemingway's "Up in Michigan."

bility." Though to possess her would certainly be a triumph for his masculine prowess, he is drawn not merely by the opportunity of showing that prowess but also by something about the girl herself: "It was that exquisite excitability that for the moment he controlled and owned."

More light on this motive is shed by the disillusionment of George O'Kelly in Fitzgerald's "The 'Sensible Thing,'" different though he and Jonquil Cary are from Dexter and Judy. After George has won Jonquil and married her, and even though the marriage gives every promise of being serene and happy, he nevertheless laments because something has gone out of the love between them:

But for an instant as he kissed her he knew that though he search through eternity he could never recapture those lost April hours. He might press her close now till the muscles knotted on his arms — she was something desirable and rare that he had fought for and made his own — but never again an intangible whisper in the dusk, or on the breeze of night. . . .

What George and Dexter want, of course, is love radiating glamor. For Dexter, Judy's glamor is enhanced, not undermined, by her fickleness, her vacillations, her moods. It is the familiar desire of the romanticist to find in the experience of love a quality of beauty of a different order, superior to that found in any other experience — the desire for some quality that will elevate the experience out of the class of the ordinary. Such a romanticizing view of love, which finds the beloved most attractive when she is "an intangible whisper in the dusk," or which is most charmed by a girl's elusiveness and unreliability, puts a premium on the unreality of the love object. It contrasts directly with the attempt to base love upon the recognition of valid virtues of character and to express love through the tranquillity and serenity of a lifelong domestic establishment.

Such a motive is less commonly the primary motivation of love than the other two needs, but in certain stories it is central, and it colors the concept of love in many stories where other motives are dominant. In the stories chosen to represent the early period, on the other hand, it is — curiously, since it is certainly familiar in romantic literature of all times — insignificant. This is not to say that the lovers in early stories do not find love a joyful and pleasing experience, but there is no story in the early canon in which the joy or pleasure or beauty of the experience is itself an issue or problem, a motivation or a basis for disappointment or suffering if frustrated.

The content of the romantic exhilaration that is sought differs from story to story. Sometimes, as in Fitzgerald's stories just mentioned, it is a sense of mystery and remoteness. The loss of this feeling probably explains why the youthful Nick finds himself no longer able to love Marge in Hemingway's "The End of Something."[10] Sometimes it resides in glittering associations of wealth, as also in the Fitzgerald stories. Sometimes it is sought in purity or loftiness of feeling in opposition to the dull, the ordinary, the sexual; this is seen in such Anderson heroes as Wash Williams and George Willard. Sometimes the quest is simply for the excitement of adventure and novelty of experience; this is certainly an aspect of Sartoris' heroic love for a prostitute in Faulkner's "All the Dead Pilots," of the discontent or boredom suffered by certain wives, and especially of the affairs of those who go abroad or to the city for love.[11] Whatever form it takes, this romanticizing motive is a compelling force in many lovers, who find it necessary to transform or uplift their homelier motives. The process is well exemplified by George Willard, who attempts to glorify an ordinary lust in the following manner:

The desire to say words overcame him and he said words without meaning, rolling them over on his tongue and saying them because they were brave words, full of meaning. "Death," he muttered, "night,

[10] One need not accept the explanations, based on class differences, that are offered in the sequel to this story ("Three-Day Blow") as to why Nick tired of Marge. See below, p. 94.

[11] See Fitzgerald's "Offshore Pirate," "Rags Martin-Jones"; Anderson, "Respectability," "Drink," "Sophistication" (George tells Helen: " 'I want you to try to be different from other women. . . . I want you to be a beautiful woman.' "); Faulkner, "All the Dead Pilots"; Fitzgerald, "Adjuster," "Benediction"; Hemingway, "Hills Like White Elephants," "Cat in the Rain," "Out of Season"; Anderson, "Seeds"; Porter, "That Tree." The idea of love as adventure is epitomized without customary inhibitions by Miss Porter's free-loving Mexicans, such as the husband Juan in "Maria Concepcion" and the Mexican girl in "That Tree" who never gives a thought to marriage. This approach to the question of love is very inviting to the hero, and it colors his attitudes, but he is never able to give himself to it wholly because of his deepseated restraints.

the sea, fear, loveliness." . . . Again, as in the alleyway, George
Willard's mind ran off into words and, holding the woman tightly he
whispered the words into the still night. "Lust," he whispered, "lust
and night and women."

Stress on the beauty of the love experience means that love
can find satisfaction in moments of brief duration: it is not always necessary to settle down for life, as in stories of the early
period. Sometimes, as in the case of George O'Kelly, in Fitzgerald's "The 'Sensible Thing,'" the passing moment may be
more of a triumph of love than would be a lifetime of marriage.
Of course a character is very likely to continue to yearn or suffer
after such a moment; but the satisfaction he gets is found in
such moments and often is looked for only in such moments. This
gives a further explanation as to why so many characters seek
only brief and casual affairs, and also why so many can allow
themselves to be exploited in the long run, since their only real
satisfactions are those of the short run. Indeed, except in some
of Fitzgerald's stories, the only successes of love that occur in
stories of the twenties are of a transitory kind; passing seductions
or even more ephemeral moments of rare communication,
unions of unpromising future, fleeting glimpses of success in
otherwise disappointing relationships, or false and basically in-
adequate reconciliations of discord.[12]

THE TWENTIES: FAILURE OF LOVE

The almost universal failure of love in stories of the twenties can
probably be attributed in good part to the prevailing idea of the
nature of love, as just described. Whereas the concept of love in
earlier stories provided the lover with ways of solving his problems, since it regarded love as unselfish and as deliberately and
practically subordinate to social and moral demands, the concept of love in stories of the twenties is almost equally certain to
lead to frustration, since it makes love egocentric, self-seeking,
and independent of the demands or realities of society.

Thus the lover who believes that love should satisfy his need

[12] Such "successes" appear in Anderson's "Nobody Knows," "Sophistication,"
"Death," "Out of Nowhere into Nothing"; Fitzgerald, "Benediction," "'Sensible
Thing,'" "Winter Dreams," "Rough Crossing"; Hemingway, "Very Short Story,"
"Up in Michigan"; Porter, "Rope," "Cracked Looking-Glass," "That Tree";
Faulkner, "Divorce in Naples," "All the Dead Pilots."

for exhilarating, romantic experience, like George O'Kelly in "The 'Sensible Thing,'" is bound to be frustrated ultimately because such experience is by nature not made to endure. The lover who believes that love should bring him appreciation at the rate at which he values himself almost inevitably fails because — in the stories treated here, at least — no one values another as highly as is hoped. This is to be expected in a society more concerned with being appreciated than with appreciating. The great stress on sexual needs also seems to spell their ultimate frustration in the society of the stories of the twenties. It leads to unbalanced situations in which one lover is looking for appreciation while the other is looking for sexual satisfaction — situations which make exploitation like that in "Up in Michigan" almost inevitable. Furthermore, when great emphasis is placed on the sexual role, the result, especially in stories of the twenties, tends to be conflict between man and woman: a man becomes vulnerable to his wife's scorn, as in Miss Porter's "That Tree" and Hemingway's "The Doctor and the Doctor's Wife"; a woman confusedly allows herself to forfeit feminine privileges she longs for or unwillingly accepts an unfeminine role in a marriage or love affair in such stories as Hemingway's "Cat in the Rain" and "Hills Like White Elephants."

The fear of love, which in stories of the twenties inhibits so many would-be lovers and frustrates their relationships, may arise from a great variety of buried causes — causes usually not specified in a story. In general, perhaps, it can be explained as the result of a character's inability to square his idea of love with that of his social or moral relation to society. The heroine of Miss Porter's "Theft" avoids love because of guilty feelings about possession in general; the heroine of Miss Porter's "Flowering Judas" fears it, and her fear is apparently tied up with guilty feelings about the abandonment of her religious and humanitarian responsibilities; the heroine of Anderson's "Seeds" rejects it because of old ideas, as they are called, that she has inherited from a Puritan ancestry, ideas that choke her existence like vines; Krebs, in Hemingway's "Soldier's Home," rejects it because, traumatized by his war experiences, he dreads the complexity of all relationships. Presumably most inhibitions of this kind are reflections of guilt feelings — the sort of feelings that make a person uneasy about self-advantageous behavior or action that would bring him personal gain. The source for such uneasiness is hardly ever indicated; it lies in the depths of the unconscious. The point, however, is that to an individual who has such feelings, the idea of love as depicted in stories of the twenties will inevitably seem dangerous by virtue of its egocentricity, its self-centeredness. The inhibited individual is inhibited precisely because he does think of love in this way. If he thought of it as characters in the early stories do, as unselfish and giving, his fear of gain or possession would cause no problem. As it is, afraid to claim things for himself because of a deep feeling that it is wrong, he is especially afraid to claim love.

It should be added, in qualification, that in many stories of inhibition written in the twenties, such as "Seeds" and Anderson's "The Teacher," withdrawal also seems to suggest (although not explicitly) a simpler sort of fear — a fear that submitting to love will put one in a position to be hurt by others. This too, which is not to be seen in the earlier stories, can be regarded as a consequence of the egocentric idea of love, which is an idea that breeds mistrust.

LOVE AS A SUBJECT OF FICTION

The love problems in stories of the early period can be described as problems of policy and tactics. Those portrayed in stories of the twenties are problems of feeling and impulse. In early stories, the lover's problems have to do with his judgment in recognizing and applying the concept of love already described. Sometimes he errs, and tragedy results, as in Mrs. Wharton's "Bunner Sisters." But he recognizes the error as something that might have been averted had he been a better judge.

In stories of the twenties, the problems of the lover are concerned not with judgment but with the feelings that arise from the frustration of those needs regarded as so important. In various ways, which will be described more fully in a later chapter, the love situations in stories of the twenties are contrived to demonstrate the inner sufferings, extravagances, and distortions of character involved in such a frustration.

Thus the love stories of the two periods both reflect and throw light upon the social differences previously described. The love problems in stories of the early period are tests of an individual's integration in his society. Those in stories of the twenties, by contrast, reveal emotional isolation in their stress upon the individual's private needs and the independence of those needs as such from rational considerations of social duty.

Such a difference suggests an obvious contrast in the way in which the human personality interests the two groups of writers. Those of the twenties are interested in their characters' feelings, inner impulses, and subconscious motivations rather than their reason and moral and practical judgments. The personalities depicted in the twenties have radically different psychological structures from those depicted in earlier stories.

A difference of such depth may be expected to have important consequences for the form and structure of the short stories of the twenties. Since it will have such consequences chiefly because of the moral implications of the two psychologies, we must examine these — we must complete our study of subject matter by looking at the moral problems in these stories — before we can turn to questions of form.

VII: THE IDEA OF MORALITY

A story such as Mrs. Gerould's "The Great Tradition" in the early period has a clear-cut, simple moral issue. The heroine, a New York society matron named Angela Boyce, is planning to leave her husband and elope to Europe. Shortly before her elopement, however, she learns that her daughter Monica has also left her husband. This puts a new light on Mrs. Boyce's plan. She had imagined her own case a "special" one, her unhappiness in marriage sufficient to justify divorce. But Monica has justified her action by the same reasoning: her case, too, is special. What Mrs. Boyce now realizes is that if both mother and daughter divorce, neither will seem "special"; together they will seem to flout deliberately the marriage traditions to which they are taking exception. As Mrs. Boyce sees it, "If Monica's case was to be special, her mother's would have to be irreproachable."

Reasoning thus, she gives up her plan and decides to stick by her marriage.

Fear of censure is not the primary cause of her decision, but rather an acceptance of what she regards as moral responsibility. Aware of her position as a respected member of society, she does not want to damage the "great tradition" of marriage, of marriage for life, for better or worse. She fears that if she elopes as her daughter does, she will encourage others to take that tradition lightly, and she does not want to influence society in that way.

The moral issue is a simple conflict between her personal claims and her obligation to the great institutions of society. The outcome is an affirmation of belief in the latter. Obviously, this moral issue is the primary issue in the story: the reader is meant to admire Mrs. Boyce for her principles and be gratified by the choice she makes. The moral issue subsumes other more specific issues that are also involved, such as Mrs. Boyce's relation to society, her attitude concerning love, matters that we have already considered.

Less obvious is the moral issue of such a short, simple story of the twenties as Hemingway's "The End of Something." Young Nick Adams and his girl Marge row out to the point on a Michigan lake to do some fishing. She sees that he is unhappy about something. Questioning brings forth the disclosure that he no longer finds love any "fun." He doesn't know why: "'I feel as though everything was gone to hell inside of me. I don't know, Marge. I don't know what to say.'" It is the end of their relationship; sadly she gets up and goes back to the boat, leaving him by the fire. His friend Bill comes into the clearing. Bill asks how he feels. "'Oh, go away, Bill!'" says Nick. "'Go away for a while.'"

The conversation between Nick and Marge has suggested that Nick has tired of her because she has learned too well the boyish things he has taught her; she has become too much of a "pal," thus losing her romantic appeal. It is also clear that he is unhappy about the breakup — miserable, perhaps ashamed — as if he had been forced in some way to do an unpleasant thing. We may infer two moral principles at work in Nick: one is what has made him break up with Marge, no matter how uncomfortable such a break might be, and the other is what makes the break uncomfortable, explaining his misery at the end — a principle that he has sacrificed to the first one. Both principles may be largely unconscious. They are the basis of his moral character, nevertheless, since they control his choices and his feelings. At the end, the two are in conflict; neither has a clear triumph — hence his discomfort.

It is less clear here than in "The Great Tradition" to what extent the author "approves" of his hero's morality. The story ends with an unresolved conflict in Nick's principles; this suggests at least some reservation in Hemingway's admiration of either principle. His very choice of Nick's dilemma as a subject, however, makes these principles fairly important in his world, at least for the moment of the story.

A general contrast between the kinds of moral issues treated in the two periods is implicit in the commentary of many literary historians: in statements that the writers of the twenties are in revolt against the conventional morality of their elders, for example, or statements that they take a more pessimistic view of life. Aesthetically, such a contrast may be most significant, for moral issues — questions of what is good and bad — are the most essential part of a story's subject matter: the story's effect depends most directly upon them.

In examining these moral issues, we may postpone consideration of the author's own attitudes — a matter more of his treatment than of his choice of subject. We may begin by looking simply at those moral problems that authors use as subjects for their stories. Some sort of morality prevails in a story's world; the story puts this morality to the test.

For convenience, the "prevailing morality" in a story may be identified with the morality of that character, usually but not necessarily the protagonist, who makes the most significant moral decisions or passes the most significant moral judgments — that character, in other words, who is most sensitive to moral issues. He is the representative, so to speak, of the most enlightened morality which that world exhibits. His "morality" is his concept of what constitutes good behavior in all circumstances; his ideas about good behavior are "moral premises" from which his particular acts and judgments directly follow. His morality may or may not clash with that of other characters or of the society as a whole. The environmental morality, however, is important only in relation to his, the morally sensitive character's, judgment. This may also diverge from the writer's and the reader's judgment. But the question of such divergence cannot be considered until the prevailing morality has been determined.

Nick Adams is much less overtly concerned about the morality of his behavior than is Mrs. Angela Boyce. He does not seem to weigh or evaluate carefully his decision; he justifies his break with Marge only on the grounds that things seem to have gone wrong inside him. Quite possibly Mrs. Boyce would say of Nick that he did not make a moral judgment at all, that his decisions and reactions were governed simply by impulse and unreasoned feelings. Nevertheless, his behavior reflects a moral evaluation, although it has operated in a different way. He has not only different premises from those of Mrs. Boyce, but also, apparently, a different idea as to what a moral premise is or how to recognize one. This different idea of his — this different conception of how a moral premise may be recognized — is typical of the moral attitudes of the twenties. It is true that few characters of either period are fully explicit about their moral premises — the distinctions they make between good and bad behavior. They show their principles mostly through particular applications — in choices they make or judgments and feelings they exhibit in response to particular situations. Even so, the morally sensitive characters differ greatly between the two periods in their idea of what a moral principle is, how it can be apprehended, and how it can be applied. This is seen most vividly in those, in both periods, who are moral perfectionists, those who show an exceptional concern for moral distinctions, seeking to refine them to the finest point, refusing to brook moral compromise.

Mrs. Boyce is the typical moral perfectionist of stories from the early period. Notice her reasoning: "If Monica's case was to be special, her mother's would have to be irreproachable." Such perfectionism — notable in the worlds of James and Mrs. Wharton as well as of Mrs. Gerould — is manifest especially in those

characters who make an extraordinary sacrifice for the sake of an
abstract principle — a sacrifice such as that of the heroine of Mrs.
Gerould's "Leda and the Swan," for example, who destroys her
dying husband's masterpiece, the sale of which is her only possible rescue from poverty, because she does not believe that the
private love which is expressed in the painting should be made
public. Such sacrifices are most striking in some of Bierce's war
stories, in stories dealing with the question of divorce, and in a
variety of renunciation stories by James and Mrs. Gerould.[1]

Moral perfectionism in stories of the twenties, on the other
hand, is shown in the compulsively stubborn behavior and attitudes of some and in the harsh judgments that others pass upon
themselves and others. Both patterns are well illustrated by
Wash Williams, in Anderson's "Respectability," in his extreme
and unyielding hatred of women, arising from disgust with behavior in his wife that reveals, at worst, stupidity and bad taste
rather than malice. Harsh judgment is seen especially in the
attitudes of some of the younger characters.[2]

The perfectionists of the early period, with the exception of
some in Bierce's stories, tend, like Mrs. Boyce, to relate their
behavior consciously and rationally to abstract principle. The
heroine of Mrs. Wharton's "The Quicksand" expresses her marital problem as a conflict between love and "principle." The
heroine of the same writer's "The Reckoning" finds it necessary
to generalize both her initial desire for a divorce and her later
resentment at being divorced into abstract principles of universal applicability: first, by advocating a general policy of less
binding marriage ties; second, by repudiating this policy, and
going back to the first husband and telling him, "I was wrong."
Several characters arrive at a moral decision or a moral discovery
only after an extended process of reasoning and argument — a
process of deduction from general premises to a particular
point.[3] A common feature, not only in stories by the writers

[1] Especially Bierce's "Story of a Conscience," "Affair of Outposts"; Gerould,
"Great Tradition," "Weaker Vessel"; Crane, "Monster"; James, "Paste," "Fordham Castle"; Cather, "Death in the Desert."

[2] See Anderson's "I Want to Know Why" and Hemingway's "My Old Man."

[3] Visible in Wharton's "Reckoning," "Quicksand," "The Choice"; Gerould,
"Great Tradition," "Leda," "Weaker Vessel," "Bird in the Bush"; James, "Mar-

already cited, but also in those by Mrs. Freeman and Garland, is an extended reasoned argument in which a character defends his own or another's behavior.[4] This concern for rationality, indeed, extends well beyond the perfectionists into many simpler characters who would never dream of asserting themselves as experts on morality. It is reflected in the great stress in the world of the early stories upon practicality or good sense: in the community co-operation in Garland's world, for example, and in the tendency to judge true love by practical considerations.

The typical earlier story depicts morality as dependent upon reason. The moral being is a rational being. Moral principles are constant, unchanging axioms whose content the moral being is expected to know, and moral problems are soluble by a process of reasoning from those premises. In the more difficult cases, apparently, they cannot be solved in any other way.

In stories of the twenties this idea of morality is generally rejected. Although occasional characters still talk of "principle" in an abstract sense, or still make attempts to universalize their own attitudes, the process of reasoning from premises does not usually determine their moral views.[5] Some characters rationalize their attitudes, but this follows, rather than precedes, the actual formulation of these attitudes. Arguments that occur are noteworthy for their absence of reasoning and even more noteworthy for their inability to cause anyone to change his position.[6]

riages." Of course, the author does not necessarily reproduce the process of reasoning involved, although he makes clear that it occurs.

[4] See Bierce's "Parker Adderson"; Freeman, "Church Mouse," "Christmas Jenny," "Solitary"; Garland, "Branch Road," "Among the Corn Rows"; Wharton, "Long Run"; James, "Paste," "Story In It," "Lesson of the Master"; Cather, "Sculptor's Funeral."

[5] Exceptions appear in Fitzgerald's "Four Fists," "Hot and Cold Blood," and, perhaps, "Adjuster," which are atypical stories in many other aspects as well. Characters talk of principle in the abstract in Porter's "Flowering Judas," "That Tree." But note that the hero of "That Tree" goes back on his supposed principles, attributing this to his "blood stream," which has "betrayed" him, and the heroine of "Flowering Judas" is controlled by her compulsions, and unconsciously judges herself in her dream.

[6] See the arguments in Anderson's "Teacher," "Hands," "Out of Nowhere into Nothing"; Fitzgerald, "Benediction," "Rich Boy," "Rough Crossing"; Hemingway, "Cat in the Rain," "Doctor and Doctor's Wife," "Hills Like White Elephants," "Out of Season," "Pursuit Race," "Soldier's Home," "Three-Day Blow"; Porter, "Flowering Judas," "Rope," "That Tree," "Theft"; Faulkner, "Divorce in Naples," "Dry September," "That Evening Sun."

When someone tries to defend his position, he will usually either assert it without argument or will support it — like Wash Williams or the heroes of Anderson's "Loneliness" or "The Philosopher" — with long personal narratives from which the listener is required to draw the appropriate moral inferences. Most of the substantial moral discoveries and moral judgments made by characters in stories of the twenties are never stated explicitly. Sometimes they may be expressed through symbols, images, or symbolic acts, as in Laura's dream at the end of "Flowering Judas" or the self-justifying narratives in "Respectability" and "Loneliness"; [7] they may be revealed only through suggestive questions a character may ask, such as those of the boy in Anderson's "I Want to Know Why," or through an expression of unhappy or aggrieved feeling, such as the boy's lament over his loss in Hemingway's "My Old Man" or Nick's distress as noted in "The End of Something." Or else they may remain totally unexpressed, becoming clear to the reader only through inferences drawn from the construction of the story as a whole, as with the discoveries in such stories as Hemingway's "In Another Country" or "The Battler."

This suggests that the first moral assumption made by the typical moral character in stories of the twenties is that the good is recognized only intuitively — that is, through the feelings, which short-cut the process of reasoning from premises. This is why a character's most crucial premises must remain largely unconscious, as Nick's are when "things go to hell inside him," and why so few characters are able to express their real judgments explicitly. It explains why even those characters who rationalize, who attempt to be logical in their moral attitudes, actually give priority to their impulses or their feelings in determining what to do, and also why so many characters, whom we shall be examining later, are caught in insolvable situations of conflicting motives and irreconcilable ambivalence: if principles are unconscious and logic is rejected in favor of intuition, an individual is deprived of his power to recognize inconsistencies

[7] Hemingway's "Cat in the Rain" and "Pursuit Race" and Porter's "Theft" also show attitudes symbolically expressed.

between his principles or to give one principle priority over another.

This basic contrast is important in the developing art of the short story since it is, as will be seen later, intimately related with some of the most prominent experiments in technique. It only begins to suggest, however, the actual content of the moral premises of the two periods — the premises, arrived at in these ways, which explain why Mrs. Boyce rejected divorce and why Nick was torn between the feeling that he must reject Marge and the feeling that it was bad to do so. These premises do most to determine the moral character of the two worlds.

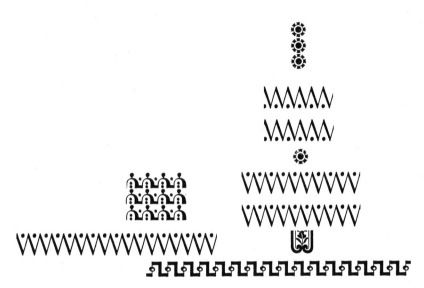

VIII: EARLY PERIOD: MORAL PRINCIPLES

The moral principles at stake in a story are revealed sometimes by the choices a character makes, sometimes by the pride he reveals or the shame he suffers, sometimes by his discoveries and judgments. They can be described as beliefs in some absolute good, transcending immediate personal interest, and stimulating or restraining conduct. In the earlier stories the moral principles at stake are to a large extent, but not wholly, implicit in the picture of social and love relationships that has already been drawn.

Such principles differ in their details from story to story. The principles which Mrs. Boyce, for instance, affirms in "The Great Tradition" when she rejects divorce differ from those affirmed by Haskins, in Garland's "Under the Lion's Paw," when he labors so hard and long trying to make himself the independent owner

101

of his farm, and Haskins' principles differ in turn from those of such a Jamesian artist as Paul Overt, in "The Lesson of the Master," who sacrifices normal personal relationships in order the better to pursue perfection in his work. By looking for common elements, however, one can distinguish at least four major kinds of moral premises, held by many or most of the characters in the early period and put to the test in their stories — premises that are distinct from the major principles similarly tested in the twenties.

ORDER AND PROGRESS

When Garland's farmer moves West to establish a democratic community, when the citizens of the communities so established strive to make the communities function better, when the citizens of other parts of the early world also seek to make society function better in ways that were considered in Chapter IV, they are all affirming belief in a common principle — in what, for want of a more precise description, can be called the orderly conduct of human affairs. They believe that human affairs can and should be conducted in an orderly manner, that good resides in the orderly disposition of things. This belief, which can also be inferred in the respect citizens show for the laws, institutions, and traditions of society, is a moral rather than a wholly practical matter: that is, a character supports the principle not merely because it may bring him personal advantages but because he regards it, in the abstract, as a good thing. It is not, for example, fear of discovery that makes two of Mrs. Freeman's heroines so remorseful about the petty thefts that need has driven them to commit, nor is it even concern for the harm (which is, after all, negligible) that they may have done to others by their thefts. Though they know that their thefts are unknown to anyone, they feel stigmatized in their own eyes for the violation of an immutable rule.[1]

---

[1] Freeman, "Calla-lilies," "Stolen Christmas." The heroine of "Stolen Christmas" reacts thus upon learning that she is to receive a steady income: " 'Five dollars a week!' gasped Marg'ret. 'My land! An' I've *stole!* ' "

It should be pointed out that in both cases the heroine is finally persuaded that her theft is forgiven because of the circumstances that drove her to it; she has, in other words, taken almost too rigid a view of her transgression. The forgiveness itself may be said to follow from a broader interpretation of what is an orderly way to conduct human affairs.

In its more active forms this principle carries with it, in the early period, an implicit faith in the possibility and desirability of human progress. The character who works in behalf of better law and order believes that it is attainable, that it can be welded out of chaos by human effort, that the history of mankind is a forward movement. In Garland's "Among the Corn Rows," the farmer's speech "voiced the modern idea"; it "declared rebellion against laws that were survivals of hate and prejudice." [2]

The universality of these principles is evidenced by their presence even in the wildest community seen in the early period, Crane's frontier world. One village takes pride in its newly acquired respectability; the story turns on this pride and the shame felt by the inhabitants when they are goaded into violence by an insulting stranger. In another story a local renegade calls off a shooting match when he learns that his opponent is married, thus betraying his surprising respect for civilized law and order even though this is a principle he scarcely understands:

"Married?" said Scratchy. . . . He was like a creature allowed a glimpse of another world. . . . He was not a student of chivalry; it was merely that in the presence of this foreign condition he was a simple child of the earlier plains.[3]

In the upper-class worlds of James, Mrs. Wharton, and Mrs. Gerould, the principle of orderly conduct in human affairs can be observed in another way: it has been refined into an intense horror of what most of these characters call "vulgarity." The people in these worlds live by an elaborate and highly polished code of fine manners, which can be seen at work in almost every scene in which they participate. These manners are their bulwark against vulgarity; one can infer, indeed, that what most of these people mean by vulgarity is simply the absence of such manners.

A sociologist might say that this horror of vulgarity is the

[2] See p. 37.
[3] Crane, "Blue Hotel," "Bride Comes to Yellow Sky." Several other stories by Crane suggest, although sometimes it is no more than a hint, a character's disposition to or yearning for law and order in violent, uncivilized surroundings — bandit country, war, the jungle of the Bowery: "Horses — One Dash!" "Five White Mice," "Three Miraculous Soldiers," "Gray Sleeve," "Experiment in Misery," "Maggie."

product of class vanity, a device that enables members of an "upper class" to justify their privileges in society on the basis of moral superiority. And so, indeed, it seems to be in some of the vain characters depicted in these stories — for example, George Gravener, in James's "The Coxon Fund," who condemns the brilliant wastrel, Frank Saltram, on the grounds that he is "not a gentleman." Yet for more serious, morally sensitive individuals, such an interpretation is at least misleading. They dread vulgarity for reasons quite other than simply to protect their own self-esteem. A study of their fine manners suggests that their general purpose is not snobbish but to make human intercourse as free of conflict as it can possibly be. This could be illustrated by any number of scenes, such as the following crucial one between mother and daughter in Mrs. Wharton's "Autres Temps," in which unpleasant questions are asked and unpleasant answers given without overt acknowledgment by either party of the unpleasantness:

"Do your visitors know I'm here?" Mrs. Lidcote suddenly went on.

"Do they — Of course — why, naturally," Leila rejoined. . . .

"Then won't they think it odd if I don't appear?"

"Oh, not in the least, dearest. I assure you they'll *all* understand." . . .

. . . "Will they think it odd if I *do*?"

Leila stopped short, her lips half parted to reply. As she paused, the colour stole over her bare neck, swept up to her throat, and burst into flame in her cheeks. . . .

Mrs. Lidcote silently watched the conflagration; then she turned away her eyes with a slight laugh. "I only meant that I was afraid it might upset the arrangement of your dinner-table if I didn't come down. If you can assure me that it won't, I believe I'll take you at your word and go back to this irresistible sofa!"

The finest manners involve, generally, a highly calculated kind of behavior based on perception of another's needs and motives and designed to put him in as favorable a light as possible. The well-mannered tend to avoid direct explanations in order not to insult the listener's intelligence; they tend to avoid direct expressions of feeling in order not to make emotional demands upon the listener.[4] Sometimes the finest courtesy may involve

[4] These tendencies are carried to a self-defeating extreme in Wharton's "Dilettante."

behavior which by ordinary standards is quite unconventional, as in the following passage from Mrs. Wharton's "The Long Run," in which the narrator discovers why the heroine — described by him as "the steadiest-minded woman I had ever known, and the last to wish to owe any advantage to surprise, to unpreparedness, to any play on the spring of sex" — had approached him in the way she had:

She had come to my house, had brought her trunk with her, had thrown herself at my head with all possible violence and publicity, in order to give me a pretext, a loophole, an honourable excuse, for doing and saying — why, precisely what I had said and done! . . .

Of course she had known all along just the kind of thing I should say if I didn't at once open my arms to her; and to save my pride, my dignity, my conception of the figure I was cutting in her eyes, she had recklessly and magnificently provided me with the decentest pretext a man could have for doing a pusillanimous thing.

What such people mean by vulgarity, then, is a kind of disorderliness in the conduct of human affairs. This is what relates their devotion to polished manners to that general faith in order and progress which is displayed in simpler forms in other parts of the world of the earlier stories. Faith in progress is implicit in their respect for fine manners as an achievement of a high civilization, the result of a civilizing process.

The nature of the abhorred vulgarity varies. The heroine of Mrs. Gerould's "Leda and the Swan," for example, abhors the vulgarity of displaying to the public her husband's expression in a painting of his private feelings for her. The hero of James's "Flickerbridge" similarly abhors the vulgarity of publicity, which he fears will destroy the fine distinction of an old English home and of the English spinster who has hitherto been shielded from modern influences. James's butler Brooksmith has become so attached to the kind of fine gentlemanly conversation that goes on in his master's house — excellent talk that he himself has cleverly and inconspicuously helped to make possible through his handling of the guests — that after his master's death he finds all other households intolerably dull and vulgar, even those of the highest society.

In James's stories, indeed, high society itself quite often turns out to be intrinsically vulgar. The finest ear for vulgarity, the finest taste (and taste and fine manners have become essentially one) is found in his artists and writers. Neil Paraday, in "The Death of the Lion," is destroyed by his exposure to a society that vulgarly tries to lionize him. Ray Limbert, in "The Next Time," finds it impossible to write a vulgar book and thus goes through life turning out masterpieces that only a handful of people appreciate. Hugh Vereker's distaste for vulgarity, in "The Figure in the Carpet," is so great that he disdains to tell anyone the intention of his works, with the result that it is a secret he takes to the grave.

For the Jamesian artist, indeed (if not so consistently for Miss Cather's artists), the ultimate bulwark against vulgarity is perfection in art. Except in "The Lesson of the Master," great art is never popular, for it can be appreciated only by the few. Popular art, vulgar art, is second-rate, as we see clearly enough in such a story as "Greville Fane." For the Jamesian moralist the antithesis of vulgarity is beauty — the beauty of art, or, in "The Beldonald Holbein," the beauty of a face that only artists are able to appreciate.

Beauty itself, for the typical Jamesian artist, is the manifestation of this principle of orderliness. The object of Paul Overt's quest, in "The Lesson of the Master," is nothing less than artistic perfection, as is explicitly stated at several points. The perfection of a lifelong unifying plan is Vereker's object in "The Figure in the Carpet." Dencombe, in "The Middle Years," is unhappy because he has not yet attained a perfection that he now sees as possible. Limbert, in "The Next Time," cannot help being a perfectionist, and this is his distinction. Perfection is order, pursued for its own sake, for its own beauty. The artist who pursues it is expressing his faith in the principles of order and of progress — the belief that better order, finer beauty, is achievable by man.

The disregard of law and order in stories of the twenties has already been described, and the disregard of fine manners is obvious to any reader. Seldom, for example, does anyone make a significant effort to prevent the embarrassment of others, and in many stories characters deliberately embarrass each other, sometimes for the sheer pleasure of it,[5] and sometimes because

[5] For example, some of Fitzgerald's partying young men and women; also the American soldiers who insult their French allies in Faulkner's "Ad Astra."

they are forced to by their feelings.[6] To be sure, the presence of a few artists in the stories of the twenties and the occasional emphasis on ritual activities show that the principle of order has not been completely abandoned. Yet the artists seem more significantly motivated by principles other than this one, and the rituals are complicated by kinds of problems, to be discussed below, that characters in the early stories do not have to face.[7]

SELF-SUFFICIENCY

"I consider myself a sight better 'n any man who lives on somebody else's hard work. I've never had a cent I didn't earn with them hands."

This is the beginning of Rob's explanation of why he moved West, in Garland's "Among the Corn Rows," quoted at greater length on p. 37. It enunciates what is probably the most impelling motive in the Western migration Garland depicts: the pride that his people take in their self-sufficiency — their ability to take care of themselves.

Such pride is especially characteristic of the rural people in the world of the early stories — in Mrs. Freeman's communities as well as in Garland's — where the rigors of life are a challenge to self-sufficiency. It accounts for Haskins' desire to be the owner of his own farm:

No slave in the Roman galleys could have toiled so frightfully and lived, for this man thought himself a free man, and that he was working for his wife and babes.

It stiffens the returned soldier-farmer in his fight against age and hardships. It explains, apparently, most of the concern about status shown by Mrs. Freeman's wives and spinsters. They dread the disclosure of poverty in the fear that it will prove them unable to take care of themselves. The aging singer who refuses to retire is motivated less by vanity than by a fierce pride which refuses to admit that she is no longer competent. An aged pauper boasts of a fictitious wealthy sister because of a confused feeling

[6] The characteristic disregard of manners in the twenties is well typified by the husband in Hemingway's "Cat in the Rain" who, good-naturedly enough but with complete lack of respect, tells his wife, to "shut up," or the heroine in "Hills Like White Elephants" who is exasperated by her lover's insincerity and threatens to scream.

[7] See chap. ix.

that wealth is a token of virtue. Note how she couches her explanation in moral terms: "'But I used to feel dretful bad an' wicked when I heerd you all talkin' 'bout things you'd had, an' I hadn't never had nothin' . . .'"[8]

Sometimes this pride hampers an individual's relationships with others. For just as it may prevent him from admitting weakness, so it may prevent him from admitting love. Here is the chief obstacle that must be overcome in most of the courtships and milder marital conflicts in the period. It does not mean that such characters cannot feel love. On the contrary, their love is usually deep and strong. But it may be concealed beneath a bristly show of independence, as in Crane's story of two brothers who pretend to be enemies until danger in war exposes their love, and who resume their hostility as soon as the danger is past. Or it may hide behind reticence or timidity, attributable to the lover's confused fear of admitting to weakness or dependence.[9]

In the early world, however, this principle is not as universal as the principle of order. In the love stories just cited, it gives way to other motives that enable love to emerge. Occasionally it may give way to some real weakness of character. Some individuals make little pretense about their weakness or dependence, but they are less typical than the self-sufficient ones; there are apt to be extenuating circumstances for weakness, such as old age; otherwise, admission of weakness or dependence is characteristic only in stories by those writers, such as Dreiser, whose subject matter tends to be atypical of the period.[10]

In stories of the twenties many characters also show great pride in their independence, but it does not usually spring from the same principle as that dramatized in the earlier stories. The

[8] Stories cited: Garland, "Under the Lion's Paw," "Return of a Private"; Freeman, "Village Singer," "Sister Liddy." See also Freeman's "Gala Dress," "Stolen Christmas."

[9] Love is concealed by a display of hostility or independence in Crane's "Little Regiment"; Garland, "Mrs. Ripley," "Uncle Ethan," "Branch Road"; Freeman, "Kitchen Colonel." Love is reticent in Freeman's "Amanda," "Scent of Roses," "Discovered Pearl," "Calla-lilies"; James, "Broken Wings."

[10] Façades give way in Bierce's "Parker Adderson," "One Officer, One Man"; Freeman, "Solitary"; Garland, "God's Ravens"; Crane, "Death and the Child"; Cather, "Death in the Desert," "Wagner Matinee." Dependent characters are noteworthy in Bierce's "Chickamauga"; Freeman, "Village Lear"; Dreiser, "Free," "Lost Phoebe," "Second Choice," "Married"; James, "Coxon Fund."

independence of wanderers like Nick Adams, of recluses like Wing Biddlebaum, of grotesques like Wash Williams, is essentially antisocial, a withdrawal from society,[11] directly opposed to the self-sufficiency generally displayed in the early stories, as can be shown by a contrast of extreme cases. Whereas Rob, in "Among the Corn Rows," for example, shows his self-sufficiency by building a farm, bringing a wife to it, and settling down to play an important part in a new community which he is helping to build, Emily, in Faulkner's "A Rose for Emily," shows her independence by refusing to pay her taxes, closing her doors, poisoning her lover, and sleeping with the corpse. Again, the protagonists of both Mrs. Freeman's "A Village Singer" and Hemingway's "The Undefeated" proudly refuse to admit that they are finished in their special fields of distinction. They differ only in the source of their pride: the bullfighter is trying to retain the glory of a champion, a figure set apart from and held in awe by the rest of society, whereas the singer is trying to retain her special niche in the local community, her right to make her own particular contribution (as church soprano) to community life. The independence of the individual in stories of the twenties, in other words, is a rebellion *against* the community and its impositions; self-sufficiency in the early stories is an assumption of responsibility *within* the community.

ACCEPTANCE OF ADVERSITY

Mrs. Gerould's "Wesendonck" concerns the discovery of another principle that appears frequently in stories of the early period. Sadie Chadwick, wife of a struggling college professor, is asked by her husband to give a dinner for Wesendonck, a great man who can do much to advance her husband's career. Sadie, who is not fond of her household duties, finds the idea intolerable and persuades herself that no wife need feel obliged to do anything she finds intolerable. Without warning, she leaves to pay a visit to her mother, not returning until after the scheduled evening has passed. When she returns, she sees not only that she has ruined her husband's chances, but that he is hurt and angry with her:

She heard the front door slam behind him.

[11] See discussion of withdrawal, pp. 48–51.

Long before Bert Chadwick returned from his laboratory, Sadie slept, from utter weariness. She had discovered that sometimes the intolerable must be borne.

The principle that Sadie Chadwick discovers here is accepted as a matter of course in other early stories, and in many cases it is an important part of their characterization. Often closely related to the principle of self-sufficiency, it is most evident in the pride with which most rural characters face the hardships of daily living. Garland's Mrs. Ripley, having returned from her trip to York County, tackles her housewifely duties without complaint: "She took up her burden again, never more thinking to lay it down." Mrs. Freeman's Hannah wears a smile even though she is being most unjustly treated by the community, and the smile helps her to avoid their pity.[12] Mrs. Freeman's Louisa, fighting for her freedom not to marry, shoulders enormous household burdens without complaint. Often such behavior moves the author to outright praise. In "The Return of a Private," Garland praises the returned soldier-farmer: ". . . his heroic soul did not quail. With the same courage with which he had faced his Southern march he entered upon a still more hazardous future." Mrs. Freeman praises the hero of "A Kitchen Colonel," an ineffectual man who has been reduced to menial tasks in the household because he fails at most things he does: ". . . and the kitchen colonel fought faithfully in his humble field, where maybe he would some day win a homely glory all his own."

Many characters reveal a similar attitude in the great pleasure they derive from trivial compensations. This also is a common pattern in the rural stories and is clearly manifested in the case of Mrs. Markham, in Garland's "A Day's Pleasure." A lonely farm wife, she takes a rare day's vacation, which threatens to be a failure since there is nothing to do in the village but sit in the grocery store and wait for her husband. But a stranger pities her and invites her in to tea. Although nothing happens at the tea and the conversation is stilted, Mrs. Markham is filled with

---

[12] "Calla-lilies": "A smile in an object of pity is a grievance. The one claim which Hannah now had upon her friends she did not extort, consequently she got nothing."

pleasure: "The day had been made beautiful by human sympathy." Much of the story's impact depends upon its demonstration of how easily Mrs. Markham is made happy, despite the drudgery and loneliness of her life. Her willingness to be pleased by the smallest favor or display of sympathy shows how humbly she accepts her lot. Similarly, Mrs. Ripley is sustained for most of her life by anticipation of the vacation trip she will someday take to York County; after the trip she is sustained by the knowledge that she has taken it. Many of Mrs. Freeman's spinsters are adepts at the invention of small pleasures that make life worthwhile: one plays cards, another delights in dressing up (in a shabby old dress), two of them cultivate flowers, another devotes herself to the writing of mortuary verse. Louisa, in "A New England Nun," is so successful at finding happiness in small things that she passes up a chance for a more active, married life:

[She set forth her daily tea] with as much grace as if she had been a veritable guest to her own self.

She would have been loath to confess how more than once she had ripped a seam for the mere delight of sewing it together again.

So too, elsewhere, Mrs. Wharton's Greenwich Village shopkeepers build a very exiciting life out of very small happenings, and Dreiser's laborers make their dreary life tolerable by imaginatively converting their shop into a ship and themselves into its officers and crew.[13]

Although some of the simpler souls, such as Mrs. Freeman's Hannah, try to school themselves to accept anything, no matter how unjust it seems, this principle tends to be limited in a fairly specific way. Obviously it does not interfere with the efforts of those who are devoted to improving the lot of their communities or the functioning of their societies. Garland's farmers, moving West, have refused to accept the claims of the "cussed European aristocracy," even though they generally make a point of resigning themselves to the hardships consequent upon their choice. Mrs. Wharton's Mrs. Lidcote does not feel it wrong to criticize the absurd grounds on which she is ostracized, even though she

[13] Stories cited in this paragraph: Garland, "Mrs. Ripley"; Freeman, "Innocent Gamester," "Gala Dress," "Calla-lilies," "Scent of Roses," "Poetess"; Wharton, "Bunner Sisters"; Dreiser, "Cruise of the 'Idlewild.'"

makes no effort to rectify the situation. The principle of acceptance, in practice, usually applies only to those misfortunes, hardships, or wrongs that are, practically or morally, difficult or impossible to rectify. It does not apply to those evils that might be remedied by human agency and according to civilized principles within the framework of society.

Thus most of the infrequent instances of refusal to accept misfortune — the bitterness of the farmers in Garland's "Up the Coolly" and "Under the Lion's Paw," the despair of the prostitute in Crane's "Maggie," the grief of Mrs. Freeman's old villager who is rejected by his daughters, the horror of Bierce's heroes who crack up in war, the contempt of James's artists for the vulgarity of their audiences — may be interpreted not as violations of the doctrine of resignation (especially as they are often accompanied by an effort toward resignation) but as moral criticism of social or personal injustice. The farmer and the prostitute implicitly criticize the economic system, which, being a system, is ideally capable of reform; the soldier implicitly criticizes war, which is the result of political deficiencies in the structure of society; the old man implicitly criticizes his daughters, who are guilty of a personal injustice; the artist criticizes vulgarity, which implies the possibility of a non-vulgar society, no matter how limited or small it may be. Reform of the system or education of various kinds could ideally prevent these wrongs; hence it is no violation of the principle to object to them.[14]

True rejections of this principle — cases in which an individual refuses to resign himself to evils beyond the reach of civilized justice or reform — are confined to certain stories by Dreiser and Miss Cather,[15] and Crane's "The Open Boat," an extraordinary story for the period, in which the characters rail against nature itself. They resent being threatened with death by the

[14] Some other kinds of seeming violations of the principle also are not really violations. The cowards in Bierce's "Parker Adderson" and Crane's "Death and the Child" show their respect for the principle in their shame of cowardice. The Gerould hero who cannot accept his son's defiance of his wishes ("Dominant Strain") and the artists in stories by Mrs. Gerould and by James who defiantly reject social conventions ("Pearls" and "Coxon Fund") obviously do violate the principle; but the astonishment of the narrator and all who behold these things testifies to prevailing beliefs.

[15] Cather, "Paul's Case"; Dreiser, "Free," "Old Rogaum," "Second Choice," "Married," "Lost Phoebe."

sea, and in defying the "seven mad gods who rule the sea" they take a long step away from their contemporaries in the direction of the stories of the twenties.[16]

The protagonists in stories of the twenties are often strikingly unable or unwilling to accept the kinds of things that characters in earlier stories accept. This does not mean that they do not value the virtue of resignation. But it is not a primary virtue, since it cannot always be practiced, usually because some other value has priority over it.

Some characters make an attempt at stoicism. The heroine of Anderson's "Adventure," for instance, "began trying to force herself to face bravely the fact that many people must live and die alone, even in Winesburg." She has a long way to go before she can match the spinster who rips out a seam for the pleasure of stitching it again; as long as it is a matter of "forcing herself" it is not comparable. Several of Hemingway's heroes submit to frustration without overt protest.[17] This, too, is not comparable to the earlier kinds of resignation; the girl who decides, in "Hills Like White Elephants," not to continue to argue with her lover merely bottles up her discontent. Likewise, Fitzgerald's hero who "accepts" the lamentable passing of his youth. Even as he says, "'I cannot cry. I cannot care. That thing will come back no more,' . . . tears were streaming down his face."[18] A mother, in Miss Porter's "He," fails in her attempt to resign herself to having an idiot son; when she is finally persuaded to send him away, she cannot resign herself to this either, castigating herself and lamenting, "Oh, what a mortal pity he was ever born." As already noted, most reconciliations between quarreling couples are attempts to suppress or ignore, rather than to face and accept, the issues of conflict; they show surrender rather than resignation. Indeed, true resignation is found in not more than a handful of stories: Anderson's "Paper Pills," "Death in the Woods," and, modified, "The Untold Lie," and possibly Faulkner's "Red

---

[16] See p. 339. This is also a reminder that American short stories have a debt to the tradition of Hawthorne and Melville.

[17] Hemingway, "Up in Michigan," "Doctor and Doctor's Wife," "Cat in the Rain," "Out of Season," "Now I Lay Me," "Hills Like White Elephants."

[18] Fitzgerald, "Winter Dreams."

Leaves." In the latter story the resignation appears ridiculous as *not* being really necessary.

Many characters refuse to resign themselves. Instead they stubbornly resent and defy any frustration. Like the hero of "The Undefeated," who refuses to admit defeat even after he has been gored in the bull ring, they obey principles that prohibit resignation.

COMMITMENTS TO OTHERS

In the early days of the Civil War, in Bierce's "The Story of a Conscience," Paul Hartroy is made to guard a Confederate spy who has been condemned to death. Exhausted, Hartroy falls asleep at his post; the spy takes pity on him and, instead of escaping and saving his own life, saves Hartroy's life by keeping his place and waking him before the officers come. Several years later, Hartroy has been commissioned and is in command of a Federal post in Confederate country, where he has given orders that any spy should be summarily shot. While talking to a sentinel one day, Hartroy recognizes and captures a spy, the same man who had saved his life on the earlier occasion. In an interview he expresses his appreciation: "'Ah, Brune, Brune, that was well done — that was great. . . . Ah, but if I had suffered the penalty of my crime — if you had not generously given me the life that I accepted without gratitude you would not be again in the shadow and imminence of death.'" Nevertheless, he orders the execution of Brune. At the moment of execution, he takes his own life; it is a renunciation of "the life which in conscience he could no longer keep."

Hartroy's decisions — both to execute the spy and to kill himself — imply a moral principle unlike those we have examined thus far. From his actions and words, we may infer that Hartroy's fundamental belief is in the sacredness of an obligation. Hartroy owes his own life to Brune, but he also owes Brune's life to the military cause. Obligated to uphold military discipline, he sacrifices Brune's life; obligated to Brune for his own life, he must sacrifice that, too, when he takes Brune's life.

A number of stories — characteristic of Mrs. Wharton, James, and Mrs. Gerould as well as of Bierce — present dilemmas that put judgment and power of self-denial or self-sacrifice to an extreme test. Ordinarily, like Hartroy, the protagonist makes the sacrifice. The common element in most of these sacrifices is the presence of commitments or obligations that must be evaluated; as with Hartroy, the sacrifice is usually made for the sake of such a commitment.

Though not all of the early stories by any means put this to the test, a commitment, a promise, a contracted obligation clearly takes precedence, in almost all cases where it is involved, over any other consideration. Few characters in stories of the early period violate this rule. If they do, they face the shock and disapproval of those around them.[19] On the other hand, faith in the importance of commitments can be read into much of the common behavior that has already been described in other connections. Garland's farmers and Freeman's villagers are committed to help their neighbors by their own dependence on the community in a world that threatens their security. Bierce's war heroes sacrifice themselves because they have contracted to do so by joining the army. Love is the most compelling commitment of all, because it is the most immediate and personal. Declarations of love and marriage vows are promises, and the lover who sacrifices his self-interest for the beloved, the husband who makes concessions for his wife, the father who yields his self-interest for the sake of his children, do so because they have so obligated themselves. The joy such characters feel in performing acts of love in no way diminishes the moral significance of their acts.

This principle is most significant as a moral issue when tested by a situation in which two or more commitments clash. Stories with such conflicts provide perhaps the most searching probe into the morality of the world of the early stories.

The simplest of such tests is seen in Mrs. Gerould's "The

---

[19] As in Gerould's "Dominant Strain" and "Pearls," James's "Coxon Fund" and, to an extent, "Miss Gunton." Some characters violate this rule, but later repudiate the violation: Gerould, "Wesendonck"; Garland, " 'Good Fellow's' Wife"; Wharton, "Reckoning"; James, "Marriages." Some secondary characters betray the protagonist: Garland, "Under the Lion's Paw"; Wharton, "Bunner Sisters"; Freeman, "Village Lear"; Crane, "Maggie"; Dreiser, "Second Choice"; Cather, "Flavia," "Death in the Desert"; James, "Abasement," "Paste," "Europe," "Fordham Castle," "Lesson of the Master," "Death of the Lion." The victims in such cases feel justified in their resentment according to the standards that have been described here.

Bird in the Bush." The promising diplomat gives up the brilliant career that was expected to do his country so much good in order to make possible a needed operation for his son. Love wins out over patriotic duty. The apparent test that has been applied here is that of immediate need: the son needs his help more than does the world:

"The world won't thank us," she went on. "What will, I wonder?" Not the deaf generations, she thought to herself, to which we all sacrifice.

"Not Geoffrey," she heard Glave saying. "He will never understand. . . . We haven't answered him. Life has answered him. Call it God, if you must . . ."

Often, however, love is sacrificed and the claim of the most dependent party is denied. The heroine of Mrs. Wharton's "The Quicksand" castigates herself for having placed love above social conscience. In "The Choice," another of Mrs. Wharton's stories, the heroine saves the hated husband rather than the lover who would rescue her. A doctor in Crane's "The Monster" sacrifices the happiness of his family rather than abandon his duty to the injured Negro who had saved his son's life. The heroes of Bierce's "A Horseman in the Sky" and "The Affair at Coulter's Notch" destroy their families in obedience to military command. The principle that accounts for these choices can be inferred with reasonable certainty by comparison with the case of Captain Hartroy in "The Story of a Conscience." Since it would have been perfectly possible for him to let his prisoner go, and since his own suicide cannot possibly help the man, the suicide can only be explained as a way to avoid *profit* in breaking his obligation to the man. He cannot keep the life that he owes to Brune since he has taken Brune's life in obedience to his military obligation. The test is clear: If commitments clash, a man should honor the one that profits him least. Only thus can he be sure that his decision is a moral and not a selfish one.

Thus the diplomat in "The Bird in the Bush" can save his son and abandon his patriotic duty because he gives up fame and glory in doing so. The heroine of "The Quicksand," on the other hand, is wrong in placing love above social conscience because the choice of love is most comfortable and pleasing. We can

infer that the wife in "The Choice" saves the husband rather
than the lover because she would profit were the husband to die.

Two or three stories show that one can be freed from a contract if the other party violates its assumed terms. This can be
inferred in those disenchanted marriages in which the spouse
turns out to be a scoundrel, whereby the protagonist is entitled
to consider divorce. But he usually gives up this idea, as further
complications in the rule of obligations make their appearance.
Thus Mrs. Angela Boyce, in "The Great Tradition" (see p. 93),
gives up when she perceives that her plan would betray not only
her duty to her husband, which she considers void, but also her
duty to society. She knows that she must not profit at the expense of that duty. A wife in Mrs. Gerould's "The Weaker Vessel" argues her husband out of his plans to leave her in a scene
that ends in this way:

"I can't prevent your fantastic infidelities, but I can and will prevent your breaking your word. You repeated the marriage-service of
your own free will. I appeal to your honor."

"You and I don't mean the same thing by honor, Evelyn; but I
don't break my word. If you're mad enough and wicked enough to
ask me to go on ratifying that old promise under the changed conditions of our lives, I suppose I shall do it."

The conception of honor to which he tries to hold her gives way
before his own respect for the rule of commitments; he cannot
escape, since she insists on stressing his personal gain at her
expense.

Although this principle is developed by James with great
subtlety and complexity in such novels as *The Portrait of a Lady,*
The Spoils of Poynton, and *The Ambassadors,* a conflict of obligations is not a major moral issue in most of his short stories in
the canon. To be sure, self-sacrifice in response to an obligation
is as common here as elsewhere in the early period: in "The Middle Years," "The Tree of Knowledge," "Paste," "Europe," "Fordham Castle," and "The Coxon Fund," where the sacrifices do
not involve direct clash of obligations to others. These stories do
show, however, an additional moral subtlety lacking in most of
the others of the period since the character who makes the sacrifice is usually thereby unscrupulously exploited. The mother in

"Europe" exploits her daughter's sense of duty to a degree that shocks observers; the husband in "Fordham Castle" submits dutifully to his virtual obliteration as a person in order to satisfy his wife's selfish ambitions. The principle, in other words, does not always lead to action that the audience is permitted to feel to be wise or just. Such stories, in which its extreme application makes the protagonist seem foolish, as also in Mrs. Gerould's "The Weaker Vessel," or stories such as Bierce's, in which it makes a character seem horrible, give some measure of the manner in which the morality of the author may deviate from that of the most sensitive of his characters. The fact remains, however, that in the stories I discuss respect for commitments is the most important moral subject and fundamental to the motivation of characters.

Like the other dominant principles of the early period so far described, this principle also is much less important in the stories of the twenties. The number of infidelities and betrayals indicates the extent to which it is actively ignored. In most of these stories the principle is simply not put to the test. Even characters who stick to their unhappy marriages or stay with unworthy lovers, such as the heroine of "Hills Like White Elephants," do not seem to be motivated by a firm conviction of loyalty. In the story where a feeling of obligation is most keen in the protagonist — Miss Porter's "Flowering Judas" — the heroine apparently sees no way to honor her conflicting duties to God, society, and humanity; instead of making a choice between them, as earlier heroines would have done, she honors none of them and sinks into a nightmare of universal betrayal. When Hawkshaw, in Faulkner's "Hair," carries out his intention of marrying the girl whom he chose as his wife when she was only a child, having spent many years paying off the debts of the family of his deceased first fiancée, he is fulfilling a contract from which he would have been excused in earlier stories, since the girl has turned out to be publicly disloyal and promiscuous. His motive is clearly more complicated than a simple respect for the principle of honoring obligations.

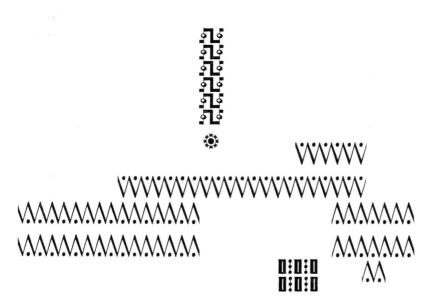

IX: THE TWENTIES: MORAL PRINCIPLES

It has already been suggested that the morality of the typical
hero in stories of the twenties tends, as with Nick in "The End
of Something," to lie below the rational and perhaps even the
conscious level. This absence of formulated moral doctrine may
obscure the strong and positive moral feelings that such an individual does have. That these moral feelings are what earlier
writers would very likely brand as "selfish" does not make them
less moral. An individual must have some ideas of good and bad
in order to decide what his self-interest is; and these ideas may
be called moral principles since they are not simply instinctive
reactions to particular situations but have a general application
as well. As in the early period, four general kinds of moral principles can be discerned in stories of the twenties, motivating

119

those typical characters who are most morally sensitive [1] — sometimes as stimuli for action, sometimes as criteria for criticism,
sometimes as bases for shame or guilt. These principles are
sharply distinct from those that dominated the early period and
give the world of the twenties a sharply different moral
character.

THE IMPORTANCE OF EXPERIENCE

George Willard's departure from Winesburg is described as "the
adventure of his life." His motive is quite different from that
which caused Joe Dagget, in Mrs. Freeman's "A New England
Nun," to leave his village for fifteen years to "make his fortune,"
after which he returned with the idea of settling down and
marrying Louisa. When the heroine of Anderson's "Seeds" goes
to the city to find love, it is clear that not any kind of love will
do. She wants a kind of love, evidently, that a small town cannot
give: love in the setting of a big city, in a setting of adventure.
When the heroine of Anderson's "Out of Nowhere into Nothing"
returns home to the farm on a visit, she is oppressed anew by
the monotony and routine of the life from which she has fled.

We have described the wanderings of the typical traveler,
the expatriate, the nomad of the twenties, as a flight from his
society, a manifestation of his desire to withdraw from the social
organizations. They can be described equally well as a pursuit
of adventure — of a novelty and variety of experience such as
the home environment cannot give. The girl on the farm and the
small-town boy hope for adventures in the city that the farm
or small town does not afford. The expatriate who skis, who
fishes out of season, who travels about from pension to pension
alone or with a wife or mistress, is obviously looking for kinds
of experiences different from those available at home. The boys
who ride freights or travel between county fairs have no appar-

---

[1] Our references to "morally sensitive" characters (see also pp. 95–96) do not
contradict our assertion here that all choices reflect moral character or moral
principles of some sort. The morally sensitive characters may be described as
those who either make the subtlest distinctions between good and evil or who
are most serious (i.e., most strict) in the application of their own principles.
Obviously some people are less tolerant of what they consider to be evil in
themselves than are others. The morally insensitive character is one who either
minds less when the conflict of his principles causes him to violate some of them
or is actually unaware of such violation.

ent motive beyond that of "seeing the world," accumulating a
wealth of new and different experiences of places and people.
The adventure motive is sometimes a source of trouble for lovers.
It may cause discord by making one of the lovers reluctant to
settle down. It may cause infidelity, or color a conception of love,
leading the rover into the pursuit of such kinds of stimulating
love experiences as we have described, a quest not usually
satisfied.[2]

The adventurer is bitterly opposed to respectability, conventionality, responsibility — all the features of civilized society
that tend to confine the range and variety of interesting experiences. This attitude is directly opposed to the earlier stress on
orderliness and responsible self-sufficiency. It is most vividly illustrated by the protagonist of Miss Porter's "That Tree" — even
though he is a somewhat lazier adventurer than most.

He had really wanted to be a cheerful bum lying under a tree in
a good climate, writing poetry. . . . He would have enjoyed just that
kind of life: no respectability, no responsibility, no money to speak of,
wearing worn-out sandals and a becoming, if probably ragged, blue
shirt, lying under a tree writing poetry.

The following episode typifies his desire to find novelty — a
"good show" — in almost anything that might befall:

He had lost his teaching job almost immediately. . . . After a
while you learn to take such things calmly. You wait until your man
gets back in the saddle or you work up an alliance with a new one.
. . . Meanwhile the change and movement made such a good show
you almost forgot the effect it had on your food supply.

In some stories the adventure motive is connected with a
character's keen awareness of death. It becomes a reaction to
the knowledge of mortality, which makes the adventurer want

[2] Some of the stories that show clearly such motives, although in some cases
they are restrained or inhibited, are Anderson's "Nobody Knows," "Adventure,"
"Loneliness," "Awakening," "Drink," "Sophistication," "I Want to Know Why,"
"Seeds," "Other Woman," "Out of Nowhere into Nothing," "I'm a Fool," "Ohio
Pagan," "The Return"; Fitzgerald, "Offshore Pirate," "Ice Palace," "Rich Boy,"
"Winter Dreams," "Rags Martin-Jones"; Hemingway, "Out of Season," "Three-
Day Blow," "Battler," "Mr. and Mrs. Elliot," "Cross-Country Snow," "Che Dice,"
"Cat in the Rain," "Hills Like White Elephants"; Porter, "Maria Concepcion"
(the character Juan), "Theft," "That Tree," "Cracked Looking-Glass"; Faulkner,
"Ad Astra," "All the Dead Pilots," "Mistral," "Divorce in Naples," "Carcassonne."

to pack in as much experience as he can before he dies. Faulkner's war stories show this. Living in the shadow of death, his soldiers accelerate the pace of their lives in a frenzy of adventurous experiences. It is not fear of death but a desire to live that motivates the wild exploits of Sartoris in "All the Dead Pilots," exploits in which he risks his life recklessly in ridiculous as well as noble causes. The following passage, by characterizing the postwar lives of these men as "dead," underscores the point that their wild wartime adventures were their only experiences of actual "living:"

But they are all dead now. They are thick men now, a little thick about the waist from sitting behind desks, and maybe not so good at it, with wives and children in suburban homes almost paid out, with gardens in which they putter in the long evenings after the 5:15 is in, and perhaps not so good at that either: the hard, lean men who swaggered hard and drank hard because they had found out that being dead was not as quiet as they had heard it would be. That's why this story is composite: a series of brief glares in which, instantaneous and without depth or perspective, there stood into sight the portent and the threat of what the race could bear and become, in an instant between dark and dark.

But the threat of death need not be so immediate as this to stimulate an individual to search for adventure. In "Sophistication," George's desire to leave Winesburg, to become a big man, to love, to encounter life, is stimulated by the sudden realization of his own mortality:

The sadness of sophistication has come to the boy. . . . The eighteen years he has lived seem but a moment, a breathing space in the long march of humanity. Already he hears death calling.

What the adventurers share is a belief that stimulating emotional experiences are important, good for their own sake. The kinds of experience vary with the individuals — they may involve seeing new places, having new relationships, encountering new dangers — but it is important to the character that they have variety and novelty, presumably because this is what makes him most conscious of life.

Some characters show a belief in stimulating emotional experience somewhat more subtle than the quest for simple novelty and variety. These people — who are perhaps simply a little more explicit about their desires than the others — seem to share with each other a desire to feel wonder or strangeness or beauty in life. Here too what provokes a sense of wonder varies. We have seen this desire in the tendency of lovers to glamorize or romanticize their love (see pp. 86–89). It is important, also, in the success drive of at least a few of Fitzgerald's ambitious young men, who find glamor in wealth and success. A similar motive can be attributed to most of Hemingway's fishermen and outdoor people, even though they are not explicit about it and other motives may be more prominent; a love for the beauty of sport and nature can be inferred from the loving way in which the details of their outdoor activities are presented.

As an issue, however, this principle is chiefly important in characters who fear or regret the loss of their capacity for such appreciation of wonder or beauty. Sometimes a character's stubborn, persistent attempt to preserve such a feeling reveals this fear, as when the boy in Anderson's "I Want to Know Why" tries to cling to the ideal purity of his love for horses and the men who love horses in circumstances that threaten that purity; in others it is revealed by an exaggerated revulsion, an obviously false attempt to deny the lost feeling by repudiating it, as in the case of Wash Williams' loathing for women in Anderson's "Respectability." Sometimes a kind of protective ritual against loss of the feeling reveals it, as in Nick's refusal, in Hemingway's "Big Two-Hearted River," to let "thoughts" distract him from his pleasure in fishing, or in the warning given by the priest, in Fitzgerald's "Absolution," after he has advised Rudolph to go to an amusement park to observe the glittering lights: " 'But don't get up close . . . because if you do you'll only feel the heat and the sweat and the life.' "

This power of appreciation is frequently seen as an attribute of youth, even though those who seek to develop it and those who dread or resist losing it seem to identify it with the very awareness of being alive: to lose it is to die. This is what relates Dexter, bemoaning the loss of his youth, in the following passage from Fitzgerald's "Winter Dreams," to Faulkner's Sartoris,

Anderson's George Willard, and the many others who seek to defy mortality by a variety of experiences:

For he had gone away and he could never go back any more. The gates were closed, the sun was gone down, and there was no beauty but the gray beauty of steel that withstands all time. Even the grief he could have borne was left behind in the country of illusion, of youth, of the richness of life, where his winter dreams had flourished.

Few earlier characters show such motivation. The adventure motive in the frontier world of Crane's stories is, as has been said, in the process of being tamed. The restlessness of some of Dreiser's and Miss Cather's characters does, it is true, foreshadow that of later characters, but this occurs in those stories — "Free," "The Second Choice," "Old Rogaum and His Theresa," "Paul's Case" — whose subject matter in general is most like that of the twenties. A few of James's characters place a strong value on experience as such (it is, of course, a major value for Strether in *The Ambassadors*), but they usually either sacrifice this principle to felt commitments, as do two of the three daughters in "Europe," or they make themselves foolish by the vulgarity with which they pursue experience, as does the son (a minor character) in "Greville Fane." A true zest for living for its own sake, taking priority over everything else, is seen in the early canon only in such an unusual character as Frank Saltram in "The Coxon Fund"; a true objection to the arrangements of the universe, which would snuff out life arbitrarily, is seen only in the castaways in the "The Open Boat" shaking their fists at the gods.

IDENTITY

Revolt against conventionality is not confined to adventure-seekers alone. When Anderson's Wing Biddlebaum, Kate Swift, Wash Williams, and others give advice to George Willard, they urge unconventionality because conventionality threatens to swallow up the individual. Their primary concern, other than their own personal problems, is that George find himself as an individual, apart from the crowd, that he see the difference between himself and others, that he know who he, uniquely, is. Thus Wing warns George in "Hands":

"You are destroying yourself. . . . You have the inclination to be alone and to dream and you are afraid of dreams. You want to be like others in the town here. You hear them talk and you try to imitate them. . . . You must try to forget all you have learned. . . . You must begin to dream. From this time on you must shut your ears to the ringing of voices."

Doctor Parcival, in "The Philosopher," tries to tell George that every individual is alone against a hostile society:

"The idea is very simple, so simple that if you are not careful you will forget it. It is this — that everyone in the world is Christ and they are all crucified."

Kate Swift, in "The Teacher," is less direct, but in trying to inspire George to see through the conventional masks to the real feelings of other people, she shows her concern with the question of identity:

"You will have to know life. . . . It would be better to give up the notion of writing until you are better prepared. Now it's time to be living. . . . The thing to learn is to know what people are thinking about, not what they say."

Wash's lesson, in "Respectability," is the most unconventional of all; for him, sexuality destroys the individual:

"I would like to see men a little begin to understand women. They are sent to prevent men making the world worth while. . . . I want to put you on your guard. Already you may be having dreams in your head. I want to destroy them."

In their advice to George these people reveal of course their own acute concern with maintaining or finding their own identities against the pressure to conform. Like the quest for varied or beautiful experiences, this concern is also a moral principle. Note the moral earnestness of the people just cited. The good man knows what he is or is what he thinks he is.

The search for identity takes two typical forms: whereas many individuals in these stories show a need to win confirmation of their identity from other people, many others show a similar need to establish or prove their identity in their own eyes.

The need to win confirmation of identity from others is, of

course, what underlies the quest for appreciation or recognition at one's own rate that is such an important motive for lovers. The frustration of this need accounts for most of the loneliness suffered in the society of the stories of the twenties. Elmer Cowley wants others to prove that he is a normal human being; Dr. Parcival wants them to acknowledge that he is a Christ-like sufferer; Kate Swift would like recognition as a passionate woman of insight. Such characters, very common in the period, want others to acknowledge the high value they place upon themselves.

The need to establish or prove one's identity in one's own eyes leads to attempts to play the part or role of some particular kind of person. This, too, has also been observed in much of the love behavior in stories of the twenties. Role-playing is not confined to the sexual roles alone. The hero of Anderson's "The Egg" tries to play the part of the popular clown; the hero of Faulkner's "Victory" adopts the clothes and manners of the English lord he would like to be. Dexter, in "Winter Dreams," can again be cited, to show how the success-pursuing character seeks to fit himself to a preconceived role, as in his young dreams he imagines himself in such a role:

He became a golf champion and defeated Mr. T. A. Hendrick in a marvellous match played a hundred times over the fairways of his imagination. . . . Again, stepping from a Pierce-Arrow automobile, like Mr. Mortimer Jones, he strolled frigidly into the lounge of the Sherry Island Golf Club . . .

A more subtle kind of role-playing may be inferred in a few of Hemingway's stories about those who place an exceptional emphasis upon the exercise of some "craft." In their loving attention to artistry — the process of executing the necessary steps, carrying out the proper procedures, obeying the rules of the game — they are fitting themselves to the role of "expert," whether the art be bullfighting, fishing, or skiing. The process is, as critics have noted,[3] ritualistic; no doubt it is this that gives

---

[3] Cowley explains "Big Two-Hearted River" in this way: "We notice that Nick Adams regards his fishing trip as an escape, either from nightmare or from realities that have become a nightmare," but "the whole fishing trip, instead of being a mere escape, might be regarded as an incantation, a spell to banish evil

it a therapeutic quality for these individuals. But performing a ritual is also a kind of role-playing. Here too the narrator's stress on the detail of the process suggests the point. Notice in the following description of a bullfight, how the critic's report helps to emphasize that Manolo is performing a ritual:

Four times he swung with the bull, lifting his cape so it billowed full, and each time bringing the bull around to charge again. Then, at the end of the fifth swing he held the cape against his hip and pivoted, so the cape swung out like a ballet dancer's skirt and wound the bull around himself like a belt, to step clear, leaving the bull facing Zurito on the white horse . . .

El Heraldo's second-string critic . . . wrote: "the veteran Manolo designed a series of acceptable veronicas, ending in a very Belmontistic recorte that earned applause from the regulars, and we entered the tercio of the cavalry."

In stories written in the early period all of the more typical characters take their identities as a matter of course. None of the self-identifying activities that have just been described are important to them — neither the quest for appreciation, the sexual role-playing, nor the drive for personal success — unless possibly the pursuit of artistic perfection by James's artists and writers might be compared with the pursuit of ritualistic perfection by Hemingway's characters. Yet James's artists are concerned with constructing something perfect, Hemingway's with performing perfectly; in the earlier cases, the interest is in the product, in the later, in the action.

In general, the principle of unconventional individualism contradicts the most crucial principles of the early period, with their stress on subordination of the self. Yet, paradoxically, the intent to confirm identity by playing a role is the chief moral force in stories of the twenties that turns characters in the direction of conventionality. For the roles they seek to play are always conventional ones; this is intrinsic to role-playing, which means fitting oneself to a pre-established part. The heroine of Faulkner's "A Rose for Emily" desires to play the feminine role that any wife in the early period unselfconsciously filled. Dexter,

spirits." (Malcolm Cowley, introduction to Ernest Hemingway, *Hemingway* ["The Viking Portable Library"; New York: Viking Press, 1944], pp. x, xix.)

in "Winter Dreams," desires to fit the conventional role of the wealthy man, to acquire exactly the same kind of respectability exhibited by Mr. Mortimer Jones.

Thus a character's need for role-playing is likely to come in conflict with his less conventional principles. This is one of the most powerful causes of frustration and defeat in the stories of the twenties. Sometimes the conventional role-playing principle acts unconsciously to inhibit the quest for adventure or appreciation, as when the heroine of Anderson's "Seeds" is unable to go through with her affair because of "old thoughts and beliefs — seeds planted by dead men," springing up in her soul; her Puritan heritage is planted, so to speak, in her unconscious and rises up to intervene in her quest. The hero of Miss Porter's "That Tree" gives up his adventurous dream and yields to his wife:

His old-fashioned respectable middle-class hard-working American ancestry and training rose up in him and fought on Miriam's side. . . . It was as if his blood stream had betrayed him.[4]

Sometimes the attempt to play a role is threatened by other principles, as when a life such as Alice's, in Anderson's "Adventure," or the minister's, in "The Strength of God," is disrupted by an explosion of feeling as a result of being unappreciated, or when the feminine desires of the heroines of Hemingway's "Hills Like White Elephants" and "Cat in the Rain" are thwarted by the fear of loneliness that keeps them in thrall to some exploiting lover.[5] Sometimes two roles come in direct conflict with each other; a classic example of this is Faulkner's Emily, whose aristocratic and feminine roles, conflicting, lead to perversity and tragedy.[6] A typical emotional condition in such conflicts is displayed in the climactic scene of Anderson's "Loneliness": Enoch, who has resorted to fantasy to play the role of a "producing citizen of the

[4] The force of conventionality also interferes with the protagonist's success or happiness in Anderson's "Hands," "Nobody Knows," "Philosopher," "Teacher," " 'Unused' "; Fitzgerald, " 'Sensible Thing' "; Hemingway, "Doctor and Doctor's Wife," "Mr. and Mrs. Elliot," "Out of Season."

[5] Conflicts of these kinds are also seen in Anderson's "Death," "Drink," "Man Who Became a Woman," "New Englander," "Out of Nowhere into Nothing," " 'Queer,' " "Thinker"; Fitzgerald, "Absolution," "Benediction," "Rich Boy," "Winter Dreams"; Hemingway, "Simple Enquiry," "Three-Day Blow," "Up in Michigan"; Porter, "Cracked Looking-Glass," "He," "Jilting of Granny Weatherall," "Maria Concepcion," "Rope."

[6] Also Porter, "Theft," "Flowering Judas."

world," tries to win appreciation and perhaps love from a neighboring woman by explaining his fantasy life to her. But he is torn between a desire to impress her as a man and a desire to win her sympathy as a suffering individual; as soon as he realizes that she understands his fantasy life, his role is destroyed and he flies into a rage:

"I became mad to make her understand me and to know what a big thing I was in that room. I wanted her to see how important I was. . . . A look came into her eyes and I knew she did understand. . . . I was furious. I couldn't stand it. I wanted her to understand but, don't you see, I couldn't let her understand. I felt that then I would be submerged, drowned out, you see."

EMPATHY

In some stories a sensitive but passive character is witness to an extraordinary display of suffering in someone else. The display may be perverse and bizarre, such as the suicide in Hemingway's "Indian Camp" or the desecration of the corpse in "An Alpine Idyll," or it may be restrained, as in the case of the major in "In Another Country." [7] In such stories, although the observer's reaction is seldom specified, the inference is that he has made an important discovery about life. Since the stress is more on the sufferer's experience and expression of pain than on the evils that cause the pain, the discovery can be described as a recognition of how little the observer knows about suffering in the world. He recognizes a barrier that stands between himself and the sufferer, a barrier raised by the sufferer's pain, which no amount of sympathy on his own part can really break down. Thus Nick, in bewilderment, asks his father why the Indian killed himself; he walks away from the "battler's" camp, troubled and anxious; he gives up trying to proffer sympathy to the bereaved major who sits staring out the window.

The implicit distress, or even horror, that the observer feels in such situations is chiefly the result of his recognition of this

[7] See also Hemingway's "Battler." Stories in which the protagonist witnesses the suffering of others constitute a special form, and are discussed further, pp. 254–58. Stories in which the observation of another's suffering constitutes an action secondary to the main action include Fitzgerald's "Absolution," Hemingway, "Killers," Faulkner, "That Evening Sun," and most of the *Winesburg* stories in which George Willard is a witness.

barrier. This is most clear in "In Another Country," which tells of Nick's growing awareness of such barriers, separating him from those who know suffering, making him feel emotionally as well as physically "in another country." The moral issue in such distress lies in the observer's presumed belief that there ought not to be such barriers, that he *ought* to be able to understand and sympathize fully with anyone's deep suffering. He has discovered a limit on his present capacity to feel for others.

This belief in the importance of empathy with others is prominent in many of the more sensitive characters in stories of the twenties. Unlike the earlier motives of service and love, it seldom leads to positive action, unless it can be inferred as a secondary motive in the love quest of some characters.[8] It is most evident when a character thinks he sees someone violating the principle or when he thinks it has failed in himself — as in the discovery stories just described.

This principle can be adduced to explain why some characters show distress when they find themselves obliged — in response to still more pressing principles — to hurt someone else, as when Nick breaks with Marge in "The End of Something," or when Krebs rejects his mother in Hemingway's "Soldier's Home." It explains the shock that many characters feel when they see others showing cruelty or callousness; the observer in such cases implicitly condemns the offender for a deficiency of human sympathy. Although the observed deficiency may on occasion involve vicious sadism such as that of Braggioni, which shocks Laura, in Miss Porter's "Flowering Judas" or that of McLendon, which shocks Hawkshaw, in Faulkner's "Dry September," more commonly it is a stupid insensitivity, like that of the matron in Hemingway's "A Canary for One," which the narrator finds irritating.[9] Sometimes such insensitivity on the part of a parent is the cause of disillusionment in the child.[10]

[8] In Anderson's "Adventure," Alice's approach to the stranger is explained as a desire to find some other lonely person with whom she can sympathize, but her quest for sympathy is more important to her than her desire to sympathize, and her motives are complicated by sexual frustration.

[9] See also Hemingway's "Che Dice."

[10] See Anderson's "Out of Nowhere into Nothing," "Chicago Hamlet"; Hemingway, "Indian Camp," "Now I Lay Me"; Faulkner, "That Evening Sun."

This principle is not, of course, inconsistent with any of the principles in stories of the early period. Obviously a character in an early story confronted with the situation that confronts Hawkshaw in "Dry September" (a lynching that he tries feebly to prevent) would react in much the same way, and indeed the reporter in Dreiser's "Nigger Jeff" is confronted with a similar situation and does react similarly. But the reporter's reaction goes beyond that of Hawkshaw; whereas the latter, having failed to stop the lynching, simply gives up and nurses whatever unspecified feelings of shock and horror may be inferred, the reporter translates his shock and horror into a news story, deliberately intended to support a theory about the apportioning of good and evil in society. He turns his observations into social commentary. In general, in the early stories, belief in human sympathy is tested by situations that call for action. In such situations, although the "right feeling" is certainly important, it is important only because it is necessary to the performance of civilized deeds; the principle of sacrifice or service is more important. In stories of the twenties a character's belief is tested by situations in which action is all but impossible; the right feeling is apparently an end in itself.

EMOTIONAL INTEGRITY

Certain typical attitudes in stories of the twenties suggest the presence of some other major moral principle, more fundamental and universal than those that have been discussed, acting as a check upon them. When Krebs, for example, in Hemingway's "Soldier's Home," in the midst of an irritating scene with his mother is asked, point-blank, "'Don't you love your mother, dear boy?'" he feels obliged to answer "No." Of course this makes things worse, and he tries to smooth it over, but the scene following his apology only makes him feel "sick and vaguely nauseated," and the story ends with his plan to leave home. Something has made it extremely difficult for him to express emotions that he does not feel.

Such an attitude is common among characters in stories of the twenties. It is, for example, Seth Richmond's problem in Anderson's "The Thinker." Typical is his contempt for "everyone

[who] talks and talks," his sense of isolation because he will not express emotions he does not feel:

When the boys with whom he associated were noisy and quarrelsome, he stood quietly at one side. With calm eyes he watched the gesticulating lively figures of his companions.

Despite his wish to experience many things and express himself, it is his horror of false expression that chiefly guides his behavior. His reluctance is so great that it blinds him even to emotions that he evidently feels, such as the desire for love, so that he fails to communicate to Helen White the feelings he has for her or to elicit from her an expression of the admiration she feels for him.

A similar attitude helps to account for Nick's difficulties with Marge, in "The End of Something," as well as similar denials of love by certain of Fitzgerald's heroes.[11] It checks the behavior of the hero of Anderson's "The Untold Lie," who realizes that any one-sided judgment of his marriage would be a lie. False expression also contributes to the annoyance of several lovers and spouses with the hypocrisy of their partners, as in the following diatribe against his wife by the hero of Miss Porter's "That Tree": [12]

The thing that finally got him down was Miriam's devilish inconsistency. She spent three mortal years writing him how dull and dreadful and commonplace her life was, how sick and tired she was of petty little conventions and amusements, how narrow-minded everybody around her was, how she longed to live in a beautiful dangerous place among interesting people who painted and wrote poetry, and how his letters came into her stuffy little world like a breath of free mountain air, and all that . . . Then she came out with a two-hundred-pound trunk of linen and enough silk underwear to last her a lifetime, you might have supposed, expecting to settle down in a modern steam-heated flat and have nice artistic young couples from the American colony in for dinner Wednesday evenings.

Although this particular narrator is unconsciously arrogant, such a horror of false expression probably accounts for the moral modesty of some of the most sensitive characters in stories of the twenties — the reticence, despite the implicit severity of

[11] See Fitzgerald's "Rich Boy" and "Winter Dreams."
[12] See also Hemingway's "Hills Like White Elephants" and "Doctor and Doctor's Wife."

their judgments, in their assertions of principle and the refusal
to make any claims to righteousness. Even a severely critical
judgment, such as that of the boy in Anderson's "I Want to
Know Why," may be expressed modestly as a question; or it
may, as in Hemingway's "My Old Man," be stated merely as a
personal (and doubtful) feeling of loss, softened by a perplexed
reference to a vague "they" who control our destinies:

> And George Gardner looked at me to see if I'd heard and I had
> all right and he said, "Don't you listen to what those bums said, Joe.
> Your old man was one swell guy."
> But I don't know. Seems like when they get started they don't
> leave a guy nothing.

The most violent judgments, such as that made by Wash Williams, in Anderson's "Respectability," tend to be passionate out-
bursts of emotion in which exaggeration reduces the element of
self-righteousness to a minimum, and many characters, as has
been suggested, refrain from uttering all moral judgments, tending to feel rather than formulate them.

Similar to the dread of false feeling is the stubborn refusal
of many characters to accept any compromise with their aims,
their desires, their beliefs. This attitude — one of the most common character traits in stories of the twenties — is expressed in
different ways in different kinds of situations. Often leading
characters into extreme positions of defiance of frustration and
adversity, it is present in the attitude of every lonely character
who refuses to be satisfied with his loneliness, every frustrated
lover or would-be lover who refuses to accept his frustration,
every frustrated pursuer of success who refuses to give up his
pursuit — the attitude, indeed, of virtually every defeated character in stories of the period.[13] But the stubbornness is especially emphasized in such cases as Elmer Cowley's continued
efforts to prove that he is not queer, in Elizabeth Willard's lifelong pursuit of love, in Anson's continuing quest for the ideal girl
despite his own admission that he will never find her, in the
bullfighter's refusal to admit defeat, the prize fighter's refusal
to accept a double-cross against him, and the betrayed wife's at-

---

[13] Exceptions are listed above, p. 113.

tempt to halt her husband's infidelities by murdering her rival.[14] It is evident, in Miss Porter's "That Tree," in the hero's insistence (despite his submission to his wife's demands) that she return to him without the blessing of remarriage — a last feeble gesture in support of his old, abandoned role of the Bohemian. Faulkner makes it especially vivid — in the perversions of Emily, the murders by the frustrated priest and the would-be Indian king, the ambitious Scotsman's refusal to concede the defeat of his aristocratic quest, and Hawkshaw's determination to marry despite the infidelities of his fiancée. In other cases, refusal to submit is expressed by suicide, by madness, by belligerency, or simply by protests, complaints, tears, and anger.[15] Resentment of frustration becomes both more extravagant and more subtle as the decade progresses: simple protest or complaint is characteristic in Anderson's and Fitzgerald's stories; bottled-up complaint, in Hemingway's; excessive and even violent stubbornness, in Faulkner's; unconsciously maintained resentment, in Miss Porter's.

Such attitudes, of course, directly oppose the principle of acceptance in early stories. The contrast is most striking in the attitudes taken toward death. Of all eventualities, death is the most certain, and there are not more than three or four characters in early stories, such as the men in Crane's "The Open Boat" or the bereaved husband in Dreiser's "The Lost Phoebe," who would think of complaining against this certainty. In the twenties, on the other hand, the thought or threat of death evokes horror and resistance. The link between mortality and the adventure motive has been noted. Also significant are the reactions to death in such stories as Hemingway's "Now I Lay Me," "Soldier's Home," "In Another Country," "An Alpine Idyll," and "The Killers" and in Faulkner's "That Evening Sun." In the first two, proximity to death in war does profound psychological damage to the protagonist, an effect duplicated earlier in only

[14] Stories cited: Anderson, "'Queer,'" "Death"; Fitzgerald, "Rich Boy"; Hemingway, "Undefeated," "Fifty Grand"; Porter, "Maria Concepcion."

[15] Faulkner's stories cited: "Rose for Emily," "Mistral," "Justice," "Victory," "Hair." Other examples: Hemingway, "Indian Camp," "Battler"; Fitzgerald, "Absolution," "Winter Dreams," "'Sensible Thing'"; Anderson, "The Egg," "Philosopher," "Respectability," "Thinker," "Teacher," "Awakening," "Loneliness"; Porter, "Theft."

two war stories by Bierce.[16] In "An Alpine Idyll," proximity to his wife's corpse has led a peasant to desecrate it, even though he "loved her fine"; this situation has no duplicate in stories of the early period. In "In Another Country," the major confesses that he "cannot resign" himself to the death of his young wife; in "That Evening Sun," Nancy is unable to conquer her panicky fear of being murdered even when this fear has exhausted her; in "The Killers," although Ole has stopped trying to run away from his murderers, his state of mind is not resignation but despair, an attitude which Nick recognizes in his final comment: " 'I can't stand to think about him waiting in the room and knowing he's going to get it. It's too damned awful.' " His friend George's reply reflects the same feeling: " 'Well, you better not think about it.' " The immediate awareness of death is intolerable; since it cannot be faced, thought of it must be avoided.

The more stubborn of the characters who have been cited show a striking fear of dilution of their feelings, a kind of either/or psychology that is also highly characteristic in the later period. They fix upon some particular value intuitively and commit themselves to it with such single-mindedness that it becomes almost impossible for them to conceive of any alternative. Such characters fit the description, already quoted,[17] of the "grotesque" in Anderson's *Winesburg*.

The typical grotesque in Anderson's stories is unable to conceive of gradations of value. Wash Williams concludes that all women are wretches because one has shown herself to be less pure in feeling than he, and Louise, in "Surrender," recoils in a similar way from men. Tom's repugnance toward women, in "Drink," has much the same origin, as does the shock of the boy in "I Want to Know Why": it is inconceivable to him how joy in horses and the clean outdoors can be compatible with pleasure in sex. In "The Strength of God," a comparable psychology accounts for the minister's dilemma prior to his crucial discovery: because he sees Kate Swift smoking in bed, he decides that she is an immoral woman, and because he is attracted to her, he figures that he is a man of lust who has betrayed his

[16] Bierce, "One Officer, One Man," "One of the Missing."
[17] P. 18.

calling as a minister. When Joe, in "My Old Man," feels that the discovery of dishonesty in his father is the loss of everything, he too shows an inability to make relative judgments.

Such an attitude helps to explain why certain characters cannot fulfil their desired roles. Anderson's Elmer Cowley is not aware of the fact that the sharp distinction he makes between normality and queerness is the cause of his unhappiness and of the queerest thing he does (namely, his attempt to prove his normality by slugging George). Mrs. Whipple, in Miss Porter's "He," is made miserable by worry and guilt because she cannot square her desire to be rid of her idiot son with her desire to be regarded (and to regard herself) as a good mother. In Anderson's "The Thinker," Seth Richmond's conception of himself as unemotional blinds him to the fact that he is yearningly in love with Helen White. The dilemma of the either/or morality is at its most intense in Miss Porter's "Flowering Judas," in which Laura's conception of her social duty seems incompatible with her conception of her religious and humanitarian duties, and all seem incompatible with her conception of what it means to love and be loved.

One consequence of this principle is the development of an extreme egotism, typical of many of the grotesques of the later period. This is especially marked in Dr. Parcival's fear that the town will lynch him (when in fact they have hardly noticed him), in Elmer's great concern as to what the town thinks of him, in Enoch's enormous rage with the woman who understands his weakness, in Billy Turner's self-pity, in the bitterness of the lover who contracts gonorrhea after being jilted.[18] Sometimes this absorption in self makes the moral basis of one's action seem obscure indeed; many of these characters may strike the reader as weak, childish, and contemptible. Yet their refusals to accept frustration reflect a positive moral principle of a sort, however foolish or misguided its particular application may be.[19]

[18] Stories cited: Anderson, "Philosopher," " 'Queer,' " "Loneliness"; Hemingway, "Pursuit Race," "Very Short Story."

[19] Although many characters in stories of the early period are fully uncompromising in their moral perfection, no more than a very few cling so defiantly to their feelings. Such attitudes, of course, run counter to most of the important

Such attitudes account for the most difficult moral dilemma in stories of the twenties: the presence of ambivalent feelings. This dilemma is as important in the moral world of the twenties as the conflict of obligations was in the early period. If a character insists on purity of feeling as a matter of principle, what is he to do when his feelings or intuitions come in direct conflict with each other?

One answer is seen in the uncompromising attitudes just described. In such cases, the character has selected one of his feelings as more insistent or more demanding than others and then has ruthlessly tried to crush ambivalence by refusing to brook any compromise. The effort is almost always unsuccessful. If the outcropping feelings do not themselves impede the character's pursuit of his aims, then his suffering is revealed by the very defensiveness of his attitude.

But some characters are scarcely able to make such a clear differentiation between the validity of their conflicting feelings. In most cases this is very frightening to them. The problem is not ambivalence as such. The mere fact of ambivalent feelings need not be greatly disturbing, as is seen in such stories as Anderson's "The Untold Lie," "Sophistication," and "The Return," in each of which the protagonist discovers a mixture of feelings in himself and is relieved or pleased to find it. In "Sophistication," indeed, the acknowledgment of a mixture of feelings is taken as a sign of maturity:

Man or boy, woman or girl, they had for a moment taken hold of the thing [the combination of melancholy, thoughtfulness and joy which the story depicts] that makes the mature life of men and women in the modern world possible.

principles of the early period, which require constantly that a character's feelings and needs be subordinated to social considerations. The chief exceptions: Freeman, "Village Lear"; Cather, "Paul's Case"; James, "Tree of Knowledge," "Miss Gunton"; Dreiser, "Second Choice," "Married," "Old Rogaum," "Lost Phoebe"; Bierce, "Occurrence at Owl Creek Bridge." Other cases of the stubborn maintaining of personal feeling are either regarded as perverse and extraordinary by others, as in Gerould's "Pearls," or involve defense of values or principles in keeping with the dominant morality of the period, as in the case of James's artists, such as the heroes of "The Next Time" and "Figure in the Carpet" who consciously or unconsciously cling to their anti-vulgarian concepts of art. Only in the exceptions listed here does it appear that a character is controlled by his feelings simply because they are his feelings, or that such a reason is considered morally sufficient in his world.

Usually, however, characters with ambivalent feelings tend to think that ambivalence itself is wrong, or that one of the conflicting feelings is wrong. This is what creates the dilemma, which is usually not solved except by makeshifts that are damaging to personality.

The damage varies in its seriousness. At the least it consists of an intense fear, such as the terrifying doubt of his sexual identity suffered by the boy in Anderson's "The Man Who Became a Woman." [20] Often the character tries to hide this dread from his own eyes, as when the couples in Fitzgerald's "The Rough Crossing" and Miss Porter's "Rope" reach makeshift reconciliations and deny that there is any trouble between them. This denied dread is evident to the reader in Anderson's "The Door of the Trap," Miss Porter's "The Cracked Looking-Glass," Hemingway's "The Doctor and the Doctor's Wife," and others. In more serious cases the fear of ambivalence leads to such self-destructive behavior as has been discussed. A character may be paralyzed in action, like the heroine of Anderson's "Seeds," who wants but will not take a lover, or the heroine of Miss Porter's "Flowering Judas," who wants to escape from the revolutionary movement but cannot make herself do so, or the heroine of Hemingway's "Hills Like White Elephants," who would like to defy her lover but will not. Or he may develop perversities of behavior ranging in seriousness from the brooding withdrawal of Enoch in Anderson's "Loneliness" through the sexual perversities of the heroines of "Adventure" and "The New Englander" to the extreme abnormality of the heroine of Faulkner's "A Rose for Emily."

All of these attitudes — the fear of false expressions, the fear of compromise with feelings, the fear of ambivalence of feelings — are united by an apparent common belief in a principle of emotional integrity, of loyalty to one's feelings and intuitions. This follows directly from the belief that morality is measured intuitively, which has been discussed, but it is not identical with

[20] The narrator claims to have overcome his fear at the end of the story and to be perfectly normal. Irving Howe interprets the story to show that this is not so, that the trauma remains, at least on the unconscious level. (Irving Howe, *Sherwood Anderson* ["The American Men of Letters Series"; William Sloane Associates, 1951], pp. 160–64.)

that belief. For it involves, in addition, the idea of honesty or sincerity, or, at any rate, of consistency. It is this that keeps the individual in stories of the twenties from being merely and happily impulsive, justifying anything he does by the argument that that is how he happens to feel at the moment. For, although he may believe in being guided by his feelings, he also feels that there is some consistent distinction between good and bad, and that his feelings therefore ought also to be consistent. Thus he is constrained to choose between his conflicting feelings, trying always to act or judge by the one that seems to him most "sincere," most true to what he thinks his real nature to be (or what he would like to have it), the feeling that seems most urgent or compelling in his emotional makeup. He may condemn some feelings as "false," as Krebs does, because they come out of a need for expediency, which seems less urgent than do other feelings that conflict with them. He may try to suppress feelings that seem to threaten his emotional consistency, as when Wash Williams tries to put down any impulse to modify his sexual idealism, or when the boy in "The Man Who Became a Woman" tries to do the same to the homosexual elements that he thinks are unnatural to him. Or he may be paralyzed because he is unable to assign priority to one feeling when he thinks that, to be consistent, he should.

Certainly few characters in the earlier stories would argue against the importance of sincerity. They take sincerity for granted because their strongest feelings are always devotion to those principles that have been attributed to them in Chapter VIII; this makes it possible for them to deny other, more "selfish" feelings, with perfect emotional equanimity. Nor would they insist, as the character of the twenties is likely to do, that sincerity is the most important virtue. Service, order, self-sufficiency, acceptance of necessity, payment of obligations — all these, they would say, are more important than whether a person acts or judges according to his truest feelings.

Of course there are exceptions to this general contrast in both periods, just as there are characters in both periods whose behavior, although consistent with that of the period as a whole, does not contrast strikingly with the typical behavior of the other period. This is not surprising, since the moral contrast between the periods is not between two diametrically opposed moral attitudes but between different emphases on moral problems. Some "exceptions" to the dominant early patterns are not significant: villains, for example, or such "shocking heroes" as those in Mrs. Gerould's "Pearls" or James's "The Coxon Fund" are at odds with the morality of the more sensitive people in the same story, a morality which is more typical. More significant exceptions, rather, are those in which the morally sensitive heroes themselves tend to reject typical principles. We see this, for example, in the intense drive to live that stimulates the hero's hallucinations in Bierce's "An Occurrence at Owl Creek Bridge" and cracks the composure of the heroes in "One Officer, One Man" and "One of the Missing"; in the great need for love that emotionally cripples the senile old men in Mrs. Freeman's "A Village Lear" and Dreiser's "The Lost Phoebe"; in the bitterness against fate shown by the correspondent in Crane's "The Open Boat" and by the heroine of Miss Cather's "A Wagner Matinee"; in the impulse that drives Paul to New York and suicide in Miss Cather's "Paul's Case" and distracts the heroine of "A Garden Lodge"; and in the yearnings, resentments, and insecurities of the protagonists of Dreiser's "The Second Choice," "Free," "Married," and "Old Rogaum and His Theresa."

A few exceptions to the dominant patterns of the twenties are found in stories in which the earlier principles are affirmed without a disturbing ambivalence of feeling. They appear in stories by Fitzgerald — "The Four Fists," "The Adjuster," "Hot and Cold Blood" — although occasionally stories by Sherwood Anderson also suggest the earlier patterns in modified ways — notably "I'm a Fool" and "Death in the Woods." Their scarcity suggests that the moral contrast is by far the most substantial difference in subject materials between the stories of the two periods. More than any other contrast yet noted, it suggests a profound, if subtle, revolution in thought.

X: MORALITY AS A SUBJECT OF FICTION

The suggestion of a subtle revolution in thought stimulates further provocative questions. Is there any way to relate the new principles to each other? Do they imply any fundamental change in the ultimate basis of the morality with which the writers of the twenties are concerned? If they do, what is its artistic significance? Is there any consistent change in the *way* morality is used as the subject of a story?

SOURCES OF VALUE

The possibility of a general change in the basis of morality brings us into an area of speculation which cannot be supported by citing particular stories. In dealing with the depiction of particular behavior we can, as we have done, legitimately translate that behavior into motives and these, in turn, into principles revealing similarities and differences between one character and an-

141

other: we have been able, for example, to compare the morality of Faulkner's Emily in many particulars with that of other characters, the heroines of "Seeds," "The Teacher," and "Flowering Judas," and to distinguish it from that of heroines in "The Reckoning," "A Day's Pleasure," and "Wesendonck," or any number of others.

Faulkner gives us no clues, however, as to the "ultimate basis" of Emily's morality. No doubt if a character's moral principles are consistent and if his morality is revealed in full, its ultimate basis will be found in his concept of the source of absolute value, to which he gives allegiance in all his acts. The particular principles that control Emily, unconscious and compulsive though they be, can be regarded as the signs of such allegiance or faith — though this, too, must in her case be unconscious or compulsive. We cannot determine what sort of faith this may be, however, since neither Faulkner nor other writers of either period attempt to go deeply enough into a character's motivations to disclose this source.

Although we cannot define Emily's ultimate faith, we may at least determine what kinds of faith can explain the particular collection of principles that she shares with other characters of her time. Insofar as Emily's morality is typical of her time and typically different from that of the earlier period, what sort of a faith or allegiance to ultimate values is suggested?

Her visible moral problems do not, in the first place, arise from faith in a supernatural God. In this she is typical: few stories of either period probe deeply enough into a character's motives to relate them to religious doctrine. This does not mean, of course, that these characters have no religious belief or even that these religious beliefs are not sometimes specifically indicated. Religious belief — or at any rate, churchgoing — figures fairly prominently in some communities in both periods: in Mrs. Freeman's world, and sometimes in James's, Miss Porter's, Anderson's. Usually, however, a character's religious beliefs are not a significant moral issue but typify his social position, his social attitudes, or some of his habits of thought and feeling — as, for instance, in Miss Porter's "Maria Concepcion," in which the primitive Mexican heroine's Christianity is one sign of the higher civilization toward which she aspires.

As an actual issue, religious faith is significant in only two or three of the earlier stories (all by Mrs. Freeman) and only a few more than that in those of the twenties. The contrast between these stories [1] parallels the contrast in issues that has already been noted. In the Freeman stories religious faith provides a simple, happy solution to the protagonist's problems, enabling her to make peace with the world in the face of death or in the encounter with human suffering. Only "Life-Everlasting" involves any doubt as to God's nature: the agnostic heroine has faith in the goodness of the universe and only needs to be persuaded by the plight of a not-completely-evil murderer that Jesus Christ was necessary to make this goodness possible. God in each case — the God of the New England church — functions therefore in making acceptance of suffering possible.

The religious problems in stories of the twenties all turn upon a conflict between taught or imposed religious doctrine and inner conviction. In the simplest cases, doctrine may be used by an antagonist (such as the wife in Hemingway's "The Doctor and the Doctor's Wife") to humiliate or control the protagonist; here the doctrine is repugnant to him, but he dare not oppose it. In more complicated cases a character changes his concept of God — usually from that of a God of wrath into one who looks benignly upon human weakness. Thus the Catholic boy in Fitzgerald's "Absolution" relieves the guilt he feels for lying in confession (the lie itself being a denial that he ever lied) by reconstructing a God who approves of him for such a sin, since it is an affirmation of "immaculate honor" — a romantic God, indeed, who is very indulgent of the boy's love of the glitter of material things. The minister in Anderson's "The Strength of God," guilt-ridden because his lust has been aroused, decides that God pities and loves (rather than condemns) the nakedness of humanity — which represents weakness and suffering rather than sex and

[1] Freeman, "Sister Liddy," "Village Singer," "Life-Everlasting"; Anderson, "Strength of God"; Fitzgerald, "Absolution," "Benediction"; Hemingway, "Doctor and Doctor's Wife," "Soldier's Home," "Now I Lay Me"; Faulkner, "Mistral."

temptation — and thereby he destroys his lust. In the most complex cases the conflict between doctrine and feeling is insolvable. The priests in "Absolution" and Faulkner's "Mistral" are driven mad by the conflict between their sexual desires and their vows. In "Flowering Judas," as previously noted, Laura's socialistic principles, her humanitarian scruples, and her original Catholicism enter into an insolvable three-way conflict that can only culminate in a dream of betrayal.

Thus the stories of the twenties differ from those of the early period in that they involve, not an intellectual doubt of God's nature, but a moral doubt. The conflict between doctrine and feeling is significant because it shows that formal religious faith does not have a clear priority as a source of values. The typical religious problem of the twenties is the difficulty of finding out what one really believes in.

But if belief in a supernatural God is not the source of the moral problems in most of these stories, neither is belief in a natural God — a God in nature but outside of man. To be sure, when Nick Adams goes fishing, in Hemingway's "Big Two-Hearted River," his obvious love of the country, his almost ritualistic performance, suggests that for him, at this moment, God is in nature, in the outdoors, the woods or (in other stories) the mountains or the snow. This familiar romantic attitude is very rare in the stories of either period. Though many characters are perhaps sensitive to the beauty of nature, only Nick and his friends ever make it a primary value. In general, God in nature is even less important to these writers than is a supernatural doctrinal God.

A few stories concern beauty-worshippers in another sense, the artists who admire not so much the beauty of nature as the beauty of man's "imitations" of nature. These artists and art-worshippers are, as has been noted, most important in the stories of Miss Cather and James.[2] In most of these the love of art comes

[2] Cather, "Flavia," "Sculptor's Funeral," "Garden Lodge," "Death in the Desert," "Marriage of Phaedra," "Wagner Matinee," "Paul's Case"; James, "Middle Years," "Greville Fane," "Broken Wings," "Tree of Knowledge," "Real Thing," "Beldonald Holbein," "Story In It," "Lesson of the Master," "Death of the Lion," "Next Time," "Figure in the Carpet," "Coxon Fund." Also Gerould, "Pearls," "Leda"; Dreiser, "Married"; Wharton, "Long Run."

into conflict with the protagonist's personal or social relations, and usually, as with Paul Overt in "The Lesson of the Master," triumphs (at least in his mind) over such relations.[3] Nevertheless, in most cases, the artist's problem is primarily a social one. I have already suggested that the pursuit of artistic perfection in stories of the early period is a high manifestation of the pursuit of order, which in other respects is a social quest. Similarly, the typical artist's problem is not the artistic struggle itself but the quest (or the longing, or the need) for the kind of society that will give greater recognition to the art he loves or to himself as an artist.[4] Ray Limbert, in James's "The Next Time," suffers from his unpopularity, Neil Paraday, in James's "The Death of the Lion," is virtually killed by an admiring public that does not understand his art, Paul, in Miss Cather's "Paul's Case," goes to New York in search of an artistic society. The issue appears in many guises, but the quarrel between the artist and society is only a lover's quarrel.

The only active artists in the canon of the twenties are the struggling writer in Miss Porter's "Theft," the frustrated poet in Miss Porter's "That Tree," and the mystical "natural" or folk poet in Anderson's "The Man's Story." Here, too, love of art is not the primary issue. It signifies, primarily, a character's social or emotional needs; writing poetry for the hero of "That Tree," for example, is only one aspect of the lazy Bohemian life he would like to lead. In "The Man's Story" it is meant to be an expression of the hero's natural, virile emotional nature. Of course, there are two or three incipient artists in stories of the twenties: George Willard wants to be a writer, and is advised by Kate Swift to get to know people's feelings first; if Nick Adams is regarded as a young man whose development is con-

[3] Exceptions — art sacrificed to society by the artist, or the artist's passion itself condemned by the most sensitive characters for its flouting of society: Cather, "Flavia," "Death in the Desert" (indirectly); James, "Coxon Fund" (several of James's stories of inferior artists are *not* exceptions to the point); Gerould, "Pearls," "Leda."

[4] Two stories directly concerned with the artist's artistic problems are James's "Real Thing" and "Story In It." Artistic problems are a secondary issue in James's "Middle Years," "Greville Fane," "Beldonald Holbein," and "Figure in the Carpet." They are not significant as such in the work of the other writers considered here.

tinued in later stories (and especially if, as critics assert, he is a part of Hemingway's picture of himself), he might be regarded as a potential artist, as is also the dreamer in Faulkner's prose poem "Carcassonne." The popular artists in Fitzgerald's "The Rough Crossing" and "Magnetism" are significant more as celebrities than as artists, although one may perhaps see some lower form of "art worship" in the fondness for the glitter of material riches, the pursuit of the "best things," that motivates Dexter in Fitzgerald's "Winter Dreams."

Such characters raise a suspicion that the artists portrayed in stories of the twenties may hold a somewhat different conception of art from that held by those in earlier stories. One suspects that, whereas James's and even Miss Cather's artists admire art primarily for the form or order that it applies to its materials, the artists or incipient artists of the twenties look to art as another way of expressing or communicating a sense of self. The stories in the canon of the twenties do not supply sufficient evidence to confirm this assumption. What is most clear is that in neither period is an ultimate faith in art for its own sake a sufficient explanation of a character's morality. Even when an artist's problems pertain primarily to his love of art, as in some stories by James and Miss Cather, these problems manifest moral issues that are not, after all, radically different from those that face characters in other stories of the two periods.

Since neither a supernatural God nor nature nor some objective ideal such as perfection in art seems to be of more than occasional and incidental significance as a source of morality, it is likely that the most plausible general source in both periods is a faith in an ultimate value existing in man. Good behavior is that which is good for this good thing in man. Whatever else might be uncertainly inferred as to the morality of most individuals in stories of both periods, they seem to resemble each other in basing their judgments of good and evil at least in part upon the idea that something in man is good of itself.

Different characters have different ideas of how they may best serve this good thing; they may feel commanded to serve man collectively, or to serve some person or group which embodies this good element, or themselves by cultivating this good element in and for themselves. All of these patterns are common, yet the contrasting principles of the two periods suggest a fundamental disagreement as to what the ultimate good thing in man is.

The most distinctive virtues of the earlier period are alike in that they are all useful or necessary to the functioning of a civilized society. A civilized society is essentially an organization of individuals who subjugate their own individuality to the interests of society for the mutual benefit of all. Respect for law and order is the most elementary virtue needed by such individuals, and the development of fine manners is simply the refinement of this in a highly advanced civilization. Responsible self-sufficiency is a virtue required of any individual in a democratic civilization, which, in passages such as that cited from Garland's "Among the Corn Rows," is regarded as a more advanced kind of civilization than others. Acceptance of adversity that cannot be corrected by civilized means is necessary to any individual who values being civilized above all else, for not to accept it would imply a criticism of the limits of civilization, which in turn would imply a higher set of values. The belief in the sanctity of obligations to others is clearly a utilitarian principle than can only be explained as a device to enable people to live and work together in trust. It seems unquestionable that the dominant general source of morality in stories of the early period is a belief that man is good because of his capacity to civilize himself. The crucial virtues are those habits and principles upon which civilization depends. The good man is the civilized man and will try to develop in himself the virtues of the civilized man.

The element common to the various distinctive virtues in stories of the twenties is not so easily defined. These virtues are alike in that they affirm the value of certain kinds of emotions. The good thing in man depends upon his capacity to feel these emotions: when he fails to have stimulating experiences, when he loses his capacity for wonder, or is unable to enjoy a satisfying self-identification, or when his integrity of feeling fails or is threatened, then he feels morally lost, guilty or damned or deprived.

The valued emotions consist in the appreciation of being alive and a feeling of integrity. The quest for variety and novelty of experience, when analyzed in stories of the twenties, is usually, as has been noted, a reaction to the awareness of mortality. So, too, the apprehension of one's identity as an individual and the development of wonder and empathy will enhance the individual's awareness that he is a living being, a creature gifted with life. Like Strether, in James's *The Ambassadors*, the typical character in stories of the twenties seems to operate under the assumption that the moral being is he who values the gift of life and makes the most of it; unlike Strether, he does not, in theory, approve of subordinating this good to his duty to others, even though his problems often make it impossible for him to make the most of his life. On the other hand, the protagonist in stories of the twenties also believes profoundly in the feeling of integrity — the sense that he is doing "right," a moral feeling, or one of restraint, acting as a check upon his pursuits.

No certain answer can be given as to why these two kinds of feelings should be stressed. But a possible answer might be that they are conceived to be the feelings that are most distinctly *human*, the kinds of feelings that distinguish man from beast. Man alone is aware that he is alive and will cease to exist, and man alone knows moral restraint. One may guess that the typical character in stories of the twenties fears that if he loses his awareness of either of these two things he will become less than human and that this is the worst evil that can befall him.

Perhaps, then, the moralities of both worlds rest upon a distinction between man and other creatures. For the earlier stories, the leading distinction lay in man's reason and, particularly, in one of its products, his ability to civilize himself. The character in stories of the twenties, not very consciously, finds this unsatisfactory. He feels that reason is fallible and that stress on the value of civilization alone will defeat itself and will ignore an earlier and more fundamental value. The world of the twenties turns to man's feelings, therefore, and finds there the unique value of man.

MORAL OUTCOME

The new morality tends to function in stories in a manner differ-ent from that of the earlier morality. There are, to be sure, stories in both periods in which a character simply affirms his principles through action, and others in which he conspicuously violates them, suffering from the violation directly or indirectly. Affirma-tion, however, is much more common in the earlier period, viola-tion much more common later. This suggests a change not merely in the kind of morality depicted but in the kind of interest that a moral issue is meant to have in a story.

The interest of the more fully developed moral problems of the early period resembles that of a puzzle. Given a certain clearly defined moral system, the interesting problem is how one can resolve certain dilemmas that will arise, such as that of an unhappy marriage, or the conflict of military and personal obligations, or the clash of artistic and social obligations. The interest is in the solution and is, in a sense, intellectual.

In stories of the twenties, on the other hand, the more fully developed moral problems have no solution, and their interest centers more directly in the question of sympathy for the bewil-dered individual. Grotesque or twisted characters are presented. Though they act in ways that seem to us childish or perverse, it becomes clear that they behave so for moral reasons. This para-dox is probably intended in part to stimulate us to make a basic re-examination of accepted moral premises, although this re-examination is apt to be largely negative, since the moral deci-sion taken leads only to frustration and suffering. But the reader is also invited, as he contemplates the morality of these twisted characters, to enlarge his sympathy and understanding for hu-mankind in general, to be more critical of ready-made moral premises and more charitable toward the feeling of others. This tolerance of people as such, it must be pointed out, tends to be qualified by an attitude of fairly stiff criticism of the ways, fruitless or destructive, in which these people apply their moral principles in particular cases. As will be seen in following chap-ters, many of the stories of the twenties are clearly designed to evoke not pity or pathos but horror or a caustic and critically comic effect. Yet it is seldom a pure horror, never a pure contempt. It has been asserted that even Faulkner's Emily is a sympathetic character and of Anderson that

The author's critical judgment which ordinarily manifests itself in selection of judgments stated or implied, is replaced in Anderson by *sympathy* — that is, in the etymological sense of that word, a "suffering with." That is especially true, since there is an autobiographical fragment in almost every one of his creations — they are creations both of his imagination and of his temperament.[5]

Keynotes to the moral interest of writers in the twenties are contained in Anderson's theory of the "grotesque," and also in the famous passage from Hemingway, which may be quoted again:

I was trying to write then and I found the greatest difficulty, aside from knowing what you really felt, rather than what you were supposed to feel, and had been taught to feel, was to put down what really happened in action . . .[6]

If the implicit sympathy for people noted in Anderson's stories is combined with the implicit criticism of "principles" in his theory of the grotesque and with the explicit concern for integrity of feeling in Hemingway's remarks, one has the elements for the primary moral interest in most stories of the twenties.

Obviously, the contrast in moral problems is closely tied to the contrasts in social and emotional problems described in earlier chapters. The social disintegration and emotional isolation depicted in the twenties reflect the shifting moral emphasis by which individualistic feeling becomes the basis for action. Together these various kinds of problems form a distinctive new complex of subject matter in the short stories.

In its most general and important points much the same complex of material was developed earlier abroad by such leading short-story writers as Chekhov, Joyce, and Katherine Mansfield. The society depicted in their stories is much like that described in American stories of the twenties, especially with respect to its internal disintegration and the emotional isolation of its members. Love means much the same kind of thing to the

[5] Frederick J. Hoffman, *Freudianism and the Literary Mind* (Baton Rouge: Louisiana State University Press, 1945), p. 253.
The interpretation of Emily as a tragic and sympathetic figure has been advanced especially by Cleanth Brooks, Jr., and Robert Penn Warren in *Understanding Fiction* (New York: Appleton-Century-Crofts, 1943).
[6] *Death in the Afternoon*, p. 2.

characters in these stories as it means to those of Anderson, Hemingway, Miss Porter, and Faulkner. Especially significant is the new kind of problem arising from a morality based on feeling, the sort of problem for example, that faces Gabriel Conroy in Joyce's greatest story, "The Dead," and certainly no major American writer in the twenties put greater stress on the question of a character's capacity to feel sensitively than did Katherine Mansfield.

The appearance of such subject matter in American stories was, for the most part, new, though even here it was not totally new. It was anticipated in the stories by Dreiser and, to a lesser extent, in those by Miss Cather and Crane, but only in certain stories and seldom, if ever, in a fully developed treatment. Of course, even in the work of the five writers of the twenties the new subject matter was not always consistently developed. It was most typical and complete in Anderson, Hemingway, and Faulkner, who show a progressive tendency toward increasingly overt, extreme, and violent manifestations of the crucial issues. Miss Porter sometimes combines the new elements with older ones or presents, in stories such as "The Cracked Looking-Glass" and "He," problems and characters that look like those typical of the earlier period but are actually strongly colored and shaped by the new issues. Curiously, Fitzgerald, the writer most often associated with the idiosyncrasies and excesses of the twenties, was the least consistently modern in the essentials of his subject matter. Although the world of such stories as "Winter Dreams," "The Rich Boy," "Absolution," and "Benediction" is thoroughly in keeping with that of his contemporaries, the world of many of his other stories is indistinguishable, except in details, from the earlier world.

Yet in most stories the basic contrast holds true with surprising accuracy. The earlier world is stable and coherent, its members in substantial agreement as to the worth of society and the principles that should guide them. The world of the American twenties, like that in stories by Joyce and Katherine Mansfield, is fragmented both socially and morally, with each man isolated, obliged to find or make for himself his appropriate place in society and the appropriate principles to guide him. Almost never does he find a satisfactory solution.

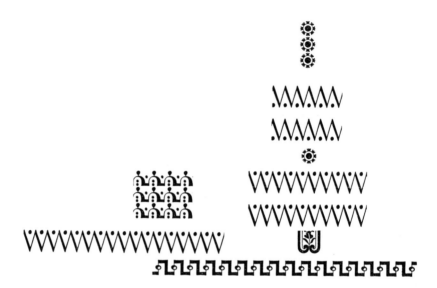

XI: THE FORMAL PRINCIPLE

"Paul's Case," by Miss Cather, is one of several stories in the early period whose subject matter anticipates that of the twenties. It deals with a boy from Pittsburgh who feels estranged from his society, finding his environment mediocre and stultifying. Much like a later Fitzgerald or Anderson hero, he wants to escape from his bourgeois world into a more glamorous one. For him glamor is to be found in New York; it is associated with artists and musicians who come on visits to his city. The story tells about his flight from home, his failure, and his suicide.

Despite the modern subject, this story does not look very much like the typical later stories. The difference is an artistic one, a matter of form and technique — a matter of plot and sequence, perhaps, or of the relationship of the parts to the whole,

152

or of the manner of narration, or of "point of view," or of all these things. Such matters bring us to the center of our inquiry: what indeed are the important artistic differences between the stories of the two periods?

This phase of the inquiry may start with the "form" of a story, that is, with the principles which give the story its unity and organize its parts. A glance at the critics of the two periods suggests the possibility of a radical contrast in form between the two periods. The later critics — those most sympathetic to the writers of the twenties — seem to differ strikingly with earlier critics in their ideas as to what a short story is. Such differences in theory, one might well think, could reflect important formal differences between the kinds of stories these critics know and admire. In the first years of the twentieth century, when the early critics began to develop theories about the short story, the prevailing view — as expressed by Brander Matthews — was that the short story should

deal with a single character, a single event, a single action, or the series of emotions called forth by a single situation. . . . The Short-story is the single effect, while the Novel is of necessity broken into a series of episodes. Thus the Short-story has, what the Novel cannot have, the effect of "totality," . . . unity of impression.[1]

This view — traceable to Poe[2] — became the basis for distinguishing the short story not only from the novel but from other kinds of short fiction as well. The primary point of difference, as the quotation shows, was the greater unity of the short story.

[1] Brander Matthews, *The Philosophy of the Short-Story* (New York: Longmans, Green & Co., 1901), pp. 16–17.

[2] "A skilful literary artist has constructed a tale. If wise, he has not fashioned his thoughts to accommodate his incidents; but having conceived, with deliberate care, a certain unique or single *effect* to be wrought out, he then invents such incidents — he then combines such events as may best aid him in establishing this preconceived effect. If his very initial sentence tend not to the outbringing of this effect, then he has failed in his first step. In the whole composition there should be no word written, of which the tendency, direct or indirect, is not to the one pre-established design. And by such means, with such care and skill, a picture is at length painted which leaves in the mind of him who contemplates it with a kindred art, a sense of the fullest satisfaction. The idea of the tale has been presented unblemished, because undisturbed; and this is an end unattainable by the novel." (Edgar Allan Poe, *The Works of Edgar Allan Poe*, ed. Edmund Clarence Stedman and George Edward Woodbury [Chicago: Stone & Kimball, 1895], VII, 31–32.)

This idea presented difficulties, of course, which these critics tried to resolve. Chief among them, perhaps, was the difficulty that unity does not come in degrees; a thing is unified or it is not unified, and the critics were well aware that even novels, like all works of art, were expected to have unity of some kind. Consequently an attempt was made to distinguish the short story in terms of its particular kind of unified effect, as in the following passage (1914):

Like the novel, the Short Story is a piece of fiction producing a unified effect. Unlike the novel, its single effect is usually an *impression* instead of a deliberate marshalling together of a large number of diverse elements into a unity.[3]

Although this explanation still presents difficulties, we need not argue what an "impression" is; what matters is that the early critics in their search for the identifying characteristic of the short story emphasized simplicity in construction, clarity in effect, and calculated directness in the production of that effect.

They put primary stress upon what they called "plot." Plot was the indispensable ingredient of the short story as a developed art form:

While a Sketch may be a still-life, in a Short-story something always happens. A Sketch may be an outline of character, or even a picture of a mood of mind, but in a Short-story there must be something done, there must be an action.[4]

The Short-story is nothing if there is no story to tell; — one might also say that a Short-story is nothing if it has no plot, — except that "plot" may suggest to some readers a complication and an elaboration which are not really needful.[5]

Despite this qualification, many early critics did insist on complication and elaboration in the short-story plot. According to one, a plot ought to contain

Preliminary situation, the Complication of the threads of the plot, and the Resolution of the complexity; i.e., the solution of the problem set. . . . Just before the culmination, the threads seem to be in an

---

[3] Ethan Allen Cross, *The Short Story: A Technical and Literary Study* (Chicago: A. C. McClurg & Co., 1914), p. 25.
[4] Matthews, p. 35.
[5] *Ibid.*, p. 32.

inextricable tangle — a knot, where all the threads of causation cross each other. Then comes the culmination. The knot is untied — or maybe cut — and the story rounds itself out into a natural conclusion.[6]

This was, perhaps, extreme; not all critics were so demanding. They tended, nevertheless, to demand that the action deal with a significant change in a situation (the short story, it was said, should deal with the most important crossroads or turning point in a character's life) and to put a heavy stress upon "climax" and "conclusion." Judgments such as the following criticism of the stories of James and Howells were, as has been noted, common:

Such stories have a real interest, but it is of a pale and intellectual sort, because there is little stirring action and almost no attempt at climax. The works of the psychological realists are certainly not improved by their lack of movement and *denouement*. The short-story should have outcome. Some element of the situation should be changed in the progress of the narrative.[7]

Such a conception of the short story was strenuously rejected by the writers of the twenties and the critics who praised them. It was, certainly, no mere eccentricity that caused Anderson to subtitle his Winesburg collection, *A Group of Tales of Ohio Small Town Life*, thereby dissociating his work from the hyphenated "short-story" of the earlier critics. The later writers and their critics put relatively little emphasis upon the "single effect" or "the unified impression." They rejected with special vehemence the notion of the primacy of plot.

Apparently they thought that they were doing away with plot. Plot was an artistic heresy, the result, according to Edward O'Brien, of "a codification by solemn lawgivers of certain elements in the somewhat meretricious detective stories of Poe and in the more brittle anecdotes of Bret Harte. . . . I state without hesitation that this respect for 'plot,' or let us call it scheming, is the curse of the American short story": [8]

Artists as serious as Sherwood Anderson and Wilbur Daniel Steele have no knowledge of this elaborate game with its complicated play, as they have confessed to me, but their work is finding its way into the

[6] Cross, *The Short Story: A Technical and Literary Study*, pp. 40–41.
[7] Albright, p. 50.
[8] O'Brien, *Advance*, p. 7.

textbooks to be duly codified in turn and to be admired for qualities which it fortunately does not possess.[9]

Katherine Anne Porter's attack on plot (1942) is especially lively:

Now listen carefully: except in emergencies, when you are trying to manufacture a quick trick and make some easy money, you don't really need a plot. If you have one, all well and good, if you know what it means and what to do with it. If you are aiming to take up the writing *trade*, you need very different equipment from that which you will need for the *art*, or even just the *profession* of writing. There are all sorts of schools that can teach you exactly how to handle the 197 variations on any one of the 37 basic plots . . . .[10]

"The least essential element of all," says O'Faoláin, "is the actual story or anecdote on which the tale hangs . . . . an anecdote is not a story if that is all the story contains. In fact, it is an interesting matter to consider just how much anecdote even a good story can stand without appearing artificial."[11]

Such remarks contain a warning to the writer against a too logical, too intellectual approach to his story, such as is implicit in the earlier stress on plot and unity. Typical of the logical approach in the earlier period is Carl H. Grabo's classification of stories into five different kinds and his suggestions as to how each of these kinds should be written. There are, he wrote, stories of action, stories of character, stories of setting, stories of idea, and stories of emotional effect. Each of these kinds has its own particular laws. See, for example, his advice to the writer of a story of character. The object is to demonstrate some particular trait, some "direction" in a character. The writer should therefore plan his story in such a way as to

place [the character] in a situation which will try him to the utmost, reveal the full potentialities of his character in the one direction . . . . In my story, therefore, I present my creation with a conflict of choices, let us say one of love and duty.[12]

[9] *Ibid.*, p. 8.
[10] Porter, *The Days Before*, pp. 134–36.
[11] Séan O'Faoláin, *The Short Story* (London: Collins, 1948), pp. 154–55.
[12] Carl H. Grabo, *The Art of the Short Story* (New York: Charles Scribner's Sons, 1913), p. 201.

Such an approach was much too artificial for the writers of the twenties. To be sure, this kind of objection had been in the air years before they came along. As far back as 1909, when Henry Seidel Canby complained — in a passage previously quoted [13] — about the artificiality of the stories of his time, he prophesied that

A less labored story must come back. The movement will be towards the ideal of Chaucer, and away from the strenuosity of Poe . . . . It is to be hoped that a new taste will rediscover the beauty of the simple, unforced tale.[14]

Although the development that followed was probably not precisely what Canby had in mind — hardly a return to the "ideal of Chaucer" — the new writers obviously wanted to give an appearance of greater freedom in matters of form and technique. What matters, for them and their supporters, is not the calculated single impression but some quality of expressiveness, which they are careful to insist is essentially indefinable. O'Faoláin's conception of the indefinable quality of a good story has been mentioned; though his remarks were made in 1948, they typify the views held by critics who admired the work of the twenties:

But the essentials of a good story are indefinable; or one uses words to define them which will have private meanings for oneself. Thus, the things I like to find in a story are punch and poetry.

. . . the stort story is an emphatically personal exposition. What one searches for and what one enjoys in a short story is a special distillation of personality, a unique sensibility which has recognized and selected at once a subject that, above all other subjects, is of value to the writer's temperament and to his alone — his counterpart, his perfect opportunity to project himself.[15]

To O'Faoláin it was "punch and poetry"; in O'Brien's view of Anderson it was "faithful discovery and impersonal compassion"; for Miss Porter it was "theme and style"; Hemingway held it to be "the thing you really felt . . . the actual things which produced the emotion you experienced." Observe, for

---

[13] See above, p. 22.
[14] Canby, *The Short Story in English*, p. 350.
[15] O'Faoláin, pp. 11, 37–38.

example, O'Faoláin's analysis of Hemingway's "The Light of the World," a story like many written in the twenties, although written somewhat later:

[The story] is overtly . . . about two whores. It is about so much more, which neither we nor Hemingway can fully understand, that he calls it 'The Light of the World.'

[It is a] warm, human story, full of emotion. Technique? Unity of place, a railway station; of Time as long as it takes to tell; of Character, two bums. Characterisation; nil. Poetry; full of it, unanalysable. Principle, idea, kernel, core, comment; it is in the title. Construction; two bums are thrown out of a bar and fall into a station, and fall out of it again, and pick up misery and pathos on the way. Form; in and out and in and out; as simple as could be. Suggestibility; nothing whatever is 'told,' except for the first sentence, and that compresses two lives in two lines and three words. Subject; a whore's despairs? Nobody ever wrote a good story without as much technique as that.[16]

It is clear that this indefinable element — the common denominator of excellence accepted by these writers and critics — is a quality of honest emotion that the writer must feel and his story must express through "poetry" or "style," that is, by intuition and suggestion rather than by intellectual contrivance. Notice the suggestion that "The Light of the World" is about much more than even the author can understand.

At first the contrast between the early and later view of the short story seems sharp and striking. All the same, it does not tell us much that is specific about how the forms of short stories in the two periods actually differ. Is the "indefinable" element which is most essential to the modern story — the personal feeling — really different from the "single impression" that the early story tried to produce? Do the stories of the twenties actually lack the kinds of "plots" which in the early period were thought essential, and, if so, what have they provided instead? The most positive difference between the two groups of critics seems to concern the writer's psychology in working out his story: the early critic asks him to work it out logically, the later critic tells him to do it intuitively. Does such a difference in approach mean that the invented forms will differ correspondingly?

[16] *Ibid.*, pp. 12, 191.

To answer such questions, one must examine the forms of the two periods by a single standard of comparison. It is not enough to insist, as we have up to this point, that the story itself shall determine how it should be analyzed. Form being defined here as the principle that unites and organizes a story, making necessary the inclusion of details in their own particular order and manner of treatment, in order to compare forms we must ask similar questions about the form of any story in either group and arrange these questions in a natural order. The primary formal principle of a story as a story (rather than as a discourse) is a unified *action* so treated as to possess some particular emotional power. This is, in fact, what most people naturally respond to when reading most familiar stories — excluding those clearly rhetorical or didactic. It is the story's essential nature as a work of art. Such, of course, is the classic view of Aristotle in the *Poetics* when he judges the particular elements of tragedy according to their ability to produce the tragic effect of pity and fear, a view that does not appear to contradict the belief of those writers and critics of the twenties who assert that the most important thing about a story is the feeling or personal emotion that it possesses. It differs from the viewpoints described above in two ways: by regarding the emotion or effect as something inhering in the action rather than as a direct expression of the author's personality (this means only that we are looking at the emotion as perceived by the reader through the particular artistic mechanism chosen by the author, without considering how much of the latter's personality enters into the picture), and by not insisting on the indefinability of that emotion.

Although not indefinable, the emotions of a story can scarcely be conceived apart from that which gives rise to them: Aristotle's pity and fear, themselves, do not exist apart from situations or actions that are pitiful or fearful. Thus for Aristotle the form of a tragedy is not simply the abstracted effect, but the whole completed unified tragic action — the tragic "Plot." Plot, so considered, is not a mechanical sequence of events moving toward a certain resolution, but a sequence defined by its specific moral and emotional movement.[17] The sequence determines the effect, and the effect is defined by analysis of the sequence.

Primarily, then, our comparison of forms should be a comparison of whatever principles in different stories are comparable in function to the plot of a fully developed tragedy. We must look at that particular sequence of happenings whose "beginning, middle, and end" best explain the power, interest, and feeling of the story, and we must look at the nature of that power and feeling as contained in the sequence. We need not insist on the term "plot" to designate this formal principle in every case, especially as the writers of the twenties thought they were doing away with plot. The term, however, is useful, as will be seen, to designate certain *kinds* of formal principles.

It is clear from the foregoing discussion that two major kinds of criteria are of paramount importance in the classification of forms. One of these concerns the sort of action or activity that the story imitates: is it about an *action*, or about an *activity* of character, or of thought, or of feeling? Such distinctions are largely meaningless unless we also distinguish according to the second major type of criterion: the nature of the effect or emotional power which the story is intended to produce.

Among the stories being studied here, the sorts of actions imitated tend to vary between two extremes which can be illustrated (in their typical, not most radical, manifestations) by a contrast between Miss Cather's "Paul's Case" and a story which in its subject and even its effect is somewhat similar, Anderson's "The Thinker."

In "Paul's Case" there are at least three distinguishable stages in which the situation changes. In the beginning the narrator presents a number of incidents to show Paul's growing dissatisfaction and restlessness in Pittsburgh: his surly behavior with his teachers and at home and his efforts to engage himself in the more exciting world of the visiting musicians and actors. Out of this situation comes his decision to escape: he steals money and flees to New York. The final stage, which follows his disillu-

[17] See R. S. Crane, "The Concept of Plot and the Plot of *Tom Jones*," *Critics and Criticism: Ancient and Modern*, ed. R. S. Crane (University of Chicago Press, 1952), pp. 616–47.

sionment with this experiment, is precipitated by the news that his flight has been discovered and that he will be obliged to return. Since this is intolerable to him, he throws himself under a train.

The unifying action is a change in Paul's circumstances as the result of the interaction between his character and external elements. The change is an irretrievable disaster that has evolved out of his initial unhappy situation: it possesses a serious effect of modified horror developing out of pathos. The effect depends upon the unfolding of this change and is shaped finally by the way in which the completed change has frustrated or satisfied our desires and fears, developed in the course of the story. Not everything in the story, to be sure, is a link in the causal chain of events that leads to the final outcome; in the first part, for instance, there are many incidents that merely illustrate the nature of Paul's initial situation before the change begins to take place. Their particular arrangement is determined by the nature of the expectations the author wants to establish. The successive situations or stages so illustrated, however, are linked causally; the story as a whole is bound together by the developing change, the real "beginning" of which is Paul's decision to leave Pittsburgh, and the end of which is his death.

In Anderson's "The Thinker" there are some interesting parallels to the problem treated in "Paul's Case." Like Paul, Seth Richmond is unhappy in his environment; he too feels misunderstood and wants to escape, although it is not Winesburg's lack of glamor that oppresses him but the emotionalism and volubility of its people. He is a quiet boy; he feels detached from everything that surrounds him and seems to lack the emotions — excitement, anger, despair, fear, love — that are so natural to everyone else. To some extent he feels contempt for the others — for everyone who "talks and talks" — and to some extent he feels envy, thinking it would be better if he could become excited about something. He wants to go to the city to escape the emotional pressure he feels — to get an undemanding job and lose himself in anonymity. Very little happens. The story begins with a summary presentation of Seth's situation, including a brief description of his house, a brief picture of his feeling as he watches the berry-pickers go by, a short biography covering the death of his father and his mother's life in Winesburg while Seth was growing up, including one or two incidents, more fully developed, in which his quiescent nature is strikingly manifest. Then a more particularized narrative begins. "On a summer evening," Seth goes to see George Willard; on the way he listens to some men arguing politics, an argument which starts a "chain of thoughts in his mind," thoughts disclosing the mixed envy and contempt which he feels. Then he finds George, who talks volubly and in an irritating manner. He leaves George and goes for a walk with Helen White, whom George has just said he intends to fall in love with. The rest of the story is devoted to Seth's walk with Helen.[18] It shows the mutual shyness between the pair and a romantic feeling growing between them as Seth tries to explain his plan to go away to the city. He does not express this romantic feeling, and Helen, who admires him as strong and purposeful, does not recognize it. She wants to kiss him, but refrains; after she leaves, he wants to run after her, but "only stood staring, perplexed and puzzled by her action as he had been perplexed and puzzled by all of the life of the town out of which she had come." Now he is overcome by loneliness, imagining that henceforth she, like the others who don't understand him, will "'begin . . . to look at me in a funny way.'"

"That's how it'll be. That's how everything'll turn out. When it comes to loving some one, it won't never be me. It'll be some one else — some fool — some one who talks a lot — some one like that George Willard."

Unlike "Paul's Case," this story shows no disaster, no irretrievable or irreversible change of any importance. If there is a unifying action, it must be the episode that begins with Seth's decision to talk to George and ends after Helen has left him. But nothing conclusive occurs: at most there is a change in his mood, a sharpening of his feeling of loneliness and restlessness, which is scarcely a new thing in his life. We do not read the story as an account of his decision to leave town, for even if the decision were not made until his walk with Helen (which is doubtful), it would scarcely explain the peculiar power of the final scene.

[18] This scene is discussed in more detail below, pp. 295–96.

Nor can we read the story as an account of a significant discovery by Seth, even though he has a somewhat keener awareness of his feelings at the end than at the beginning.

What affects us most in the story, certainly, is the demonstration in Seth's final thought, not of what he has learned but of what he has failed to learn. The power of the story resides in the episode, which is a concrete manifestation of certain *unchanged* facts about his relationship with himself and others. The story tells us that he is not unemotional, as he thinks; he longs to fall in love with Helen White, and it would be an easy matter to win her love, if he could acknowledge his own feeling toward her. The story is a disclosure of the way in which Seth defeats himself because of his misconception of himself and his effect upon others. It is not an initial or a final defeat, but a characteristic one. The story is a revelation of a static situation through an episode which is a materialization of that situation. As in "Paul's Case," the specific effect is a complex kind of pathos.

In "Paul's Case" the unifying action may be called a *plot*, in "The Thinker," an *episode*. The essential difference is in the importance of change in unifying the action. We may define a plot as a form whose effect depends upon the unfolding of some complete and irreversible change in the depicted situation; its parts are linked causally to bring about such a change. An episode, on the other hand, is not a completed action. The term itself implies a large action of which the episode itself is only a part. Thus, to say that a story is unified by episode is to say that any change which takes place within the episode is significant less for its own sake than as a part of some large situation. This larger situation is the source of the effect. It is essentially fixed or static, or if changing, it is changing in an indefinite way — that is, it may be a momentarily fixed condition of instability. Thus in "The Thinker" we are moved less by a contrast between beginning and end than by the absence of contrast between beginning and end.

In a sense, then, an episode, unlike a plot, is not an imitation of an *action* at all, since action means change and the change involved in an episode is not complete. Episodes are imitations,

rather, of *activity*, open-ended, with an indefinite beginning and
end. Completeness and unity exist, in other words, not in the
imitated action itself, but in the representation of action by
the author; when he has revealed all he needs to reveal about
the situation in order to produce the desired effect, the story
ends.

As will be seen, the plots and episodes in the stories being
studied vary greatly in the magnitude, substance, and complexity of the actions or activities that they imitate. The fundamental change in "Paul's Case," for example, is a change in
fortune — a disaster. In other plots the change may be far less
comprehensive: many stories have plots, for instance, in which
the only change is the making of a choice by the protagonist, and
in others the only change may be the acquisition of some significant knowledge — a discovery. Similarly, episodes may be so designed as to stress different kinds of activity in the fixed situation.
"The Thinker" culminates in a display of the characteristic attitude in Seth (a kind of choice) that accounts for his situation;
others may stress the feelings or thoughts that a character has
about his case.

All such distinctions, as well as the many further discrimina-
tions that can be made concerning the structure of the unifying
action or activity, tell us little if we do not distinguish between
the kinds of effects that the structure is intended to evoke. The
production of the effect is the ultimate determinant of a story's
form and the most significant differential between forms.

It should be emphasized that the term" effect," as used here,
does not mean the vague and variable emotion that readers may
actually feel, differing from one reader to another and one reading to another. It means, rather, the precise emotional power
that the author has put into the story for the "ideal" reader. As
such, it exists in the structure and devices of the story, and
theories as to its nature can be defended or challenged by reference to this structure and technique. The ambiguity, the vagueness, the disturbing awareness of shadowy, not-quite-tangible
feelings, the fear that any statement one might make about the
effect of a story would be a crude oversimplification — all these

feelings which the reader of any really good story always experiences are not the signs of actual vagueness, imprecision, or
ambiguity in the effect; when they are not the result of our
own failure to grasp the story, they spring from the enormous
complexity of its emotional intention, a complexity that far out-
strips our meager vocabulary. The terms we use — anger, pity,
fear, horror, and the like — signify merely broad kinds of feelings
commonly evoked in universal situations. The effect of a particular story, on the other hand, is a very specific combination
of emotions caused by a very specific combination of circumstances, and it differs from that of any other story.

This study is not concerned with a complete description of
the specific effect of any single story. What matters here are the
contrasts between the two periods in the "dominant effects" of
the various kinds of stories. The dominant effect of a story is the
final one, which all the various elements of the story combine to
produce. It is not, of course, separate or distinct from the various
subordinate or secondary emotions that may be felt in the course
of the story, but is a composite of them, determined by and sub-
suming them.

The most useful primary distinction between kinds of effects
produced by stories in our canon is probably that between painful and directly pleasurable ones. Aristotle's tragedy and comedy
are extremes of these two kinds, the one arousing the painful
emotions of pity and fear, the other producing pleasure in the
contemplation of the ridiculous, which is defined as a species of
the ugly that does not cause harm. Of course these extremes are
opposites and easily distinguishable from each other, but the
presence in our canon of stories that attempt to combine painful
and pleasurable effects shows that the distinction is not quite as
obvious as it seems. Furthermore, tragedy as well as comedy
gives pleasure; otherwise we could not bear to contemplate it.
The essential difference may be a difference in the relation between the reader's pain and his pleasure. In the "painful" story
the pleasure arises through the catharsis of pain; it develops out
of the experience of a painful emotion that has reached a complete development. This requires, in the action, a vivid and im-

mediate development of misfortune, suffering, or harm strongly contrary to the reader's desires — disaster such as that in "Paul's Case," suffering such as that in "The Thinker." In the non-painful story, on the other hand, pleasure comes out of the avoidance of or escape from the threat of a painful experience; the painful possibilities are thwarted or defeated short of full development. Misfortune or suffering may exist in such a story, but the reader's concern about it is diverted. The form is such that it puts the misfortune at a distance, emotionally and morally.

It should be reiterated that the effect does not exist apart from the action, and can scarcely be described in the abstract. Terms such as pity and fear are defined in relation to action: pity is the feeling we have whenever we see what we judge to be somebody else's undeserved misfortune, fear is our expectation that evil will befall ourselves or, as in a tragedy, those like ourselves, or those with whom we have identified ourselves. Just as there can be many kinds of undeserved misfortune, so there can be many kinds of pity, and a description of the nature of the undeserved misfortune is perhaps more useful in characterizing the effect than any number of adjectives attached to the term "pity." This fact makes all the more important the precision with which one describes the nature of the unifying action or activity: an episode makes its effect in a different way from that of a plot; the effect of a plot of changing fortune is different from that of a plot of choice; the presence or absence of such elements of structural complexity as Aristotle's reversal and discovery has great significance. Especially important is the moral relationship between the reader and the protagonist — the one whose experience is the unifying action of the story.[19] Before the effect can be described or the form identified, it must be determined whether the author intends the reader to feel superior or inferior to the protagonist, or to feel that what happens to the protagonist is just or unjust, or to sympathize with him or admire or despise him. In most stories in the canon, the protagonist has mixed qualities, elements both of superiority and in-

[19] See Appendix C, p. 391, for my definition of "protagonist" and a brief discussion of stories with multiple protagonists.

feriority. Here, as in other matters, the identification of the form depends upon which elements are the dominant ones, or those most effective in making the action what it seems to be.

The conclusions in the following chapters are based upon a classification of the stories in the canon according to their principles of form, analyzed according to such criteria as have here been suggested. Such a classification is, admittedly, somewhat hazardous, since there are few stories that do not offer some problems in analysis. In most cases, to be sure, these problems relate only to minor matters of detail within a story: the general formal nature is perfectly clear. The greatest difficulty, no doubt, is that of making equally clear the terms by which this formal nature is described, so that the reader who knows the story can see in an instant what is meant. This difficulty, however, is not serious enough to necessitate the abandonment of the classification, which is the only means whereby the formal developments in stories of the twenties can actually be demonstrated.

The formal classification of the stories in the canon is presented, therefore, in full, in Appendix B, p. 385. Descriptions of the specific terms used in the classification, as well as explanations of all significant qualifications and interpretations of its meaning, are included in the following pages.

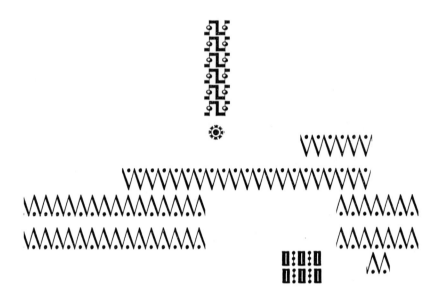

XII: COMEDY AND ROMANCE

Mrs. Freeman's "A Village Singer" — a simple, characteristic, not especially distinguished story of the early period — is full of suffering for the protagonist. It deals with an old woman, Candace Whitcomb, who after forty years as the church soprano is retired against her will. Bitterly resentful, she tries to cause difficulty for the girl who has replaced her; while her successor is trying to sing, Candace's voice, competing from next door, is heard through the open window of the meetinghouse. The minister and Candace's nephew (engaged to her successor) try to reason with her and scold her; they are astonished by her anger, which makes her threaten to cut off the nephew in her will. Soon, however, she falls ill. On her deathbed she relents; she calls in the nephew and the girl, tells them that they will inherit all her things, and asks the girl to sing for her. The story concludes with

168

a comment that shows that she has not completely given up her pride, when she mildly criticizes the girl's singing: "'You flatted a little on — soul.'"

The story is a simple example of the kind of form that produces not a primarily painful effect but a directly pleasurable one. It puts the misfortune or suffering at a distance from the reader by diverting his attention to more pleasurable elements. This can be easily demonstrated. Although the story ends with the implication that Candace will soon die, this misfortune can scarcely be regarded as the real outcome of the story since it develops from perfectly natural causes that have nothing to do with the preceding action. Somewhat more significant is the suffering that she endures upon retirement and that motivates her behavior through most of the story. But this suffering, too, is not a consequence of the action in the story; it is "given" in the initial situation as one of the circumstances out of which the action is to develop. It does not increase during the story; on the contrary, it is mollified. How, therefore, the suffering could be considered the primary source of the effect is difficult to see. A study of the action makes clear what is perfectly obvious from the summary already given: the primary change that takes place and into which all the parts of the story fit best is the change in Candace's attitude toward retirement and her successor. The interesting conflict in the first part of the story is between herself and those she thinks are trying to keep her out: her successor, the minister, and her nephew. She resists until the imminence of death breaks her down. Finally she yields.

Such a plot distances misfortune primarily because the change of attitude that takes place is what the reader (as well as all the more sensible characters in the story) wants. Her final attitude is "better" than her original one — more reasonable and more generous — even if less colorful. What's more, she feels better as a result of it: the change in attitude actually reduces her own suffering. Besides these primary sources of pleasure, the story further minimizes the immediacy of suffering by stressing what is ridiculous in the way Candace expresses her suffering. Most striking is her extraordinary attempt to interfere with her successor's success by singing through the meetinghouse win-

dow, to the consternation of the people inside; this emphasizes
the absurdity in the situation by turning our attention from Candace's pain to the inappropriateness of what she does.

Two-thirds of the stories in the early canon are "directly
pleasurable" in this sense, putting misfortune at a distance.[1]
Only in stories by Bierce, Dreiser, and Miss Cather — not the
most characteristic writers of the period — are such stories less
common than painful ones, and in writers such as James, Mrs.
Freeman, and Garland they constitute much more than two-
thirds of the selected stories.

In the twenties such forms become considerably less important, relatively speaking. Just over half of the stories of this
canon are of this kind, with the proportion greatest in stories by
Fitzgerald and Faulkner, smallest in stories by Anderson. Non-
painful stories are still important, of course, but not so exclusively so. The non-painful stories of the twenties, furthermore,
use effects and structures untried in the early period and spread
over a wider spectrum of possibilities.

The non-painful stories of the early period are ranged between typical extremes represented by Mrs. Freeman's "A Wayfaring Couple" and James's "Paste." "A Wayfaring Couple" is
in a form that may be termed "romance." "Paste," whose action
more closely fits the definition of the "ridiculous," may be called
"comedy." In stories of the early period, romance is more common than comedy, and is especially prominent in the work of
Mrs. Freeman, Mrs. Wharton, Mrs. Gerould, and, to a lesser
extent, Garland. Comedy is more frequent in the work of James.
Neither form is as common, however, as an intermediate form
that characterizes half of all the early non-painful stories, the
romantic comedy, of which "A Village Singer" is an excellent
example. In the twenties all these forms are much less important
than they were before, with the sharpest relative decline occurring in comedy and romantic comedy.

The characteristic effect of a comedy such as James's "Paste"
seems to involve two chief sources of pleasure which provide
an interesting contrast to the sources of pain in a classic tragedy.

[1] The classification of individual stories according to the various formal
principles described in this and the following chapters on form is given in
Appendix B.

Instead of pity for the undeserved misfortune of the protagonist, we feel satisfaction in the justice of deserved misfortune suffered by the comic agent. Instead of fear of threatening evil in seeing the oncoming misfortune of someone like ourselves, we enjoy the security of witnessing a display of foolishness to which we are superior. The story, which James described as a twist on the idea of Maupassant's "La Parure," deals with a girl who is given a pearl necklace by a priggish cousin. He insists that the necklace, left by his stepmother along with other gaudy bits of costume jewelry, is not genuine. The young man wants to believe that the necklace is false, for if it were genuine it would raise ugly doubts about the respectability of his stepmother. But one of the girl's friends, seeing the necklace, insists that the pearls are real. Against the advice of her friend, the girl scrupulously returns the necklace to her cousin, who vows that he will prove it an imitation. Though she hopes that he will give it back to her, he tells her, somewhat later, that, having had the necklace appraised and proven false, he has destroyed it. Months later, she discovers her friend wearing the pearls; the friend says she bought the necklace in a pawnshop and it is genuine. The girl realizes that she has been duped, that her cousin, having discovered the pearls to be genuine, has secretly sold them to the friend, thereby making a profit while at the same time expecting to keep the profitless truth from the heroine.

The girl's loss of the pearls, though painful to her, is hardly a serious disaster; much more important is her discovery that she has been tricked. This is the essential change that unifies the action — a process culminating in the embarrassing and humiliating discovery of a foolish mistake, which, in the typical Jamesian way, results from the heroine's excessive scrupulousness. It is a "plot of discovery," the discovery constituting a comic comeuppance for the girl. This comeuppance is an appropriate punishment, more embarrassing than destructive, for the mistake. At the same time it liberates our pleasure in the ridiculous. The source of this pleasure — as always when we enjoy the ridiculous — is obviously the surprised recognition (occurring when the discovery is made, although in other comedies it may recur constantly throughout the story before the climactic recognition) of our own superiority to an inferior character in an inferior position. The manner in which we are made to enjoy such a feeling is important, for obviously not every display of the consequences of a character's mistakes will produce such an effect. One might expect the display of inferiority to provoke indifference unless it is made important to us in some way. One way is to stress the harm it does, as in serious stories of fear and horror. But the harm the heroine does to herself in this story is not sufficiently serious to alter our feeling that it was deserved. Another way — the comic way of "Paste" — is to make the character's mistake reflect on her own sense of self-importance — the vanity, the pride she takes (in this case) in her scrupulousness. Perhaps it is the challenge to the ego which this vanity presents that makes us enjoy the heroine's discomfiture. As a result, we feel both of the responses appropriate to comedy: the confirmation of our own superiority and the satisfaction of our punitive desires, of our sense of justice.

It is true that the heroine of "Paste" is far from unsympathetic; at another level the reader identifies with her and is disappointed when she fails to get the pearls. This, however, is a secondary complication in the effect, more characteristic of Jamesian comedy than of early comedy in general; it is a further means, added to the heroine's own vanity, of making her discomfiture important to us. As in many of the best comedies, the comic pleasure here involves our own discomfiture as well as hers, for in order to perceive and enjoy her inferiority, we must raise ourselves to a higher plane of moral judgment than that upon which we originally identified with her.

The characteristic effect of a romance such as "A Wayfaring Couple" is somewhat simpler. The protagonist is a young wife. Her husband is deprived of his job in a New England factory by another man's jealousy, and the young couple have to move elsewhere to find work. For a long time they travel on foot from village to village without success. The husband falls ill in an abandoned house where they have stopped. His wife now displays the courage and strength that the whole trip has brought out in her; she finds a carriage and, stepping between the shafts, pulls her husband to a doctor in the nearest town:

. . . her face was wonderful with the love and strong patience shining through it. Those days of watching over this honest, distressed soul, whose love for her was so unquestioning, had caused all the good elements in her nature to work out a change in it. This was Minty's true flower time. Everything worthy in her was awake and astir and glowing. She, dragging her sick husband over the rough country road, like a beast of burden, was as perfect a woman as she ever would be in this world. She seemed to rise triumphant by this noble abasement from any lower level where she might have been.

When she gets to town people are so impressed that their natural "New England suspicion" falls away. They help the couple; the young man recovers, and they give him the job he needs; Minty is taken into the town and eventually becomes the heroine of a folk song.

The plot involves two changes. The primary one, which embraces the other, is the good fortune that Minty wins, as complete as such a change can ever be. Much of its effectiveness, however, depends upon the other change, the growth of Minty's character under stress. The obvious intent of the story is to please the reader in the fullest possible way with the spectacle of Minty's growth and the rewards given to her as a result. The story resembles "Paste" in satisfying the reader's demand for justice, the justice in this case being not deserved misfortune but deserved good fortune. Unlike "Paste," the story carries no suggestion of absurdity in the character. Instead of feeling superior to her, the reader comes to admire her; instead of being discomfited in the sympathy he has given her, the reader finds that sympathy amply justified by her growth and success. Thus, although the reader's feeling of security (the opposite of fear) is not threatened, neither is it positively developed, as in a comedy. This is the essential characteristic of the "romantic effect" as defined here: satisfaction of the reader's desire for justice, flattering the reader not by elevating him above an inferior character but by justifying the sympathy or admiration that he wants to feel — confirming his moral judgment of things. It is a gratification of the reader's desire for the triumph or vindication of what he considers good. Although such a definition ignores, of course, many qualities commonly associated with "romance," the term is nevertheless appropriate to such an effect; it is certainly the characteristic effect in many if not all great works that are commonly called "romances."

Romantic comedy, as illustrated by "A Village Singer," combines elements of romance and comedy to produce an effect perhaps even more flattering to the reader than are the others. The story resembles a romance in that it stresses the heroine's discovery of the best moral attitude. She redeems a previous error and thus justifies the reader's sympathy. The strength of her passion is treated in a characteristically romantic way, too — sympathetically, wonderingly, more or less admiringly, a treatment that also tends to justify the reader's sympathy. On the other hand, her passion and error, if not intrinsically comic in origin, are, as has been suggested above, expressed in an unquestionably comic way. Our attention is called by her behavior to her vanity, her harmless self-importance, which gives us the comic pleasure of superiority, heightened, of course, by the almost equally comic consternation of the people around her.

This sort of effect is distinguished from romance and pure comedy by its combination of comic security (the surprised feeling of superiority) not with the punitive satisfaction of a comeuppance but with the romantic vindication of our sympathy for the heroine. The story invites us to admire a character at the same time that we enjoy her comic inferiority. This is what makes it most flattering to the reader: it is a patronizing or sentimental effect, delighting in the goodness of those who are comfortably inferior to the assumed reader's own level of moral sophistication.

ROMANCE

Romances in the early period constitute almost one-quarter of the entire canon. They include a variety of kinds of unifying action, the great majority of which are plots rather than episodes. Most of these plots fall into two classes: plots culminating in deserved good fortune for the protagonist, as in "A Wayfaring Couple," and those culminating in an admirable choice by the protagonist, without conspicuous deserved good fortune.

Except for two of Garland's strongest stories, "A Branch

Road" and "A 'Good Fellow's' Wife," the romance of good fortune in the early period is seen exclusively in the work of Mrs. Freeman, where it is fairly common. These plots resemble that of "A Wayfaring Couple" in that the protagonist eventually triumphs decisively over real or threatened adversity. The adversity itself varies somewhat in seriousness, from the real disgrace that befalls the heroine's husband in "A 'Good Fellow's' Wife" to the threatened loss of a fiancée in "Amanda and Love" and "A Branch Road." In any case, it is overcome: the disgraced husband is helped by his wife to redeem himself, and the fiancée is won back. In all cases but two, the triumph is preceded and made possible by some significant change of character or attitude on the part of the protagonist. In stories such as "A Wayfaring Couple" and "A 'Good Fellow's' Wife," in which the initial adversity is not, to any serious extent, the heroine's fault, this change is gradual — a growth of strength and courage, which brings about good fortune finally through its effect upon others — upon the impressed townspeople in "A Wayfaring Couple," upon the weak and errant husband in "A 'Good Fellow's' Wife." In most cases, the initial adversity is the result of the protagonist's own error or blindness and the good fortune the result of his discovery of that error and the consequent change in his attitude, as, to cite the simplest case, when the hero of Mrs. Freeman's "A Discovered Pearl" realizes his mistake in overlooking the good neighbor girl, proposes to her, and wins her. Such growth or change in attitude lends a complexity of interest to the romantic effect that is lacking in the two plots without it. In these two, "Louisa" and "Calla-lilies and Hannah," the heroine is not morally to blame in any way for her adversity (except through the action of her very goodness); the story shows her quietly patient and courageous response to it. In these stories it takes an act of chance to bring about the final good fortune, although in "Calla-lilies" chance is assisted by the salutary effect of the exposure of the heroine's virtues to the young man most capable of rescuing her.[2] Even when chance assists,

[2] Mrs. Freeman's story "Calla-lilies" is complicated by the excessive modesty and self-effacement of the heroine, which must be overcome before she can claim the good fortune that comes her way.

however, the reader is made to feel that the good fortune is a deserved reward for virtue. The effect is simpler only because the reader feels less need, in the course of the story, for vindication of his sympathy; the question is purely and simply whether the character's environment will give him the reward that he deserves.

In the plots of choice the effect depends upon an action which, in one important sense, has less "magnitude" than that of good fortune. This does not mean that the action is necessarily less intricate or elaborate in its sequence of incidents, but rather that the change that takes place is less consequential, less tangible or material, inasmuch as it does not involve the character's basic state of fortune in a primary way. The effect in such stories, similarly, does not turn upon the question of rewards for the character but depends chiefly upon the vindication of the reader's sympathy for him.

The romantic plots of choice, distributed in the early period among several writers and most prominent in stories by Mrs. Gerould, Mrs. Wharton, and Mrs. Freeman, can be illustrated by Mrs. Wharton's "The Reckoning." The heroine, Julia Westall, has become a "radical" with respect to divorce as the result of the failure of her first marriage ten years before; she has become an advocate of easy divorce and of marriage based upon a mutual agreement to break off as soon as either party wearies. Thus she justifies her divorce from her first husband, Arment; her second marriage, to Westall, has been undertaken on the basis of her new ideas. The story deals with the "reckoning" that must follow: she discovers that Westall now intends to make use of their agreement in order to divorce her and marry some one else. Thus she becomes aware of the cruelty of her adopted theories and of her own treatment of Arment:

The law? What claim had she upon it? She was the prisoner of her own choice: she had been her own legislator, and she was the pre-destined victim of the code she had devised. . . . *She* had been allowed to go free when she claimed her freedom — should she show less magnanimity than she had exacted? . . . The law could not help her — her own apostasy could not help her. She was the victim of the theories she renounced. It was as though some giant machine of her own making had caught her up in its wheels and was grinding her to atoms. . . .

There are the makings here of a tragic plot of misfortune: an error, a considerable loss, and, too late, the discovery of error. The emphasis, however, is not upon downward movement; the entire history of her first divorce and her remarriage is told in flashbacks as a part of her thoughts. The primary sequence deals only with her discovery of Westall's intention to leave her and her reaction to this; what matters is the recognition of her error and the resulting revision of her attitudes. At the end of the story she demonstrates the change in her attitude by paying a call on Arment and admitting the wrong she has done him. Thus the loss of fortune becomes the means to a change in attitude on her part, and it is this change that constitutes the fundamental unifying action. It is essentially a choice: a decision to reject one set of principles, which she had previously held, in favor of another set. It is precipitated by the problem facing her as the result of her previous behavior, and it is manifested most concretely by her apology in the final scene. Despite the misfortune, the choice is obviously meant to seem admirable and wholly satisfying to the reader; it "corrects" her error, whose consequences have been vividly demonstrated. Thus it vindicates her in the reader's eyes — a positive effect that transcends or supersedes whatever painful concern he may also feel for her misfortune.

Such romantic plots of choice fall into two categories: Plots of "correction" and "renunciation." "Correction" plots, like that of "The Reckoning," turn upon a character's revision of a mistaken attitude he has held. This revision may take place after the disclosure of unfortunate consequences of the original attitude, as in "The Reckoning," in which case the choice provides us with a certain punitive satisfaction, or it may follow some more favorable manifestation of a mistake, as when the hero of Garland's "God's Ravens" discovers that his neighbors are really kind, warmhearted people after all. The correction of attitude is usually manifested in a gesture, as in Mrs. Westall's apology, although it may appear in nothing more tangible than a thought, as in the last sentence of Mrs. Gerould's "Wesendonck": "She had discovered that sometimes the intolerable must be borne."

In "correction" plots, the protagonist overcomes what the reader is encouraged to regard as a fault. In most cases (most obviously in "Wesendonck") the initial error is one that the reader will condemn without question; the conclusion that the heroine reaches at the end is no more than what the reader has known from the start. In such stories the reader feels justified not only in his desire to sympathize with the erring heroine but in his (perhaps complacent) initial assumptions about the moral issues involved. The misfortune that the character may suffer in the process is necessary to clear the character of any suspicion of getting more than he deserves because of his error, and varies in seriousness according to the seriousness of the error. Thus in such stories as Mrs. Freeman's "A Solitary" and Garland's "God's Ravens," in both of which the character's initial error is an excessive suspicion and aloofness from his neighbors, the new more humane attitude involves no loss at all and is such a happy one as to be almost a reward in itself. The most complex effect in a correction story, however, is seen in James's "The Middle Years." Here the hero's original erroneous attitude — his fear of the approach of death before he can complete his work — is treated so sympathetically, and his character is developed on such a high plane of moral and human sensitivity, that his final moral discovery may surpass what the reader has been expecting or desiring. He ends, in a sense, "better than we are," thus gratifying our sympathies on a higher level than that of "Wesendonck." Here the effect verges on exaltation; it depends, that is to say, upon an enlargement of the reader's moral view as he reads the story.[3]

[3] This is not to say that every reader inevitably learns something as he reads the story. The moral enlargement is "built into" the story, so to speak; the expectations and desires which the story develops are based on an expanding moral view as the story proceeds.

One other correction story, Mrs. Gerould's "The Miracle," also deviates from the usual pattern, though not so significantly as does James's "Middle Years." The heroine's change in attitude is initiated unconsciously; she discovers in herself new resources of maternal feeling toward a stepson, resources that she did not think she possessed. The change in "Middle Years" is precipitated in part by unconscious processes, an inner change in the hero's feelings.

In this respect the story has a resemblance to the second category of romantic plots of choice: plots of "renunciation." These somewhat rarer plots differ in that there is no specific error in attitude to be corrected in the final choice. The character, through no fault of his own, is faced with a dilemma that he must solve. This he does, according to the characteristic morality of the time, by renouncing his own selfish interests. The heroine of Mrs. Gerould's "Leda and the Swan" destroys the painting which, if sold, could save her from poverty at the cost of the violation of her code of privacy; the hero of Mrs. Gerould's "The Great Tradition" renounces her plan to elope in order to fulfil her responsibility to society; the hero of Mrs. Gerould's "The Bird in the Bush" renounces his great ambitions in order to make possible a life-saving operation for his son. In such stories the intention is clearly something like that of "The Middle Years": we are meant to be impressed by the fine morality which the protagonist brings to his choice. The misfortune involved in the sacrifice has one obvious function — to make the sacrifice more impressive. Unfortunately, the modern reader is likely to be somewhat less impressed by these cases than by "The Middle Years," partly because the protagonists of these stories have little emotional depth (they exist for us largely through their reasoning about the issues that confront them) and partly because the principles they affirm are perhaps less impressive to us today than when the stories were written (seeming excessively finicky in two cases and all too obvious in the third).

One romantic plot of choice in the early period — Bierce's "A Son of the Gods" — does not quite fit either of the two categories as they have been described. It resembles a renunciation story, but with an important difference. It deals with the noble sacrifice of a young officer who gives his life voluntarily on a scouting mission, thereby saving most of the rest of the troops. Emphasis is placed, not on the dilemma facing the hero — he simply makes his choice and carries it out — but on the botch which the troops make of his sacrifice, for in their enthusiasm for his act many of them move into the exposed position which he had tried, with his life, to warn them against. This adds a bitter element (almost horror) to the effect, magnifying and enriching the dominant romantic admiration.[4]

The four remaining romances in the early period are episodes. As in "The Thinker," the action is less significant for any permanent change that it brings about than for its demonstration of some constant characteristic of the protagonist's situation. These episodes resemble "The Thinker" further in that they are all "episodes of choice": the significant demonstrated characteristic is the chosen attitude or manner of behavior that the protagonist displays in his situation.[5] The difference is that the attitude so demonstrated emerges not as a blind or faulty one but as wholly admirable. Garland's "A Day's Pleasure" illustrates this. As was noted earlier, the story describes a lonely, hard-working farm wife's rare day of vacation in the village: the day starts badly because there is nothing to do, and the woman's loneliness seems reinforced, but the situation is saved by the kind action of a matron who invites her in to tea. As was also pointed out, by showing how easily she can be made happy by the smallest of kindnesses the story demonstrates the depth of the heroine's acceptance of her hard lot. Nothing permanent, of course, is accomplished by this action. The development of the effect, however, is perfectly clear: pity for the heroine's suffering is converted into admiration for the basic goodness of her attitude in misfortune — her attitude of acceptance, which the episode brings out. Just as in the more complex plots of renunciation, our sympathy is rewarded by this demonstration of virtue.

The four episodes are all similar in their basic elements: the situation contains considerable quiet suffering; the episode demonstrates the protagonist's goodness amid this suffering; and the

[4] The story might be classed with the painful stories, with a form approaching the tragic, but I do not believe that such a description is as accurate as that given here. Although the foolishness of the men tends to make the protagonist's sacrifice a vain one, it also serves to magnify, by contrast, his own nobility; in addition, it constitutes a tribute to him, significant since the men had laughed at him when he first appeared. See quotation, p. 329. These lines reinforce my impression that we are meant to be stirred first and most by the protagonist's greatness; the disaster, brought about through the men's own admiration of this greatness, adds poignancy to it but does not become the primary concern of the story as a whole.

[5] See below, p. 206, n. 1, and p. 260.

suffering itself is "distanced" from the reader by this display of goodness, its function being primarily to make such a display possible. The virtue in each case consists primarily of the character's modest and courageous acceptance of his lot, with emphasis on courage in such a story as "The Return of a Private" and on self-effacement in such a story as "A Kitchen Colonel." The latter shows that in such episodes, the romantic character need not necessarily be a superior being in all respects. Here the hero is a weak, henpecked man, a failure in almost everything he does. The weakness is nothing, however, in comparison to the goodness demonstrated in the characteristic sacrifice which the episode describes.[6]

In stories of the twenties, there are barely half as many romances as in the early period, although this loss is less significant than it may seem because of the general decline of non-painful forms. Even so, the displacement of romance is greater, proportionately, than the general decrease in the importance of non-painful stories.

Only a very few of these stories — Fitzgerald's "The Four Fists," "The Adjuster," and, to a less marked degree, "The Ice Palace" — resemble at all closely the common earlier forms. Apart from these, only two of the romances of the twenties have plots, and, of the rest, only two are episodes of choice similar to those of the early period.

One of the two "plot" stories is Miss Porter's "Maria Concepcion." It can probably be classified as a plot of good fortune, although vastly more complicated than earlier stories of this type. The heroine escapes danger, is purged of jealousy, and

---

[6] Mrs. Freeman's "Scent of Roses" shows a version of this pattern slightly more complicated than usual. Of two sisters, the elder, whose beauty is waning, contents herself with growing roses while the younger's beauty blooms. A former admirer of the elder sister returns to the village after a long absence. Because of his shyness it is assumed that he is now more interested in the younger sister. Eventually, he manages to reveal that it is the elder sister whom he loves. They are married, and the younger sister now turns patiently to the same pursuit with which the elder sister had consoled herself.

The ironic turn of the story suggests that the two girls should be regarded as a multiple protagonist (see Appendix C, p. 391), the action being an episode manifesting their similar manner of behavior (choice). This choice may be described as the modest, graceful, uncomplaining way in which the girls accept both the good and the bad fortune that befalls them.

wins peace, after a thorough humbling of her pride, but this end is only reached after she has gone through a far more terrible experience than faces any of the earlier romantic protagonists. In a passion of jealousy she commits murder; the horror of what she has done and the fear of the consequences precipitate the change in attitude leading to her final good fortune. The story has thus a much stronger tragic quality than do the earlier stories; yet tragedy for the heroine is averted; through her suffering, she is better off at the end than at the beginning. She has gained through "self-abasement," to use Mrs. Freeman's term in "A Wayfaring Couple."

The other "plot" story — Hemingway's "The Undefeated" — is like the earlier stories in showing the hero's noble behavior in the face of a given misfortune, there being, however, a significant difference in what is presented as noble. The aging bullfighter, gored in the ring in his attempt to make a comeback, refuses to admit defeat, refuses to be retired, although it is perfectly clear that he can never fight again. There is little question that the intensity of this man's pride is meant to seem admirable, despite (or perhaps because of) its defiance of the realities of nature.

This plot differs also from the earlier romantic plots in the way the choice is manifested. There is no change of attitude here, nor any dilemma for the protagonist to solve, although his behavior does manifest a choice between alternatives. The hero, rather, reiterates at the end the same choice that he had made at the beginning — the choice not to admit defeat. The circumstances in which this choice is made have changed: in the beginning there was still a possibility of success, but at the end there is none. The nature of the choice has therefore changed in one important way: whereas it was still a moderately reasonable one at the beginning, at the end it is not.

Of the eight romantic episodes in the twenties, at most only three romanticize virtue in the manner of the earlier episodes. Two of these — Hemingway's "Cross-Country Snow" and "The Revolutionist" — somewhat resemble earlier episodes of choice. They differ from them in the underplaying of the disclosed virtue. "Cross-Country Snow," which treats Nick's last ski outing

with a close friend before taking his pregnant wife back to the
States, culminates in a scene in which Nick quietly manages to
suggest that he is resigned to leaving, that he does not feel the
bitterness his friend expects him to feel, even though there is
no pleasure quite like skiing with a friend. "The Revolutionist,"
more difficult because of its brevity and seeming simplicity, may
also belong to the same class, although it contains no such clearly
defined episode of revelation. The protagonist is a young revolutionist from Hungary who has met the narrator in Italy; he lives
in danger; at the end he is caught and interned in Switzerland.
Most emphasized in this little sketch are his pleasure in normal
civilized living, his love of art and of the mountains, his idealistic faith in world revolution, and his shyness, attitudes that he
maintains despite the dangers threatening him and the horrors
to which he has already been subjected. Most striking is the
contrast between his nonbelligerent personality and the violence
of both his life and his faith. Such faith and such courage emerge
as admirable in the circumstances, although there is no explicit
suggestion of praise by the narrator.

The third episode romanticizing virtue — Anderson's "Death
in the Woods" — differs essentially from the other two in its
structure in that the principle that unifies the story is not an episode in the life of the protagonist but an attempt on the part of
the narrator, who has witnessed the circumstances of the protagonist's death years before, to grasp and communicate the nature
of the feeling the event produced in him. The essential point he
wants to make is his feeling for the beauty, perfection, and simplicity of the life and death of a totally self-effacing old woman
whose whole existence was given to the feeding of "animals and
men." The treatment is not chronological; it includes a fairly
detailed description of her death in a snowstorm in the woods
and the ritual dance of the dogs around her as she is dying, a
summarizing biography of her life, and, at the end, an explanation of how and why the narrator has pieced together from
various sources the facts of the old woman's life. In a sense such
a story is not an "episode" at all, unless one regards as an episode
the narrator's experience in trying to do justice to his feeling
about her. In this regard the story, like "The Undefeated," re-

sembles structurally other stories in the twenties which usually produce a quite different effect.[7]

Most romantic episodes in stories of the twenties turn on the protagonist's perception of a feeling that he has about his situation. The hero of Anderson's "The Untold Lie" recognizes that his feeling about his marriage is not totally unhappy; the hero of "Sophistication" experiences for a moment the combination of joy and sadness which, according to the narrator, is necessary to mature living in the modern world; the hero of "The Return" gets a glimpse of what it means to be emotionally unfettered, to throw his habitual caution to the winds. Such stories may be called "episodes of discovery" since they depict the emotional quality of situations through episodes in which the characters themselves become keenly aware of that emotional quality — episodes rather than plots, because the protagonist's experience brings no permanent change of any kind. He does not learn anything about his situation that he did not know; rather, through being made to look at it in a certain way, he experiences a temporary intensification of feelings about it.

The effect achieved in this way has, however, a fundamentally different quality from that of the earlier romances, as may be seen in Hemingway's "Big Two-Hearted River." This story describes in detail Nick's experiences and feelings on a fishing trip. As was pointed out in an earlier chapter, certain details suggest that the trip serves a therapeutic function for Nick, and there is some emphasis upon the whole process as a kind of purging ritual for him. It is clear that the primary intention is simply to make the reader share vicariously Nick's joy in this experience. The reader is meant not merely to see and judge but actually to experience, as intimately as art allows, Nick's feelings. Such a sharing of the protagonist's feelings may be called a "sympathetic effect," and it may have any sort of quality, depending upon what kinds of feelings are being shown.[8]

The sympathetic effect of "Big Two-Hearted River" is romantic because the emotions depicted are romantic. The essence

[7] See discussion of "exposed situations," p. 236.
[8] For this term I am indebted to R. S. Crane.

of the romantic effect is gratification of our desire for the reward or vindication of what we admire as good. Nick's ritual
exhilarates him; it expands his appreciation of life through its
purgation of the unspecified but presumably unpleasant and dis-
organized emotions of his ordinary existence in society. It exhilarates us, then, in the same manner.[9] This appreciation of life is
a romantic gratification, resulting, in Nick, from his recognition
that good abounds all around him. Words such as "wonder,"
"joy," even "exaltation," are appropriate to describe such a feeling. It differs from the effect of more conventionally romantic
stories in that it is evoked not by some victory of good over bad
in a conflict that we witness outside ourselves (what might be
called "objective romance") but by an enlargement of our own
emotional horizons whereby we become conscious of the good
and beautiful in an experience we are undergoing. This enlargement — a specific effect of this story, not to be confused with the
enlargement we may feel as the result of reading any good story
— is caused by our sympathetic identification with a character
whose own horizons are thus enlarged.

Except for Faulkner's "Carcassonne" — an even more direct
depiction of a character's state of feeling in a situation whose
objective nature is only vaguely suggested — none of the other
episodes of romantic discovery depends for its effect quite so
exclusively upon sympathetic identification. The three Anderson stories resemble in some ways the more traditional romances
of moral discovery and correction — except, as has been said,
that the changes are not permanent. Yet we are gratified less
because the hero finally measures up to standards of which we
approve than because the enlargement of his emotional horizons
suddenly enables us to identify ourselves with him sympathetically (as we could not, so fully, earlier in the story). Thereby we
can share the exhilaration or pleasure or relief in his experience,
as in "Big Two-Hearted River."

[9] The story can be criticized on the ground that the horrors from which
Nick is escaping are not dramatized; as a result, the full impact of Nick's
escape can scarcely be felt by the reader. In this regard, the story is more
effective in the context of the collection in which it originally appeared (last
in the volume *In Our Time*), the preceding stories suggesting vividly the sorts
of horrors involved, than when it is considered in isolation.

COMEDY

Comedies — such as "Paste" — are less common than romances in the early period. Most of these are by James, whose tendency is somewhat less romantic than that of the other writers. The early comedies may be divided into two main groups, the "objective" and the "sympathetic." In objective comedy, the primary absurdity resides in the protagonist himself, as in "Paste." In sympathetic comedy it resides in the protagonist's environment.

A distinguishing feature of all objective comedy in the early period is the presence of a comeuppance for the protagonist's absurdity, necessary to provide the proper comic punitive satisfaction. Not all these stories have as complete a comeuppance as has "Paste" — one in which the protagonist finally perceives, in a more or less humiliating way, his comic error. The stories of full comeuppance are all plots of discovery. This means that the essential action, the completed change that controls all else in the story, is an emotionally meaningful process of learning whereby the protagonist becomes aware of things he did not know before, without any significant consequences beyond the discovery itself. No change of attitude, no choice, no act (beyond what may be useful simply to indicate that a discovery has been made) is implied in a discovery plot, which differs nevertheless from the discovery episodes discussed above in that something has been actually learned that can permanently alter a character's feelings about the situation. In the comic discovery plots, the protagonist learns that he has been making a fool of himself; the discovery is humiliating and embarrassing to him, although the narrator seldom needs to specify this explicitly. It is an appropriate comeuppance for comic error, since it satisfies both our punitive desires (aroused by the display of that error) and our desire to feel superior to that which is ridiculous.

The discovery plots all begin with some act by the protagonist which either constitutes or reflects his comic error.[10] The subsequent action involves either a development of conse-

---

[10] The beginning of the plot and the beginning of the story are not, of course, identical. In "The Other Two," for example, the plot begins when Waythorn brings his wife to live in New York in the mistaken belief that his marriage will not be haunted by the ghosts of her two previous marriages. The story itself begins shortly after this moment.

quences from that error (as in James's "The Marriages") or a re-iteration of the error, until circumstances are forced to the point where the character discovers the mistake.[11] In Mrs. Wharton's "The Other Two" and Miss Cather's "The Marriage of Phaedra," as in "Paste," the error is the assumption that others are as scrupulous or proper or disinterested as one's self; the discovery is the realization that one has been duped — wilfully, in "Paste," unintentionally in "The Other Two" — a fact that exposes the somewhat self-righteous vanity of the otherwise natural initial assumption. In James's "The Marriages," the plot of which is more elaborate and complex than in the other stories, the discovery is considerably grimmer. Here the heroine acts to prevent her father's plan to remarry by telling the woman he intends to marry that her mother had never been happy with her father. Her motive, she thinks, is family loyalty, deeper, she supposes, than her father's. Her plan works: the wedding is called off, after which it becomes increasingly clear that she has done great harm by her act, having hurt not only her father but also her brother, who had an interest in the wedding. Finally, filled with remorse, she goes back to the woman, confesses her lie, and begs her to take her father back. But the woman laughs, telling her that it is now too late, that she is going to marry someone else. Then she reveals that she had never believed the girl's lie and that she had called off the wedding because the father had refused to repudiate his daughter for telling it. The comeuppance is in this final discovery by the girl, a discovery that explains all the previous action. She learns in effect that her father

[11] Mrs. Wharton's "Long Run" is a comeuppance story with a pattern somewhat different from others described here. It deals with the degeneration of a promising young man, who falls into conventionality and dullness following his cowardly refusal to elope with a woman who had argued eloquently in favor of boldness and daring. Since she too becomes conventional, the story might be read as a story of misfortune as the result of the error of his choice, although it is told in such a way as to constitute a plot of discovery, and the emphasis upon the recognition of the cowardice beneath the young man's reasonable and chivalrous pretensions serves to distance the actual misfortune and stress instead the comeuppance of his vanities. The story begins with a description of what Merrick has become, raising a mystery as to how he got that way. The action proper begins when Merrick starts to tell the narrator his story — a story of essentially comic error and discovery. The actual "change" in Merrick's character, as described at the beginning, is not the outcome of the story but a cause of the outcome, which is his humiliating recognition of his mistake.

has been more generous and loyal toward her than she toward him and that while she has been hurting him in the name of love, he has sacrificed and suffered for her. The previous action is all a manifestation and consequence of this contrast between them, of which she has been unaware. What counts most is not the suffering, not the heroine's misfortune or that of her family, but her discovery of the vanity that has caused her to harm others. The story becomes comic by virtue of the emphasis upon that vanity in the final discovery; the fact that this follows rather than precedes the revelation of the harm she has done serves to distance the harm and produce a comic effect. The relative grimness arises from the greater-than-usual emphasis on the harm, with a consequent greater emphasis on the punitive aspect of the comic effect and lesser emphasis on the pleasurable absurdity of the comic object.

In some objective comedies, the comeuppance does not involve a full discovery of the error. Most of these stories are plots of choice, so classified because the error tends to persist, even to the end. The action is unified by a change something like that in "The Undefeated": the same attitude or choice is manifested through irreversibly changing circumstances. James's "The Lesson of the Master" illustrates this kind of plot at its most complex. The story deals with a promising young writer, Paul Overt, who, as his name suggests, is open and trusting. He is persuaded not to marry by an aging "master," Henry St. George, who convinces him that marriage would interfere with the development of perfection in his art. When Overt returns from a trip, he discovers that the master himself is about to marry the girl Overt had given up. At first the young man believes he has been duped — and if the story ended here it could be called a conventional discovery plot. But the master insists that he has done so only because he has given up his own art, and Overt decides to believe him. It is this final decision that constitutes the reiteration of the comic error, the refusal to accept the full humiliation of a full discovery. This point is made clear in the last lines of the story. The young man, recognizing that his conclusion is valid only if St. George actually does give up his art, tells himself that if the master should write another great book, he will know that he has been swindled. The narrator then tells us that this is not so; if the master were to publish another book,

I may say for him . . . that . . . he [Overt] would really be the very first to appreciate it: which is perhaps a proof that the Master was essentially right and that Nature had dedicated him to intellectual, not to personal passion.

The "intellectual passion" is Paul Overt's comic vanity, which not only enables him to be swindled but keeps him from admitting it or resenting it even when he knows he should.

In such a plot of comic choice, the comeuppance is the defeat that the protagonist suffers before the final reiteration of his comic attitude. The defeat is the result of the comic error; it provides a satisfactory punishment, even though the character refuses to acknowledge his absurdity, because it involves a deserved loss, of which he is aware. The reiteration of his absurd attitude at the end is the sign of his awareness of the loss, a reaction to the humiliation to which his error has subjected him, a reaction in which he tries to deny or evade the humiliation. It also makes doubly clear the nature of the comic error. The reader feels no need for further punishment of this error when it is thus reiterated, because it has already been punished: all the possible humiliation that it could bring to the protagonist has already been brought about.

The comeuppance and reiterated choice take different forms in different stories. In Mrs. Gerould's "The Weaker Vessel" they are combined: the defeat is the hero's renunciation of his plan to leave his wife; the reiterated absurdity is the lofty rationalization he gives for his surrender.[12] In "The Beldonald Holbein" the heroine's defeat is the discovery by her society of the rare beauty of the "homely" companion whom the heroine had employed as a foil for her own beauty; the reiterated absurdity is the hero-

[12] Mrs. Gerould's "The Weaker Vessel" resembles superficially this author's plots of romantic renunciation. The main signs that the intention here is comic are the indications, at the beginning, of the hero's fears that he will be talked out of his plan and his determination not to be, the inconsistency between the principles by which he justifies leaving his wife and the principle that decides him to stay, with the relative shallowness of the latter, the fact that his wife has no moral claim on him, as he has demonstrated in his argument, the sophistry in her arguments, and, of course, the hint in the title that it is weakness, not strength of moral principle, that defeats him.

ine's failure to appreciate that beauty, her dismissal of the companion, and the reassertion of her vanity by hiring another companion. In James's "Europe" the defeat looks, from one viewpoint, like a victory. The heroine grows to tremendous old age pretending to encourage the life-consuming desire of her three daughters to travel to Europe, while actually preventing them from going by her conveniently timed illnesses. The youngest daughter, Jane, escapes; the others, Becky and Maria, remain bound; they become old themselves, and Becky dies. The defeat is the old lady's loss of her daughters; the reiterated absurdity, her failure to admit how she has lost them: thus in her senility she insists that Jane, who has gone to Europe, is dead and that Becky, who is dead, has gone to Europe.[13]

Sympathetic comedies have a variety of plots. James's "The Death of the Lion" concerns a loss of fortune (although the misfortune is subordinated to the comic manner in which it takes place); "Mrs. Medwin" is a plot of good fortune; "The Figure in the Carpet," "The Next Time," and "Flickerbridge" are plots of choice. Mrs. Wharton's "Autres Temps" is a discovery plot. In each case, the action involving the protagonist, whatever its specific nature, has the effect of exposing the absurdity of a

[13] James's "The Real Thing" belongs in this class, and his "The Coxon Fund," an unusually long story, is also somewhat hesitantly placed in it. "The Real Thing" shows a comic choice persisted in by the double protagonist: the unshaken belief of an impoverished but aristocratic couple in the self-evidence as well as the superiority of their inborn aristocratic heritage. This, they suppose, qualifies them to serve as artist's models of aristocrats like themselves. Although they fail as models and accept this defeat with graciousness, they never understand why they have failed; even though they take money from the artist to go away, they never give up their belief in their quality, a belief that sustains them through all their humiliations.

The protagonist of "The Coxon Fund" is probably best regarded as "multiple" — the little group of admirers of Frank Saltram, a brilliant personality and talker who also happens to be a lazy, unproductive scoundrel and parasite. One member of the group, which has long supported Saltram, acquires the power to administer a fund to help some needy "earnest and loyal seeker." Deciding to ignore the evil things that are said about Saltram, she administers the fund to him. Its effect is to destroy his brilliance completely, and after his death no one else appears whom the fund can be used to help: "But what are these accidents, which I should perhaps apologize for mentioning, in the light of the great eventual boon promised the patient by the rate at which the Coxon Fund must be rolling up?" The comic vanity, in brief, is the impractical idolatry displayed by the group, an attitude which persists after their failure with Saltram, despite the narrator's own increased skepticism.

society that is more ridiculous than he and of administering thereby a kind of moral comeuppance to that society. The heroine of "Mrs. Medwin" does this in a tangible way: she exploits for her own ends English society's gullible fascination with Americans. The heroine of "Autres Temps" discovers the ridiculous reasons why society has banished her and states these reasons to a man who stands on a middle ground between her and that society. The hero of "Flickerbridge," on the other hand, administers a comeuppance by passing judgment on society and by breaking his engagement to the girl who, in his eyes, represents it. The actions of "The Death of the Lion" and "The Next Time" are comic because they put to shame a society that cannot appreciate its true artists, or appreciates them for the wrong reasons. The great but frail writer is lionized to death in a story that stresses his admirers' total misunderstanding of his worth and of what they are doing to him. The writer in "The Next Time" unintentionally exposes the folly of the public by his persistent lifelong inability to write anything but masterpieces (an unconscious reiterated choice) when he is trying to write bad popular works that will support him. In no case does the society become aware of the comeuppance of its folly; the comeuppance is rather the exposure of that folly to the sympathetic protagonist or, when he is its victim, as in "The Death of the Lion" or "The Next Time," to another character, a neutral.

The comic pleasure in such stories results from our sympathetic identification with the protagonist in his moral relation to society. Our desire for justice is satisfied by the moral comeuppance in the exposure, even though the protagonist may suffer in the process. Our pleasure in superiority to the ridiculous depends on our identification with him — our sudden pleased recognition of his superiority to the rest of his world. If, as in "Mrs. Medwin," the protagonist herself is also somewhat ridiculous, so much the better: our pleasure is thereby increased.

James's "The Figure in the Carpet" is the most complex plot of this kind. The story deals with the writer Hugh Vereker's decision to keep secret the motivating, unifying principle that runs through all his works, after he has revealed to one admirer that such a principle does exist. The story, told from the point of view of that admirer, concerns his efforts to discover the secret in a variety of ways, all of which are defeated. In the end the secret is carried to the grave. This is a frustration or misfortune for the narrator, certainly, but he could hardly be called the protagonist since the whole interest turns upon the fate of Vereker's secret — whether it will be disclosed to the world, of which the narrator is merely the representative. The action as a whole is thus essentially the acting out of Vereker's decision to punish his admirers for their obtuseness; the choice is made not at the end but at the beginning, and the story describes the execution of that choice, the carrying out of all the consequences implicit from the moment Vereker first made the decision.

In the development of this tale, the reader identifies himself with the narrator. When he fails to discover the secret, we realize, as in so many of James's stories, that to an extent the joke is on us; in order to appreciate it, we must move to the "higher level" of the agent who has discomfited the narrator — the level where James himself stands, with Vereker. We cannot fully identify ourselves with Vereker because we do not know his secret. He remains above us, and we laugh at ourselves for our inability to achieve his level, our failure to achieve an ideal superiority.

Only six stories from the twenties have been classified as either objective or sympathetic comedy, according to the definitions used here. This is an even more striking decline than that of the romances. Four of the six are essentially "objective," with comeuppance for a comic protagonist. Of these, Anderson's "The Egg" and Fitzgerald's "Magnetism" have plots of reiterated absurdity after the comeuppance, whereas Fitzgerald's "Bernice Bobs Her Hair" has a discovery plot of comeuppance. These stories vary in the degree to which potentially serious elements contribute to the effect. In "Magnetism" the hero's comic humiliation is fairly trivial: he discovers to his embarrassment how irresistibly attractive he is to women whom he does not wish to attract; he gets out of one difficulty caused by this handicap (a kind of unconscious comic choice) and at the end is about to be faced with another. In "The Egg," on the other hand, the hero's humiliation has strong overtones of pathos, in addition to which the narrator manages to suggest levels upon levels of seriousness by exploring the symbolic implications of the hero's situation. These elements enhance rather than destroy the basic comic effect: the symbolic implications suggest the broad universality of the comic situation, and the pathetic implications increase the protagonist's importance and add a discomfiting element to what otherwise might seem a trivial farce. Hemingway's "Cat in the Rain" differs from the early objective comedies in that it is an episode (rather than a plot) of discovery, in which the heroine's frustrated feelings are sharpened into comic embarrassment and humiliation when an expression of whim is taken literally by an uncomprehending bystander.[14]

Anderson's "A Man of Ideas" and Hemingway's "Che ti Dice la Patria?" are two very different kinds of sympathetic comedies. Anderson's minor story has a simple plot of good fortune in which the hero scores a triumph of which his world does not think him capable, thereby making that world look ridiculous. Hemingway's story has a discovery plot in which, in four episodes parallel to each other rather than causally related, the hero perceives the folly of attitudes that have infected some Italians under the new fascist regime. In a manner characteristic of the twenties, the narrator never explicitly acknowledges his discovery; it is left entirely to the reader's inference.

ROMANTIC COMEDY

More common than either comedy or romance in stories of the early period is romantic comedy. A favorite subject of Mrs. Freeman, Garland, and Crane, romantic comedy is represented in some thirty-five stories in the canon. Even Bierce, most of whose Civil War stories are painful, is represented in the canon by one such story ("George Thurston"), and only Mrs. Wharton, whose

---

[14] The wife expresses her implicit desire to play a more feminine role by asking for the cat she sees shivering outside the window of the hotel. The comeuppance occurs when the gallant hotel manager, trying to please, produces another cat. It is the grotesque inappropriateness of his gesture that makes the story a comic one, despite its overtones of pathos. The story is more properly considered an episode of discovery than a story of plot, since the event scarcely brings any new knowledge of the vanity of the wife's hopes, but simply alters for a time the feelings she has about herself. See above, p. 184, and below, pp. 198, n. 18, 228, 251–52, 254–58, for descriptions of other kinds of episodes of discovery.

stories tended to pure romance and traditional comedy, is unrepresented.

As was explained earlier in this chapter, such stories combine the comic pleasure in harmless inferiority with a romantic satisfaction in the vindication of our sympathy for the protagonist rather than with a punitive satisfaction in comeuppance. Whatever comeuppance the absurdity may call for is absorbed in the romantic justification of the protagonist: either his virtue triumphs over absurdity (his own or that of others), as in "A Village Singer," or it excuses or justifies it.

Many of the romantic comedies deal with changes of attitude like that in "A Village Singer," in which the protagonist corrects an earlier error. Some of these may culminate in a positive reward of good fortune (as in Mrs. Freeman's "A Gala Dress"); some—plots of choice—do not ("A Village Singer" and Mrs. Freeman's "A Poetess"). The basic action of such plots is romantic, but a comic element is introduced, residing usually in the mildly ridiculous simplicity of the otherwise good protagonist. This comic simplicity may appear either in the expression of the error itself (as in "A Village Singer") or in the manner in which the discovery is brought about (as in "Life-Everlasting"). The latter provides a clear example of how an action can appear to the reader as both admirable and comic. The good, kind, simple heroine is converted from agnosticism to faith by a criminal's demonstration of goodness. To Mrs. Freeman's readers, this change was certainly regarded as thoroughly admirable and ample justification for the sympathy felt for the heroine. At the same time, even though the reasons for her change have a certain subtlety, the occasion and the simple manner in which the heroine describes her change were certainly meant to seem naïve to those readers who, while approving, would doubtless be made conscious, with sympathetic amusement for the heroine, of their own greater sophistication. In stories such as "A Poetess" and "Sister Liddy" there is also a pathetic element that functions, as in some of the romances, to enhance or make compelling the romantic element.

A second group of romantic comedies consists of stories with good-fortune plots simpler than those described above; the protagonist himself makes no significant error that needs to be discovered. The "reversal" in such stories is the discovery by others of the character's true deserts, as a result of which they give him his deserved reward. This pattern is seen at its simplest in such a story as Mrs. Freeman's "Christmas Jenny," in which a town's inquiry ("really a witch-hunt") into the life of a kindly eccentric old recluse is thwarted when a neighbor stands up in her defense:

"But I know one thing — if she did git kind of twisted out of the reg'lar road of lovin', she's in another one, that's full of little dumbies an' starvin' chippies an' lame rabbits, an' she ain't love-cracked no more'n other folks."

Embarrassed and impressed by this plea, the townspeople reverse themselves and instead shower Jenny's cabin with Christmas gifts. Jenny's goodness has worked indirectly, through the agency of the appreciative neighbor, to bring her recognition and rewards. In other cases the protagonist wins through her own direct efforts, as in Mrs. Freeman's "The Revolt of 'Mother.'" Deprived by her husband of the new house she wants, the heroine takes matters into her own hands by appropriating for that purpose the new barn he has built, doing this at a time when he is out of town. Faced with this *fait accompli*, he has to yield: "'Why, mother . . . I hadn't no idee you was so set on't as all this comes to.'" In such stories the just reward to the protagonist provides the romantic element; the comic element lies usually in some aspect of the process that must be gone through before this reward is given. Usually it is the blunt directness of the protagonist's effort, which ludicrously oversimplifies the issue and works because its very simplicity catches everybody by surprise. This is true not only in "The Revolt of 'Mother'" but also in such stories as Mrs. Freeman's "A Church Mouse" and "An Innocent Gamester" and Garland's "Among the Corn Rows," in all of which the environment is the primary source of the comic quality in the effect. The simpler stories, such as "Christmas Jenny," are similarly comic because of the naïveté and simplicity of the neighbors who give the heroine her reward.[15]

[15] Mrs. Freeman's "Gentle Ghost" is the simplest of all the romantic comedies of this kind. A family is frightened by what sounds like a ghost. After a

A third, smaller, but important, group of romantic comedies consists of stories with plots of discovery culminating in a mild sort of comeuppance for the protagonist. Here, unlike the other stories discussed, the basic action is more comic than romantic, but acquires a romantic quality through the nature of the circumstances that give rise to the comeuppance. For, in contrast to the discovery of having been duped in a story such as "Paste," the discovery in such stories as James's "The Abasement of the Northmores," or "The Tree of Knowledge," or Miss Cather's "Flavia and Her Artists," is that things are actually much better in the world than the skeptical or doubtful protagonist had supposed. In "The Tree of Knowledge" and "Flavia," he discovers unsuspected powers of devotion and loyalty in others, putting his own somewhat uncharitable attitudes to shame; since he gains nothing himself, the comic element is a little stronger than in such a story as "The Abasement of the Northmores," or, for that matter, Crane's "A Gray Sleeve," in which he discovers that others have a kindlier attitude toward himself than he had supposed. A Yankee soldier, subjected to the hatred of the men in a Southern family, discovers that the girl in the family appreciates him. Here, to be sure, the romantic conclusion is reached too easily to make a very good story, but "The Abasement of the Northmores" is more effective: the heroine, after the failure of her own efforts to make the public acknowledge the superiority of her deceased husband to his more successful rival in public life, discovers that the balance is righted automatically when the publication of the rival's inane letters reveals his full vacuity. The story concludes, it is true, with a decision by the heroine not to press her advantage any further against the humiliated rival family; this choice seems less significant as a change in attitude (in a plot of choice) than as a sign of acknowledgment of her discovery. In Dreiser's "Married," also placed in this class although very different in its material, the romantic-comic discovery has a more serious or pathetic quality: the essential dis-

time, they discover that the sounds are the cries of a poor waif, to whom they give a home. If the child is the protagonist, the story is a simple account of the way in which her just need for a home is satisfied, romantic because of this good fortune and the pathetic situation that gives rise to it, and comic because of the manner in which the family discovers her.

covery is that a young husband's insecure wife has firmly rooted
emotions and is deeply dependent on him. The emotional quick-
ening that this produces in him is clouded somewhat by his
realization that he will constantly have to renew the emotional
support he gives her.

A fourth, still smaller, and largely uncharacteristic, group
consists of stories with plots of choice in which the choice is
romantic not because it corrects an error but because it involves
behavior that is astonishing and contrary to normal expectations.
Some of these — Bierce's "George Thurston" and James's "Brooksmith" and "Miss Gunton of Poughkeepsie" — involve a reiteration of choice through changing circumstances (as in "The
Undefeated"); others — Mrs. Gerould's "Pearls" and Mrs. Freeman's "A New England Nun" — involve actual reversals of previous behavior and apparent attitudes. In each case, the comic
element lies in the inappropriateness of the choice to the circumstances — a soldier adopts a heroic battle stance as he is dying
in a ridiculous accident; a butler rejects all available positions
in upperclass society because they do not provide the cultural
enrichment obtained in one position he had held; a young
American girl rejects a prince rather than yield the tradition of
her country that her fiancé's mother should write to her first;
an artist abandons his devoted and dependent family to pursue
an artist's life in the South Seas; a spinster who has waited fifteen
years for her fiancé to return rejects him because she has become
accustomed to the placid serenity of her single state. Although in
the latter two choices there is a hint of a caustic element,[16] the
misfortunes are rendered non-painful by final emphasis upon
the exceptional devotion to an ideal which motivates the protagonist's extraordinary choice.[17]

[16] See Chap. xiii.

[17] The heroine of Mrs. Freeman's "New England Nun" shows no such
positive devotion to an "ideal" as do the others. The heroine gives up her
"birthright" — her right to marriage — for the sake of the placid serenity to
which she has become accustomed. The romantic quality is more diffuse, implicit in the generosity and consideration she shows for others while making
her choice and in the sympathetic attitude of the narrator toward her. One
detects wonder in this attitude, which implies admiration directed towards the
courage that Louisa shows in changing her mind and her calm refusal to regret
the sacrifice of her birthright. Such a sacrifice in the stories of the twenties,
of course, would emerge in a far different light.

In addition to the plots just discussed, a large number of early romantic comedies — eleven stories — are episodes. A majority of these are by Crane, the only writer of the early period who commonly relied on this form. But since Garland, James, and Dreiser also wrote occasional romantic-comic episodes, with the result that more than a third of all the early episodes are romantic comedies, there seem to be grounds for thinking that in the early period generally the romantic-comic episode was considered more acceptable, more in accord with dominant practices, or at least easier to write, than other kinds of episodes.

One kind of romantic-comic episode is represented only by three stories by Crane, of which "The Bride Comes to Yellow Sky" is the most celebrated. Since these episodes show a very specialized sort of construction, dissimilar to anything else in either canon, they may be passed over quickly: the protagonist experiences a mild comeuppance in the escape from sudden danger by the use of means that accidentally present themselves and that seem inappropriate to his conception of himself as a certain kind of man.[18] Most romantic-comic episodes, however, are episodes of choice. As with romantic episodes of choice such as "A Day's Pleasure," most of these display behavior that reflects the goodness of the protagonist. The comic element resides in the fact that this virtue is applied in inappropriate circumstances in a harmless way, so that the reader becomes aware of absurdity. This is seen in its clearest and simplest form in Garland's Ripley stories and Crane's "The Little Regiment," in each of which the protagonist's pride in his self-sufficiency causes him

---

[18] In Crane's "Bride Comes to Yellow Sky," the town marshal escapes being killed by a frontier primitive out on a drunken shooting spree by introducing his wife; as noted above, p. 103, this baffles his opponent; in "Horses — One Dash!" the hero escapes bandits by fleeing on horseback in the night; in "Five White Mice" the hero escapes bandits, who have knives, by drawing his gun, the advantage of which had apparently not occurred earlier to him. These stories are not classified as good-fortune plots becase they obtain their strongest impact not from the hero's escape from danger (which comes about through circumstances unplanned by the hero) but from the manner in which he escapes. This manner of escape is not a sign of choice, indicating character, but an accidentally discovered advantage that surprises and, to an extent, chagrins the protagonist. For this reason, we classify these stories as episodes of discovery: see also pp. 184, 193. The effect is primarily a sympathetic one (see p. 184): we share the protagonist's mixed relief (romance) and chagrin (comedy). The comic quality is enhanced by the absurdity of the foiled opponent.

constantly to conceal love or other good qualities behind a crusty pretense of independence. The episode in each case turns upon an event subjecting him to special stress, whereupon the real love that he feels emerges for a time, to be put down again as soon as the stress is over. In other instances, a girl in wartime brings her natural feminine goodness, curiosity, and tenderness to an exciting and dangerous wartime adventure; a soldier displays great heroism and subjects his life to mortal danger while filling a bucket of water; laborers in a shop devote imagination to the task of maintaining a mutual fantasy whose purpose is the denial of the hard realities of their existence; and a husband nobly persists in the renunciation of his claims to love and social identity for the sake of a selfish social-climbing wife who denies his very existence. James's "The Story In It" differs from the other romantic-comic episodes of choice in that the heroine's behavior itself is almost wholly admirable, the comic element residing in others, who expose their absurdity to the reader by their judgment of the heroine. It deals with an argument between a virtuous woman and a man and his mistress as to whether a virtuous woman can be the heroine of literature; the sophisticates say no, but the heroine proves her point by citing her own case, the unlawful, "interesting passion" that she has kept under total restraint. Even though the man discovers that he himself is the object of this passion, he scoffs at the idea, but the reader is led to believe that the heroine has scored her point and made foolish and shallow the other's ideas of adventure and romance.

In the twenties, romantic comedy — represented by twelve stories — has declined in importance just as sharply as, or more so than, pure romance. It is true that twelve stories constitute a significant portion of the canon, but this does not approach the significance of romantic comedy in the early period, when half of the non-painful stories and almost a third of the entire canon were of this type. The decline in importance is accentuated by the relative insignificance of some of the new romantic comedies, some five minor stories by Fitzgerald in his most "commercial" vein: "The Offshore Pirate," "Rags Martin-Jones and the Pr–nce of W–les," "Hot and Cold Blood," "Gretchen's Forty Winks," and

"Head and Shoulders." Except for their more broadly farcical quality and some differences in subject matter, these stories adhere to familiar earlier patterns: plots of deserved good fortune achieved by comic means, plots of correction of comic errors, and the like.

Others (a majority of which are by Faulkner) show a variety of unifying principles, most of which are not especially characteristic of the period. Anderson's "I'm a Fool" and Faulkner's "Divorce in Naples" are essentially correction plots, differing from earlier correction plots such as "A Village Singer" by their greater emphasis on comic comeuppance. The protagonists of both stories are defeated, one in an attempt to win a girl by fraud, the other in an attempt to protect the virginity of a young buddy on his ship. These comeuppances differ from those of objective comedies of the earlier period such as "Paste" by virtue of the greater emphasis upon the protagonist's acknowledgment of the comeuppance: the emphasized self-castigation in Anderson's story "I'm a Fool" and the delay in Faulkner's "Divorce in Naples" before the protagonist is willing to restore his friendship with his "fallen" friend. The romantic element in both stories is achieved by this emphasis, which suggests a salutary change of attitude, but one more subtle than those in the early stories. Faulkner's "All the Dead Pilots" and "Hair" are also classed as stories having plots of choice; here a character reiterates his chosen attitude through irrevocably altered circumstances, as in "The Undefeated" and such earlier romantic comedies as Bierce's "George Thurston," James's "Brooksmith" and "Miss Gunton of Poughkeepsie." Thus, in "Hair," Hawkshaw the barber persists in carrying out his assumed obligations to the family of his dead fiancée and to the young girl whom he has chosen to replace the fiancée, even though both obligations have been clearly voided by changing circumstances. The romantic-comic pattern is obvious here: the barber's single-minded loyalty to his purposes is admirable, whereas the disregard of the circumstances that have made those purposes meaningless — disregard capped by his marriage to a girl who has become a tramp in the years since he first selected her — is a comic absurdity. In "All the Dead Pilots" the same essential combination, the appli-

cation of admirable virtue to ludicrously inappropriate circumstances, is developed in a plot whose specific sequence of
episodes follows a somewhat different kind of pattern, anticipated in the early period only by "George Thurston." The story
deals with various escapades and adventures of a young pilot in
the war and ends with his death in battle. This outcome is not
a direct result of the previous action; the narrator himself suggests that the episodes do not form a causal sequence when he
says, in the passage already quoted,

. . . this story is composite: a series of brief glares in which, instantaneous and without depth or perspective, there stood into sight the
portent and threat of what the race could bear and become, in an
instant between dark and dark.

The outcome is an appropriate conclusion to the situation that
the previous episodes dramatize — the war, the imminence of
death, to which Sartoris is reacting with a wild zest and a reckless bravado. The plot, then, is his persistence in this attitude
to the moment when death takes him. As the narrator makes
abundantly clear in his comments, this attitude is admirable for
its intensity and vitality; the comedy lies in the triviality of the
objectives to which Sartoris dedicates himself — most notably,
his rivalry with a superior officer over a whore. Unlike "Hair,"
the comedy is complicated by a caustic element (see chap.
xiii) arising from the horror of the external situation facing
Sartoris.

The romantic comedies that are, formally, most characteristic of the twenties are three episodes of choice. Faulkner's
"Ad Astra" resembles "All the Dead Pilots" in dealing with the
buoyant unconventionality of soldiers at war; here, too, there
is the same comic triviality of objectives pursued with admirable
spirit in a potentially terrifying situation. But the choice is manifested in a single episode illustrative of the fixed situation; it
does not culminate in death, as in "All the Dead Pilots." The
other two episodes of choice, Hemingway's "The Three-Day
Blow" and "Ten Indians," resemble other important stories of
the twenties whose effect is less romantic: stories of adolescent
initiation into the problems of adult life. As will be seen, stories
of initiation have several forms and produce several different

kinds of effects, of which the romantic-comic effect of "The Three-Day Blow" and "Ten Indians" is the rarest. The hero — Nick Adams in both stories — encounters the pain of losing a girl: in one case, he has broken with her himself; in the other he is the victim of her infidelity. In each case the emphasis is upon his reaction to this situation.[19] The most striking thing about this reaction is Nick's effort to sustain more painful feelings about his misfortune than are natural to him in the circumstances. This emerges at the very end of each of these episodes, at which point it suddenly becomes clear that Nick's grief is largely artificial and self-encouraged. The effect depends ultimately upon the revelation of this fact, which is comic because of the vanity of Nick's self-dramatization and romantic because of the innocence that shows through, relieving his distress even as it undermines his attempt to have grown-up feelings. Thus at the very moment when he suddenly becomes most clearly comic, he also becomes most attractive, and we feel that our sympathy for him is justified.

All but one or two of the non-painful stories in the early period fall between comedy and romance, as outlined earlier in this chapter. Virtually all, even the so-called pure comedies, contain at least a moderately romantic element, which is often enhanced by an element of pathos. The most usual comic error is an excess or misuse of virtues, of positively admirable qualities, and the comic protagonist is nearly always treated with affection rather than contempt. Many of these stories thus acquire a distinctly sentimental quality, most marked in some of those by Garland and Mrs. Freeman. In certain of the more serious romances, especially those by Mrs. Gerould and Mrs. Wharton, there also appears a fairly strong didactic quality, most marked

[19] In "Ten Indians" this emphasis is achieved in a less direct way than in "Three-Day Blow," which concentrates directly upon Nick's reaction throughout the story. In "Ten Indians" the first and longest part of the story is concerned with establishing Nick's mood prior to the revelation of his sweetheart's infidelity; the holiday celebration and the drunkenness of the nine Indians have the effect of enhancing for Nick his feeling of alienation upon the discovery about his girl (the "tenth" Indian). The conclusion of the story, which deals directly with Nick's reaction to the discovery, acquires power from this preparation. The opening has the additional advantage of showing Nick's extreme youthfulness, which plays such an important part in our final view of his reaction.

in the correction stories and the dilemma-renunciations, in which the moral issue threatens to take precedence in interest over the specific situation and the individual character. Nevertheless, it is in the romances, comedies, and romantic comedies that the early stories in general are most consistently strong, a strength most evident in the work of James, who of the early writers is the least romantic and most stringently comic. Perhaps his formal superiority is best disclosed in his skill in the invention of comic forms whose full effect depends upon the discomfiture of the reader by making his sympathy for a character itself the butt of comedy, achieving thereby a depth and richness of effect unmatched by the stories, more flattering to the reader, of Garland and Mrs. Freeman.

In the twenties, on the other hand, these forms are uncharacteristic. The most striking difference between the romances and comedies of the twenties and those of the earlier period is the virtually complete disappearance of plots of good fortune — an abandonment of what was certainly the easiest, surest, and most obvious way to achieve a fully romantic effect. Also striking is the all but complete disappearance of plots of corrected attitudes, except in the minor stories of Fizgerald. Apart from the latter, it is noteworthy that in such correction stories as do remain, such stories as "Divorce in Naples" and "I'm a Fool," the emphasis is more on the mistaken attitude than on the positive new attitude that corrects it, with the result that the didactic element that marked so many earlier stories of this type virtually disappears. One might infer from these changes that in the stories of the twenties there is a tendency to avoid the romantic effect: indeed, even in those romances and romantic comedies that have been noted, the most obvious sources of romantic effect are in general avoided.

The most characteristic romantic effect in the twenties depends, to a considerable extent, upon the reader's discomfiture, in much the manner of James's comedies, but differs from the latter in that the reader is invited to find good in that which he might ordinarily find ridiculous or evil instead of finding absurdity in that which he is disposed to admire. The effect depends upon a revision of the morality with which the reader begins his reading. Thus in such stories as "Hair," "All the Dead Pilots," "The Undefeated," and others, irrational or violent or rebellious and unconventional attitudes are praised for the intensity and pride they evidence. In "Maria Concepcion" the reader finds himself in sympathy with a murderess. Simple episodes such as "The Three-Day Blow" and "Ten Indians" also depend for their effects upon a new kind of moral complexity. Whereas pathos in the early stories was a means to enhance the romantic effect, here pathos is exposed as sentimentality, and this enhances the comedy; the romantic effect depends upon the natural, innocent vitality that tends to reduce the protagonist's comic suffering.

Despite such developments as these, it is probably significant that only in the categories of romantic comedy and comedy (among our major classifications of forms) do the writers of the twenties still tend to produce stories of plot. Their departure from earlier practices in these categories is, in other words, less marked than in others. This is further evidence, apart from the actual decline in the numbers of such stories, of the uncharacteristic nature of these forms in the twenties. One is tempted to infer a connection here: it may be that the effects of pure and even romantic comedy require fairly fully developed plots (or seemed to so require to the writers of the twenties) — perhaps because of the need for punitive comeuppance — and it may be that the rejection of romantic comedy and the more striking rejection of pure comedy is tied to the decline of interest in stories of plot.

The decline of these forms can also be explained in another way: the writers of the twenties had new things to offer. One of these was a new kind of "comic effect," quite different from any that have been discussed thus far and unanticipated in the early period by any more than one or two stories. This new comic effect may, for lack of a better term, be called "caustic." Though no more common numerically, the caustic forms are far more representative of the new movement than the romances, romantic comedies, and traditional comedies that have been discussed in this chapter. They deserve separate examination.

XIII: CAUSTIC STORIES

The "caustic" forms — most distinctive of the non-painful stories of the twenties — extend the non-painful spectrum observed in the early period in a direction opposite to that of romance. In contrast to the romantic stories, which dealt with good characters in just situations, the caustic stories deal with inferior characters in ugly situations. Although not primarily painful, the purely caustic stories, like the pure romances, often push close to the limits of the non-painful.

The caustic effect in the twenties can be illustrated by Hemingway's "The Doctor and the Doctor's Wife," a story, characteristic of this author, which demonstrates how close some stories of the twenties come to the line that separates painful from non-painful. In this — or Anderson's "An Awakening" and "I Want to Know Why" or Hemingway's "The End of Some-

205

thing" and "A Very Short Story" — the line is so thin that one hesitates before calling the effect non-painful; one knows that many readers will be too much moved by the pathetic or fearsome implications to agree that they have been effectively distanced. Yet one sees in these stories an effort to distance misfortune unlike anything the painful stories show. Though the reader does not find such clear and obvious "humor" as in traditional comedy, he is nevertheless detached from the object in an ultimately pleasurable way.

"The Doctor and the Doctor's Wife" is an episode of choice.[1] Nick's father, Dr. Adams, is first seen collecting and sawing into firewood some logs washed up on shore. The logs belong to a logging company, but we are told that it is common practice for people to take them since it is unlikely that the company would bother to recover them. One of the doctor's helpers, an Indian named Dick Boulton, insults the doctor by accusing him of stealing. The doctor is offended, and a fight threatens, but instead he turns and goes up to the house. His wife, an ardent Christian Scientist, is resting in her room, "with the blinds down." She questions him about what has happened; he tells her that Boulton tried to pick a fight to get out of working off his medical bills. His wife challenges this explanation: " 'Dear, I don't think, I really don't think that any one would really do a thing like that.' " The doctor starts to go out for a walk. She asks him to send Nick to her. Then, "The screen door slammed behind him. He heard his wife catch her breath when the door slammed. 'Sorry,' he said, outside her window with the blinds drawn." He gives Nick her message, but when Nick says he would rather come along with his father, the doctor does not stop him.

The episode is full of frustration for the doctor. But the story is designed to lay stress less on the unhappiness that the doctor endures than on his manner of making himself unhappy. His

[1] An episode of choice is one in which the constant element emphasized in the treatment and organization of the episode is some attribute of the protagonist's moral character — some constant or habitual choice of behavior which he makes and which is exemplified in the episode. Anderson's "Thinker," discussed above, pp. 161–64, to illustrate the general nature of the episode story, is an episode of choice. See also below, p. 260.

pride in his virtue has been hurt by Boulton and is then further hurt by his wife, with her bland assumption that he must be more to blame than Boulton. Her expectation that her husband must have lost his temper and her assertion that no one would do what he accuses Boulton of doing are deeply insulting, for they imply that the doctor is belligerent, suspicious, and depraved at heart. But though he had flared up in response to Boulton's insult, he makes no response to his wife's worse insult, except for two small signs of suppressed feeling — slamming the door and taking Nick with him. We infer great anger, but he has clamped down on it almost completely. The contrast between his reactions in the two situations shows that he has been defeated by his wife, and the reason for this sense of defeat is clear in the light of the touchiness displayed in the first scene: he is cowed by her self-righteous attitude of moral superiority. His problem is evident: it can only be that he would like to be an upright, virtuous man but knows that he is not. He is enraged by Boulton and intimidated by his wife because of the guilty feeling that he is not as good a man as he should be.

The final emphasis is on the doctor's reaction to his wife's criticism — obviously an habitual reaction, an habitual choice. Although the objective treatment seems to leave it up to each reader to decide for himself whether this choice is a serious error, like Seth's in "The Thinker," or a ridiculous one, it should not be assumed that Hemingway did not have a precise effect clearly in mind. Our conclusion is that the doctor deserves what he gets (despite the arrogant self-righteousness of his wife) — that he is more nearly ridiculous than pitiful in the situation of this story, if not in all aspects of his character. This conclusion arises from the objectivity of the author's presentation of the seemingly trivial causes of the doctor's suffering — a way of distancing the doctor's feelings and throwing emphasis upon the vanity of the motives whose frustration makes the doctor suffer. Unlike "The Thinker," in which Seth's error, honest and innocent, deprives him of the satisfaction of fundamental needs, the doctor's story reveals the suffering of a wounded, ineffectual vanity; it is a story of affectation.

The effect in such a story depends on several facts: the pro-

tagonist is suffering more or less; this suffering is the direct result of some distortion in his attitudes and is therefore needless;
and there is nothing admirable in that aspect of his character
which causes the distortion. The absence of notably admirable
qualities in the character weakens any serious pity we might
feel for his suffering; on the other hand, since his deficiencies are
not destructive or harmful to any but himself, they do not provoke serious fear or horror. The progression of feelings is from
sympathy or potential pity toward a destruction of sympathy:
the final effect involves a judgment that he deserves his suffering, that he is "getting what's coming to him."

Here the judgment does not give a sense of punitive satisfaction, as in the comeuppance of a traditional comedy. It indicates
the presence of an "underlying justice" which keeps the story
from becoming painful or pitiful. But the primary effect, made
possible by this, depends upon a violation of justice on a more
immediate level, a violation that gives pleasure because of its
absurdity, its harmless ugliness. This painless violation of justice
is the essence of the caustic effect. In Hemingway's story it is
simply the failure of the doctor to recognize his own errors;
though he suffers, he experiences no comeuppance; the suffering, indeed, is the very sign of the unchecked triumph of his
deficiencies. The reader's pleasure is, as in comedy, a feeling of
superiority over that which is absurd, the absurd here being the
pointless triumph of weakness and ignorance and vanity from
which the reader has been emotionally detached.

A simple caustic story thus may be described as one that develops the reader's pleasurable sense of superiority over the inferior object without developing a comparable satisfaction of
his demand for justice. It differs from the traditional kind of
comedy, which develops both elements, and from romance,
which primarily satisfies justice. Of course, the reader must not
be allowed to get the impression that the crucial ugliness or inferiority reflected by the injustice is a threatening evil; hence the
need for an "underlying justice," although this does not provide
a positive punitive satisfaction in its own right.

No early story is classified as primarily caustic. The closest
approach to the caustic quality in the early period is a stringency

in certain of those objective comedies containing an element of
unsatisfied justice, such as Mrs. Wharton's "Autres Temps," Mrs.
Gerould's "The Weaker Vessel," and some of James's comedies,
especially those in which the comeuppance is incomplete, as in
"Europe." The Jamesian characteristic of discomfiting the reader
by raising the "level" of the comedy so as to force him to see absurdity in a character with whom he would like to sympathize
is also a caustic element in a dominantly comic effect.

In the twenties, on the other hand, the caustic effect is the
dominant one in almost half of the non-painful stories in the
canon. It appears in its purest form in Hemingway's "The Doctor and the Doctor's Wife," "Out of Season," "Mr. and Mrs.
Elliot," "A Very Short Story," and "A Simple Enquiry." The
temptation is to speak of these as more or less "nasty" in effect
(as Philip Young did when he characterized "Mr. and Mrs. Elliot" as "amusing but rather nasty")[2] or to describe the effect as
"contempt." It is, of course, a kind of contempt that gives pleasure. Among the stories just mentioned, the effect is probably
most contemptuous in "Mr. and Mrs. Elliot" and "Out of Season," both dealing with hypocritical and baffled prigs. "The
Doctor and the Doctor's Wife," on the other hand, as also perhaps "A Very Short Story," pushes more closely to the serious
and pathetic, since other characters besides the protagonist contribute to his discomfiture: there is no question in the former
story, for instance, that the doctor's own vanity and hypocrisy
are exceeded by those of his wife. In "A Very Short Story" the
hero is cruelly jilted by his fiancée. Yet the final stress is not on
his suffering but on his vanity: this, surely, is the effect of the
final sentence which curtly informs us that he has contracted
venereal disease from a shopgirl, a sordid misfortune that we
cannot help thinking he has brought upon himself through self-
pity. The pathetic element makes the character sufficiently interesting for us to enjoy our contempt; the hero's self-pity is a
function of the sexual vanity, which is the primary source of the
reader's contempt.

All of these stories except "Mr. and Mrs. Elliot" are episodes

[2] Philip Young, *Ernest Hemingway* ("Rinehart Critical Studies"; New York:
Rinehart & Co., 1952), p. 1.

of choice. The latter, a story of sexual failure in marriage, is more properly described as having a plot of choice reiterated through changing circumstances: even after the failure in the marriage, the couple refuses to acknowledge that there is anything wrong with their attitudes. The failures in the other stories do not change the circumstances sufficiently to alter the nature of the protagonist's reiterated choice.[3] They function, rather, simply to reveal that nature, which becomes most clear in the display of the character's bafflement. In each case the choice involves a discrepancy between a character's pretensions and his actual behavior or motives, usually involving sex and caused by his cowardice or timidity. In "A Simple Enquiry" the protagonist is implicitly homosexual; what makes the story caustic is the over-simplifying attitude he brings to emotional problems. He is an Italian major who tries to find out if his orderly is homosexual by questioning him directly. He is relieved by the orderly's denial, because "life in the army was too complicated," but at the end realizes that his inquiry has not solved anything: "The little devil, he thought, I wonder if he lied to me." The crucial caustic element here is not so much the exposure of the major's ill-concealed approach to the boy as the way in which the major's tired longing for simplicity in human relations blunts his purposes and exposes him to embarrassment — behavior that is ridiculous because he is scarcely aware of its futility.

Although the simple caustic effect is characteristic of Hemingway's stories, more commonly among the work of writers of the twenties the caustic effect is modified in some way. In a few stories with plots and episodes of choice (like those just discussed) a sympathetic quality in the hero so mitigates the dominant caustic effect as to justify our terming them "caustic

[3] These failures are signs of the choice: the doctor bottles up his anger; the young sportsman in "Out of Season" gives up his attempt to fish out of season because he lacks the courage to be the kind of man he would like to be. All of these episodes of choice, except "A Very Short Story," deal with a single incident. In the latter, the episode involves the protagonist's reaction after being jilted; this reaction is summed up very briefly in one indirect statement of action at the end of the story. The preceding part of the story is devoted to dramatizing the situation prior to the jilting and summarizing the jilting itself. The brief narrative treatment of the "change" involved in the jilting minimizes the effect of this change *as* change and throws emphasis on what is unchanged in the protagonist's situation between beginning and end.

romances," self-contradictory as this term may seem. These stories — notably, initiation stories such as Anderson's "An Awakening" and "I Want to Know Why" and perhaps Hemingway's "The End of Something," as well as stories of needless self-destruction such as Faulkner's "Victory" and "Red Leaves" — resemble certain romantic comedies characteristic of the twenties: initiation stories such as "The Three-Day Blow" and Faulknerian stories of romantic absurdity such as "Hair" (see above, pp. 200–202). They differ from such romantic comedies in that the mitigating romantic element is not sufficient to justify the absurdity; although the reader is made to admire the innocence, the idealism, the courage, or the determination of the protagonist, this admiration is forced to yield to a caustic perception of insufficiently corrected or punished inferiority. As in the simpler caustic stories, the caustic effect is produced by a demonstration of the needless way in which the protagonist's vanity or ignorance makes him suffer. Pity is diminished as the hero's tendency to embrace his own suffering becomes apparent. The romantic quality enriches the caustic effect by adding to the discomfiture of the reader's sympathies when the caustic quality becomes clear.

In both romantic-comic and romantic-caustic initiation stories, the young hero, exposed to the unpleasant realities of life, fails to achieve a mature understanding of them. The reader understands the situation much better than the protagonist does; the inferiority of the latter is measured by this insufficiency in his understanding. But in a romantic comedy such as "Ten Indians" or "I'm a Fool" the child's innocence and natural healthiness soften his suffering, whereas in caustic romances such as "An Awakening" and "I Want to Know Why" they play only a negative part: the hero cannot be consoled. Similarly, the hero of "Hair" or "All the Dead Pilots" is motivated by such a passion as to mitigate or even eliminate any apparent suffering, whereas the intense "romantic" passion of a story such as "Victory" provides no compensation and leaves the hero miserable.[4]

[4] The general difference between the caustic romance and the romantic comedy may be the destructiveness of the hero's choice in the caustic romance.

Faulkner's "Red Leaves" is also classified as a caustic romance, although the hero is more resigned to his fate than is the hero of "Victory." This resigna-

The most common non-painful stories in the twenties are not such relatively simple caustic stories and caustic romances as those just discussed, but a group that may be called "caustic comedies." Like the simple caustic stories, these give pleasure primarily through a ridiculous violation of justice, which here too lies in the uncorrected or unpunished assertion of an ugly or inferior element. The difference is that the ugly element, instead of being a needless vulnerability to suffering caused by vanity, is a failure to recognize the presence of misfortune or evil. This failure is contemptible — in contrast to the admirable accommodations of many earlier romantic heroes — because it issues from deficiencies of character, traits of weakness, cowardice, stupidity, or moral blindness, which provoke a punitive desire on the reader's part. The failure of the action to satisfy this punitive desire is the basis of the caustic effect. Such stories are rendered painless in a variety of ways.

In one story — Hemingway's "A Canary for One" — the protagonist does harm to others without being aware of it. The story deals with a mother who has prevented her daughter from making a desirable marriage. Her motive is not malice but stupidity; she means well by her actions and cannot understand the injury she is causing. The story is an episode in which she inadvertently exposes her folly to a stranger on a train (the narrator). The episode distances the misfortune she causes by concentrating on the folly of her misconception.[5]

tion is not comparable to the great indifference that is shown by the heroes of such "romantic comedies" as "All the Dead Pilots" and "Hair." "Red Leaves" concerns the childlike dependence of a slave upon his environment and upon the traditions which prevent him from carrying through his intended (and very easy) escape from the ritual death that his society has ordained for him. It is caustic by virtue of the needless destruction involved in his death, yet the inconsistency of the hero and the emphasis not on his suffering but on his peculiar way of pursuing his "objectives" keep the story from being truly painful or pathetic.

[5] The last sentence reveals that the narrator himself is preparing for a divorce. His own difficulties point up still more vividly the mother's simpleminded view of human relationships; and the fact that the narrator is an American makes an ironic comment on the mother's belief that "Americans make the best husbands."

[6] The prize fighter in "Fifty Grand" agrees to throw a fight in exchange for a bribe which will enable him to retire from the ring and settle down. During the fight he discovers that his opponent is also determined to throw the fight — that he has been double-crossed by the crooks with whom he has made his deal. The opponent, attempting to lose the fight, fouls him; the hero, equally

5

In three stories—Fitzgerald's "Dalyrimple Goes Wrong,"
Hemingway's "Fifty Grand," and Faulkner's "A Justice"—the
protagonist does intentional harm to others. All have plots of
conspicuously undeserved good fortune: the burglar gets
elected to Congress; the prizefighter double-crosses the public;[6]
the murderer and terrorist sets himself up as a just and wise
ruler. Their victories are rendered painless by the failure of
those who have been cheated to realize that they have been
cheated: the ultimate absurdity is theirs, not that of the protagonists. These stories differ from such an earlier sympathetic comedy of good fortune as "Mrs. Medwin," since the protagonists
are morally inferior to the society they defeat—this is what
makes the victory seem undeserved. Rascal defeats fool: it is
the pattern of the true rogue story, differing from the classic
pattern (and becoming caustic thereby) mainly in its lack of a
final comeuppance for the rogue. In such stories, as the world is
discomfited so is the reader. Yet the exposure of the world's
failure has a typical caustic underlying justice: if the world is
unable to appreciate that it is being hoodwinked, it deserves to
be. This, on a secondary level, tends to make the rogue somewhat sympathetic, even romantic, a quality implicit in the very
word "rogue," enhancing the essential caustic effect.[7]

Most of the caustic comedies of the twenties are stories in
which a character is indifferent to the harm he does himself or
blind to his own misfortune. The unsatisfied punitive desire—
source of the caustic effect—is the desire that the protagonist
recognize his misfortune or acknowledge the suffering appropriate to his situation. It is rendered non-painful by the fact that
no one in the story is aware of harm in this behavior, as a result
of which pity and fear are precluded. The "underlying justice,"
in other words, is that the protagonist deserves the worst that he

---

determined to lose, musters sufficient courage and strength to foul his opponent
in return, thereby winning the fortune he had been hoping for. His victory
is an "immoral" one—hence the caustic effect. The story, however, has a more
strongly sympathetic and romantic quality than do the other rogue stories named
here because the defeated crooks are more depraved than the prize fighter and
because his desire to win his fortune is so intensely and even courageously
pursued.
[7] The caustic quality noted in Mrs. Gerould's "Pearls" (p. 197) is closer
to that of the rogue stories than to that of any of the other common caustic forms.

is getting because he is not aware that it is bad. As has been said, this ignorance arises from deficiencies rather than from virtues of character.

The stories of this kind fall into two groups. In one, which includes such episodes of choice as Anderson's "The Man Who Became a Woman" and "Nobody Knows," Fitzgerald's "The Baby Party" and "The Rough Crossing," and Miss Porter's "Rope," the protagonist denies the existence of a problem (usually marital or sexual) which actually exists and which, if acknowledged, would make him suffer. The episode in each story first manifests an eruption of the problem and then ends with a demonstration of the character's effort to deny its existence. The nature of such problems and the manner of their denials have been discussed in an earlier chapter.[8] The effect is non-painful because the character's refusal to suffer precludes pity and caustic because the refusal reflects emotional cowardice; we judge it cowardly rather than courageous because it offers no permanent solution but is all too clearly an evasion of what clearly remains as a potential source of suffering.[9]

The second group consists of stories with plots of choice such as Anderson's "Out of Nowhere Into Nothing," Fitzgerald's "Benediction" and "The Rich Boy," and Miss Porter's "That Tree."[10] The distinctive and caustic feature of the final choice here is that the protagonist deliberately and wilfully ignores the suffering that this choice is almost certain to bring. In the first two stories, in both of which the protagonist decides to embark on an unpromising love affair, there is what is probably an intentional romantic element that slightly modifies the effect: the unwise decision shows courage in the heroine's determination to have love at any cost. Yet the reader cannot avoid seeing in this courage a shortsighted desperation and indifference to ultimate consequences which precludes much pity and hence much real

[8] See especially, pp. 71, 77, 138.
[9] The caustic quality noted (p. 197) in Mrs. Freeman's "New England Nun" is more like that described here than that of the other caustic forms.
[10] "Out of Nowhere into Nothing" and "Benediction" are dilemma-choice plots (see p. 260). Fitzgerald's "Rich Boy" is a reiteration of choice after circumstances have changed. Porter's "That Tree" is a change of attitude in which a certain basic error (the protagonist's tie to his wife and his belief that he can please her and yet maintain his integrity) is reiterated.

admiration of the choice. In "The Rich Boy" and "That Tree"
the romantic element is less marked, since the significant choice
involves, not courage, but a surrender to weakness, to the deepseated vanity or need which prevents the character in the one
case from facing the realities of his situation, in the other from
upholding his principles, and in both from profiting by his
experiences.

What relates the caustic comedies more closely than the
other caustic forms to traditional objective comedy is the
stronger and less equivocal nature of the underlying justice that
makes the story non-painful. Although the basic caustic element
— the display of absurdity in an unpunished or uncorrected evil
— remains undiminished, the absence of suffering means that
there is less discomfiture for us in judging the action ridiculous
than there is when we must decide that the suffering is deserved
(as in the simple caustic stories). The comic quality in the
effect arises, most probably, from some secondary punitive satisfaction that we get simply from passing this judgment on the
absurdity of the action.

Thus, we see that the chief contributions of the writers of
the twenties to the art of the non-painful American short story
are the development of caustic effects — effects which give less
satisfaction to the reader's demand for easy justice than romance
and traditional comedy — and of romantic and comic effects discomfiting to the reader — effects to be seen in such stories as
"The Undefeated" and many of Faulkner's stories of wild, irrational heroism, requiring the reader to revise his conventional
ideas of what is good and sensible in order to admire the virtues
that are placed before him. The easy sentimental romantic comedy and the sentimental or didactic romance which functions
(like "Wesendonck") to confirm the reader's settled moral views
are rejected; the writers of the twenties are scrupulous in their
attempt to avoid giving pleasure by flattering the reader.

It must be said, though, that in rejecting the dominant non-
painful forms of the early period, the writers of the twenties
turned their backs not only on what was weak and ineffective
in the early canon but also on what was best. The highest
achievements of the early period were, almost certainly, the

fully developed comedies — especially those of James, although Mrs. Wharton was also very effective in these forms. The writers of the twenties have nothing to offer that is quite comparable. The caustic effect of the twenties is a "curtailed" comic effect; while effectively attained in episodes, it falls short of what a fully developed Jamesian comic plot can give. In James's stories one finds the same elements that most sharply distinguish the non-painful stories of the twenties from their run-of-the-mill predecessors — the same implications of seriousness and the same tendency to disturb the reader's moral complacency — and they make James's effects as rich and complex as those of the twenties. In addition, the Jamesian stories, in their larger actions, provide a more nearly complete satisfaction of the reader's demands for justice and comic pleasure than is achieved in the twenties in all but a few of the very best stories by Faulkner and Miss Porter. The primary contributions of the writers of the twenties, on the other hand, are in the painful or serious forms.

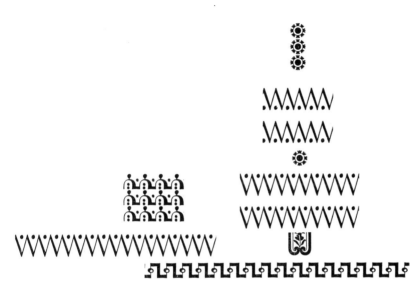

XIV: TRAGEDY AND PATHOS

Comedies, romances, and caustic stories account for a little
more than half of the stories in the canon of the twenties.
Though slightly more numerous, they are less significant than
painful stories for two reasons: first, they have lost in numbers
whereas the painful stories have gained, and second, they form
a less homogeneous group, displaying a broader diversity of occasional forms covering a wider spectrum of effects than do the
painful stories. The major tendencies noted in the non-painful
stories, furthermore, reflect tendencies that are seen more clearly
and far more consistently in the painful stories. The heart of
the new movement of the twenties is in its painful stories.

Though not wholly satisfactory, the term "painful" is less
ambiguous than "serious" and less misleading than the more
specific term "tragic." It is applied to stories whose primary

217

effect is an involvement of the reader's emotions painfully in the imitation of evil, misfortune, or suffering. The reader is sufficiently identified with the agents in the story (although not necessarily the protagonist or even specific individuals) to suffer vicariously, the suffering taking the form of such various emotions as pity, fear, horror, and indignation. The distinction between such emotions and those of the comedies, romances, and caustic stories is usually perfectly obvious; in stories where it is not obvious, the classification is based, as has been demonstrated in the foregoing analyses, upon the final effect — upon whether the painful element exists primarily to enhance the pleasure of the effect of justice, vindication, or absurdity or is developed for its own sake.

The aesthetic pleasure of a painful story depends upon the purgation or catharsis of painful emotions that have been developed to the maximum. The pleasure of such a catharsis differs from the direct pleasure of comedy or romance in that it is caused most essentially, apparently, not by the removal of evil in the action but by our recognition that the action is an imitation — that the experience is aesthetic, not "actual." This does not mean that any attempt to imitate a painful object will automatically produce a satisfactory catharsis. Our emotional involvement must terminate once we perceive the whole form of the story; otherwise we have the unpleasant and inartistic effect that Croce called "feeling in its immediacy." The termination requires some sort of settling, some sort of disposition of the painful elements in the action; they must be checked or stabilized in some way. This checking or stabilizing is not a thwarting of evil, a positive conquest of the bad in situation or character, as in a romance, but merely the reassertion of an appropriate state of order or justice after the complete fulfilment or exhaustion of the evil source.

Only three early writers — Bierce, Dreiser, and Miss Cather — are more consistently "serious" in this sense than otherwise. The others are all far more commonly non-painful. In the twenties, by contrast, only Fitzgerald is less commonly painful than not; Miss Porter and Faulkner strike a fairly even balance; in Hemingway painful effects are somewhat more and in Anderson much more common than non-painful ones. The new painful forms are, furthermore, strikingly and significantly different from those that were popular earlier. The latter fall into a few clearly distinguishable categories, most of which were the specialty of one author or a small group of authors — for example, the horror stories of Bierce. No particular kind of painful story was common to any large group among the earlier writers. In the twenties, on the other hand, new and subtler forms are developed, and though writers continue to have specialties, each is related closely to the others by many common elements.

PAINFUL EFFECTS

In general, the stories of both periods involve the reader painfully in either or both of two ways. On the one hand, the reader's moral sense may be painfully aroused by the spectacle of injustice. He recognizes that the victim of misfortune has a moral or just cause and suffers vicariously when the victim's deserts are ignored; he feels this while remaining otherwise detached from or superior to this victim, since he is aware of the difference in circumstances and character between the victim and himself. On the other hand, the reader may be painfully affected through his perception of likeness in character or situation between the victim of misfortune and himself; in this case, he feels a threat to his security, his well-being, his complacency, arising from his direct identification with the victim.

These two kinds of painful effects correspond, of course, to the two emotions that Aristotle identified as the components of the tragic effect: pity and fear. Critics have objected to the barren "narrowness" of these terms to describe the rich emotional content of the tragedies in our heritage. As has been pointed out, they refer to categories of feeling rather than to specific feelings. They signify merely the two ways in which the reader of a tragedy becomes painfully involved in the subject: the moral involvement, which is detached, and the intimate identification, which is not detached.

That the painful stories of both periods produce feelings of pity and fear does not mean that they are tragic in Aristotle's sense — that they produce a fully developed catharsis of both

emotions. A few, perhaps, do. Most subordinate one component
to the other, developing a strong effect of pity with little fear
or a strong effect of fear with little pity. The catharses vary
accordingly.

Three general types are distinguishable in our stories — the
story of pity, the story of fear, and the tragic story that combines
pity and fear. The fundamental differences between them can
be seen most clearly in three examples from the early period,
where the effects tend to be less complex than in the twenties.
The tragic combination can be illustrated in miniature by such
a story as Bierce's "One Kind of Officer." The story deals with
an officer of the Civil War who in foggy weather is commanded
by his general to bombard any troops that appear in front of
his position. It is clear at the beginning that he has tried to argue
with this order, but he is told, "'Captain Ransome, it is not permitted to you to know *anything*. It is sufficient that you obey my
order. . . .'" Thus, when troops are detected in front of the position, Ransome's battery begins firing. After a time his lieutenant protests, but Ransome says to him the same words the
general had uttered to him. At the end of the battle it is revealed
that the troops that have been attacked belong to his own side;
in the investigation that immediately follows, Ransome admits
that he knew this but supposed that it was none of his business.
He refers to the general who had given the order, but the general
is dead. He calls then upon the lieutenant who had heard the
order given, but the lieutenant (probably angered by his own
rebuke) denies all knowledge. Recognizing that he is without
defense, Ransome gives up his sword and prepares for execution.

The story contains in brief form many of the essentials of
classic tragedy; the captain, hitherto an admirable officer, suffers
a great disaster, a great loss of fortune, brought about by his
own error, which springs from a defect in his character. The
error is his insistence in carrying out orders despite his knowledge that they are mistaken and reflects the angry pride that has
been insulted by the general. The conclusion involves his discovery of this error, which comes about when the lieutenant fails
to support him; although the full content of the discovery is not
explicit, the reader can infer from the dignity of his surrender

that he recognizes the falsity of his moral position. The discovery follows the disaster and functions as discovery in tragedy usually does — to maximize the disaster by making the protagonist fully aware of what it is and to redeem the character in the reader's eyes by making him aware of what we have known, thus to make possible tragic stature on his part. This recovery of full moral stature in misfortune provides catharsis by terminating the fear and justifying the pity the reader feels for him. Once the misfortune has run its course, the hero is able to obtain the best possible outcome that is left to him: knowledge and dignity in surrender.

The alternatives to this tragic combination in the stories of both periods differ from the tragic primarily in their lack of a comparable tragic discovery. This is highly significant in that it "limits" the catharsis or, to put it more accurately, leads to the maximizing of one rather than both of the emotions of pity and fear, whose catharsis is then achieved in a different way.

The kind of story that develops pity with little fear — what may be called the story of pathos — can be illustrated in simple form by Dreiser's "The Lost Phoebe." The story deals with an old man in a rural community whose wife has died. Because of this, he feels lost. Gradually his mind begins to go; he forgets that she is dead and imagines that she has merely gone away for a time. He begins to roam the countryside looking for her, asking all his neighbors each day if they have seen her. Finally, one day, he has a vision of her; going forth to meet her, he plunges to his death off a cliff. As with tragedy, this story deals with misfortune and suffering caused in part by the error of the protagonist. This error is essentially a kind of overdependence upon his wife, which makes it impossible for him to cope rationally with existence after her death. In contrast to tragedy, there is no discovery of this error. The error lowers the stature of the hero — it makes him in a sense, inferior to us, the readers, since we can see very clearly things he does not see. The error is such, and the plot is so constructed, as to maximize the pity — the effect of undeserved misfortune — and minimize the effect of destructive evil. For though the error prevents him from coping with his misfortune, we are more struck with the suffering he endures than with his own blame for that suffering. This effect is enhanced by our awareness that his misfortune is the result, primarily, of external forces: not merely the natural death of his wife but his own frailty — his senility — for which he can hardly be held morally responsible. Thus, even as we recognize the difference between him and us, even as we feel safe and secure and superior to him, we suffer pity on his behalf. The pity is greatest at the end, when we see him take one further and fatal step into the fantasy caused by his suffering. The catharsis, in this case, is in the relief provided by our realization that his suffering is over and that he thought, at the end, that he was happy. As will be seen, this is a more elaborate catharsis (possessing a more romantic coloration) than is usual in such stories; more commonly the catharsis of a pathetic story is achieved simply through our final recognition that the pity we are disposed to give is justified. It results, that is to say, from the elimination of fear or negative feelings we may have had about the protagonist; it depends upon that detachment which is characteristic of unmixed pity, whereby our own security is enhanced by our ability to pity others.

The story that develops fear with little pity may be illustrated in extreme form by Bierce's "A Horseman in the Sky." A soldier in the Civil War has enlisted on the opposite side from his father. While on sentry duty, he shoots an enemy officer whom he had noticed on horseback observing the site of his camp. The officer has a spectacular death: the horse plunges with him over the cliff. The story concludes with the return of the sentry to camp. His sergeant asks him about the horseman's death; the soldier quietly informs him that the horseman was his own father. The reader of the story no doubt pities the sentry for being placed in a predicament where he had to make such a choice. The pity, however, is secondary. Far more important is an element stressed by the organization of the narrative: the astonishing choice that the sentry has made, the nature of which, though prepared for by the narrative, is not revealed until the final lines — the choice to kill his father rather than shirk his military duty. The reader finds such a choice perverse and unnatural, and the perversity is emphasized by the seemingly calm manner in which the soldier makes his choice. The effect is fear turning to horror — fear being what we feel in the expectation of destructive evil, horror being what we feel when confronted with its materialization. Both of these emotions result from our initial identification with the protagonist; the catharsis, which occurs when the fear turns to horror, comes about through the abrupt and final termination of this identification — through our moral recoil from the protagonist when we see what he has done.

These three examples display what appear to be the more useful differentiae for distinguishing major differences among the painful stories of the two periods. The discovery of disastrous error, with the recovery of stature implicit in it, provides the fundamental distinction between the tragic hero and the heroes of stories of pathos and fear. The story of pathos in general deals with a hero whose misfortune seems more clearly undeserved as the story proceeds; the final catharsis is the detachment that enables the reader to pity him securely. The story of fear or horror in general moves in an opposite direction: the reader, by his identification in the action (either with the protagonist or, if the protagonist is evil, with his victims), is brought face to face with destructive evil; the final catharsis comes about through his recoil from this evil, through the severance of identification.

TRAGEDY

Changes between the two periods may be seen by considering each of these three types separately. The rarest is tragedy. Except for "One Kind of Officer," only Mrs. Wharton's "The Choice" shows the pattern that seems to be necessary for a fully tragic effect: a real disaster or loss of fortune caused by an error, followed by a discovery, too late, of the error. In "The Choice," the heroine and her lover are tempted to kill the heroine's husband when he draws near the boathouse where they are talking. They set a trap into which he falls, and the lover then attempts to rescue him. Faced with a choice of saving lover or husband, the heroine saves her husband. The disaster is the death of her lover, who had been the only consolation in her unhappy marriage; the discovery is her recognition that she cannot be a murderess, expressed by her decision to save the husband first. The story ends with a remark by the husband pointing up the irony of the misfortune:

"Poor Austin! Poor Wrayford . . . terrible loss to me . . . mysterious dispensation. Yes, I do feel gratitude — miraculous escape — but I wish old Austin could have known that I was saved!"

In the twenties there are no tragedies, no stories approximating the formula used here. As will be seen, two general features of construction prevent situations of misfortune and suffering from becoming fully tragic in the stories of the twenties. One has already been noted: the universal absence of a full discovery of error by the protagonist. The other is the widespread avoidance of plots of real loss of fortune: the preference for episodes without significant change prevents a full development of pity and fear with a catharsis of these emotions.

This does not mean that in a looser and more popular sense of the term there are no tragedies among these stories, but the strict definition is valuable in enabling us to perceive more accurately the significant differences between the painful forms that do exist and to describe more precisely their characteristics and effects. Thus, in the early period, more especially, the actions of several stories approximate what is generally considered tragic — Crane's "Maggie: A Girl of the Streets," Miss Cather's "Paul's Case," Bierce's "The Story of a Conscience," Mrs. Wharton's "Bunner Sisters." Their deviations from the strictly tragic are more important to the purposes of this study.

PATHOS

A pathetic story has been defined as one that produces pity with little fear. We feel that the protagonist's misfortune is undeserved, but we are sufficiently detached from him not to feel in his fate a threat to our own well-being.

In the early period, only eleven stories have been classified as dominantly pathetic. This is a small number, but it acquires significance from the fact that these eleven are distributed among six writers, with only Bierce, James, and Mrs. Gerould unrepresented. In the twenties, pathetic stories number twenty-three — almost a quarter of the canon — all but four by one writer, Anderson. Hence the primary significance of the pathetic

forms in the canon of the twenties depends upon the significance
of Anderson in the new movement. In his work pathetic stories
are far more common than is any other kind.

Romantic Pathos

The pathetic stories in the early period tend to differ from
those of the twenties in two major respects. They have a strong
romantic element lacking in most typical pathetic stories of the
twenties, and they are likely to be stories of plot, whereas those
of the twenties are mostly episodes.

The early stories of romantic pathos are of two kinds. Some,
like "The Lost Phoebe," have plots of misfortune. The dominant
action is a movement from potential if not actual happiness into
an irredeemable misfortune or disaster. In most cases, the beginning itself is not particularly happy: the old man in "The Lost
Phoebe" has lost his wife; the old man in Mrs. Freeman's "A
Village Lear" is ignored and rejected by his daughters; the girl
in Crane's "Maggie: A Girl of the Streets" lives in an intolerable
slum society. The misfortune varies in complexity and in the
depth of suffering endured: the heroes of "The Lost Phoebe"
and "A Village Lear" die while experiencing an hallucination of
the happiness and love that they have lost; the heroine of "Bunner Sisters," an old lady, loses her sister and faces loneliness and
hopeless poverty; the heroine of "Maggie," who has been driven
to prostitution by her misfortunes, commits suicide. By contrast,
the misfortune suffered in Garland's "Under the Lion's Paw" is
relatively mild; a farmer who has been struggling to become the
owner of his own farm is cheated by a usurous landlord and faces
the total defeat of his hope.

The misfortune comes about in a variety of ways. In "Bunner
Sisters," "Maggie," and "Under the Lion's Paw," the action is
started by the protagonist, who makes a move intended to improve his situation. His act, though his motives are worthy, is a
mistake — in each case he trusts someone too much — and leads
to a sequence of events culminating in his downfall. The protagonists of "A Village Lear" and "The Lost Phoebe" are passive
victims. The essential sequence here is not a causal chain of
developing consequences but a gradual intensification of the

suffering that they endure in their situations. Although death is the outcome of this suffering in "The Lost Phoebe," in "A Village Lear" death comes from natural causes and is significant not as the final outcome of the plot but as a complication that brings the hero's suffering (on his deathbed) to a maximum. In one important respect, even the protagonists of these two stories are guilty of "error" and cause their own misfortunes — an error that is expressed not through a decisive act, as in "Bunner Sisters," but through a pattern of continuing behavior. The error in this sense is the vulnerability, the excessive dependence that makes both old men unable to cope with the situations that face them. It is a moral and psychological error that causes the character to misinterpret and misevaluate the things that are happening to him. The same sort of error is revealed in "Maggie" after she discovers her initial mistake of eloping with a scoundrel; she is unable to cope with the situation that confronts her, with the result that the situation becomes increasingly intolerable.

The error is essential to the pathetic effect of these stories, for if there were no error, if these were stories of perfect innocence and goodness defeated by gratuitous evil, our attention would be absorbed by the spectacle of the triumph of evil, and we would feel primarily horror or, as Aristotle says on this point, shock. While the character is making his error, he is, in that crucial respect, inferior to the reader: this inferiority is an essential means toward that detachment without which we do not feel pity. At the same time and despite this inferiority, the misfortune in these stories emerges as worse than the inferiority deserves. The error itself is mild — there are many extenuating circumstances — whereas the consequences in suffering are intense. This in itself is enough to provoke pity, and in most cases the contrast between error and suffering is accentuated by the fact that other characters exploit or deny the protagonist without good reason. In all the stories in this group, there is thus a strong element of innocent victimization of the protagonist: he is a victim of slums, of usurers, of deceit, of neglect, of his own senility.

The developing misfortunes in these plots of misfortune undoubtedly also provoke some fear in the reader, thus giving the stories a "quasi-tragic" quality lacking in most other pathetic stories. The reader dreads the misfortune that seems to be approaching. These stories differ from full tragedy, however, in significant ways. The failure of the protagonist in most cases to discover his error means that the tragic fear can never be developed to its full potential. For tragic fear, as has been said, depends upon our intimate identification with the protagonist, whereby we dread the evil that threatens him. In a tragedy this identification will be greatest at the moment of discovery (which destroys the ignorance that had tended to separate us from the protagonist); at this moment the fear is materialized, whereby it may now be converted into horror and pity and be relieved at the same time. In the pathetic stories, the absence of discovery keeps us detached from the protagonist; the possible horror is not achieved, and the dominant effect remains simply pity. In "Bunner Sisters" and "Under the Lion's Paw," it is true, the protagonist does makes a discovery of his basic error. The discovery does not make these stories tragic, however. In "Bunner Sisters," the protagonist remains, even after discovery, too small and inferior a character for us to feel a sufficiently tragic fear or horror; she is, despite her goodness and innocence, too lacking in sophistication, passion, or intelligence for her error to be terrifying. In "Under the Lion's Paw," in which the protagonist's stature is greater, the misfortune itself is not sufficiently grave to provoke a sense of tragic horror, even though it provokes strong pity.

The romantic quality in these earlier pathetic stories becomes most clear when they are contrasted with the typical pathetic stories of the twenties, to be discussed below. Its source is a kind of negative goodness in the protagonist, visible chiefly in his response to his suffering: the reader becomes aware that, despite his ignorance, weakness, or inferiority, he is reacting to his suffering in the best possible way, and in this respect deserves our admiration. (This too serves to reduce our intimate identification with him.) In plots of misfortune, the romantic element is most significant at the end: the "catharsis" of the pity is provided by a kind of romantic satisfaction that remains after the misfortune has run its course. For at the end of each of these stories, as in most great tragedies, the hero is, in a sense, repaid for his suffering by the best possible remaining termination: an illusion of happiness as he dies, perhaps, or an affirmation of dignity in accepting his defeat, or, as in "Maggie," in her refusal to bear any longer the intolerably corrupt way of life forced upon her. Such endings relieve our pity by a fairly positive manifestation of final justice done to the goodness of the protagonist, which, of course, is a romantic effect.

The remaining stories of romantic pathos in the early period are all episodes of discovery. Two of these, Garland's "Up the Coolly" and Crane's "An Experiment in Misery," are "generalized discoveries" — a kind of construction, rare in the early period, that was to become far more important in the twenties, when it was used ordinarily to produce effects quite different from those achieved by Garland and Crane. These two stories are, then, more appropriately discussed below in connection with other generalized discoveries.[1] The other two episodes of discovery are Miss Cather's "A Death in the Desert" and "A Wagner Matinee," each of which, like most episodes of discovery,[2] deals with an episode in the life of the protagonist that brings no permanent change in his situation or even his attitude or knowledge of his situation. The event, rather, has the effect simply of focusing the protagonist's attention more strongly than usual upon what he has lost or failed to win, thus sharpening for a time the suffering he feels. The episode is, in a sense, a "re-discovery" of his situation.

For the reader, the action of the episode, the protagonist's re-discovery, has the effect of revealing to us the nature and source of his suffering in his fixed situation at a moment when this nature and source are most in evidence. The story does not produce, of course, the effect of fear of impending misfortune that is produced by plots of misfortune; it simply develops pity as the undeserved suffering becomes more and more clear. The basic ingredients of this pity are much the same as in the more complex plots: the suffering is made possible by a weakness, a vulnerability, a mild deficiency sufficient to detach us from the most intimate identification, and yet it strikingly exceeds any-

[1] See pp. 254, n. 13, and pp. 254–58.
[2] See p. 193, n. 14, and pp. 251–52, 254–58.

thing that such a deficiency would make us wish upon the character. As in the more complex stories, the catharsis has a romantic quality, although it cannot here involve any termination of the misfortune (an episode, by definition, brings no permanent change). What we see at the end is that the character responds well to his suffering; our appreciation of this undoubtedly provides a certain romantic vindication of our feelings which is sufficient to take the edge off, or the painfulness out of, our pity.

Not more than two stories in the twenties seem clearly classifiable as romantic pathos. One of these — Anderson's "Unused" — is the only full-fledged plot of misfortune in stories of the period. It is somewhat comparable to Crane's "Maggie" in its over-all construction as well as in certain important aspects of its subject matter, and though its heroine's deficiency — her inability to cope with her situation — is more marked than Maggie's, the final effect is similar. The story is not only uncharacteristic of the period, but also, unfortunately, one of Anderson's least successful stories, marred by a lack of economy, a deficiency in probability and characterization, and a failure to dramatize some of the important elements upon which the effect depends. The other — Anderson's "Paper Pills" — is more conveniently discussed in another place.[3]

Caustic Pathos

The distinctive nature of the pathetic effect in the twenties can be illustrated in fairly extreme form by Anderson's "Respectability." The story begins with an account of Wash Williams in Winesburg — sloppy, dirty, full of hatred for women. Then he tells George his history — how he once idolized a woman, his wife, who was unfaithful to him, and how he sent her away when he discovered her infidelity. It was not this that made him bitter, for he still loved her and was willing to take her back. But when she sent for him and he went to her, she made the mistake of entering naked the room where he waited. So infuriating was this to him that he tried to kill her mother, who had suggested to the girl this method of winning him back. He has loathed all women ever since.

[3] See p. 236.

The distinctive feature of such an episode is that it moves from a display of what is ugly or grotesque in a character to a revelation of the depth of suffering that he endures. The effect is a far cry from the innocent pathos of "A Village Lear" or "The Lost Phoebe." The suffering is not the result of innocent weakness or vulnerability that makes the hero incapable of coping with external evils; it is, primarily, a function of his own moral character, of the perverse egotism and distorted feeling that make him idealize love impossibly and resent so bitterly any insult to his masculine dignity. These things not only make possible his suffering, as in the typical story of romantic pathos — they also provide for it. The moral distortion is evident from the start; the reader has to be shown why he should not feel contempt for this man. The picture of the moral distortion is maximized only at the end, when we take the full measure of the man's grotesque passion. But the final event has a more significant impact than this: it also succeeds in converting into pathos our original caustic or fearful or negative view of him. This it does by making clear the reasons for Wash's suffering. Perceiving them, we become aware that, for all Wash's faults, his suffering is greater than his errors morally deserve.

Such an effect may be called "caustic pathos," meaning that the final pity develops out of or transforms an initially antagonistic or caustic effect. The characters of such stories are more to blame for their sufferings than the heroes in the earlier stories of romantic pathos; the stories are so constructed to turn our attention away from their blame to whatever is most pitiable in the case.

In all but two of the caustic-pathetic stories of the twenties this is done through an episode rather than a plot,[4] most of which are of a kind that may be called "episodes of suffering." Like "Respectability," these complete the revelation of the protago-

[4] The exceptions are Anderson's "Death," a plot of choice involving a change in attitude brought about by the approach of death, and "Unlighted Lamps," which is probably best regarded as a discovery plot with a double protagonist. In the former story the change in attitude (the emergence of the heroine's death wish) does not affect her longing for love, which is simply reiterated in a different way. The reiteration is pathetic and relieves the caustic element in the heroine's previous situation. (See further description of this story, p. 70.) In "Unlighted Lamps" a father and daughter, in the face of death, make the discovery that

nist's misfortune by a demonstration of the depth of his suffering, but they differ from "Respectability" — which has a different sort of construction — in that this demonstration is accomplished by an actual change in the protagonist's way of expressing his suffering. This change, of course, is less significant for its own sake than as a sign of the constant suffering that he endures. It gives a beginning and end to the episode: the suffering itself is constant and is the primary object of interest.

Two different kinds of episodes of suffering are common in stories of the twenties. In the more complicated kind, the manner of expression changes twice. First, there is an eruption or explosion of uncharacteristic behavior in the protagonist — behavior reflecting suffering that he has been feeling for a long time. This is ultimately put down; the character returns to something like his previous way of life. Though superficial changes may result from the explosion, the inference is that the fundamental suffering remains.

Most of these eruptions are compulsive and irrational, true wellings-up of feeling; many of the most typical, such as those in Anderson's "The Teacher," "Adventure," "The Strength of God," and "The New Englander," are summed up elsewhere in these pages.[5] Also in this group are such stories as Anderson's

they have never properly expressed or understood the love of each for the other. The father dies; since the discovery is made too late for the misunderstanding to be retrieved, the effect is pathetic.

Only two early stories are considered to be stories of caustic pathos. Both of these — Crane's "Death and the Child" and Dreiser's "Free" — are plots of discovery. The protagonist of "Free" becomes aware of the fact that it is too late for his romantic fantasies to come true; the protagonist of "Death and the Child" becomes aware of the fact that he is a coward. Both are painful discoveries. The pathos in the former is obvious, but in the latter it depends upon the highly suggestive evocation in the final incident of the hero's shame, when a small child innocently asks him if he is a man.

[5] "The Teacher," see pp. 125–26, 399; "Adventure," see pp. 71, n. 13, 113; "Strength of God," see pp. 135, 143–44; "New Englander," see p. 71, n. 13. "Adventure" may be mentioned to illustrate the borderline between a plot of change and an episode. The narrative begins when the heroine, Alice, is engaged; it tells of her jilting, her gradual acceptance of that fact, her deepening loneliness and despair, before the final episode in which she appeals to a stranger for love. This could conceivably be described as a plot of changing attitudes — a plot of unconsciously motivated choice — precipitated by growing frustration. I prefer to regard it as an episode of suffering, since the final episode has the effect of illuminating and clarifying all that has gone before. It makes us see the various phases of her increasing despair as manifestations of a constant condition of

"Mother," in which Elizabeth Willard's hatred for her husband causes her to contemplate his murder; Anderson's "The Philosopher," in which Doctor Parcival is panicked by the unreasonable notion that the town is going to lynch him; and Miss Porter's "The Cracked Looking-Glass," in which the heroine's need for romance and love sends her on a futile trip to Boston to see a sister who isn't there and to flirt with a young man whose approaches she indignantly rejects.

In several of these stories, the conquest of the eruption gives the protagonist a feeling of emotional purgation — most marked in "The Strength of God" and "Mother." Even here, the indications are that the fundamental problem has not been solved when the eruption of feeling is stemmed; it has only been repressed; we still feel that the protagonist is fundamentally unhappy.[6] More often, the unresolved misery is quite obvious in the repression, as in Kate Swift's tears, Alice Hindman's resolution to "face bravely" her loneliness, Rosaleen O'Toole's plea to her aged husband after her return from Boston:

". . . if anything happened to you, whatever would become of me in this world?"

"Let's not think of it," said Dennis.

"Let's not, then," said Rosaleen. "For I could cry if you crooked a finger at me."[7]

In the simpler kind of episode of suffering, there is but one significant change in the expression of the protagonist's suffering. This may be a shift of a somewhat deranged character into a more obvious state of derangement, as when Elmer Cowley, in Anderson's "'Queer,'" concludes that he has proven his normality by slugging George Willard without provocation. More commonly, the change is a gesture by which the protagonist attempts to accommodate himself to his unhappy situation. The gesture

sexual frustration and suffering; emphasis shifts from the seemingly changing elements to the unchanging ones.

[6] The chief source of this judgment is, in "Strength of God," that the hero's explanation of his liberation, couched in mystical terms, does not show that he understands the reasons for his earlier behavior, even though his new fervor is perfectly sincere; the fervor itself strikes us as a sign of deep inner suffering. In "Mother," the heroine is inarticulate, unable to express her true feelings toward her son.

[7] Stories cited: Anderson, "Teacher," "Adventure"; Porter, "Cracked Looking-Glass."

of accommodation itself — or the need to make such a gesture — is the most poignant evidence of the character's suffering. In Anderson's "The Door of the Trap," "The Other Woman," and "Drink," it is the chief or only sign that suffering is present in a quiet, self-contained individual: a married man reveals his frustrations by kissing and then asking a student whom he has informally "adopted" to leave because she seems to tempt him; a man about to be married has a brief affair with another woman, regarding it as a kind of mystical experience that enables him to approach his marriage in a happier state of mind; a gentle boy, in whom childhood experiences have developed a fear of sex and love, tries to adjust himself to the repression of his natural impulses by going on a solitary drinking spree during which he has fantasies of love, his ostensible motive being to satisfy his curiosity once and for all. The reader infers the fear of life that makes him think he can be satisfied by this experiment.

The gestures function a little differently in Hemingway's "Up in Michigan" and "Soldier's Home" and in Miss Porter's "He," also episodes of suffering. Liz Coates covers with her coat her callous and rather brutal seducer, who is now asleep, and walks home alone in the cold — a poignant gesture making clear the tenderness of her feelings. Krebs, whose need for a simple, passive life is frustrated by his parent's expectations and demands (he has been "psychologically wounded" in the war), leaves home — an act that is his way of adjusting his basic good will toward his parents (his desire not to hurt, to please if possible) to the suffering that makes life with them intolerable. Mrs. Whipple tries to adjust to the problem of having an idiot son who is a burden to her and the family by sending him away to an institution; her tears and self-reproaches when she does so are evidence of the guilt she feels because of her repressed desires to be rid of him, conflicting with her conscious desire to love him as she thinks a true mother should.

In all of these episodes of suffering, of whatever kind, the writer must solve the problem of how to make the final manifestation of suffering sufficiently compelling to overcome the initial caustic or negative view of the character. What causes us to feel that Kate Swift's or Elmer Cowley's or Liz Coates's suffering is indeed worse than each deserves? The specific device seems to vary in the different constructions: in the stories of eruption, one feels that the termination, conquest, or suppression of the eruption has the effect of overcoming its horror and of liberating pity; in the stories of accommodating gestures, the attempt to adjust to suffering which the gesture reveals liberates pity; here, however, the initial caustic quality is usually less marked and is not itself clear until the gesture reveals the source of the character's suffering; in stories such as "Up in Michigan" and "Soldier's Home" the good intentions of the character as revealed in the final gesture have the same effect. In all cases, therefore, the final release of pity is provided for, apparently, by the unexpected emergence or clarification of some virtue in the protagonist at the very moment when his suffering is most clearly disclosed. In this respect these stories resemble the earlier stories of romantic pathos: the difference is that the virtue so brought out is generally less striking and obvious and that it has to counter a caustic or doubtful view of the character such as we did not feel in the earlier stories. The virtue indeed can be minimal; perhaps all that is needed to convert a caustic character into a pitiful one is the display in his suffering of just a little more goodness than we had previously seen in him.

This seems enough, also, to achieve a catharsis in such stories that is subtly but significantly different from that of most of the early stories of romantic pathos. In the early period, catharsis depended on the termination of misfortune or the emergence of fairly positive romantic satisfaction, both of which tended to *relieve* the pathos that had been developing in a fairly unqualified way throughout the story; in the story of caustic pathos, the emergence of pity is itself sufficient to produce catharsis. No doubt it is the presence of the caustic element in the preceding parts of the story that makes this possible — which causes us to feel an emotional completeness in the reversal of our feelings. The pathos at the end of such a story is a settled judgment, a relief because it is less threatening to us than the caustic or negative feelings that had been evoked previously.

A few episodes of caustic pathos — including "Respectability" — have a significantly different construction from that of the

episodes of suffering and indeed from most of the episodes of
any kind that have been thus far discussed. In the majority of
the episode stories of the twenties and nearly all those of the
early period, whatever the effects they produce, the illuminating
or unifying episode is itself an integral part of the situation
revealed, a direct manifestation of the situation. The protagonist
himself is at the center, acting, suffering, feeling. In such stories,
bystanders like George Willard, in "The Teacher," may appear
as part of the technical machinery enabling us to witness the
hero's behavior dramatically, but the central impetus in the
episode is either what the protagonist does or what happens to
him. Only a few stories deviate from this method and are unified
not by an episode featuring the protagonist but by one centering
in a bystander, who discovers, interprets, clarifies, or otherwise
responds to the protagonist's situation. The exposing episode is
itself not an integral part of the situation that it reveals but
exists for the sole purpose of revelation. Such stories may be
called "episodes of exposure." Other episodes thus far discussed
expose the situation by a manifestation of its essential elements
in action, but here the only action is the external exposure of
the protagonist's situation by or to the bystander: more than in
any other stories that have been considered, the machinery or
technique of representation provides the story's unity.

Although one caustic comedy and two celebrated horror
stories of the twenties may be included in this small but important group of episodes of exposure, most of the examples are
stories of caustic pathos like "Respectability." [8] Their construction varies considerably. In "Respectability" and "Loneliness" it
is quite simple: the episode centers in the protagonist's own
explanation to the bystander of the pertinent history that has
accounted for his present situation. Although his narrative may
in itself constitute a coherent action, its plot is not the story's
plot, since the suspense has been altered by the treatment of the
circumstances surrounding the narration. "Respectability" consists of two parts: first, an externalized representation of the

[8] Apart from those of caustic pathos, the episodes of exposure are, from the
early period, Miss Cather's "Sculptor's Funeral" (see p. 246); from the twenties,
Faulkner's "Mistral" (see p. 250) and Hemingway's "Killers" (pp. 249–50) and
"Canary for One" (p. 212).

protagonist's situation, then the interview between the protagonist and the bystander, who acquires a deeper understanding
of the protagonist's situation by learning its causes. In "Loneliness," to be sure, this two-part construction is not so clearly
defined, since the story begins with the narration of the past,
directly presented, and postpones the representation of the
present situation until the middle. But by the conclusion the
reader has become very much aware of George Willard as listener and of the hero's struggle to make his feelings clear; he
becomes aware of the act of exposure, of the hero's narrative as
an explanation of his feelings rather than as the account of an
organically whole or completed action.[9]

Anderson's "Seeds" and "Tandy" are variants of a different
kind of exposure episode. In these the illuminating episode does
not consist in the discovery by a bystander of the protagonist's
situation, although this may be a preliminary, but in the expression by a bystander of an explicit or implicit judgment of that
situation. "Tandy," which culminates in a sympathetic judgment
of the alcoholic hero, is a simple and unimpressive example.
"Seeds" is more complex, but also culminates in an indirect and
sympathetic judgment by two bystanders who recognize the
universality of the heroine's problem.

Closely related to the exposure episodes is Anderson's
"Hands," which, like the same author's story of romantic pathos,
"Paper Pills," might be called an "exposed situation."[10] Such a
story differs from an episode of exposure in that the bystander
virtually drops out or becomes one with the author. The narrative has no plot; the narrator juggles the chronology of the hero's

[9] Such stories differ from others in which the protagonist tells his story to a
bystander. In Anderson's "Philosopher" and Mrs. Wharton's "Quicksand," the
hero's narrative not only manifests suffering but also accounts for a later choice.
In Mrs. Wharton's "Long Run," the protagonist's narrative is the plot of the
story — essentially a plot of discovery, told in the first person. Preliminary dramatization is used to establish the proper kind of suspense, to shift emphasis from
the protagonist's misfortune to his discovery — his comeuppance. See p. 187, n. 11.

[10] Other exposed situations are those dramatized in Anderson's "Death in
the Woods" (see pp. 183–84), Faulkner's "Rose for Emily" (see p. 243), and, in
stories of the early period, James's "Greville Fane" and Bierce's "Occurrence at
Owl Creek Bridge" (see p. 243). "Greville Fane," "Death in the Woods," and
"Rose for Emily" are closer to exposure episodes than are the others, since the
narrator is a bystander — though his narrative is not organized according to a
chronological sequence of discovery.

life; nor is it a manifesting, integral episode. In "Hands" the order of presentation is essentially the same as in "Respectability": first there is an externalized depiction of the hero's situation, followed by a summary narrative of its causes. The only difference is that Wing, who has begun to talk to George, stops short in fear; then the author takes over and tells his story for him. This difference from the pattern of "Respectability" is a fairly minor one, a technical difference necessitated chiefly by the difference in Wing's character from that of Wash's rather than by a difference of unifying principle.

It is clear that in general the source of the caustic-pathetic effect in these exposure episodes and exposed situations is similar to that in the episodes of suffering. The use of a bystander makes even more striking the movement from the grotesque to the pitiful aspects of the hero's life. Pity is liberated by our increased understanding of the sources of suffering, which now seem to exceed what the protagonist deserves because we know of the goodness that has been thwarted. In "Tandy," to be sure, the method is a bit simpler and more direct: the little girl's expression of admiration for the drunkard replaces the investigation of the sources of his suffering: it tells us, in effect, that there is something to admire in him; if we believe this, then we will pity him. In "Seeds" the understanding of the sources of suffering is provided only partially by a history of the heroine's past; the most essential thing is the judgment by the bystanders that she is suffering from a universal kind of psychological sickness. In all cases, however, the result is the same. Pity replaces our negative feelings about the situation and, since it is a settled and detached judgment, relieves us of our painful emotional involvement.

XV: FEAR AND HORROR

A story of fear or horror has been defined in the preceding chapter as one that develops and fulfils the reader's fear of threatening evils. It depends upon the reader's intimate identification with agents in the action, but differs from the story of pathos in that fear gives way not to pity but to horror — to the appalled recognition that the feared evil has come to pass, is inescapable and triumphant. It differs from tragedy in that this horror, which in tragedy is mixed with or yields to pity, is itself the end, the only catharsis being our recoil from the horror, the termination of that identification upon which the horror depends.

In the early canon, although such stories are more numerous than are stories of pathos, they are not more significant or characteristic. The larger number is explained by the strong preference of Bierce for horror stories; among the other early writers, only

Crane, Dreiser, and Miss Cather produced important stories of this sort, and their evocation of horror is distinctively different from that of Bierce. Here, as in so many other respects, these three writers anticipate the developments of the twenties, when stories of fear and horror become by far the most important kind of painful story in the work of all writers except Anderson.

SIMPLE HORROR

"A Horseman in the Sky"—used in the preceding chapter to distinguish the horror story from other kinds—and most of Bierce's other horror stories possess a simpler, purer, and more obvious quality of horror than do other stories in the canon. They are thus uncharacteristic of either period. Yet they are not insignificant. Related to the horror tradition of Poe, which was important in the earlier history of the short story, they help us to measure the distance between the later, subtle kinds of horror and the more traditional kinds. They are useful in another way, too; their relative simplicity exposes vividly important mechanisms for the evocation of horror that are present in the later stories in a much less obvious way.

In Bierce's horror stories, the source of the horror may be either in the protagonist himself, as in "A Horseman in the Sky," or in the terrible fate that befalls him, for which he is not to blame. The former might be called "horror of character" or "moral horror," since it depends on a moral choice made by the protagonist; the latter might be called "sympathetic horror," since it depends on our sympathetic identification with the protagonist in his encounter with a dreadful evil external to himself.

With one exception,[1] all of Bierce's stories of moral horror

[1] The exception is Bierce's "One of the Missing," classified as a plot of misfortune. The final effect is not so purely and simply one of moral horror as it is in the other stories. The hero is caught in a trap (a collapsed house) with a gun pointing at his head. Unable to move, he becomes panic-stricken and at last contrives to kill himself. The story develops sympathetic horror (see discussion of sympathetic horror, below); the protagonist's breakdown converts this to moral horror. The total effect involves both the hero's final choice and the misfortune prior to this choice.

The story can be classified as simple horror rather than horror modified (see p. 244) because the character of the protagonist does not determine the initial misfortune. This contrasts with Cather's "Paul's Case," which has a plot of misfortune which arouses modified horror, and Hemingway's "Killers," where sympathetic horror becomes moral horror.

have plots of choice, even though they end, without exception, in disaster for the protagonist. The disaster is only the concrete sign of the protagonist's horrible choice, which is the primary thing: in stories such as "A Horseman in the Sky" and "Killed at Resaca," for example, the disaster is deliberately and knowingly chosen by the protagonist, who, in the former, kills his father with full knowledge and, in the latter, deliberately sacrifices himself in battle. In a story such as "Parker Adderson," the disaster is, in a sense, "given," and is a cause for the horrible choice: the protagonist here has been condemned to death at the beginning of the story, and his choice — the collapse of his indifference to death, his breakdown into cringing cowardice — follows. The choice itself may be any one of three kinds: it may be the solution to a dilemma, such as that which faces the sentry in "A Horseman in the Sky" or the captain in "The Affair at Coulter's Notch"; it may be a change in attitude under stress, such as the breakdown of Parker Adderson or that of the hero of "One Officer, One Man," who commits suicide because he cannot stand the terrors of his first night on the battlefield; or it may be a reiterated choice, as in "Killed at Resaca," in which the hero makes a continuing effort to get himself killed in order to prove his bravery — and is successful.

Each choice is horrible because it is perverse, unnatural, sharply deviant from what is normal, human, or good. To be sure, few of these choices are quite as monstrous as that of "A Horseman in the Sky." The most usual sort of perversity is self-destructiveness: destruction of those one loves, or of one's own life, or, as in "Parker Adderson," of one's dignity as a man. All the same, the spectacle of suicide is not necessarily sufficient to evoke in us a feeling of fear or horror — as the caustic stories have demonstrated. Bierce's stories evoke horror rather than contempt, partly because of the great magnitude and completeness of the self-destruction, partly — perhaps mainly — because we have been led to identify ourselves with the protagonist before his perversity is revealed. In all cases but "Parker Adderson," which is probably less effective as a story of horror, this sympathetic identification is maintained until the very end, at which point the horrible nature of the perverse act is abruptly disclosed. Indeed, in order not to destroy this identification too soon and thus mitigate the horror, the author may deliberately withhold crucial information — for example, by not telling us whom the sentry had shot or who was in the house bombarded by the captain until after he has described the performance of these acts. The intensity of the horror varies according to the kind of perversity involved: in "Killed at Resaca" and "One Officer, One Man" it issues from traits ordinarily fairly normal or natural — fear of one's first battle, or the desire to prove oneself to a scornful woman. In such cases, the horror of the excess to which these traits are carried is enhanced by something pitiful, something unjust, in the situation in which the character finds himself. We pity; this makes the horror of what he does to himself seem more important. The horror is felt at its most intense when an act of such terrible destructiveness as that of the captain in "The Affair at Coulter's Notch" is combined with vivid indications of the hero's suffering. This magnifies our awareness of his perversity. As has been suggested, the best general description of "catharsis," here a relief from horror, is that at the close of the story we recoil from the hero; we sever our identification with him.

In stories of *sympathetic* horror, the protagonist, in all significant respects, is morally neutral — as in sympathetic romances, sympathetic comedies, and other stories with sympathetic effects.[2] Since he is "ordinary" — not distinctive morally — we tend to identify ourselves with him in his experience and share vicariously his feelings, which are the natural, appropriate feelings for the situation. The causes for the action are entirely in the environment. The action itself is terrifying or disastrous, a gratuitous evil that befalls him. Identifying ourselves with him, we dread the approach of that evil and are horrified when it strikes. The catharsis apparently may result from nothing but the exhaustion of that evil — we have seen the worst; nothing more is possible — but in "The Mocking-Bird" and "An Occurrence at Owl Creek Bridge," the death of the protagonist provides a further relief by severing our identification with him.

Each of Bierce's three sympathetic horror stories has a dif-

[2] See p. 184.

ferent kind of plot. The simplest is "Chickamauga," which is best described as having a plot of discovery. A small boy, playing in the woods while a battle is raging nearby, comes home — after an encounter with a troop of crawling wounded men with whom he tries to play games of war — to find his house burned and his mother killed. The story deals not with the development of this misfortune, with which the boy's actions have nothing to do, but with his discovery of its existence: the misfortune in a sense is "given" from the beginning of the plot. The effect depends upon this discovery — a terrifying discovery of the evil that has befallen him. A question arises as to why such a story is horrible rather than pathetic: why is not the dominant emotion pity for the boy, whose misfortune is certainly "undeserved"? What happens, of course, is that horror subsumes or absorbs our pity, which is a relatively detached emotion. The evil is too great, too shocking. Our identification with the boy, which depends primarily upon the fact that the boy is totally innocent of what befalls him, is too great to allow us to feel detachment. Oddly enough, the one respect in which he is unlike the reader — the fact that he is a child — increases our identification with him, since it emphasizes his innocence of blame and magnifies the gratuitousness of his misfortune.[3]

Of the other sympathetic horror stories by Bierce, "The Mocking-Bird" has what may be called a plot of misfortune since it goes a step beyond the hero's discovery of an intolerable misfortune: having made this discovery, he commits suicide. There is an actual worsening of his misfortune in the story, for which he is not to blame; the effect depends upon our identification with him and the horror is relieved by the suicide, which indi-

[3] This contrasts with the function of "innocence" in the protagonist of a pathetic story such as "Village Lear" or "Lost Phoebe." In these the hero is not innocent in the most important sense, for what we have called his innocence — his lack of sophistication, his absence of bad intention, his vulnerability — is actually a major cause of suffering, whereas the boy's innocence in "Chickamauga" merely enhances — it does not cause — his suffering. The "innocence" in "Village Lear" is a positive trait, not a neutral one, and makes us aware of the difference between the hero and us; it leads us to judge his misfortune as undeserved but not to identify ourselves with him. The innocence in "Chickamauga," on the other hand, since it is not a primary cause of suffering, functions not to detach us but to enhance our identification with the hero, thus producing an effect of horror instead of pathos.

cates his own recoil from it. "An Occurrence at Owl Creek Bridge," probably Bierce's most celebrated story, is a rare kind of "exposed situation." [4] The horror depends upon the revelation at the end — made possible by a sudden shift in point of view — that a man who had supposed he was escaping death was at that moment dying in the hangman's noose. Identifying ourselves with him in his fantasy of escape, we do not know that he has not escaped until we are suddenly informed that he is dead. The horror here lies in this disclosure of the falsity of the hero's fantasy, a disclosure that not merely crushes our hopes for his escape but makes us realize that these hopes were blind from the beginning. The horror of this revelation depends in good measure upon the vividness and intensity with which these hopes of escape are developed before they are crushed.

In the canon of the twenties there are three stories whose primary effect may resemble the simple horror of those of Bierce, although this formal similarity is obscured by the many obvious material and technical differences. These include Faulkner's celebrated "A Rose for Emily," which has been mentioned in an earlier chapter. [5] The story is classed with the exposed situations, the narrator freely rearranging the chronology of events in order to build a pattern of external clues to the nature of Emily's way of life that will increase the shock and horror of the revelation offered by the final clue. The essential fact so exposed is the perversion that ruled her years in seclusion. Although some critics like to find in Emily's pride and her defiance of the town certain elements that give her "tragic stature," [6] the story can scarcely be called a tragedy in view of the obvious arrangement of parts to emphasize, not her fall and discovery (she makes no discovery), but the hitherto concealed perversity of her choice. The stature she possesses functions (as do whatever implications of universality and "Southern significance" the story may have) to enhance the moral horror of her choice — to make it the more horrible by making her the more important.

Also in the class of simple horror stories are Faulkner's "Dry

[4] See pp. 236–37.
[5] See pp. 42–43.
[6] E.g., Brooks and Warren. See p. 150, n. 5.

September" and Miss Porter's "Magic." Episodes of choice in which a character demonstrates his perversity in a characteristic action that does not change it, both of these stories differ from all the others that have been observed in that the perversity is not so much self-destructive as harmful to others; these stories have the two most destructive and least attractive protagonists in the entire canon. One is the leader of a lynch mob, the other the owner of a brothel who keeps prisoner the girls who are its inmates. The construction of these stories differs also in that the perversity is not suddenly revealed at the close but is apparent almost from the start. As a result there is an intense and growing fear (especially in "Dry September") of the danger threatening the victim and, when the victim is defeated, the final increment of horror necessary to complete our recoil is a demonstration of the protagonist's incorrigibility. In "Magic" this is achieved when the brothel owner attributes to magic spells the influence that compels the return of the girl who has tried to escape, and, in "Dry September," when the lynch leader, at home, treats his wife with brutality.

HORROR MODIFIED

In an earlier chapter Miss Cather's "Paul's Case" was mentioned as producing an effect of "modified horror." This term, which may be applied to most painful stories of both periods that are not primarily pathetic, is used here to indicate an effect quite different in quality from the simple horror of Bierce's stories or Faulkner's "A Rose for Emily." While the difference is partly a matter of degree — Bierce's stories are more violent, although there is violence of a kind in "Paul's Case" — it may also involve the complexity of the issues. In "The Affair at Coulter's Notch," the issue confronting the hero is a simple question of military duty versus family love; in "Paul's Case," subtle questions about maturity, reality, and the gratification of passions enter in. This explanation will seem only partly adequate. The main difference results, apparently, from the manner in which the source of fear or horror is revealed.

Miss Cather's story differs from Bierce's "A Horseman in the Sky" in what it makes the reader go through before the final horror. The source of horror in "Paul's Case" is his suicide, which reiterates in fatal form the self-destroying errors he has been making throughout the story. In Bierce's story we are ignorant of the protagonist's perversity until the final deed is known; the effect of pure horror depends upon our sudden, startled perception of dreadful evil in a character who invites us to identify with him. In "Paul's Case," on the other hand, we are thoroughly familiar with Paul's mistakes, his motives, his suffering; we are tempted to pity him, and even after his suicide there is a strong residue of pathos, a wish to believe Paul an innocent victim of undeserved misfortune. We recoil in horror only because he lacks the ability to discover his error even when its consequences are clear; we find, in other words, that his undeserved misfortune is more deserved than at first we had supposed. This would reduce or destroy our sense of pity, as in a caustic story such as "The Doctor and the Doctor's Wife," were it not that at the same time we also see the misfortune as worse than we had supposed. Our awareness of suffering is increased, not lessened, and though it is not sufficient to "excuse" the hero, it makes him important enough for us to be horrified by what he is doing to himself. Our escape is not the pleasurable detachment of contempt but the recoil of horror.[7]

The essential difference between the two kinds of horror might be summed up as follows: Simple horror involves the emergence of grotesque evil in a character or world that initially appears to be morally neutral: the identification from which we recoil is based essentially upon that moral neutrality;[8] horror

---

[7] The apparent similarity between this and the non-painful, caustic reaction is essentially in the disclosure that a seemingly pitiful protagonist does not merit the pity we have been disposed to give. In the caustic story this judgment is pleasurable; in the horror story, painful. The reason can only be that in the serious story our desire to pity is frustrated; in the caustic story we are allowed to gratify our desire to withhold pity, we have, in the serious story, invested more in the protagonist's moral cause. We do so, presumably, because his misfortune is indeed more serious and more to be pitied; there is justice in our desire to pity. The shock we feel is based on a continuing desire to pity, which means that on a secondary level we do indeed continue to pity. In the caustic story, on the other hand, if we do feel a continuing secondary pity (as we may, on reflection, for the doctor in Hemingway's "The Doctor and the Doctor's Wife"), it is insufficient to make his actions shock us, though it may add discomfiture to our contempt for him — an appropriate enrichment of the caustic effect.

[8] The "secondary pity" we may feel for protagonists like Coulter and Emily

modified involves the emergence of a stronger evil than we had foreseen in a character or world in which the effects of evil are already apparent and which had originally seemed to be pathetic (or romantic): the identification from which we recoil is based on the pity that we continue to feel. It has been said, of course, that pity involves not identification but detachment, and yet pity does involve identification in one sense: it is a moral if not an emotional identification. Though we feel ourselves personally detached, we identify ourselves with the victim's cause. If, however, we find that his cause is less just than we had supposed, we are shocked and respond with horror. Paul's suicide is an unjustifiable act by a character we have been prepared to pity. This act destroys our hope that he will do better, and, thereby, our hope of achieving a "settled judgment" that his case is pitiful.

Such an effect is closer to the tragic combination of pity and fear than are any of the other forms of pathos and horror that have been considered here. Like tragedy, it develops to the limit a horror that arises out of the violation of our moral identification with the protagonist, upon which our pity is based. It stops short of tragic catharsis, since the protagonist makes no discovery sufficient to re-establish this moral identification and convert the horror into a more settled pity. Left with an unsatisfied desire to pity the character, our pain is relieved only by our recoil from the horror, the termination of our identification with him.

Like stories of simple horror, those of "horror modified" may be divided into stories of moral horror (horror seen in the character of the protagonist) and of sympathetic horror (horror seen as encroaching upon the protagonist from without). In the early period, the horror is moral in eight stories of modified horror, sympathetic in four. Of the stories of moral horror, "Paul's Case" has a plot of misfortune, "The Sculptor's Funeral," also by Miss Cather, is an episode of exposure, with a whole town as protagonist (the episode centering upon the exposure to a visitor of the

follows rather than precedes the full development and catharsis of horror. We pity these people after we have recovered from the shock of learning what they have done, so to speak. Such a judgment thus serves to magnify the seriousness of their deed — it enhances the horror in retrospect — but it does not contribute to our moral identification, upon which the horror is based, as pity does in stories of horror modified; it does not change the nature or source of the horror we feel.

narrowness and bigotry of the town), and the rest are stories of choice—four plotted stories, two stories of episode.

Perversity in early stories of choice varies greatly. It can be as mild as that of the heroine in Miss Cather's "The Garden Lodge," an attractive, generally sympathetic woman who suppresses the warm, live, passionate side of her nature in favor of the coldly rational and practical side; the reader's recoil here is most moderate and subtle, based almost entirely upon a perception of how the heroine's choice constricts her spirit and hurts her psychologically. It is horrible only because the general picture of this woman is so favorable; she is displayed in such a sympathetic and attractive light as to make this mildly self-destructive tendency seem a serious matter. On the other hand, the perversity can be violent and abnormal, as when the protagonist of Bierce's "The Story of a Conscience" [9] condemns to death the spy who had saved his life and commits suicide to pay off the debt.

These two stories—as also Bierce's "An Affair of Outposts" and Crane's "The Monster"—differ from both "Paul's Case" and most of the stories of the twenties in the nature of the element that modifies the horror. In "Paul's Case" the horror is modified by a pathetic element, excessive suffering caused by an evident error in attitude; in "The Garden Lodge," "The Story of a Conscience," and "The Monster," the modifying element is better described as romantic, since the emphasis is placed so much more strongly on what is admirable in the character and correspondingly less on the suffering he undergoes. The reader is aware that the protagonist's choice is made with the highest, the most noble of motives; the source of the final shock is far less a tension between repulsion and pity than between repulsion and admiration, horror and romance, perverse self-destruction and noble renunciation in the manner of "A Son of the Gods" or "The Great Tradition." The heroine of "The Garden Lodge" does not want to threaten the security of her home or the happiness of her husband; the hero of "The Story of a Conscience" is making the supreme sacrifice to the sacred principle of keeping faith—the principle of obligation. The implicit horror is most

[9] See pp. 114–15.

subtle: we recognize it at the end of "The Garden Lodge" when we discover that the husband himself would like his wife to be less practical, less coldly rational; at the end of "The Monster" when we discover that the doctor's proud devotion to principle will sacrifice the happiness even of his own children; [10] and in "The Story of a Conscience" because our feelings insist that such an extreme devotion to principle is inhuman. These feelings become more clear when we realize that, as in other stories of simple horror by Bierce, the hero's dilemma is based on an exaggerated, literal interpretation of military rules which, in this case, he himself has established.

Much closer to the common patterns of the twenties are Dreiser's "The Second Choice" and "Old Rogaum and His Theresa" — one having a plot of reiterated choice, the other an episode of choice with a double protagonist — in which the horror develops because the self-destructive stupidity of the protagonist, his ignorance of his natural but unconscious drives and needs, makes it impossible for him to escape the suffering to which he has condemned himself.

Like these stories of Dreiser, most stories of moral horror in the twenties approach the effect of non-painful caustic stories, primarily because the self-destructive perversity reflects other unattractive traits, weakness, stupidity, and an excessive vulnerability to frustration. Anderson's "The Thinker," mentioned in an earlier chapter, is a case in point, although the perversity is perhaps milder than that depicted in Hemingway's "Hills Like White Elephants" and "A Pursuit Race." All of these stories differ from the caustic in one important respect: the suffering displayed is far more serious, if not necessarily more intense. It is a frustration not of a character's vanities and pretensions but of desires and needs that are made to seem natural and important and universal. The heroine of "Hills Like White Elephants" is forced into an abortion she does not want by a lover who pretends a love for her that he does not feel; her misfortune is real — the horror lies in her willingness to accept it. The hero of "A Pursuit Race" is a dope addict completely incapacitated for the

[10] Our recognition of this and our feeling of horror do not mean that we are necessarily able to recommend any morally satisfactory alternative, although we do realize that pride and resentment are as important in the doctor as is principle.

functions of life; the horror lies in his acceptance of his fate. In "The Thinker," Seth's desire to experience emotional involvement is made important by his baffled sincerity — it is a real and natural need — whereby his failure to recognize the existence of his emotional involvement with Helen White strikes us, subtly, as a serious perversity.

The stories just cited are episodes of choice. The perversity is demonstrated in a characteristic choice that indicates an essentially unchanging attitude in an unchanging, if unstable, situation. The episode is so designed as to culminate in a manifestation of this choice after a preparation in which the pitiful aspects of the situation are made clear. It thus involves a sequence directly opposite to that of the typical pathetic episodes of suffering, a movement not from representation of the character's perversity toward a more sympathetic depiction of his suffering, but from the suffering toward the perversity. "Hills Like White Elephants" accomplishes this most economically. Unlike "The Thinker," in which the episode is preceded by a summary narrative establishing the situation out of which it arises, in "Hills" the movement from the manifestation of suffering to that of perversity is accomplished within the episode itself, a single short scene presenting an argument between the lovers in a railroad station.

Two of the remaining stories of modified moral horror written in the twenties have plots of choice, and the other two are episodes of exposure. Of the plots of choice, Anderson's "Surrender" is, in its essentials, similar to the episodes of choice just discussed and differs in that the story is an account of the development from childhood of the heroine's perverse attitude — her bitter hatred of men. Faulkner's "That Evening Sun" is a plot of reiterated choice; the perversity that emerges is the absolute despair into which the heroine sinks when threatened with death, after others have abandoned any effort to help her. "The Killers," like Faulkner's "Mistral," is an episode of exposure: the situation is revealed to us not through a manifestation of its essential elements in the protagonist's own experience but by an episode in which a bystander becomes aware of those essential elements. The most essential and last-discovered ele-

ment is the protagonist's perversity, which, as in "That Evening
Sun," is his despair. In these episodes of exposure — as also in
"That Evening Sun" — the final moral horror is modified by the
preceding development not of pathos, as in the episodes of
choice, but of fear in regard to the protagonist. The reader,
sharing the bystander's implicit feelings, experiences an evolu-
tion of sympathetic horror into moral horror. As a result, the
final horror, though modified, is much more obviously horrible
than in the other stories of modified horror. In "The Killers,"
Nick and George discover first that Ole is going to be killed by
gangsters; the horror they feel is on his behalf. When Nick goes
to Ole, he discovers that Ole has turned his face to the wall, that
he has yielded to absolute despair. The horror of this attitude
caps the horror that has been developing on his behalf and
causes our final recoil from the situation.[11] In "Mistral" sympathetic horror also turns to moral horror, but in a different way.
Here the first effect developed is fear in the bystanders, a pair
of American hikers in Italy; they fear that the protagonist, a
priest, is capable of murder and has committed murder, and that
now he may do so again. At the conclusion the hikers discover
that the priest has no intention of murdering again; they see
him in a copse, lying on the ground and moaning in a terrible
agony of jealousy and frustration. This discovery turns the priest
into an object of moral horror.[12]

Probably the most important of the painful forms distin-

[11] This view of "Killers," with Ole as protagonist, is contrary to the usual
view, which sees Nick as the protagonist. If the story is considered a chapter in
"The Adventures of Nick Adams," then of course Nick is the protagonist, but
considered as an independent whole it seems much better explained as an
episode of exposure whose whole object is the depiction of Ole's situation.
This does not mean, of course, that all other stories in which Nick is witness to
horrifying events — such as "Indian Camp" and "Battler" — are similar. See the
discussion of these stories, pp. 254–58. Each story has to be judged on its own
merits.

[12] An alternative view would be that the priest becomes sympathetic, in
which case the story might have to be classified with the stories of caustic pathos.
I cannot, however, feel much pity for him at the end; his moaning in the copse
seems even stranger and more abnormal than his murderous bent. It affects me
with horror, and I strongly suspect that it was intended to and that the reason
for this horror is that we have witnessed the loss of dignity of a priest; when he
was seen as a dangerous murderer he had a kind of great ominous stature, but
when he rolls upon the ground he loses this and reveals his weakness, which,
in the light of his earlier actions, is horrifying.

guished in stories of the twenties are those represented by a group of thirteen stories in which the effect is not moral but sympathetic horror modified, analogous to such stories of simple horror as Bierce's "Chickamauga" and "An Occurrence at Owl Creek Bridge." The horror arises from our sympathetic identification with the protagonist's feelings during a horrible experience. There are not more than three or four comparable stories — stories of sympathetic modified horror — in the early period. The thirteen stories in the twenties are, without exception, stories of discovery: the protagonist perceives or learns something about his situation or the world in which he lives. The effect is sympathetic because he is morally neutral with respect to this discovery; hence we identify ourselves with him, and it is an effect of fear or horror because what he discovers is fearsome or horrifying. This fear or horror is modified in a number of ways, depending upon the kind of discovery involved.

Some of these may be called "personal discoveries." They imply the protagonist's increased understanding of a misfortune of his own, and are anticipated in the early period by Crane's "The Blue Hotel," a story in which a multiple protagonist becomes aware of shared guilt in the murder of an obnoxious visitor to their town, and Crane's "An Episode of War," in which an officer's experience in being wounded and losing an arm is presented through details that emphasize the emotional quality that the experience had for him. The stress in the latter story is, apparently, on his perception of the half-terrifying, half-soothing contrast between the great misfortune that has befallen him and the casual, stable, almost serene aspects of the surrounding world.

"The Blue Hotel" has a genuine discovery plot: "An Episode of War," on the other hand, is an episode of discovery. In the twenties the discovery episode is the more characteristic. The reversal in such a story (the point at which the protagonist achieves knowledge) is less important for its own sake than is the situation that it clarifies; the contrast between the protagonist's initial ignorance and final knowledge is less important than the final knowledge itself — and in most cases is very slight.

Whereas in the discovery plot the protagonist learns essential "facts" about his situation, terrible or fearsome things that he did not know, in the discovery episode he learns little or nothing new, at least in a general way. The episode functions primarily to bring home more vividly to him (and to us) the emotional significance of his situation; it makes the situation more concrete. He acquires, indeed, not knowledge but feeling; his discovery is at the emotional level only and not at the intellectual level.

Hemingway's "My Old Man" has a plot of discovery. It culminates with a boy's specific, horrible recognition, brought to completion after his father's death, that his father was a crook (the boy has lost him morally as well as physically). Miss Porter's "Flowering Judas" is an episode. Nothing happens during Laura's evening with Braggioni, the Mexican revolutionary leader whom she detests, except the gathering together of her various feelings of disillusion, fear, and guilt, culminating in a dream after her visitor's departure that expresses these concentrated emotions in the vivid symbols of the unconscious. In an episode such as Miss Porter's "The Jilting of Granny Weatherall" the approach of death to a proud old ex-pioneer woman stimulates a delirium of memories and thoughts that in their juxtaposition implicitly evoke in her the long-suppressed feeling that life has jilted her, just as she was once, years ago, jilted at the altar. In Miss Porter's "Theft" an incident with an arrogant thief is juxtaposed in the heroine's mind with a number of incidents with friends; the result is to make her more than usually conscious of her irrational guilt in the possessing of things and her misery in the self-deprivation that results. In Hemingway's "Now I Lay Me," the narrator's feeling of alienation from humanity, which has emerged in a war-induced breakdown that makes him afraid to sleep in the dark, is intensified by a conversation with a well-meaning friend who does not understand his problem. All that is "discovered" in such stories is the protagonist's emotion about his situation, an emotion evoked by the juxtaposition of various things that happen to him not through his own choice — highly evocative things suggestive of the emotionally meaningful elements in the situation. This emotional content is seldom explicitly described; it is left to the reader to infer what it must be as he identifies himself with the protagonist in the latter's passive experience. The horror in such discovery episodes is caused by this vivid evocation of the protagonist's own horror. It differs from the pathos of episodes of suffering, described in a previous chapter, in that the reader is made, not to judge the protagonist as pathetic from the signs of his suffering, but to share his own apprehension of the suffering itself by the evocation of its circumstances as he sees them.

The modification of horror in these stories arises from the fact that the misfortune itself — unlike that of a simple horror story such as "Chickamauga" — is the result of some pitiable error or weakness or vulnerability in the protagonist. The reader can pity the protagonist for his misfortune — the trap that Laura is in, the deprivations suffered by the heroine of "Theft," — since he is detached from its causes. But he is not detached from the specific action of the story, the discovery, the emotional experience of the protagonist; in relation to this, the misfortune is an immutable "given" fact and the reader shares the intensification of his suffering — the dread or horror — as the nature of this misfortune becomes clear to the protagonist. The story breaks down our detachment and our pity by intimately involving us in the protagonist's feelings.

Fitzgerald's "Winter Dreams" and "The Sensible Thing" demonstrate how mild and muted sympathetic horror or dread can sometimes be, so mild in these cases as to raise problems in analysis. On the most superficial level these are success stories, romances. The success in each case is sharply mitigated by a discovery of the loss of youth and of youthful joy, which is obviously given supreme importance in each story. The intended import of this discovery is not easy to define. At first one may suspect pathos, since the protagonists themselves feel such pity for themselves, such difficulty in holding back their tears. Yet one cannot feel pity for them; it is difficult to regard the loss of youth as undeserved misfortune, especially in young men with such excellent prospects as these two have, since it is a fortune that no young man can evade. Apparently the author expects the reader to recognize the experience as familiar — to identify himself with rather than to judge the character in his confrontation of a sad truth about life. Then the young men's tears become more meaningful; they are the device by which Fitzgerald tells us that the loss of youth is indeed worth weeping about. Undeserved or not, it is a misfortune; this, as in the other stories of sympathetic modified horror, is all that the author wants us to feel. If we find it difficult to share the young man's fears and grief, the difficulty may be due to the execution of the story — perhaps to Fitzgerald's own youthful assumption that such "horror" merely needs to be mentioned to become apparent, or to his assumption that it is not necessary to dramatize graphically the bleak process of aging as well as the brightness of youth in order to make us dread the loss of youth.

Besides the various "personal discoveries," there is also a significant group of stories of sympathetic horror which may be described as "generalized discoveries." These are stories in which a neutral protagonist discovers frightening or horrible things about life in general rather than about a specific personal misfortune of his own. Such generalized discoveries are anticipated in the early period by Crane's "The Open Boat" and Dreiser's "Nigger Jeff." [13] In the twenties, they are a specialty of Hemingway (such stories as "Indian Camp", "The Battler", "In Another Country", and "An Alpine Idyll") although Fitzgerald's "Absolution" (seen as Rudolph's story) and Faulkner's "Crevasse" also belong in the same class. All of these, except "Nigger Jeff," are episodes of discovery. The latter — which has a discovery plot — differs in that the protagonist, a young reporter, actually learns a fact that he had previously denied — the fact that nature does not always mete out justice according to one's deserts.

[13] Garland's "Up the Coolly" and Crane's "Experiment in Misery" are also stories of generalized discovery, but their effects are more like those of stories of romantic pathos than of horror modified (see p. 228). What the protagonist observes in each is not only the presence of evil or suffering but the existence of courage and heroism in the face of misfortune. This is not stated explicitly, to be sure, but it is evident in the behavior of the sufferers — in the farmer's pride, which remains strong despite the bitterness of his complaints about his life; in the almost casual way in which the Bowery derelicts maintain a standard of behavior despite the wreckage of their lives.

As in all stories of generalized discovery, we share the protagonist's implicit emotions. What we share is not a feeling of horror but a feeling of pity and admiration.

In the generalized-discovery stories the protagonist (whose character is not essential to the situation whose meaning he discovers) is personally detached from somebody else's misfortune, which he happens to observe. He sees an Indian husband driven to suicide, presumably because he cannot stand his wife's suffering as she undergoes a Caesarian without anesthetic. He sees a former prize fighter, half-demented and belligerent, withdraw from society to lead a hobo's life. He sees a wounded Italian major, grief-stricken and unable to resign himself to the unexpected death of his young wife. He sees a peasant who has mutilated his wife's frozen corpse, which he has had to keep in his shed all winter, unable to bury her until the spring thaw. In such stories, the narrative is so organized as to emphasize not so much the particular suffering of the person observed as the emotional significance to the protagonist of observing it. Each of Hemingway's stories — which show the pattern fully developed — first presents the protagonist (always Nick or a first-person equivalent to Nick) in some particular, uncomfortable relation to a world that is strange to him: as a young boy called upon by his father to witness a childbirth that goes wrong, or, somewhat older, being thrown off a freight train by a railroad guard in a lonely region, or, as a soldier, becoming aware of the distance between him and the young war heroes he meets in a Milan hospital. It is while he is most keenly aware of the strangeness of this world that he witnesses the suffering of a character whose existence had previously meant little to him.

The specific discovery (as in the episodes of personal discovery) is never explicitly stated. At the most, there may be a statement such as that in "In Another Country": Nick felt "sick for him" (the major). At the end of "Indian Camp," on the other hand, Nick "felt quite sure that he would never die," a feeling that by itself might suggest that he has failed to make any discovery at all. The reader must infer discovery in order to account for the sequence of events; he must find the connection between the observed misfortune and the uncomfortable situation that is first established for Nick. "An Alpine Idyll" is typical. At the opening, Nick is returning from spring skiing with a feeling that he has been skiing too long — that there is too much sun, that the high mountain spring seemed "unnatural," that it is not good to do anything for too long. In the second part, at the inn, he sees and hears about the peasant who has been unable to bury his wife until the melting of the snows. It is discovered that the corpse is disfigured because the peasant, who had propped it up in his shed during the winter, had got into the habit of hanging a lantern from the open jaw. The priest and innkeeper are shocked. "'It was very wrong,' said the priest. 'Did you love your wife?' 'Ja, I loved her,' Olz said. 'I loved her fine.'" The obvious connection between the two parts of the story might be called "thematic"; just as Nick has been skiing too long, so the peasant has been living near his wife's corpse too long. The story is not an abstract exposition of a theme, however, but an account of a meaningful experience for Nick, and we call it "meaningful" because there is discovery in it. Our inference is that the peasant's behavior brings home to Nick the full horror of a certain human condition that he had vaguely felt in his own reaction to skiing. He had received a hint of what morbidity lies in pursuing a pleasure too long; in the peasant he sees what the morbidity of an intolerably unnatural and painful situation can do to a simple man.

The discovery is "generalized" since the particular thing observed leads to the recognition of a general quality in the hero's world. The specific nature of the discovery in most of these stories has been touched upon: in each Nick discovers his own inexperience with kinds of suffering that life can, quite arbitrarily, provide; he sees, as he observes the reaction of the sufferer, how intense and destructive such suffering can be; and he sees, above all, how completely it cuts off the sufferer from human understanding, sympathy, or consolation. Neither he nor anyone else can help the peasant, the major, the prize fighter, the Indian husband. He can only watch with sympathy and fear while the victim isolates himself from human community. He can only feel "sick for him." The discovery is horrifying because Nick knows that only good luck has kept him safe from similar suffering, that he shares the same potential vulnerability, that perhaps all men do.

It is, of course, an emotional rather than an intellectual discovery of fact. The very circumstance that several such stories, each embodying much the same basic discovery by the same character, can be read in sequence without lessening the impact of each helps to demonstrate this. We need not assume that Nick did not know that life contains arbitrary suffering which cuts the sufferer off from others; the particular experience simply makes more concrete the full horror or terror implicit in such knowledge. Even in "Indian Camp" this is so: Nick has heard of suicide — else he would not understand how the Indian had died; we know, also, despite his final thought (that he will never die), that he will always remember the terror of the experience.

The modification of horror in stories of generalized discoveries is such as to make the term "horror" as popularly understood seem somewhat less apt than the term "dread." As in most other stories of modified horror, the modification depends upon the established familiarity of something in which a fearful quality is exposed. In the generalized discoveries we are made to feel potential horror in the face of facts about life that we know to be universal, normal rather than abnormal, despite their grotesque manifestations: the potential horror of the arbitrariness of fate, the everpresence of suffering and death, the barriers that separate sufferers, the inevitability of growing old. Since the protagonist himself has not suffered from the consequences of these universal facts, the horror remains only potential, and the story remains one of fear rather than of completed horror.

This raises a problem as to the kind of relief or catharsis offered by such stories. If the evil facing us when we identify ourselves with the protagonist is more potential than actual, if the fear that we feel is not developed into full horror with its resultant recoil, how do we obtain relief sufficient to convert the painful emotion into a pleasurable artistic experience?

A partial source of relief is no doubt the same thing that keeps the dread from becoming a fully realized horror. This is the evidence, even while the protagonist is making his frightening discovery, that the world, despite its terror, is also a place of life — the assurance that what we have seen is part of the natural order of things, which cannot be condemned. The detachment of the protagonist from the scene is useful to this effect: in "The Open Boat," for example, the oiler is drowned, but the correspondent is rescued, to his immense relief and the enhancement of his appreciation of life. Hemingway's stories have such an implication, as can be seen in "Indian Camp," for example, when Nick, despite the horror of what he has seen, responds at the end to the waking morning and believes that he will never die, as if, by engaging his emotions, the very terror of his experience had somehow made him more aware and more appreciative of life. By placing the fearful experience in a context of continuing life, the author provides relief from the feeling of dread that he has evoked.[14]

In addition to this source of resolution — essentially romantic — the generalized discoveries also seem to relieve the painful emotion by a subtle means that functions also in stories of personal discoveries and, perhaps, to an extent, in the other painful forms as well. In such stories of personal discovery as "Flowering Judas" and "Theft," one feels a certain catharsis in the very process of understanding the emotion that the story is developing. Laura's terrifying dream, for example, has a liberating effect clearly dependent not alone on our recoil from the horror that it contains but also, and perhaps primarily, upon our feeling of success in interpreting its symbols and identifying the emotion that it expresses. Much as in life itself, we are liberated from feelings of dread and other painful emotions by recognizing, identifying, and achieving an understanding of those emotions. In stories of generalized discoveries, the very act of recognizing the feeling that gives coherence to the juxtaposed elements involves a mastery of that feeling and hence a liberation from it.

This suggests a possibly important reason (in addition to the technical reasons to be discussed in a later chapter) why such stories leave so much of the discovery to the reader's inference. For if understanding a feeling is one way to liberate oneself from it, then a writer can intensify the effect by delaying the *process* of understanding. One way to do this is to require the reader to reach understanding unaided; if he has to make difficult inferences in order to understand the feeling, then both the feeling itself and the purgation of that feeling will be more intense and satisfying.

[14] I am indebted to a former colleague, Walter Blinstrub, for pointing out this element in "Indian Camp."

XVI: MAGNITUDE AND COMPLEXITY

The meaning of the assertion that the writers of the twenties were doing away with plot is clear. One of the most obvious tendencies revealed in the foregoing comparisons of forms is the reduction of the magnitude of the action that unifies a story. This reduction of magnitude does not, to be sure, necessarily involve a reduction in the absolute magnitude of the story or even of the length of time or elaboration of incident necessary to bring the change about. It means simply that less changes between beginning and end; the movement and contrast between these two points is less significant to the effect. A table in Appendix B, giving the distribution of the various kinds of plots and episodes in the work of the writers of the twenties, reveals a striking tendency not merely to write far more episodes and far fewer plot stories than their forebears but to write plots and episodes unified by smaller kinds of change or action.

259

Other things being equal, a change in fortune is more tangible, more significant in its effects, than any other kind of story development, especially if it includes character change and discovery. In the twenties such plots are almost entirely eliminated. Among other kinds of plots, those involving change in attitude or a solution to a dilemma — what may be called plot of "reversed" choice, constituting by far the most common kind of unifying principle in the early period (accounting for almost a third of all the stories) — are also much less significant in the twenties, as are plots of discovery. The former are no more common and the latter much less common in the twenties than plots of "reiterated" choice, which, of all the general kinds of plots observed, depict what is probably the least consequential change, since the character learns nothing and his motives remain unaltered.

Although in episode stories change is secondary, many of the episodes of the twenties likewise depend on more reduced actions than do those of the early period. A majority of the episodes of both periods are what might be called episodes of "character"; discussed heretofore as "episodes of choice," their object is an imitation of character in action designed to evoke a moral judgment of the character. In stories of the twenties, however, there is a marked increase in the significance of episodes essentially less "active" than these. Most notable are the episodes of discovery, which are unified ultimately by what may be called "thought" (adapting Aristotle's term) — that is, by the feelings or reflection of a neutral character in a specific situation. Thought in this sense is a less active principle than character; it could be described as the material of which character is formed. The episodes of discovery emphasize this material rather than the character that it forms; they emphasize, in other words, the passive experience of a protagonist to whom things happen and make no attempt to show the protagonist as an active agent. The development in the twenties of the episode of suffering — even though this is a kind of episode of character — is a movement in the same direction, character being seen in a more passive relationship to its environment than in the episode of choice. The reduction of action is carried still further in episodes of exposure and exposed situations, since their unity lies not in progressive activity of any kind but in the narrator's devices of revelation.

The advantages of such a development are not self-evident; readers unaccustomed to the modern short story are quite likely to miss them, as did those early hostile critics who described the stories of the twenties as mere "sketches" and objected that "nothing happened" in them. One might well suppose that a reduction in the magnitude of action would constitute a reduction in power. A tragedy, for example, is the more powerful (other things being equal) the greater the contrast between the initial good fortune and the ultimate misfortune and degradation.

It should be noticed that although the writers of the twenties were willing to sacrifice the kind of gross power that may be attained through magnitude of action, they were less willing to sacrifice those other essentials of a "good plot" that do most to give the story interest and intensity. The structural features most generally useful in enabling a plot to make its effect are probably similar to those by which Aristotle distinguished a "complex" tragic plot from a "simple" one. These features — reversal, discovery, tragic deed — maximize the effect of the action as action by putting all the most essential tragic materials into the most active possible form. Reversal maximizes the effect of the essential change by abruptly overwhelming the forces that have resisted the change; discovery provides for the greatest possible change in the causes of the tragedy by eliminating the error or ignorance that was most to blame; and the deed externalizes in the most violent way the suffering or the tragic relation between the hero and his world that is the result of that error.

Of course, there are no Greek tragedies in the twenties and few, if any, in the early period. If one looks in these stories for reversals, discoveries, and deeds comparable to those of tragedy, one might well conclude (even if examination be confined to painful stories) that the writers of the twenties have sacrificed "complexity" as well as magnitude: reversals are not found in the episode stories because such stories are not organized to present a completed change; full discoveries — discoveries of basic error — almost totally disappear, even the discovery stories themselves being far more frequently episodes than plots; and the "deeds" are less drastic, as one can see by comparing Paul's suicide with Seth's decision to leave town.

This, however, is a false way to measure the complexity of an action. The equivalents of tragic reversal, discovery, and deed should be sought in relation to the particular intent of the form. Thus, an episode may be "complex" in its own way; it may have its own kind of reversal that involves, not an irreversible final collapse of forces, but an illuminating moment in which the important constant in the static situation reasserts itself and brings the episode more or less abruptly to a conclusion. Virtually all stories in both periods are complex in this sense. In "The Thinker," for example, the reversal comes at the moment when Seth fails to understand Helen's actions and assumes once again that he will never be loved; in "Hills Like White Elephants" it occurs when the girl stops quarreling with her lover and says that she feels "fine"; in "Indian Camp" it occurs when the boy sees that the Indian has committed suicide; in "Flowering Judas" it comes with Laura's dream. In the exposure episodes it comes when the bystander suddenly grasps the nature of the situation he is witnessing. Even the exposed situations give the effect of an artificial reversal, as it were, because the narrator deliberately withholds crucial information until the moment when it will best make its proper effect. There is such an artificial reversal in "Hands" when the narrator turns to Wing's past, in "A Rose for Emily" when the narrator reveals what was found in Emily's bedroom after her death, in "Paper Pills" when the narrator tells us the story of Dr. Reefy's marriage. Among the earlier writers, Bierce was especially fond of such manipulations, using them not only in such an exposed situation as "An Occurrence at Owl Creek Bridge" (the sudden revelation of the truth about the hero's predicament is withheld until the end) but even in such plot stories as "A Horseman in the Sky" in which the revelation of what the hero has done is arbitrarily delayed. until after the hero has been shown doing it.

In this respect, then, the new stories are as complex as the earlier ones. Yet there is an obvious attempt in some of them to muffle or veil the reversal. This is most marked in Hemingway's stories. In "Big Two-Hearted River" the development is so grad-ual as to make it impossible to select any one point in the actual text as the significant point of reversal; the reversal lies in the completion of Nick's ritual, the fulfillment of his objective, and the termination of his experience: only at this point do we, the readers, perceive the direction in which the whole experience has tended. In other stories, such as "The End of Something" or "Cross-Country Snow" the reversal — here the expression of an attitude — is so understated by the hero that the reader scarcely realizes its significance until he has finished reading. In still others, such as "A Very Short Story" and "The Revolutionist," the reversal is underplayed by the narrator, who uses the unusual device of presenting it in a brief narrative statement which con-trasts with the dramatic treatment in the earlier part of the story. Such devices make a story look simpler than it really is, an effect that Hemingway and Anderson seemed especially eager to achieve. The narrator of Anderson's "Death in the Woods" con-cludes his tale by calling it a "simple story," as if to distract attention from the fact that its construction is as complicated as that of any story in the period. Although such devices can be explained as an attempt to achieve an appearance of greater naturalness and less artificiality, they also function in a more positive way to heighten the dramatic effect: a reversal gains in impact when the reader's perception of it is difficult and delayed.

Most of the forms of the twenties require that the protagonist fail to make an essential discovery of his errors; the effect of "The Thinker," for example, depends upon Seth's failure to recognize the feelings he and Helen share. Although such essential dis-covery — common in the early period — has nearly disappeared, the function of discovery as a complicating element is served by other means. The complexity that discovery introduces into an action is a change from some significant ignorance to knowl-edge: what was not known becomes known. It is an externaliza-tion of the causes of the action, just as the "deed" is an ex-ternalization of the consequences. This function need not be served by the protagonist's own discovery; it can be served by a discovery made by agents representing his "milieu."[1] Thus in "A Rose for Emily" this function is served not by Emily's discovery but by the discovery made by the townspeople. In "The Thinker" Seth exposes his error to Helen White, even though she is incapable of understanding it. Examination of the canon reveals that in virtually all stories in which the protagonist himself does not make a fundamental discovery, secondary discovery in the milieu takes place.[2]

Even discovery by the milieu need not necessarily be the intellectually and morally complete revelation that we associate with tragic discovery. In the early period, to be sure, it usually is: the hero of "A Horseman in the Sky" reveals his patricide to his friend, who expresses shock; the suffering in "Paul's Case" is exposed to the world by his suicide. Most of the early stories that lack personal discovery by the hero are told from external points of view, a technique that in itself throws special emphasis on the process of discovery.

In the twenties, on the other hand, the function of discovery as a complexity in the action is often served by the merest hint or suggestion of an increase in fundamental knowledge. Just as the protagonist's discovery in such episodes as "Theft," "The Jilting of Granny Weatherall," or "Flowering Judas" is intellectually incomplete, so often is the discovery made by the secondary character who represents the milieu. In the *Winesburg* stories, for example, the secondary character is often George Willard; although he recognizes horror or pathos in the cases he witnesses, he usually does not understand what he has learned as well as the reader does. As with the discovery episodes, this has a double value: his failure to understand heightens the pathos or horror of the story, while his partial understanding, his partial grasp, his beginning of discovery, provides a sufficient complexity to give the action the power that a discovery pro-

---

[1] I am indebted to a former colleague, Kenneth Telford, for the suggestion of the function of discovery made by representatives of the protagonist's "milieu."

[2] This is true of both periods, even in those stories in which the protagonist himself makes no significant error that is later discovered; when, in such cases, there is no discovery by the protagonist of the nature of environment, as in Hemingway's "Alpine Idyll," then there usually is a discovery of the protagonist's virtues, rights, and needs by his "milieu," as in such early romantic comedies as "Christmas Jenny" and "The Revolt of 'Mother.'"

vides. In some cases, somewhat more subtle, the discovery hinges on the characteristic division of a character into conscious and unconscious elements: here, as when the heroine of Anderson's "Adventure" is shocked by her own acts, the protagonist himself perceives his case as if he were an unrelated bystander to himself or a part of his own milieu (although unable to make the more fundamental discovery of error that would actually resolve the situation). In the subtlest stories, the exposure or discovery is only potential. Relief of tension in such cases depends upon our expectation that an ultimate exposure is inevitable. This is the pattern, unmatched in the early period, of such stories as Hemingway's "Hills Like White Elephants," Fitzgerald's "Benediction," Anderson's "Out of Nowhere Into Nothing," "Nobody Knows," "I Want to Know Why," and many others, some of which contain an immediate partial exposure as well. The reader of "Hills Like White Elephants" expects, for example, that when the heroine's fears are more fully materialized, she will perceive more clearly the horror of the choice she is making now: much of the power, indeed, depends upon our realization that this is to come. The story also shows another common pattern in the twenties — exposure to an agent who is himself deficient in some way and hence unable to perceive the real import of what is exposed to him. In "Hills" this agent is the girl's lover, who sees her surrender without recognizing the horror of it and tries to exploit it to his own advantage. The few stories which lack even such partial discoveries as these achieve the effect of discovery by narrative manipulation, just as in the artificial reversals discussed above. They usually coincide with these artificial reversals since, in such stories as "Hands" and "Paper Pills," they consist of the narrator's sudden revelation of withheld information, a revelation that brings the depiction of the situation to an end.

The function of the third element of complexity — the "deed" — is fulfilled in every story by external action appropriate to the moral situation. The comic act, the horrible act, the pathetic manifestation — all these are present and, if anything, even more highly developed (though again, often more subtle) than in the early period. The episode itself, in an episode story, is an ex-ternalization of this kind. The greater completeness of such externalizations in stories of the twenties can be seen by the greater reliance that writers are able to place upon reader's inferences as to what is being externalized: no writer in the twenties has to tell us, as does Mrs. Freeman in "A Kitchen Colonel," that the depicted episode brings a humble glory to the protagonist (see quotation p. 328). The fact that the deeds are often less violent — which has been noted above in the contrast between Seth's and Paul's ways of manifesting their sufferings — does not mean that they are less complete externalizations of the issues.

These tendencies — the reduction of magnitude of action and the refinement of complexity — make possible the development of richer and more delicate effects within the confines of short-story length. If the writers of the twenties sacrificed the power of a large and consequential action, they gained evocative intensity in their depictions of subtle states of character and thought. For the most part (although not in their rejection of Jamesian comedies) this was pure gain, for the "large" actions of the early period tend to lack intensity and richness, to lack complex development of character, thought, and feeling, and, despite their sometimes greater immediate force, to be simpler, less penetrating, less profound. They tend, in other words, to be "thinner." Even such a stunning masterpiece as Bierce's "The Affair at Coulter's Notch" is fundamentally simple: the character's only problem is whether to obey his commander's order to bombard his own house — a direct conflict between military duty and love. The horror we feel in his choice is correspondingly simple.

By using the small action, the illuminating episode, as a unifying principle, the writers of the twenties reduced the amount of activity or incident necessary to bring their stories to completion. Thus they had more scope for the development of character and thought — they were freer to choose for their stories situations involving such elements. It was an attempt to sharpen and concentrate the focus of the short story — to find the magnitude of unifying principle most appropriate to the absolute magnitude of the short story, most capable of yielding that sort of concentrated richness that we are accustomed to find in great art. In the course of this attempt they brought the short story much closer to the nature of the lyric poem. Sometimes they went too far in this direction, as in the overstrained and unimpressive prose poems that Anderson included in his volumes of stories. Generally, however, they kept the integrity of the short story as an imitation of individuals in specific relationships; the more lyrical quality came from the concentration of this imitation upon the states of character, mind, and feeling of these individuals.

The analyses in the preceding pages may give some idea of the nature of the subtler and richer effects thus obtained. Apart from the reduction in magnitude of the plot itself, the most obvious formal tendency is the trend toward more painful effects. But the increase in the relative number of painful stories is no more telling than the changes that took place within both broad categories of effect—the painful and the non-painful. The general tendency in both is a shift from the romantic side of the spectrum towards the caustic-fearful side—from stories that tend to flatter the reader toward stories that discomfit him. This is seen in the radical reduction of pure romances and romantic comedies and in the virtual disappearance of stories of romantic pathos; it can also be seen in the kind of discomfiture that is involved in those romantic stories that the twenties produced— stories such as "The Undefeated," "Hair," "All the Dead Pilots," and the like, full of overtones of horror or caustic or comic elements that the reader must transcend before he can respond to the romance. The realm of non-painful effects in stories of the twenties is dominated by caustic comedies and the pure caustic —types which push closer to what is painful and disturbing to the reader than does the flattering romance. Similarly, stories of pathos are almost exclusively "caustic pathos," obviously more painful and disturbing than stories of romantic pathos in the early period. There is, also, the increased importance of stories of fear and horror—not the simple horror of Bierce, which in the very purity of its shock provides an easy catharsis, but the modified horror of Hemingway, Miss Porter, and others, an effect that involves the reader's painful emotions much more insidiously and relieves them less obviously and less immediately. Even the earlier equivalents of these, the earlier stories of modified horror —"A Garden Lodge," "The Monster," "The Story of a Conscience"—depend more on romantic elements to modify the horror than do those of the twenties.

Such a shift is a direct consequence of a more critical representation of character than was common in the early period. There is scarcely a protagonist in the early period who is not presented, if not admiringly, at least lovingly or tenderly. In the twenties, apart from the neutral protagonists of the discovery stories, there is scarcely a hero who lacks a defect that is in some way contemptible or grotesque. In the early period, except in the horror stories of Bierce, most error of character can be rectified by the protagonist, whether or not he discovers it in time to avoid its consequences. In stories of the twenties, most error is so deeply rooted in the protagonist's moral character as to be undiscoverable, and so cannot be corrected. The undiscoverable errors of the twenties are, furthermore, less readily excusable than those that appear in the early period. In the early comedies they tend, usually, to involve little worse than the misapplication of attractive virtues. In the early pathetic stories, too, and even in most of the horror stories, they tend to be the result of the protagonist's goodness, innocence, trustfulness, loving kindness, or sense of duty and responsibility. In stories of the twenties, except in some of the child protagonists, the undiscoverable errors, however they may be compensated by virtues, indicate less attractive traits: cowardice like that of the doctor in "The Doctor and the Doctor's Wife," exaggerated emotional vulnerability like that of Wash Williams in "Respectability," faulty self-understanding like that of the heroine of "He." Perhaps the broadest general contrast in moral stature between the protagonists of the two periods is indicated in the way the early protagonists, nearly always, impress us with their emotional dignity, whatever their faults, the protagonists of the twenties, nearly always, lack this quality, whatever their virtues. The predominant defect in character in stories of the twenties is the individual's inability to cope with or understand his feelings.

Yet the reader is not permitted to laugh with easy contempt at these characters. The stories are painful; emotionally, the reader is intimately involved in their fates. Even those stories which lead to feelings of contempt — the caustic stories — arrive at this result usually only after first involving the reader's sympathies. In the other kinds of stories of the twenties such involvement is still more obvious, and it contrasts strikingly with the affectionate detachment or the respectful distance one feels from the earlier heroes. Ultimately it depends, in almost every case — whether the dominant effect is comic, caustic, pathetic or horrible — on either or both of two qualities in the character or his situation. One of these is common to the protagonists in stories of both of the periods: nothing less than an implicit goodness, a romantic element subordinate to and yet essential to the non-romantic effect. This is a major modification in the later effects as they have been described. Despite the more critical treatment of character, despite the great shift from dominantly romantic effects to dominantly caustic ones, despite the increased effort to disturb the reader's complacency, the characters in stories of the twenties possess, in most instances, positive virtues strong enough to make us care very much about what they do or what befalls them. These virtues are not the same as those of the early period. We admire the characters in stories of the twenties for such virtues of feeling and respect for life as have been described in Chapters IX and X. We admire Wash Williams for the passion and integrity of his feelings about love, and we admire the adolescents of the twenties for the purity of their desires. Even though these virtues seldom triumph as virtues did earlier, and though our appreciation of them is seldom the final result of a story, there is "affirmation" nevertheless: it appears when our contempt is turned to pity, as happens so often in reading Anderson's stories, but it is also produced by quite different stories — when pity is turned to contempt, scorn, horror, or fear. For these effects depend upon our perception of admirable values violated; in their catharsis we feel these values — the new values of the new period — reaffirmed indirectly. Although one can readily agree with the observations of critics that earlier stories were "optimistic" — this being another way of describing the manner in which they flatter the reader — one has strong reservations about calling the stories of the twenties "pessimistic," unless one simply identifies pessimism with a rejection of the earlier values.

The other common quality that makes a character in a story of the twenties interesting to the reader or involves the reader in his fate is the likeness between character and reader in some significant respect. The element of likeness is one of the most potent sources of effectiveness in these stories: though the characters tend to be somewhat less attractive than those of the early period, they are at the same time more familiar—even when they are grotesque. Their problems are more intimate, more pressing and pertinent; this is what makes it possible for us to identify ourselves with characters who in so many respects invite censure. Note, for example, the difference between the reader's relationship to Garland's Western villages and farms and the reader's relationship to Winesburg, Ohio. Garland has an Eastern reader, the "city-bred visitor," clearly in mind: he says as much in two different stories. His people come from another world and the author is their spokesman. One feels no such distance from Winesburg, Ohio; Anderson, with his familiar references to the drygoods store, the pike, the berry-pickers, and the like, reinforces the impression he wants to give that the reader himself comes from Winesburg. It is a way of emphasizing the universality of his characters. In this regard, the most important characters in stories of the twenties are the protagonists of the various kinds of "sympathetic" stories — the neutral characters such as the narrator of "In Another Country" or the passive discoverers of their own situations such as the heroine of "Theft." In these stories of thought and feeling, in which the whole object is to evoke in a reader the emotional state of the character, the reader's involvement is complete.

As he enters the world of each story, the reader's contempt, horror, scorn, and fear struggle with and issue from his intense involvement in the action. One is mindful of the marked and consistent effort of the writers of the twenties to blend effects of opposite kinds, almost as if they wished to eliminate the difference between painful and non-painful, romantic and caustic, pitiful and horrible. Of course they do not really wish to strike out such differences, for this would mean destroying effect rather than enhancing it. But they know, better than any of the earlier writers except James (who knew it best of all), that emotions are most fully comprehended when their dependence upon their opposites is most clear. They know that just as love and hate or anger and joy or contempt and admiration are twins in the emotional life of man and are not fully understood until the twinship is seen, so the mastery of emotions sought by art depends upon a similar recognition. This is, as Croce said, what distinguishes the artistic depiction of emotion from "feeling in its immediacy"; it is the source of catharsis. The stories of reduced action in the twenties move thus to a high level of emotional complexity and subtlety, and this is certainly their chief aesthetic advantage over the simpler plots devised by earlier writers.

Although such formal developments became important in the United States in the twenties, they were not new in the art of the short story. It is not the purpose of this study to trace the origins of these tendencies, apart from our chosen writers, but it may be pointed out that similar tendencies are discernible in the work of other writers who belong on the family tree of the modern short story — most notably Chekhov and Joyce. We associate Chekhov, for example, with the episode that reveals a static situation: some of his stories — e.g., "The Student" — are virtually as motionless as any in the twenties; a story such as "An Upheaval" is a typical episode of exposure of a miserable situation; "The Lament" is a clear and obvious example of an episode of suffering. Many of his stories — "Gooseberries" is an example — reveal interestingly what may be an early stage in the development of the revelatory episode: a story in which an extensive summary narrative is included within the framework of a particular situation which is also developed in detail. The included narrative in this story is itself a reduced plot — a plot of choice rather than of fortune.

Even so, the stories of Chekhov do not look like the characteristic stories of the twenties; they belong to another time. The difference is most obvious in technique, a matter to be discussed in the following chapters. The Chekhovian world is also radically different, despite the modernity of its emotional problems. The chief formal difference from American stories of the twenties is that Chekhov's stories tend to be more purely pathetic — more romantic and less caustic — than was usual in the twenties, although a story such as "A Trifle From Real Life" resembles very much in its effect the characteristic muffled and modified horror of the twenties.

The stories in *Dubliners* most nearly anticipate the stories of the American twenties. Much has been made of the Joycean epiphany and its influence on the short story in all languages. The epiphany, a moment of revelation, when "amid the most encumbered circumstances it suddenly happens that the veil is lifted, the burthen of the mystery laid bare, and the ultimate secret of things made manifest,"[3] was used by Joyce in two kinds of stories, both familiar in the twenties. One was the discovery episode, represented in *Dubliners* by "The Sisters," "An Encounter," "Araby," "A Little Cloud," "A Painful Case," and "The Dead." The revelation is to the character himself; the thing discovered is frustration or paralysis or disillusion or the death of the spirit; the effect ranges between pathos and dread. In the others the epiphany is a direct revelation to the reader by means of an episode: there is pathos in such episodes of suffering as "Eveline" and "After the Race," modified horror in such episodes of choice as "Counterparts," "A Mother," and "The Boarding House," a fairly pure caustic effect in such episodes of choice and exposure as "Clay" (tinged with pathos) and "Two Gallants" (with much less pathos), and caustic comedy in such stories as "Ivy Day in the Committee Room" (multiple protagonist) and "Grace."

The artistic foundations of the new movement of the twenties had been laid abroad; certainly such a European forerunner as Joyce was more significantly related to the American movement, directly or indirectly, than such American forerunners as Crane, Dreiser, or Miss Cather. Nor was it only the Americans who carried on or extended the developments of Joyce and Chekhov; at the same time Katherine Mansfield was writing stories in very much the same tradition in England. This is not

[3] Harry Levin, *James Joyce: A Critical Introduction* ("The Makers of Modern Literature"; Norfolk, Conn.: New Directions, 1941), p. 28.

to minimize the significance of American developments. *Dub-liners* is an exercise in certain new forms with certain new techniques, both effective and significant within a limited range, applied to a subject matter also of limited range. The modern writers treated in this study enlarged the Joycean forms, intensified them, varied them, and invented new forms that departed from them.

It has been said that the Joycean writer was driven to the development of "epiphanies" because modern life was too complicated to be treated in the conventional ways: "The writer," says Harry Levin, "no longer hoping to comprehend modern life in its chaotic fullness, was searching for external clues to inner meaning." [4] No doubt many influences urged the modern writers to develop new forms — forms obviously much more suitable to the new kinds of subject matter they wanted to treat. One might as easily, however, put it the other way and say that conceptions of new forms led writers to new subjects. The explanation most pertinent to a study of artistic developments is simply that the writers of the twenties were trying to produce more compelling and more memorable works of art. Most of the tendencies noted in these chapters are efforts in that direction. The enrichment of effect with the occasional sacrifice of power, the disturbance of the reader with the refusal to flatter him or offer easy relief for his emotions — the primary purpose of these developments was certainly to give the reader a deeper aesthetic pleasure. The disturbing emotion is vividly evoked; the catharsis is slow and difficult, but in the end more satisfying.

[4] *Ibid.*, p. 28.

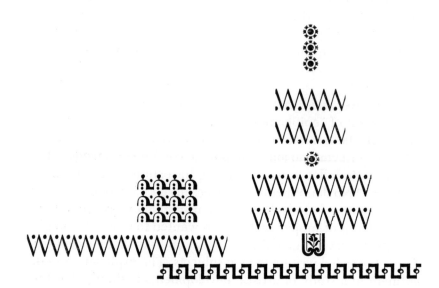

XVII: DRAMA AND NARRATIVE

Stories such as Hemingway's "Hills Like White Elephants" and "The Killers" have often been praised for artistic qualities that have little to do with the points thus far discussed. Much is made, for example, of the fact that both of these stories are told almost entirely through dialogue of a most terse and economical kind, or of Hemingway's famous power of "understatement," or of the loaded effectiveness of such moments as the following exchange between the girl who is going to have an abortion she doesn't want and the lover who wants her to have it:

"You've got to realize," he said, "that I don't want you to do it if you don't want to. I'm perfectly willing to go through with it if it means anything to you."

"Doesn't it mean anything to you? We could get along."

"Of course it does. But I don't want anybody but you. I don't want any one else. And I know it's perfectly simple."

274

"Yes, you know it's perfectly simple."

"It's all right for you to say that, but I do know it."

"Would you do something for me now?"

"I'd do anything for you."

"Would you please please please please please please please stop talking?"

The potency of such a scene in such a story depends not merely upon the author's invention of a plot or episode and characters interacting in such a way as to produce a certain effect; it depends also upon the manner in which the author tells about or "represents" this action and these characters. It depends, in other words, upon what may be called the story's techniques of representation, which may be distinguished from the story's form as discussed up to this point. The form exists for us, of course, only through the techniques — until it is represented we cannot perceive it; yet the kinds of techniques used, the ways in which forms are made to exist, may themselves vary in ways that are not exclusively dependent upon the form.

The most typical commentaries on the artistry of the new writers of the twenties concentrate upon their experiments with technique. Many critics tend to lump together under the heading "technique" the elements of form and technique that are here considered separately. This results, often, in disregard for such formal questions as have been considered in the previous chapters and a reduction of a writer's artistry solely to his manner of representing things. Certainly there is general agreement that the new stories display significant technical departures from the old. It will increase our understanding of the new movement to examine the new techniques independently of formal questions — to accept the forms as "given" and look directly at the kinds of things the author did to make them tangible.

In practice, no doubt, most writers conceive of a story's form and the technique of presenting it simultaneously: decisions as to the one lead to decisions as to the other, and the process can go in either direction. Analytically, however, we can regard problems of technique as *following* the writer's decisions about his action, characters, and intended effect. Having made his decisions as to form, every writer of fiction has to face the following problems of technique:

First, the problem of the *Narrator*, or "point of view" — who is the narrator, and what relation or what "access" does he have to the events of the story?

Second, the problem of *Particularity* — to what extent will the elements of the story be treated through particular details, to what extent will they be summed up or generalized?

Third, the problem of *Order* — what principles will govern the order in which the materials of the story are revealed to the reader?

Fourth, the problem of *Economy* — to what extent will elements of the story be left implicit, to be inferred by the reader from other elements that are treated explicitly?

Fifth, the problem of *Language* — what kinds of words, what "levels" of usage, what kinds of embellishments (such as figures of speech) will the author put into the mouths of his narrator and characters?

The last of these problems — language — will not be considered in this book. To all appearances, most significant variations in diction reflect individual differences between authors but not general differences between the two periods. Those whose use of language is most distinctive — James, for example, or Hemingway — do not seem to be significantly matched or imitated by the other writers of their periods. Generally speaking, there are in both periods writers who tend to some elaborateness of diction, complexity of sentence structure, and syntax — writers such as James, Mrs. Wharton, and Faulkner — others who, with simpler sentence structure, abound in metaphor — Crane, Fitzgerald, and to some extent Miss Porter — and others who aim for clear simplicity — Garland, Bierce, Hemingway.

One clear difference in language between the two periods is notable and obvious. This is the disappearance of dialect from the speech of the characters or — to put it more accurately — the disappearance of typographical indications of dialect: misspellings and apostrophes. Crane, Garland, and Mrs. Freeman are especially devoted to such devices, which are almost wholly dispensed with in the twenties, although a writer such as Faulkner still uses syntax, grammar, and vocabulary to suggest dialect differences. No doubt other, more subtle differences characterize the two periods — the language, we are told, is constantly changing — but such differences, which a linguist might note, do not, in all probability, have much to do with the developing art of the short story as such.

The other four problems are of great significance to the short-story writer, and differences in the way they are met can be readily detected. As will be shown, all of these problems are aspects of the fundamental technical question that every writer of fiction has constantly to face: the question of what to present by *dramatic* means and what by *narrative* means. In one way or another this question faces him with practically every word he writes.

In the literal sense, the treatment of an action is *dramatic* whenever the words are those of the characters themselves, directly quoted as in dialogue or "dramatic scenes." It is *narrative* whenever the author uses his own words to describe, sum up, or analyze the elements of the story. The dramatic method has the obvious advantage of being more truly a depiction, representation, or imitation of things, producing in the reader a stronger sense of immediacy or contact with the characters. The narrative method has the advantage of enabling the author to cover material rapidly and to present elements of a subtle or intricate nature that a dramatic method could present only in a bulky or awkward manner.

A story is, by definition, fundamentally a narration. Actually, of course, most stories — virtually all stories in the two periods being considered here — employ a combination of both methods: they are narratives that contain dramatic portions, passages, or scenes in which the narrator becomes a dramatist and quotes directly the things the characters said. Obviously the writer of fiction finds it desirable at certain points to utilize the advantages of drama and at other points to sacrifice these to the advantages of narrative. His biggest technical problem always is how best to exploit the advantages of both for his own purposes.

How he decides, at any point, depends upon the effect he wants to produce. The desired effect is determined by the form he has chosen; the purpose of the technique is to make that form as vivid and clear as possible so that it will exert its proper effect.

This does not mean that a given form will automatically pre-determine a given set of technical choices. True, we cannot easily imagine, with any good story, a technique better adapted to the form in all its detail than the technique actually used. We can conceive of an accumulation of technical knowledge — a succession of discoveries of ways of achieving effects not pre-viously achieved — whereby forms can be realized that could not be realized before. New ways of utilizing dramatic methods to achieve vividness and narrative methods to achieve propor-tion and emphasis, and hence clarity, make possible the effec-tive rendering of new forms that the older techniques could scarcely manage. Certainly the innovations of form in the twen-ties were made possible by the experiments with technique.

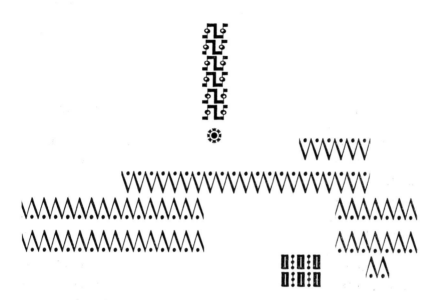

XVIII: THE NARRATOR

Since fiction is narrative it must have a narrator. This, of course, is the fundamental distinction between fiction and drama. The decisions as to what to narrate directly and what to treat dramatically belong to the narrator, whether or not we regard him as identical to the author.

Some critics prefer to reduce the main questions of technique in fiction to one of point of view, that is, the question of the choice of narrator. For our purposes, this is less fruitful than other technical matters. True, the author's first technical decision usually concerns the identity of the narrator and the point from which he views the action. But we may distinguish between the narrator's point of view and the manner in which, given that point of view, the author chooses to tell the story. The narrator's point of view, then, is the vantage point from

279

which it is presumed he has acquired his total knowledge of what goes on in the story. In most cases, his viewpoint is retrospective, and in most cases he has nearly full knowledge of everything in the story. But even after his point of view is fixed, he has important decisions to make concerning the best way to tell his tale. Given his knowledge, he has to decide what part of it to present through narration, what through dramatic means. Between the stories of the two periods, we shall find more significant differences concerning such decisions than concerning the original selection of narrator and point of view.

The point can be illustrated with Bierce's story, "An Occurrence at Owl Creek Bridge." Throughout most of the long final section of the story, the narrative appears to be from the point of view of the protagonist, who is having an hallucination of escape from the hangman's noose. At the end, the point of view shifts: suddenly we are outside the hero, watching him dangle dead in the noose. The narrator's point of view, in the story as a whole, then, is not the hero's; it is, rather, omniscient, enabling him to go inside the hero's mind when it suits him and outside when it suits him. It is not the choice of narrator that determines such a treatment; it merely makes it possible.

The narrators of most stories in both periods are omniscient in this sense. They posses knowledge both greater than that of any character in the story and greater than that of any conceivable passive witness on the stage who stands in relation to the action as the audience stands in relation to a play. Needless to say, the choice of such a narrator does not make for a dramatic effect in itself.

Yet it is possible to make a choice of narrator which is, itself, dramatic in a limited sense. The point of view of the narrator of "The Killers" is almost perfectly dramatic. He reports only what can be seen and heard on three successive stages. The result is that the story reads very much like a little play. With not more than one or two exceptions (notably the comments: "He had never had a towel in his mouth before" and "He was trying to swagger it off") the narrator's commentary could be compared to stage directions in a play — terse descriptions of physical action and of setting and costume. It is not absolutely dramatic: the gaps in time within the scene reflect the presence of a narrator deciding what to omit, and the placement of the "stage directions," as well as the choice of stressed details, indicates a narrator's mind at work.

The "stage-manager narrator," totally lacking in the early period, is, even in the twenties, a rarity. Indeed, apart from "The Killers," only Hemingway's "Hills Like White Elephants" and Miss Porter's "Rope" use this device. "Rope" shows a curious tendency to mute the dramatic quality by reporting the entire dialogue in indirect quotation, substituting "he" or "she" for "I" and dispensing with quotation marks.

The stage-manager narrator of the twenties may be regarded as the extreme result of restrictions which other, more or less omniscient, narrators tend to impose upon themselves. These are not the consequence of the choice of narrator but of the narrator's own choices and hence are more appropriately examined in a later chapter. Nevertheless, the author may attain some dramatic quality by the choice of another kind of narrator — one who is himself a participant in the action, a character on the stage. This is the so-called first-person narrator. In first-person narration, the author is, at least ostensibly, completely withdrawn; the story is literally a speech by one of the characters — a dramatic act of a sort.

In the early period, the first-person narrator was, except in stories by James, a rarity. Apart from James, the device is used in only nine stories in the early canon.[1] In each of these the narrator is an observer or witness to the action; in no case is he the protagonist. In the twenties, by contrast, first-person narration is almost three times as common as before. Furthermore, although the narrator is in most cases an observer of the action, in eleven stories he himself is the protagonist.[2]

[1] Bierce, "Son of the Gods," "Killed at Resaca," "George Thurston"; Dreiser, "Cruise of the 'Idlewild'"; Gerould, "Dominant Strain," "Pearls"; Wharton, "Coming Home," "Long Run"; Cather, "Wagner Matinee."
[2] He is the protagonist in Anderson's "I Want to Know Why," "Man Who Became a Woman," "I'm a Fool"; Hemingway, "My Old Man," "Alpine Idyll," "Che Dice," "In Another Country," "Now I Lay Me"; Porter, "That Tree"; Faulkner, "Ad Astra," "Mistral." He is an observer of the action in Anderson's

One suspects that the writers of the twenties were using this method to achieve a more dramatic effect. Such a method seems so obvious that one wonders why the earlier writers, who had a highly developed technique, were unwilling to use it. It is not enough to say that the forms they conceived were not generally adaptable to this technique. This no doubt was true, but it leaves unanswered the question why they so seldom, then, used forms that were adaptable to it. A more cogent possible explanation may be discerned in the following passage from Henry James, although the discussion applies to the novel rather than the short story. Actually, James was much more fond of the first-person narrator than were any of the other earlier writers, yet he made strong arguments against its use:

Suffice it, to be brief, that the first person, in the long piece, is a form foredoomed to looseness . . . Strether [in *The Ambassadors*] . . . has to keep in view proprieties much stiffer and more salutary than any our straight and credulous gape are likely to bring home to him, has exhibitional conditions to meet, in a word, that forbid the terrible *fluidity* of self-revelation . . . I had thus inevitably to set him up a confidant or two, to wave away with energy the custom of the seated mass of explanation after the fact, the inserted block of merely referential narrative.[3]

Another passage, closely related to this, further clarifies the danger of the first person: "The 'first person' then, so employed, is addressed by the author directly to ourselves, his possible readers." The first person, in other words, when it invited the author to introduce a "seated mass of explanation after the fact, the inserted block of merely referential narrative," actually becomes the very opposite of dramatic, for the narrator, instead of

---

"The Egg," "Death in the Woods," "Seeds"; Fitzgerald, "Rich Boy"; Hemingway, "Canary for One," "Fifty Grand," "Revolutionist"; Porter, "Magic"; Faulkner, "All the Dead Pilots," "Divorce in Naples," "Hair," "Rose for Emily," "That Evening Sun." Among these, "That Tree," like "Rope," is unusual in that what is essentially first-person narration is presented as indirect quotation. A few of these stories venture beyond the obvious confines of first-person narrative. In "Death in the Woods," "Rich Boy," "All the Dead Pilots," and "Hair," things are told which the narrator could scarcely have witnessed or learned without the aid of considerable creative imagining. Obviously the authors of such stories are eager to exploit the advantages of both first- and third-person narrative.

[3] James, *The Art of the Novel*, pp. 320–21.

being separated from the author, becomes one with him. The "fluidity" and "looseness" that James fears amount to a failure of dramatization, a failure to impose sufficiently the kinds of restrictions that a dramatic treatment demands.

It seems likely that most of the early writers feared similar dangers even in the "short piece." This conclusion is supported by the total absence in their stories of first-person *protagonists* (except, again, in some by James). Wherever the first-person *witness* is used, he provides a viewpoint external to the essential action, approximating that condition of drama whereby the audience witnesses everything from the outside.

Two kinds of action appear to have been considered suitable for such a treatment: the extraordinary, heroic public action, played out in full view of an anonymous crowd (Bierce's "A Son of the Gods" and "George Thurston"), and that kind of private action that involves a choice extraordinary for the extreme depth of perversion of values that it reveals. The latter treatment (e.g., Mrs. Gerould's "Pearls" and "The Dominant Strain") depends heavily upon interviews between the hero and the narrator, the latter an undisguised *ficelle* motivated by a strong curiosity as to what is going on in the hero's mind. In general, then, in all but James, the first person in the early period is restricted to stories dealing with acts that are meant to be astonishing, amazing, or remarkable in some way; it is used as a device to transmit to the reader this feeling of astonishment, often by direct statement of the narrator's own feelings of amazement.

In James himself, and in the writers of the twenties, the expansion of the use of the first person probably means less a disregard for the looseness that James feared than discovery of ways to exploit more fully the dramatic advantages of such a method. To explain this discovery, we must reconsider our original definition of the difference between the dramatic and narrative methods.

It is not the simple literal distinction between the two methods that makes such a significant difference in their effects or their advantages. A playwright, indeed, frequently has a very similar kind of choice to make — a choice as to whether to represent a particular action or to let an authoritative character narrate. The authoritative character himself becomes an author and stands between us and the action, just as does the narrator in a story. The crucial question, as far as the illusion of drama is concerned, is not so much a question of first- or third-person narration as of the intervention of the author's voice between the action and the reader. Nor does it matter much that the author's voice is veiled in the voice of an "authoritative" character; if the character represents the author the effect is not greatly different from the effect if the author speaks directly in his own person. Thus it is that James can say that "the 'first person' then, so employed, is addressed by the author directly to ourselves, his possible readers."

The essential difference between the dramatic and narrative methods, then, depends upon the extent to which an authoritative voice intervenes between the action and us. If first-person narration is potentially dramatic because the author has given way to a character in the telling, it will be all the more dramatic when the narrator's account and judgment of things differ from what may be presumed to be the author's "true" judgment of them. The most striking difference between the first-person narrators of the two periods is that in most of the later stories the reader is aware, to varying degrees, of the narrator's *fallibility*; he is obliged to read between the lines or make inferences beyond the conclusion of the story.

Some stories, to be sure, continue to use the older pattern: a narrator is witness to events of an astonishing or extraordinary kind.[4] In such cases, the narrator may or may not show some degree of fallibility in his treatment. In Miss Porter's "Magic," for example, it is marked: the hairdresser seems to believe that the prostitute was brought back to the brothel by a magic spell, but the reader knows better. In others, such as "Seeds," the narrator shows little fallibility; the dramatic effect depends simply upon the narrator's external viewpoint of the protagonist's case. Such a story continues to utilize dramatic possibilities recognized by the earlier writers — namely, that the first

[4] As in Anderson's "The Egg," "Death in the Woods," "Seeds"; Fitzgerald, "Rich Boy"; Hemingway, "Fifty Grand"; Faulkner, "Hair," "All the Dead Pilots," "Rose for Emily"; Porter, "Magic."

person is convenient for a dramatic treatment of the process of learning things. But whereas earlier first-person narrators discovered things about other characters, many of the later ones discover things that are significant to their own situations. Here the fallibility of the narrator is always evident, revealed in his failure to make explicit the discovery that can or should be made in the circumstances. In the episodes of discovery, the discovery is realized only on the intuitive level. In other stories, the character actually fails to understand what the reader understands, as for example when the boy in "I Want to Know Why" is baffled by his ignorance of the force of sexuality in grown men. Such a failure serves to distinguish character from author, thus providing the reader with the essential dramatic illusion of gazing directly upon an action: in episodes of choice, especially, wherein the display of incomplete understanding itself is a manifestation of crucial choice, the narration is truly a "dramatic act."

In many cases the fallibility of the narrator may be only an illusion; it does not always indicate a real defect of understanding on his part. When the narrator of Hemingway's "Che ti Dice la Patria?" concludes his picture of his trip through Italy with the following disclaimer — "Naturally, in such a short trip, we had no opportunity to see how things were with the country or the people" — we conclude that he is being deliberately ironic, that he has strong opinions and feelings about what he has seen, and that he is adopting an appearance of fallibility in order to achieve some sort of effect. "Fallibility" of this sort is thus not a consequence of the author's choice of narrator but of the narrator's choice as to the manner in which he will tell his story.

A third choice of narrator which makes for a dramatic effect is that of the narrator whose point of view is confined throughout the story to a single character. Ideally, he tells only what that character might know, think, or judge. The reader will tend, in such a case, to identify the narrator with that character, thus receiving an effect similar to that given by a first-person narrator. Narrators more or less limited in this way are not uncommon in stories of the early period; they are the usual thing in James's and Miss Cather's stories and are common also in those by Crane, Mrs. Wharton, and Mrs. Gerould. Seldom is the limitation very strict. The narrator frequently takes advantage of third-person detachment to give information or make judgments that the character himself could scarcely make; the stories could not be translated into the first person without drastic alterations. Although Dreiser's "Free," for example, has one of the most limited points of view in the entire canon, being largely an account of the hero's thoughts and recollections, it contains passages such as the following, which makes judgments that the hero himself could not make: "And yet being conventional in mood and training and utterly domesticated by time and conditions over which he seemed not to have much control . . . he had drifted, had not taken any drastic action." Dreiser's "Nigger Jeff" contains such characterizations as this: "With the cruel instinct of the budding artist he always was . . ." Although Crane's "The Open Boat" is presented largely from the viewpoint of the correspondent, it includes deviations into the experience of other characters, such as "none of them knew the colour of the sky," or "as for the reflections of the men, there was a great deal of rage in them. Perchance they might be formulated thus. . . ." James is usually very strict in limiting his point of view, but even as he does so, the reader is always aware of the author's presence, if not as a source of knowledge at least as a personality, as in the following passage from "The Tree of Knowledge":

He couldn't tell Mrs. Mallow — or at least he supposed, excellent man, he couldn't — that she was the one beautiful reason he had never married; any more than he could tell her husband that the sight of the multiplied marbles in that gentleman's studio was an affliction of which even time had never blunted the edge. His victory, however, as I have intimated, in regard to these productions, was not simply in his not having let it out that he deplored them; it was, remarkably, in his not having kept it in by anything else.

The number of stories with similarly limited narrators is not greater in the twenties than before, but many of these stories are stricter in the limitations imposed.[5] In such stories, especially

[5] Especially in Anderson's "Nobody Knows"; Fitzgerald, " 'Sensible Thing,' " "Winter Dreams"; Hemingway, "Battler," "Big Two-Hearted River," "Cross-

those by Hemingway, the narrator has no access to anything beyond what the protagonist himself would have seen or understood. Each of these stories could have been written in the first person without any severe violation of logic. The effect is thus similar to that of a first-person story, possessing the same dramatic advantages. Such stories put a similar emphasis upon discovery; several of them even show the same kind of fallibility in the character from whose point of view the story is told, as in the following examples from Hemingway:

In the early morning on the lake sitting in the stern of the boat with his father rowing, he felt quite sure that he would never die.[6]

In the morning there was a big wind blowing and the waves were running high up on the beach and he was awake a long time before he remembered that his heart was broken.[7]

The narrator here, one feels, differs from the protagonist only in his greater articulateness, which enables him, not to state things that the protagonist would not know, but to describe what the protagonist thinks and feels in ways that might be beyond him.[8]

Because of the close resemblance between these stories and those in the first person, it is difficult to determine why one method should have been used in one story, the other in another. There is an advantage in using a narrator to articulate an inarticulate character's feelings, as in the stories of young Nick Adams. Beyond this, the author may have felt that a first-person account in such stories, by its retrospective quality, might have dissipated the immediacy of the depiction of the confused state of mind of a child. In some cases, also, remnants of the conven-

---

Country Snow," "End of Something," "Indian Camp," "Ten Indians," "Three-Day Blow"; Porter, "Jilting of Granny Weatherall," "Theft"; Faulkner, "Carcassonne." Of these, the limitation of the narrator is least in the stories by Fitzgerald, which contain passages as detached from the hero as the following excerpt from "Winter Dreams": "This story is not his biography, remember, although things creep in which have nothing to do with those dreams he had when he was young. We are almost done with them and with him now."

[6] Hemingway, "Indian Camp."

[7] Hemingway, "Ten Indians."

[8] Thus the narrator in Anderson's "Nobody Knows" refers to George Willard as "the young newspaper reporter" and describes George's feelings thus: "He became wholly the male, bold and aggressive. In his heart there was no sympathy for her."

tional fear of the first person may account for the refusal to
use it; "he" has a more objective sound than "I." [9]

The first-person and quasi-first-person narrator are more
important in stories by Hemingway and Faulkner — in each case
accounting for more than half the writer's total output — than in
those of the other writers of the twenties. Elsewhere the narrator continues to retain a certain freedom in his point of view,
a limited omniscience, just as in most of the stories of the early
period. Thus, although one sees, more frequently than earlier,
an attempt to achieve a more dramatic effect by the choice of
narrator, the methods thus far described concern only a fairly
small number of stories in the canon as a whole and are only
preliminary to far more significant kinds of choices that the narrator himself, whether first-or third-person, restricted or omniscient, has to make in the actual telling of the story.

[9] Miss Porter's experiments in "Rope" and "That Tree" suggest such an
unwillingness to use "I." By making constant use of indirect quotations, these
stories retain the advantages of first-person narration without using it. In the
canon, "Magic" is the only first-person story by Miss Porter.
The choice between first-person and restricted third-person narration depends ultimately on the very particular effect which the writer intends his story
to have. Appendix D illustrates some of the reasons which may determine such
a choice, contrasting Hemingway's "An Alpine Idyll" and "Cross-Country
Snow."

XIX: DRAMATIC PARTICULARITY

The presence of a narrator distinguishes a story from a play. But the narrator, as has been said, is free to use the techniques of drama in various ways in order to achieve the vividness of a play. We think of the story as "dramatic" in the literal sense whenever the narrator uses dialogue, speaks with the words of his characters, for this is what is done in plays. As we have suggested, the use of dialogue is not the only source of dramatic vividness in a story: the crucial point, rather, is the extent to which we are aware of a narrative voice interposing itself between the action and us. The narrator may become a dramatist in the literal sense in scenes of dialogue, but he may also present his narrative in such a way that it exhibits qualities that we ordinarily associate with drama, qualities that contribute to the vividness characteristic of a play and can contribute a similar vividness when incorporated in narration.

289

The writers of the twenties attempt to increase the dramatic vividness of their stories by such means. One way is by increasing the particularity of their narratives. One of the distinguishing features of drama is that everything is rendered through particularized actions and speeches. A dramatist does not have the narrator's privilege of generalizing a number of events (e.g., "Louisa used china every day . . ."), of summing up the consequence of a series of actions (e.g., "for fourteen out of fifteen years the two had not seen each other, and they had seldom exchanged letters"), or of explaining the actions that he shows (e.g., "she caught his meaning in a flash" or "said Joe, sympathetically"), unless he turns one of his characters temporarily into an authoritative narrator.

Dramatic action is particularized in two senses. In the first place, it is unique: every event is a single event that happens at one moment in time, no matter how many similar undepicted events may be assumed to have occurred at other moments. In the second place, it is coherent: not only does time move forward, but it moves forward without skips. As long as the curtain is up, all the components of a developing action, all the particulars in a time sequence, must be revealed.

Such particularity is hostile to brevity. The primary advantage of narrative over drama is that it enables the writer to cover the equivalent amount of ground more swiftly and concisely than drama does. The subject of a short story is characteristically too diffuse to sustain a fully dramatic treatment of all its elements. The writers of both periods had to decide what parts of their stories they wished to present through particulars, what parts through generalization and summary.

Most stories of the twenties give us an impression of being more particular in their treatment than do their predecessors. We feel a more dramatic effect, a greater vividness, not only in such a story as "The Killers," which is almost all dialogue, but also in a story such as "Flowering Judas," which has almost no dialogue. Asked to explain our impression of dramatic vividness in the latter story, we may well cite the concreteness of its parts, the particularity of its treatment. But we are still dealing with impressions. If we examine the stories of the two canons in detail, we find that the difference between them is less a quantitative matter—less a difference in the particularization that the stories contain—than in the kinds of things that they particularize. This can be seen by examining separately the dramatic scenes and the narrative portions of these stories.

SCENE

Most stories in the early period follow a standard pattern in their employment of dramatic and narrative methods, regardless of whether the narration is first-person, restricted, or omniscient. In this pattern, dialogue is organized into "dramatic scenes." These are of variable length but tend to be coherent and unified, well-defined in their beginnings and endings. They resemble more closely than anything else in the story the scenes of a play. They are more particularized, in both our senses of the term; the speeches are the particulars, and they exist in a coherent relationship, as in a play.

In most early stories these dramatic scenes are the main "props" around which the stories are built. The writers ordinarily use three or four or more major scenes, separated and prepared for by passages of narrative, also of variable length. The pattern is so familiar to readers of short stories that it hardly needs demonstration. It is illustrated in Appendix E, which consists of a line by line breakdown of two stories into their narrative and dramatic portions. One of these, Mrs. Freeman's "Calla-lilies and Hannah," consists of four major dramatic scenes separated by narrative which in several places yields to short dramatic scenes of a transitional nature. The other, James's "The Middle Years," has longer narrative passages which culminate in three fairly short but significant dramatic scenes and two major dramatic scenes.

In the early period exceptions to this general pattern are not common. A few stories, notable only in Bierce, are almost entirely narrated; the scenes they contain are brief and fragmentary.[1] A few approach the other extreme, centering in a single

[1] Notably, Bierce's "Chickamauga," "Horseman in the Sky," "Son of the Gods," "Occurrence at Owl Creek Bridge," "One of the Missing"; Cather, "Paul's Case," "Garden Lodge" (to some extent); Crane, "Open Boat"; Dreiser, "Free," "Lost Phoebe."

dramatic scene with relatively little narrative introduction and explanation.[2] The characteristic pattern of three or four major scenes is especially prominent in the work of Mrs. Freeman, Garland, and James.

This general pattern is repeated in many stories of the twenties, but there are a good many more exceptions, and these often deviate strikingly from the usual pattern. In a few important stories the dramatic portion is enlarged so that it almost completely overshadows the narrative. This pattern has already been noticed at its extreme in "The Killers," "Hills Like White Elephants," and "Rope"; it is approached also in such stories by Hemingway as "The Three-Day Blow," "The Battler," and "A Pursuit Race." Yet this literally dramatic treatment is exceptional in the twenties. Many stories dispense entirely, or almost entirely, with dramatic scenes. Most of the *Winesburg* stories are, by earlier standards, short on dramatic scenes; such stories as "Paper Pills," "Adventure," and "The Strength of God" (except at the very end) are almost entirely narrated. The same is true of such other well-known stories by Anderson as "I Want to Know Why" and "The Man Who Became a Woman." Nor is this merely an idiosyncracy of Anderson. Hemingway's "Big Two-Hearted River" is devoid of dialogue, and such technically significant stories as Miss Porter's "Flowering Judas" and Faulkner's "A Rose for Emily" contain only extremely brief and fragmentary dialogue passages embedded in an over-all narrative texture.

In general, then, the tendency of the writers of the twenties is to cut down on the number of dramatic scenes. In addition to the ten or twelve stories with virtually no scenes of dialogue at all, at least twenty contain or develop only a single scene.[3]

---

[2] Bierce, "Parker Adderson"; Gerould, "Weaker Vessel"; Wharton, "Dilettante." Even these stories contain large segments of narrative. To these may be added some stories, primarily narrative, which are kept within the confines of a single incident: Bierce, "Chickamauga," "One of the Missing," "Son of the Gods"; Crane, "Experiment in Misery," "Open Boat"; Cather, "Wagner Matinee," "Garden Lodge."

Other interesting departures from the usual pattern appear in Bierce's "Story of a Conscience" and Mrs. Wharton's "Long Run" and "Quicksand." Each contains within the frame of a longer dramatic scene a long first-person narrative.

[3] Stories of the twenties without dialogue, or using only limited dialogue:

Though this scene may be virtually the whole story, as in "Hills Like White Elephants," usually it follows an introductory summary narrative, which may be fairly extensive or, especially in the later stories, quite brief. A less extreme reduction is that of stories whose treatment is confined to a single short incident composed of two or more short, closely related scenes; this pattern, which was in the early period the most common departure from the dominant pattern, remains as frequent in the twenties as it was earlier.[4] Including these, it is possible, though the contrast is less drastic than some that have been noted, to list more than forty stories — almost half the canon — which differ from the prevailing earlier practice by their reduction of the number of dramatic scenes.

As the number of scenes is cut down, the scenes themselves are less fully and elaborately developed. This cannot be demonstrated easily, but the tendency can be suggested by some contrasts between typical scenes characteristic of the two periods.

Typical of the early period is the extract from a scene in "Under the Lion's Paw," quoted in Appendix F. Perhaps the most important distinguishing feature of the early scenes, as demonstrated by this illustration, is the effort to maintain a playlike coherence: the scenes unfold with only a minimal number of breaks or skips. This has some important consequences. Often it means the introduction of material relatively unimportant to the unfolding of the story as a whole. Greetings and introductions of one person to another are recorded; partings must often

Anderson's "Death," "Death in the Woods," "Hands," "Man Who Became a Woman," "Paper Pills"; Hemingway, "Revolutionist," "Big Two-Hearted River"; Porter, "Flowering Judas," "Jilting of Granny Weatherall," "Magic"; Faulkner, "Rose for Emily," "Carcassonne." Others that consist of or develop only a single scene: Anderson's "Adventure," "Awakening," "The Egg," "Loneliness," "Strength of God," "Teacher," "Thinker"; Hemingway, "In Another Country," "Now I Lay Me," "Soldier's Home," "Up in Michigan," "Alpine Idyll," "Battler," "Cat in the Rain" (scene divided), "Cross-Country Snow," "End of Something," "Pursuit Race," "Simple Enquiry," "Three-Day Blow."

[4] Early period: Bierce, "Affair at Coulter's Notch," "One Kind of Officer," "Story of a Conscience"; Crane, "Bride Comes to Yellow Sky," "Five White Mice," "Horses — One Dash!"; Garland, "Day's Pleasure," "Return of a Private"; Wharton, "The Choice," "Quicksand," "The Reckoning"; Cather, "Sculptor's Funeral"; James, "Story In It." Twenties: Anderson, " 'Queer,' " "Unlighted Lamps"; Fitzgerald, "Baby Party," "Benediction"; Hemingway, "Canary for One," "Doctor and Doctor's Wife," "Killers," "Out of Season," "Ten Indians"; Porter, "Theft"; Faulkner, "Ad Astra," "Dry September."

be accounted for; a character may rise and prepare to leave several speeches before the scene ends. But even when this is avoided, coherence demands that the important exchanges in a scene — the crucial revelations, decisions, expressions of feeling, or whatever may be its *raison d'être* — should develop naturally. Hence the preliminary exchanges that lead the conversation to these crucial points must also be recorded, and the transitions between one point in the dialogue and another must be made. Though this procedure may develop more suspense than do greetings and partings, and is used by a writer such as James to produce a masterful development unmatched in later stories, it too threatens, in the work of most of the other writers, to load the scene with dramatized material of minor significance. In addition to this, coherence imposes special demands upon realistic writers who want their scenes to be lifelike: hence Garland finds it necessary not merely to suggest that two conversations are going on at once, but to reproduce alternately portions of both, though the point thereby dramatized has little to do with the essential action, character, or thought in the story. So too must he throw in kinds of irrelevant interjections — "'Hain't Ike got home yet, Sairy?'" — whose purpose of suggesting the irrelevance of live talk is itself not particularly relevant to the primary purposes of the story as a whole.

Another feature of the fulness of elaboration in many of these early scenes is illustrated, in the passage quoted, by the abundance of Mrs. Council's sympathetic and kind remarks. The point that she is full of generosity and kindness is established not by one but by a whole series of instances. The effect is to reduce large parts of the scene to a purely emphatic function. The action is not advanced nor does suspense develop here; nothing new, nothing that the reader does not already know, is added by such reiterations. Yet Mrs. Council's kindness, although not irrelevant, is definitely a secondary issue in the plot, useful to typify the good will of Haskins' new neighbors, which is demonstrated by many other instances more pertinent to Haskins' problems. Often in the early period large parts of a scene will be devoted to emphasizing just such secondary points as these.

In stories of the twenties an effort is made to cut out dead weight in the internal construction of scenes. This is done in several ways. In many stories the principle of playlike coherence between speeches is rejected. The author deliberately skips in his reporting of dialogue; the reader is encouraged to believe that only the essential parts of a conversation are being reproduced. Left out are the greetings, introductions, lifelike distractions, even the buildups and transitions between essential points.

Such a technique is obvious in the early stories of the decade. Notice, for example, how many *Winesburg* scenes involving George Willard fail to reproduce anything that he says. The technique can be illustrated in detail by an examination of the scene between Seth and Helen that concludes "The Thinker." The introduction ignores the usual greetings: "It was Helen White who came to the door and found Seth standing at the edge of the porch. Blushing with pleasure, she stepped forward, closing the door softly." The scene that follows, which includes narrative descriptions of the night and of Seth's memories and feelings, covers five pages in the original text — approximately one thousand words. A complete transcript of the dialogue in this scene, including all the quoted speeches, with other elements omitted, is much shorter and reads as follows:

Seth: I'm going to get out of town. I don't know what I'll do, but I'm going to get out of here and go to work. I think I'll go to Columbus. Perhaps I'll get into the State University down there. Anyway, I'm going. I'll tell mother tonight. [After hesitation] Perhaps you wouldn't mind coming to walk with me?

[They walk]

Helen: That's Belle Turner. I didn't know she had a fellow. I thought she was too old for that.

Seth: George Willard's in love with you . . . . He's writing a story, and he wants to be in love. He wants to know how it feels. He wanted me to tell you and see what you said.

Seth: Mother'll make a fuss, I suppose. She hasn't thought at all about what I'm going to do in life. She thinks I'm going to stay on here forever just being a boy . . . . You see, I've got to strike out. I've got to get to work. It's what I'm good for.

Helen: What will you do up there?

Seth: Everyone talks and talks. I'm sick of it. I'll do something,

get into some kind of work where talk don't count. Maybe I'll just
be a mechanic in a shop. I don't know. I guess I don't care much. I
just want to work and keep quiet. That's all I've got in my mind
. . . . It's the last time we'll see each other.

    Helen: I think I'd better be going along . . . . Don't you go with
me. I want to be alone. You go and talk with your mother. You'd
better do that now.

Such a transcript makes clear how much probable dialogue has
been left out. All dialogue lead-ins are omitted; questions are
asked, their answers left to inference, and answers are given to
questions left to inference. Most striking is Helen's extraordinary
silence, which, if this were a literal transcript, would certainly
have been discouraging to Seth. What she does say helps to
make clear the important point: not that she is silent but that
she is inarticulate, unable to express the feelings that Seth's decision has provoked in her. Nor are the references to George and
Belle Turner mere lifelike distractions; they dramatize the timidity and indirectness of Seth and Helen concerning the idea of
love that is on both their minds. As for Seth's reiterations of his
intention, the suppression of all other dialogue makes it stand
out (as Mrs. Council's reiterations did not) as the only thing
that Seth can articulate clearly. His manifest resentment and im-
patience reveals indeed something quite different from what he
is actually saying. It is clear that he is suffering, that he has
feelings, is lonely, and almost in love with Helen White — all
things that he does not consciously realize. The spotlighted reiterations reveal by indirection the most important issue in this
scene, namely, he has failed to express his feelings to Helen because he does not know what those feelings are.

    Here, then, much of the secondary content of a dramatic
scene is replaced by narrative, leaving only the most essential
elements for a fully dramatic treatment. In the early period, to
be sure, a somewhat similar suppression of secondary elements
is found in some of the shorter secondary dramatic scenes, as,
for example, the first scene in "The Middle Years," in which dialogue plays a significant part only at the end. Except occasionally in stories by James, the speeches, even in such scenes, are
not spaced throughout the narrative as here and they tend, in

James as in the others, to have a coherent relationship to each other even when they are separated by narrative. More significant is the point that the scene quoted from "The Thinker" is the major, climactic scene in the story; scenes of equivalent importance in the early period were hardly ever treated in this manner.

In many of his most typical scenes Anderson goes further than this; the narrative tends to take over almost completely. A scenic quality is retained through the use of particular incidents in a particular time and place, but only the climactic verbal acts are quoted. An illustration of this is provided by the climactic scene from "The Teacher," quoted in full in Appendix G. It is easy to imagine how one of the earlier writers might have handled such a scene, reproducing at least a portion of the passionate talk of "life," steering perhaps to some talk of love in the abstract so as to make Kate's provocative utterance plausible, an exchange as George approaches her, an exclamation at the repulse, perhaps another exchange, and certainly a reproduction (tamed to conform to the proprieties of the time) of George's swearing at the end — all tending to a great enlargement of the scene.

Other writers of the twenties are less likely to economize by such simple devices. In most scenes from such stories as Hemingway's "The Killers," "Hills Like White Elephants," and "Soldier's Home," for instance, there is no implication that any talk has been omitted. Though beginnings and ends of scenes may be truncated (as they were also, of course, in many of the earlier stories), the ideal of playlike coherence seems to have been retained or revived. Yet the scenes give an impression of economy lacking in earlier stories. A transcript of the complete dialogue of the crucial scene in Hemingway's "The Doctor and the Doctor's Wife," included in Appendix H, shows this. Though the full significance of the speeches quoted is not clear out of context, every speech is directly pertinent to the doctor's highly uncomfortable emotional state and the lack of understanding on his wife's part — the crucial issues of the story. Every speech contributes to the suppressed conflict between them; at the same time, it is clear that no speeches have been omitted, nor is there any sacrifice in the effect of lifelikeness.

Such economy in the use of particulars in a dramatic scene is not to be accounted for simply by superior mastery of the art of dialogue. It is true that this and other scenes by Hemingway achieve an unprecedented effect of naturalness, but it is not true that Hemingway was a greater master of dialogue than James was. The natural effect depends rather upon a more rigorous limitation of the scenic method to certain kinds of materials. It is a safe assertion that dialogue in stories of the twenties tends to be limited to the expression of a character's emotions or of those verbals acts that do most to influence his emotions.[5] These emotional states are, as has been shown in earlier chapters, the crucial issues of the most characteristic stories in the twenties. What has happened is that the writers of the twenties have attempted, with greater rigor than earlier writers, to limit scenes of dialogue and dramatized speeches only to the most crucial moments of the plot or episode. There is relatively little verbal development — change caused by and evolving through the exchange of speeches — and the expository and emphatic functions that some speeches in the twenties fulfil are performed simultaneously with the unfolding of the crucial emotional action. A story such as "Hills Like White Elephants" simply shows this tendency carried to an extreme. Though the story is almost entirely dialogue, no speech is merely expository. Every speech expresses and furthers the conflict; the necessary background to the conflict — the facts that the characters are lovers, that she is pregnant, that she is to have an abortion which he urges but she does not want, that they have already decided on it — is entirely implicit in the conflict itself as it develops.

The most obvious purpose of this tendency to reduce the particulars in dramatic scenes is to achieve greater brevity in the representation of the action. It also enhances the emphasis in the story. For that which is dramatized stands out; if there is less dramatization of secondary material, the things that are

---

[5] It is true that relatively few stories of the twenties actually achieve such complete concentration; the practice is a tendency, not an absolute achievement. It is most nearly brought off in Anderson's *Winesburg* stories and Hemingway's "End of Something," "Three-Day Blow," "Indian Camp," "Up in Michigan," "Soldier's Home," "Cat in the Rain," "In Another Country," in Faulkner's "That Evening Sun" and "All the Dead Pilots," and in Porter's "Rope."

dramatized become, by contrast, all the more vivid. One feels, when looking at the results, that the writers of the twenties wanted a sharper contrast, a sharper emphasis, and were willing to sacrifice the dramatic vividness of some of their materials in the belief that the dramatic effect of the story as a whole depends less on how much is dramatized than on what is dramatized. Of course, the earlier writers realized this, too, as can be seen in their practice of pivoting their stories around "key" dramatic scenes; the writers of the twenties have refined the principle further by pivoting the scenes themselves around "key" dramatic passages.

NARRATIVE

Even though the final dramatic quality of a story may depend more on how the essentials are handled than on how other elements are handled, one can hardly expect that reducing the number and particularity of dramatic scenes will enhance the total dramatic effect if this is the only technical change. The writers of the twenties were aware that if they were to sacrifice certain sources of dramatic vividness for the sake of brevity and emphasis, they must compensate for the loss by providing drama in other ways. Hence they made up for the reduction of dramatic scenes by a refinement of techniques in the narrative portions of the stories. They tried, in almost every story, to give to these narrated parts more of the qualities normally associated with drama than the narrations in earlier stories usually possessed. And just as the dramatic scenes were rendered less significant, both in their particularity and as particulars in the story as a whole, so the narrative segments became more particularized than before.

This particularizing of the narrative segments, unfortunately, is more difficult to demonstrate than the changes in the use of dramatic scenes. The narratives in the early stories are also highly particularized in their depiction of action. Such passages as the following — a characteristic account of a series of unique events — are frequent:

Suddenly one of the doors flew open, and a little figure shot out. She went down the corridor with a swift trot like a child. She had on nothing but a woollen petticoat and a calico waist; she held her head down, and her narrow shoulders worked as she ran; her mop of soft white hair flew out. The children looked around at her; she was a horrible caricature of themselves . . . . [The other inmates] demonstrated that Sally had torn her bed to pieces, that it had been very nicely made, and that she should be punished. (Freeman, "Sister Liddy")

Just as frequent are passages such as the following, especially in the stories of Mrs. Freeman, Mrs. Wharton, Mrs. Gerould, and Garland, if not of Bierce and Crane:

Louisa used china every day — something which none of her neighbors did. They whispered about it among themselves. Their daily tables were laid with common crockery, their sets of best china stayed in the parlor closet, and Louisa Ellis was no richer nor better bred than they. Still she would use the china. She had for her supper a glass dish full of sugared currants, a plate of little cakes, and one of light white biscuits. Also a leaf or two of lettuce, which she cut up daintily. Louisa was very fond of lettuce, which she raised to perfection in her little garden. She ate quite heartily, though in a delicate, pecking way. It seemed almost surprising that any considerable bulk of the food should vanish. (Freeman, "A New England Nun")

Although there are particular details of a kind in such a passage, most of the actions are generalized or summed up. They are not unique events, nor are they presented in terms of unique component events. The following is another typical illustration:

Haskins worked like a fiend, and his wife, like the heroic woman that she was, bore also uncomplainingly the most terrible burdens. They rose early and toiled without intermission till the darkness fell on the plain, then tumbled into bed, every bone and muscle aching with fatigue, to rise with the sun next morning to the same round of the same ferocity of labor. (Garland, "Under the Lion's Paw")

In the following passage, although the events are unique, they are not particularized; that is, the reader is made aware — especially through such expressions as "a note of jubilation," "mitigated the distress," "learned of her mother's decision," and "no one understood this decision" — of a scene not explicitly recorded:

There was a note of jubilation in the air, for the party had "gone

off" so extraordinarily well, and so completely, as it appeared, to the
satisfaction of Mrs. Lorin Boulger, that Wilbour's early appointment
to Rome was almost to be counted on. So certain did this seem that
the prospect of a prompt reunion mitigated the distress with which
Leila learned of her mother's decision to return almost immediately
to Italy. No one understood this decision; it seemed to Leila absolutely unintelligible that Mrs. Lidcote should not stay on with them
till their own fate was fixed, and Wilbour echoed her astonishment.
(Wharton, "Autres Temps")

The narrative here is summary narration: a chain of particular
events is summed up in one sentence or phrase.

Of course, the difference between summary narration and
particular narration is relative. When words are the medium for
representing action, the only fully particularized treatment is the
dramatic speech; all other actions (represented with full particularity in the drama or cinema by spectacle or sound effects, i.e.
by nonverbal means) can always be broken down, theoretically,
at least, into smaller and finer components, so that every narrative description of an action is, in a sense, a summary. There is
a difference, nevertheless, in the degree of particularity between
such passages as those just quoted and the following, from Hemingway's "Indian Camp":

Across the bay they found the other boat beached. Uncle George
was smoking a cigar in the dark. The young Indian pulled the boat
way up on the beach. Uncle George gave both the Indians cigars.

They walked up from the beach through a meadow that was
soaking wet with dew, following the young Indian who carried a
lantern. Then they went into the woods and followed a trail that led
to the logging road that ran back into the hills. It was much lighter
on the logging road as the timber was cut away on both sides. The
young Indian stopped and blew out his lantern and they all walked
on along the road.

The effect of greater particularity is probably to be attributed
primarily to the kinds of acts that are summed up, largely physical in this case. They are of a kind so common and normal to
the experience of every reader that he can immediately visualize
their component parts as soon as the act is identified: a man
smoking a cigar, a man pulling a boat up on a beach, men walk-

ing through a meadow, a young man carrying a lantern and
stopping to blow it out. Contrast "Uncle George gave both Indians cigars" with "The prospect of a prompt reunion mitigated
the distress with which Leila learned of her mother's decision
to return almost immediately to Italy." The much greater complexity of unspecified detail in the latter passage is obvious, involving as it does a complex interaction of personalities in a
situation charged with tension. The reader is aware that the
unspecified scene between Leila and her mother might have
developed in a number of different possible ways, that significant
component parts of the summarized action are, in other words,
variable. True, Uncle George may have given the Indians cigars
in a number of different ways, but the manner in which he did
this is insignificant in the emotional context of the scene as a
whole.

Yet this particular contrast, taken by itself, is misleading.
It is true that one can find more passages like the one from Hemingway in stories of the twenties than earlier — especially in
Hemingway's stories. But one can also find many passages that
seem to be no more particularized than the passage from Mrs.
Wharton's story. The scene from Anderson's "The Teacher,"
quoted in Appendix G, might be used to suggest that there has
been little change at all between the two periods in this regard.
Statements such as the following are just as "summary" as those
from "Autres Temps":

For an hour she sat by the stove in the office talking of life . . . . She
became inspired as she sometimes did in the presence of the children
in school. A great eagerness . . . had possession of her. So strong
was her passion that it became something physical. (Anderson, "The
Teacher")

In the following passages recurring events are generalized as
freely as in Garland's or Mrs. Freeman's stories:

No great underlying purpose lay back of his habitual silence, and
he had no definite plan for his life. When the boys with whom he
associated were noisy and quarrelsome, he stood quietly at one side.
With calm eyes he watched the gesticulating lively figures of his
companions. He wasn't particularly interested in what was going on,

and sometimes wondered if he would ever be particularly interested in anything. (Anderson, "The Thinker")

Or:

For years she had been what is called "stage-struck" and had paraded through the streets with traveling men guests at her father's hotel, wearing loud clothes and urging them to tell her of life in the cities out of which they had come. (Anderson, "Mother")

Or:

She is not at home in the world. Every day she teaches children who remain strangers to her, though she loves their tender round hands and their charming opportunist savagery. She knocks at unfamiliar doors not knowing whether a friend or a stranger shall answer . . . (Porter, "Flowering Judas")

Yet there is certainly a difference between the two periods. Partly it is a difference in the functions performed by the summed-up action, a matter to be considered in a later chapter, and partly the result of the increased use of a technique similar to that of breaking up the coherence of dramatic scenes. Just as the dead weight is often removed from scenes by means of skips and omissions, with narrative interposed to bridge the gaps, so the typical new narration achieves concreteness through frequent shifts from general statements to briefly indicated particular acts and briefly quoted speeches from many unrecorded dramatic scenes. Such a narration, in fact, is often a composite of fragments of many particular scenes or incidents, joined by brief summary passages. In the more extreme cases (for example, Faulkner's "A Rose for Emily" and Miss Porter's "Flowering Judas") the effect is to break down almost completely the distinction between scene and narrative, which was formerly always so clear-cut. In all cases it lends to the summary narrative a vividness and immediacy usually associated with the dramatic method.

This technique may be best shown in long passages, but its nature can be suggested by a few brief quotations. The passage from Anderson's "The Thinker," quoted above, is directly followed, without paragraph division, by a particular idea which has the effect of throwing all the previous generalizations into the context of Seth's thought at that particular moment:

Now, as he stood in the half-darkness by the window watching the baker, he wished that he himself might become thoroughly stirred by something, even by the fits of sullen anger for which Baker Groff was noted.

The next sentence is even more particular, quoting Seth's thought in his own words:

"It would be better for me if I could become excited and wrangle about politics like windy old Tom Willard," he thought, as he left the window and went again along the hallway to the room occupied by his friend, George Willard.

The passage quoted from "Mother" likewise leads directly to a particular incident reported in a single sentence: "Once she startled the town by putting on men's clothes and riding a bicycle down Main Street." This is one of Anderson's most common techniques. Often a passage may contain several such shifts, as in the following paragraph of alternately generalized and particular events:

Resolutely the minister put the thoughts of the woman in the bed out of his mind and began to be something like a lover in the presence of his wife. One evening when they drove out together he turned the horse out of Buckeye Street and in the darkness on Gospel Hill, above Waterworks Pond, put his arm about Sarah Hartman's waist. When he had eaten breakfast in the morning and was ready to retire to his study at the back of his house he went around the table and kissed his wife on the cheek. When thoughts of Kate Swift came into his head, he smiled and raised his eyes to the skies. "Intercede for me, Master," he muttered, "keep me in the narrow path intent on Thy work." (Anderson, "The Strength of God")

Similar shifts can be illustrated in all their veiled abruptness by the following passage, which quotes speeches directly but makes the time of utterance vague by suggesting that the speeches were often repeated:

If the prisoners confuse night and day, and complain: "Dear little Laura, time doesn't pass in this infernal hole, and I won't know when it is time to sleep unless I have a reminder," she brings them their favorite narcotics, and says in a tone that does not wound them with pity, "Tonight will really be night for you," and though her Spanish amuses them, they find her comforting, useful. If they lose patience and all faith, and curse the slowness of their friends in coming to their rescue with money and influence, they trust her not to repeat everything, and if she inquires, "Where do you think we can find money, or influence?" they are certain to answer, "Well, there is Braggioni, why doesn't he do something?" (Porter, "Flowering Judas")

Faulkner's "A Rose for Emily" is unusually rich in its alternations between general and particular. The following passage casually introduces what is actually a major event in a grammatically subordinated position, as if it were only an illustration of a point:

She carried her head high enough — even when we believed that she was fallen. It was as if she demanded more than ever the recognition of her dignity as the last Grierson; as if it had wanted that touch of earthiness to reaffirm her imperviousness. Like when she bought the rat poison, the arsenic. That was over a year after they had begun to say "Poor Emily," and while the two female cousins were visiting her.

"I want some poison," she said to the druggist.

Such "false" subordinating serves a special function in this story, since we are not at this point supposed to know why she buys the poison; but it is also a common technique for introducing important action even where there is no special reason for concealing its importance, as in the following passage from Anderson's "Paper Pills":

One of them . . . talked continually of virginity. . . . The other . . . said nothing at all but always managed to get her into the darkness where he began to kiss her.

For a time the tall dark girl thought she would marry the jeweler's son [the one who talked of virginity]. . . . Then she began to be afraid of something. . . . She dreamed that he had bitten into her body. . . . She had the dream three times, then she became in the family way to the one who said nothing at all . . .

These examples demonstrate clearly the major principle that governs the distribution of particulars in a generalized narration: As in the dramatic scenes, particular treatment is used to bring out the more important points. Although the particulars are often introduced as if they were merely illustrations of the general points just made, actually they are seldom merely that, even in the examples from Anderson. What they show is by no means implicit in the general statements that surround them and is usually more important in terms of the action as a whole. Seth's quoted thought shows his discontent with what he is, which is not suggested at all by the statement that he "sometimes wondered if he would ever be particularly interested in anything." The minister's prayer alters the nature of the resoluteness indicated at the beginning of the paragraph. The speeches of Laura and the prisoners tell us much more about her relationship with them and Braggioni than anything covered by the summary statements. Even Elizabeth's riding through town on a bicycle goes well beyond what is indicated by the preceding characterization of her as "stage-struck" or her interest in the traveling men and their cities.

Although such techniques of particularizing a summary narrative are by no means new, they are far less easy to find in the earlier stories. There are, in James for example, passages, such as the following from "The Middle Years," which combine summary and particular statements:

Even for himself he was inspired as he told what his treasure would consist of; the precious metals he would dig from the mine, the jewels rare, strings of pearls, he would hang between the columns of his temple. He was wondrous for himself, so thick his convictions crowded, but still more wondrous for Doctor Hugh, who assured him none the less that the very pages he had just published were already encrusted with gems. This admirer, however, panted for the combinations to come and, before the face of the beautiful day, renewed to Dencombe his guarantee that his profession would hold itself responsible for such a life. Then he suddenly clapped his hand upon his watchpocket and asked leave to absent himself for half an hour. Dencombe waited there for his return, but was at last recalled to the actual by the fall of a shadow across the ground. The shadow darkened into that of Miss Vernham . . .

The passage summarizes the exchanges of a dramatic scene, the details being parts of a linked chain of events, whereas the typical alternations cited in the passages from the twenties are scattered components of situations temporarily static. In the Jamesian passage one is aware, also, not so much of alternations between general and particular as of a gradually increasing particularity. This leads, shortly after the quoted passage, to a dramatized dialogue between Dencombe and Miss Vernham; thus, as with most characteristic shifts from summary to particularized narration in the early period, the shift here is a stage-setting device in preparation for the dramatized scene that is to come. More typical of the later technique is this passage from the same story:

What he saw so intensely today, what he felt as a nail driven in, was that only now, at the very last, had he come into possession. His development had been abnormally slow, almost grotesquely gradual . . . The art had come, but it had come after everything else. At such a rate a first existence was too short — long enough only to collect material; so that to fructify, to use the material, one should have a second age, an extension. This extension was what poor Dencombe sighed for. As he turned the last leaves of his volume he murmured "Ah for another go, ah for a better chance!"

This example does not match the extremes illustrated in the passages quoted from Anderson, Miss Porter, and Faulkner. One does not find the swift, almost violent shifting back and forth from general to particular: the only shift here has been carefully prepared for by the previous sentence. Nor does the quoted speech in this passage carry as heavy a burden of revelation as that carried by Seth's quoted thought, the minister's prayer, or the speeches of Laura and the prisoners. Dencombe's thought has already been described fully in the previous sentences; his expression of it in words adds nothing to our actual knowledge of it, but merely makes more vivid the strength and quality of his feeling. It is, in fact, simply a more particularized representation of the action indicated in the previous sentence: "This extension was what poor Dencombe sighed for."

The most particularized narratives in the early period occur in certain stories by Bierce and Crane, such as "Chickamauga," "One Kind of Officer," "A Mystery of Heroism," "An Episode of War," and "The Open Boat," but they do not approach the particularity achieved in such stories by Hemingway as "Big Two-

Hearted River," "Indian Camp," or "Cross-Country Snow," nor the completeness of dramatization of such stories as "The Killers," "Hills Like White Elephants," and many others. We do not find in these or other earlier stories any such radical intermixing of general summary and particular treatment, breaking down the distinction between scene and narration, as in most of the stories of Anderson and Miss Porter (in addition to "Flowering Judas" see especially "That Tree," "The Jilting of Granny Weatherall," and "The Cracked Looking-Glass") and sometimes Faulkner (see, for example, "All the Dead Pilots" and "Divorce in Naples"). Only in stories by Fitzgerald does one fail to see any consistent appreciable difference in this aspect of technique from what was practiced by the best of the earlier writers.

The intent of these experiments clearly was to attain, swiftly, gracefully, and without the clumsy bulkiness of overdramatization, a greater dramatic vividness for the new kinds of actions characteristic of stories of the twenties. The techniques described are used most distinctively in the depiction of static situations or actions treating a change in a character's feelings or emotional state. Here — in the treatment of such materials as were most likely to be summarized or generalized in the early period — the new particularity of the twenties is most strikingly evident.

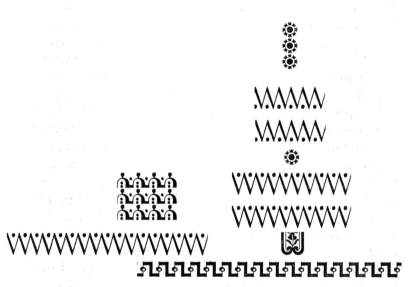

XX: ORDER

Another problem facing the narrator of a story is that of order. The simplest order is chronological — happenings revealed in the sequence in which they occurred. This is also the most dramatic order, being inevitable on the stage. While a play may begin *in medias res*, when it does (and thereby depends upon narratives speeches to bring in the past), it sacrifices some of the peculiar time-immediacy of the dramatic method. Dramatic exposition is tied to a continuous unbroken forward movement in time, and only by artificial conventions such as the lowering of a curtain or the changing of a scene can this be interrupted. The narrator, on the other hand, has all the action before him at once, so to speak, since his viewpoint is retrospective. He can arrange or rearrange the order of his events as he sees fit.

The problem of arrangement may be distinguished from the fundamental and prior problem of formal construction. The latter is a matter of invention and includes the determination of the order in which the actual events are made to follow each other so as to produce the proper effect. The technical problem of arrangement is a matter of exposition: what order of presentation is desirable to make the formal construction most vivid and clear? In actual composition, these two problems coalesce. In critical analysis it is useful to distinguish them — to examine, for example, the order followed in a story such as "A Rose for Emily" with respect both to how it maximizes the effect of horror, as has been observed in an earlier chapter, and how it maximizes the vividness and clarity of the situation. The time order is distorted to provide a succession of increasingly horrible clues as to the nature of Emily's life-situation. This succession is the form of the story; it is made possible only by certain techniques in the handling of time, certain principles of representation that enable the writer to distort time in order to achieve a particular effect.

Most stories in the early period are chronological in their over-all organization. The scenes upon which they depend are presented in the order in which they happened and are themselves internally chronological; and the intervening narrative is also primarily chronological. And yet nearly all these stories show certain limited and standard deviations from chronology in significant matters of detail.

The most obvious of these are "flashbacks," usually in the form of summary narratives in the past perfect tense. They present action that has occurred prior to the opening of the story. They may occur anywhere, but the most usual place is early in the text following an opening scene. Typical is the flashback from Mrs. Freeman's "A Village Lear," which begins as follows and continues for four pages:

Old Barney Swan had sat upon that shoemaker's bench the greater part of his time for sixty years. His father before him had been a shoemaker and cobbler; he had learned the trade when a child, and been faithful to it all his life.

Sometimes preliminary material is revealed more dramatically: the information is delivered by one of the characters in the course of a dramatic scene. Such scenes frequently have an effect

similar to that of the author's flashback, since their function is
limited largely to the revelation of prior material. A typical instance is the following from Mrs. Freeman's "Calla-lilies and
Hannah," the beginning of a dramatized flashback that continues for a page:

"'Tain't safe for you to go there, unless — you want all your things
— *stole*."

"Why, does she ——"

"She stole some money from John Arnold up here a year ago.
That's a fact."

"You don't mean it!"

"Yes. She was sewin' up there. He left it on the sittin'-room table
a minute, an' when he came back it was gone. There hadn't been anybody but her in the room, so of course she took it."

"Did he get the money back?" [Etc.]

Of course, Hannah did not steal the money. This is revealed
later in a scene that begins in the following way and which, although it furthers the action, also functions as a flashback:

"Hannah, look here; you knew I took that money, didn't you?"
She nodded.

"And you let everybody think you did it; you never said a word
to clear yourself . . . I want to tell you the whole story, how I came
to do it. It wasn't quite so bad as it looked . . . ." [Etc.]

The extreme awkwardness that could sometimes be reached in
a dramatized flashback is suggested by the following excerpt
from Bierce's "The Story of a Conscience":

". . . You sat in a corner and his orders were to kill you if you
attempted to rise."

"But if I *asked* to rise he might call the corporal of the guard."

"Yes. As the long silent hours wore away the soldier [on guard]
yielded to the demands of nature: he himself incurred the death
penalty by sleeping at his post of duty."

"You did."

"What! you recognize me? you have known me all along?"

Sometimes, especially in stories by James and Mrs. Wharton,
extended flashbacks are given dramatic justification by being
incorporated into the character's thought at a particular moment. Even these often have the effect of retrospective explana-

tion by the author, as in the following passage from "Autres Temps":

No, she didn't, as a rule, mind the past, because she was used to it and understood it. It was a great concrete fact in her path that she had to walk around every time she moved in any direction. But now, in the light of the unhappy event that had summoned her from Italy, — the sudden unanticipated news of her daughter's divorce from Horace Pursh and remarriage with Wilbour Barkley — the past, her own poor miserable past, started up at her with eyes of accusation, became, to her disordered fancy, like the afflicted relative suddenly breaking away from nurses and keepers and publicly parading the horror and misery she had, all the long years, so patiently screened and secluded.

Flashbacks of these various kinds are prominent in many of the early stories — in almost half of those by Bierce, Garland, and Mrs. Wharton, and in more than half of those by Mrs. Freeman. Crane alone does not use this device.[1] The early critics in general regarded a beginning *in medias res* as proper, as can be seen in the description by one such critic of the way a modern writer would have handled the plot of Irving's "Rip Van Winkle":

[He] would have begun with Rip's return from the mountain. He would have directed the reader's attention, first of all, to the mysterious problem presented by the sudden emergence of a stranger who did not know that the Revolutionary War had been fought. . . . The story would thus have gained in intensity of interest, in artistic unity, and in economy of details.[2]

[1] Stories of the early period which include directly presented flashbacks: Bierce, "Horseman in the Sky," "Occurrence at Owl Creek Bridge"; Freeman, "Kitchen Colonel," "Louisa," "New England Nun," "Revolt of 'Mother,'" "Village Lear," "Discovered Pearl," "Pot of Gold"; Cather, "Wagner Matinee," "Garden Lodge," "Flavia"; James, "Broken Wings," "Abasement," "Europe," "Fordham Castle."

Stories with flashback material present in dramatic scenes: Bierce, "Affair at Coulter's Notch," "Killed at Resaca," "Story of a Conscience"; Freeman, "Calla-lilies," "Scent of Roses," "Solitary," "Up Primrose Hill"; Garland, "Among the Corn Rows," "Under the Lion's Paw," "Up the Coolly," "Mrs. Ripley"; Wharton, "Long Run," "The Choice," "Quicksand," "Dilettante," "Coming Home"; Cather, "Marriage of Phaedra."

Stories in which flashbacks appear as thoughts or memories of one of the characters: Cather, "Death in the Desert"; Dreiser, "Free," "Second Choice"; Freeman, "Discovered Pearl"; Garland, "God's Ravens," "Return of a Private"; Wharton, "Autres Temps," "The Reckoning"; Gerould, "Leda"; James, "Flicker-bridge."

[2] Smith, pp. 13–14.

In James's stories the flashback structure is especially complex. Although more sparing in his use of large block flashbacks than were many of his contemporaries, James had a tendency to dot his narrative with short flashbacks, brief reversals of chronology going back not to a time before the story began but to a time shortly before that being discussed at the moment. "The Middle Years," for example, has many passages like the following:

Later he knew he had fainted and that Doctor Hugh had got him home in a Bath-chair, the conductor of which, prowling within hail for custom, had happened to remember seeing him in the garden of the hotel. He had recovered his perception on the way, and had, in bed that afternoon, a vague recollection of Doctor Hugh's young face, as they went together, bent over him in a comforting laugh and expressive of something more than a suspicion of his identity. That identity was ineffaceable now . . .

Or the following from "The Tree of Knowledge":

Within six months again, none the less, his fear was on more occasions than one all before him. Lance had returned to Paris for another trial; then had reappeared at home and had had, with his father, for the first time in his life, one of the scenes that strike sparks. He described it with much expression to Peter . . .

Such treatment of what most of the other writers would have been content to present chronologically in a simple summary narrative probably reflects James's great desire to be as "scenic" as possible; the flashbacks are incorporated in scenes that they help to explain and are justified in most cases as aspects of the character's thoughts or relevant memories during the scenes.

In addition to the flashbacks, in which time is actually reversed in the telling, stories of the early period display numerous momentary, less obvious, interruptions in the chronological movement. An examination of any story in the early period will reveal such interruptions, both large and small, and in most stories they are frequent. Most delays of this sort are passages of description and passages that explain or analyze a character and situation. Their abundance and variety can only be hinted at by a few examples chosen at random. In Bierce's "A Horseman in the Sky" time stops while the author makes clear precise details of setting that are later to be important:

The clump of laurel in which the criminal lay was in the angle of a road which after ascending southward a steep acclivity to that point turned sharply to the west, running along the summit for per- haps one hundred yards . . . . Had he been awake he would have commanded a view, not only of the short arm of the road and the jutting rock, but of the entire profile of the cliff below it. It might well have made him giddy to look.

Garland holds time still while using a description of setting to explain a man's act of singing:

In the windless September dawn a voice went ringing clear and sweet, a man's voice, singing a cheap and common air. Yet something in the sound of it told he was young, jubilant, and a happy lover.

Above the belt of timber to the east a vast dome of pale un- dazzling gold was rising, silently and swiftly. Jays called in the thickets . . . [etc.] No wonder the man sang! ("A Branch Road")

Time also stops while the same author explains the implications of a speech that a character has just made:

This working farmer had voiced the modern idea. It was an ab- solute overturn of all the ideas of nobility and special privilege born of the feudal past . . . [etc.] ("Among the Corn Rows")

Even in Crane's "The Open Boat," which is more strictly chrono- logical than most stories of the period, passages such as the following momentarily interrupt the chronological advance: "Many a man ought to have a bathtub larger than the boat which here rode upon the sea." Again: "It is fair to say that there was not a life-saving station within twenty miles in either direction; but the men did not know this fact." And of course there is no chronology in passages of generalized narration, which, as has been seen in the previous chapter, are common in most early stories.

Though the speeches in dramatic scenes are chronological, almost every scene contains explanatory interruptions of the time movement, ranging from miniscule and momentary halts — e.g., "The words she met him with were the last she could have imagined herself saying when they had parted. 'How in the world did you know that I was here?' He caught her meaning in

a flash" — a long analyses of the thoughts and feelings of characters in response to speeches, such as are frequently found in
stories by James.

A few stories, such as Mrs. Gerould's "Pearls," withhold
chronological development until after a generalizing introduction by the narrator. A few, such as Mrs. Wharton's "The Long
Run," begin the narrative so near to the end of the action that
the story is almost entirely flashback. Occasionally the whole
story is "framed" by a scene that did not begin until the action
is completed: flashback through memory is enlarged to constitute nearly the whole story, as in James's "Greville Fane," suggesting a rudimentary stream-of-consciousness technique.[3] Such
variations, however, are uncommon. The prevailing pattern in
the period consists of a loose chronological arrangement, with
occasional extended flashbacks and numerous shorter interruptions and delays in the narrative.

Most of these interruptions of chronology are expository,
clarifying or emphasizing particular points in a narrative whose
basic line of suspense is chronological: what will happen next?
They are useful for the sake of economy, enabling the writer to
proceed more quickly and without loss of the reader's interest to
the crucial events upon which the effect depends. In a few
stories, a deviation from chronology provides an effect that a
purely chronological order could not give. Crucial information
is held beyond the point where it would have been revealed in
a purely chronological treatment, in order that it may be revealed later in a more startling way. This is common in Bierce's
stories, as has been seen in our discussions of "An Occurrence at
Owl Creek Bridge," "A Horseman in the Sky," "The Affair at
Coulter's Notch," and "One Kind of Officer." Such a device, a
stock feature of the popular "surprise endings" of the time, is
employed chiefly when the interest lies in the external revelation of some exceptional choice made by a character. Although
acceptable to the serious writers of the period, such a device is
an uncommon departure from the usual methods.

These methods may strike many readers as an inevitable

[3] Other stories showing patterns similar to those described in this paragraph
are Bierce's "Story of a Conscience," Dreiser's "Free," and James's "The Next
Time."

part of the apparatus of most short stories. As at the turn of the
century, a majority of popular stories today contain similar flashbacks and breaks in the flow of time. In the twenties, too, many
stories — a distinct majority — do not depart radically from these
methods. Nevertheless, a large group of stories representing important new tendencies do.

Two developments, seemingly opposite, occur. Certain
stories severely tighten the chronology of the narrative, thus approximating more closely one of the conditions of a play. Others
seem to throw chronology to the winds, using quite different
principles of order. In addition, some stories suggest both con-
tradictory tendencies.

Hemingway makes the strongest effort to adhere strictly to
chronology. Although many of his stories — for example, "Hills
Like White Elephants" — depict episodes that must have had
antecedents, characteristically he neither interrupts the chronology for a flashback of any kind nor traces the past by expository dialogue. In "Hills," what the reader knows of the past is
learned almost entirely by deduction from the present situation,
assisted by such indirect allusions as the following: "'And if I do
it you'll be happy and things will be like they were and you'll
love me?'" The allusions to the past are a trifle more explicit in
"The End of Something," when Nick says,"'I've taught you
everything,'" or in "Three-Day Blow," when Bill says, "'You
were very wise . . . to bust off that Marge business,'"[4] or in
"The Killers," in these remarks: "'He must have got mixed up in
something in Chicago . . . Double-crossed somebody. That's
what they kill them for.'" But all these brief and sketchy allusions are important parts of the immediate forward movement
of the action, revealing the past only incidentally.

The tight chronology of Hemingway's narrative is well illus-

[4] Hemingway's "Three-Day Blow" does contain two flashbacks. Notice their
brevity and their close relation to Nick's thought at the given moment:
"His original plan had been to go down home and get a job. Then he had
planned to stay in Charlevoix all winter so he could be near Marge. Now he
did not know what he was going to do."
"The big thing was that Marjorie was gone and that probably he would
never see her again. He had talked to her about how they would go to Italy
together and the fun they would have. Places they would be together. It was
all gone now."

trated in a typical passage, already quoted, from "Indian Camp" (p. 301). In this, each sentence refers to a point in time later than that of the preceding sentence, although the intent of the whole story is merely preparatory to the crucial action that is to come. Even such a story as this cannot avoid some interruptions of the chronology. Observe the following passage:

Inside on a wooden bunk lay a young Indian woman. She had been trying to have her baby for two days. All the old women in the camp had been helping her. The men had moved off up the road to sit in the dark and smoke out of range of the noise she made. She screamed just as Nick and the two Indians followed his father and Uncle George into the shanty. She lay in the lower bunk, very big under a quilt. Her head was turned to one side. In the upper bunk was her husband. He had cut his foot very badly with an axe three days before. He was smoking a pipe. The room smelled very bad.

This description brings to a temporary halt the chronological development of the story. It even contains in sentences two, three, and four a miniature flashback, the only one in the story. Yet even this static description maintains a subtle illusion of continuing movement. The arrangement of these details, which does not follow any of the customary principles of static description, suggests the order in which they entered Nick's consciousness. To be sure, one might expect him to be conscious first of the woman's scream (sentence five). But Nick has been prepared before arriving at the cabin to see the woman in labor. The facts of sentences two, three, and four are things of which he is just becoming aware; it would be natural for him to think of them as he enters, noticing the old women and the absence of the men. Only then can he recognize the scream for what it is. Now he sees her more closely; first he locates her, then sees that she is big, then that her head is turned away. Looking up, he sees her husband, whose presence calls to mind the ax accident, about which Nick must have heard. Only after he has thus oriented himself does Nick become aware of the smell. Such an analysis suggests why, even in flashbacks, one has no impression of the stoppage of time; though it is not explicitly stated that the sequence is Nick's thought, the details are portrayed so naturally that one accepts it as such.

Equally strict chronology is followed in a large majority of Hemingway's stories. In only a few is it delayed, and in "The Doctor and the Doctor's Wife" it is interrupted by a paragraph and a half of explanation shortly after the story begins. "The End of Something" begins with a sketch of Horton's Bay in the "old days" and brings the reader up to the present in this fashion: "Ten years later there was nothing of the mill left except the broken white limestone of its foundations showing through the swampy second growth as Nick and Majorie rowed along the shore." The old mill and the old days are clearly on Nick's mind as he rows, although it is Majorie who makes the connection explicit: "There's our old ruin, Nick."

A few of Hemingway's stories depart from these principles. Of special interest are those written in the first person, suggesting a retrospective viewpoint. The episodes are now all safely in the past, as the very use of the first person helps to suggest. Occasional comment adds to the effect:

So while now I am fairly sure that it [my life] would not really have gone out, yet then, that summer, I was unwilling to make the experiment. ("Now I Lay Me")

There was a time when none of us believed in the machines, and one day the major said it was all nonsense. The machines were new then and it was we who were to prove them. ("In Another Country")

The girls at the Cova were very patriotic, and I found that the most patriotic people in Italy were the café girls — and I believe they are still patriotic. ("In Another Country")

Even such stories, despite their seemingly reminiscent quality, imply a rigorous chronological movement underlying the reminiscent effect and giving dramatic impetus to the story. This can be recognized in "In Another Country," perhaps the most complicated example, since the reminiscent illusion is here very marked.

Much of the narrative in this story is generalized; actions that have been often repeated are summed up in single statements: "We were all at the hospital every afternoon, and there were different ways of walking across the town through the dusk to the hospital." Furthermore, the internal order in many places seems to follow analytical rather than chronological principles, as in the following comparison of the various friends who accompany the narrator to the hospital:

The three with the medals were like hunting-hawks; and I was not a hawk . . . . But I stayed good friends with the boy who had been wounded his first day at the front, because he would never know now how he would have turned out . . . perhaps he would not have turned out to be a hawk either.

The major, who had been the great fencer, did not believe in bravery . . .

A study of the total content of the story suggests a chronology, not of particular events, but of successive stages of feeling or perception. In this regard the treatment is not retrospective; there are no advance intimations that a discovery is to be made. Explicit indications of the passage of time between these stages are for the most part omitted; as he perceives how the thought has shifted, the reader becomes aware of the chronology (traced in detail in Appendix I).

Although strict chronology is most evident in Hemingway's work, in a number of other stories of the twenties the method is almost as strict.[5] Even the more conservative (i.e., loosely chronological) stories reflect this tendency in their effort to make interruptions of time less obvious and less frequent. The old-fashioned extended flashback, coherent in itself and purely expository in nature, has virtually disappeared. New ways of bringing the past into the present have been discovered. The extreme practices of Hemingway only reflect what was a general tendency in the work of all the writers of the time.

A considerable number of stories in the period suggest a seemingly opposite trend. Here the order of revelation is so much at odds with the order in which things happened as to suggest that the writer wished, above all, to avoid a chronological representation. In such stories the treatment may be called analytical rather than chronological, and analytical principles

[5] Typical of the extremes in this direction are stories by other writers of the canon: Anderson, "Nobody Knows"; Fitzgerald, "Ice Palace," "Rough Crossing," "Winter Dreams" (although there are some passages of commentary); Porter, "He," "Rope"; Faulkner, "That Evening Sun."

also govern large segments of other stories with an overriding but suspended or long-delayed chronological principle. Stories of these types are especially characteristic of Anderson, Faulkner, and, to a lesser extent, Miss Porter.[6]

Because it seems to violate the dramatic principle suggested at the beginning of this chapter, this development presents an interesting problem. Sometimes the analytical order is given some dramatic justification by the character of the agent who shapes it: the sequence in Miss Porter's "The Jilting of Granny Weatherall" suggests the flow of free association in Granny Weatherall's mind. But the time sequence of such associations can hardly be the final determinant of order, for free association is by definition formless. Usually, furthermore, no such artifice is present. In such stories as Anderson's "Hands" and "Paper Pills" and Miss Porter's "Flowering Judas" the narrator himself bears the full responsibility for the disordering of detail.

Such treatment is used chiefly in episodes of exposure and exposed situations, wherein the inverted chronology itself provides the "form," and in certain episodes of choice and discovery. In the latter the analytical method is applied only to the situation out of which the discovery or the exemplified choice is to arise and gives way to chronology before the end. The analytical method is thus used to represent a static situation; it is one of the ways of directing the reader's attention to constant elements in a sequence of events.

The disordering of chronology is controlled, in most cases, by either of the two principles that have been implied above in the discussion of episode forms: the development and satisfaction of suspense as to the *causes* of a given situation, or as to the character's peculiar or distinctive *reaction* to it. The former is typified by "Hands," the latter by "A Rose for Emily." In "Hands" the development of suspense is handled in an obvious way. The author makes fully explicit the suspense and all the transitions from one stage to the next:

⁶ Primarily analytical in treatment: Anderson, "Hands," "Paper Pills," "Respectability"; Porter, "Flowering Judas," "Jilting of Granny Weatherall," "That Tree"; Faulkner, "Hair," "Victory," "Rose for Emily." Analytical treatment of large segments of a story is seen in most of the *Winesburg* collection (typically, a short, chronological episode concludes an extensive analytical exposition).

The story of Wing Biddlebaum is a story of hands.

The story of Wing Biddlebaum's hands is worth a book in itself. Sympathetically set forth it would tap many strange, beautiful qualities in obscure men. It is a job for a poet.

As for George Willard, he had many times wanted to ask about the hands . . . . He felt that there must be a reason for their strange activity.

Let us look briefly into the story of the hands. Perhaps our talking of them will arouse the poet who will tell the hidden wonder story of the influence for which the hands were but fluttering pennants of promise.

Here, as in Anderson's "Respectability," the question is answered finally by an extended chronological summary of past events. In later stories, such as "A Rose for Emily," the probing is piecemeal, fragmented, though the basic suspense is similar. In general, a provocative aspect of the character's situation is first presented to arouse some fundamental, suspenseful question as to what the situation involves; then the author presents the evidence which develops this question and finally answers it, doing so by means of a variety of artifices, ranging from uninhibited freedom, in "Hands," through the stream-of-consciousness, in Miss Porter's "The Jilting of Granny Weatherall," to the intricate recollection of clues, in "A Rose for Emily."

The impact of such an arrangement of detail is undeniable. A chronological treatment here would inevitably be weak and anticlimatic. The achieved vividness suggests that these writers, while ignoring the principle that a play always moves forward in time, were intent on utilizing a dramatic principle of order.

The nature of this principle may be discovered by a contrast between the analytical method of these stories and that of scientific analysis as ordinarily understood. The most obvious difference is that in science the conclusions are always stated explicitly, whereas in these stories the answers are only suggested through the evidence of particular concrete events. But this (the concern of the next chapter) will not make the *order* more dramatic; it would suggest that the writers, having found other means of dramatization, are now able to use a less dramatic

kind of order. But the order of the analytical stories itself differs
from the order in scientific analysis in at least one important
respect: although the movement in all these stories is from
"signs" to "fundamentals" (or, more accurately, from "signs" to
"more fundamental signs") — i.e., is superficially inductive — it
is governed not by logical, orderly principles but by the development of a particular suspense and curiosity in the reader, a
matter which should not be allowed to affect scientific thinking
(although it may be pertinent to scientific writing). The epitome of such a movement is the pure detective story. The serious
stories of the twenties lack only the detective himself to make
explicit and self-conscious the process of discovery that the
reader undertakes.

Walter Blair has pointed to this process of discovery in "A
Rose for Emily," contrasting it with the more conventional process of discovery in a story such as "The Killers," in which a
character himself makes the discovery chronologically.[7] The
dramatic quality of the process depends upon a feature of dramatic order that is fully as inevitable in a play as is chronology:
the fact that one gets to know only gradually the characters, the
mainsprings of their actions, and the depths of their feelings in
the successive unfolding of the various things they do and say.
The drama also moves from signs to more fundamental signs in
the revelation of character and in the establishment of probability, a movement essential to its nature as "imitation," since this
is the way in which we apprehend the nature of people in life.
This quality of drama is exploited by the analytically organized
stories of the twenties as a means of giving narration more of
the qualities of a play.

Stories such as Faulkner's "A Rose for Emily" and Hemingway's "Indian Camp" develop to a high point the analytical and
chronological kinds of order. In the early period, the analytical
kind extensively disrupts the chronology in only one story,
Henry James's "Greville Fane," where it is used to comic effect.

[7] Walter Blair, "U.S.A.: 1914 to the Present," *The Literature of the United
States: An Anthology and a History*, Vol. II: *From the Civil War to the Present*,
ed. Walter Blair, Theodore Hornberger, and Randall Stewart (Chicago: Scott,
Foresman & Co., 1947), p. 872.

It is approached in such stories as Mrs. Wharton's "The Quick-sand" and "The Long Run," in which the past is revaluated through extensive flashbacks or memories. Not until the twenties does the break with chronology become a natural device in the short story, used boldly and without the strain that had been shown in efforts, such as Mrs. Wharton's, to conceal it. It is the one major technical device used by writers of the twenties that Joyce's stories do not anticipate; the most natural precedent that suggests itself is in the work of Conrad, but there it appears less in his short stories than in his novels.

The abandonment of chronology may be appropriate to those forms — always based on static situations — whose chief interest is not chronological but analytical. The critical theorist, however, may find some justice in the argument that the analytical order is artistically less satisfying than the perfectly chronological. It has been noted that a play combines the advantages of both methods. Theoretically, the highest virtuosity is displayed by those stories whose foremost interest is analytical but in which the treatment is chronological. This is the combination attempted in all episode stories of both periods: the episode is the chronological analysis of the fundamental situation. But in most cases the episode is not trusted to do its work alone. In the early period, for example, it is necessary for the author to explain it, to use summary and generalized narration to make clear the point that the immediate episode is indeed illustrative of a larger situation:

[Abel was] a very unfortunate and unsuccessful man through his whole life. (Freeman, "A Kitchen Colonel")

The kitchen colonel fought faithfully in his humble field, where maybe he would some day win a homely glory all his own. (Freeman, "A Kitchen Colonel")

The thought of the long, long day, and the sickening sameness of her life, swept over her again. (Garland's "A Day's Pleasure")

The common soldier of the American volunteer army had returned. His war with the South was over, and his fight, his daily running fight with nature and against the injustice of his fellow-men, was begun again. (Garland, "The Return of a Private")

Writers of the twenties, too, continue to use such devices to suggest the relation between a specific episode and a larger situation. This appears especially in the pattern characteristic of Anderson (as in "The Teacher" or "The Thinker") wherein a fairly extensive first part mixes generalizations and particulars to depict the situation out of which the particular episode arises in the last part. But such devices disappear — reflecting an increased virtuosity — in some nine stories by Hemingway that have been noted in the previous pages; here a nearly perfect chronology is applied to an analytical purpose (these stories are all episodes); the episodes carry the whole burden of revelation.[8] The background and the future extension of the situation are largely implicit in the scene itself without direct indication by either author or characters.

Only Hemingway increases simultaneously both chronological and analytical tendencies in the same story. But the abandonment of chronology in later stories such as "A Rose for Emily" or "Flowering Judas" indicates the presence of materials more intricate than was common in Hemingway's episodes. In less complex (later) stories such as Faulkner's "Dry September" and Miss Porter's "Rope" the two methods are again combined. Obviously the order of revelation was one of the most fertile fields of experimentation for all the writers of the twenties in their efforts to dramatize the new forms they had conceived.

[8] "Big Two-Hearted River," "Canary for One," "Cat in the Rain," "Cross-Country Snow," "Doctor and Doctor's Wife," "Hills Like White Elephants," "Killers," "Out of Season," "Simple Enquiry."

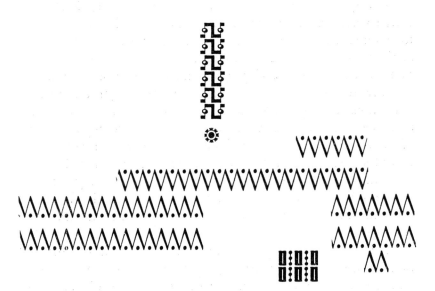

XXI: ECONOMY

Many stories of the twenties show no marked extension beyond earlier practices of the techniques that have been discussed. Even so, the more distinctive of such stories manage to produce an over-all dramatic illusion of greater vividness and immediacy. Stories such as Anderson's "Loneliness" and "Adventure," for example, despite their discursive narrator, their loose chronology, their relative scarcity of dramatic scenes and particularized narration, carry a strongly dramatic impact. Others, such as Miss Porter's "Flowering Judas" or Faulkner's "A Rose for Emily," which do employ many of the devices that have been discussed, achieve more dramatic effects than these devices alone seem able to account for.

The explanation probably lies in the way economy in the representation is achieved. Both the narrator and the dramatist are

325

faced with the problem of choosing the statement that suggest
the most in the briefest possible manner, but the typically dramatic way of achieving economy differs from the typically narrative way. The narrator has the power to abstract things —
to summarize or generalize actions, to specify character, to
analyze thought, to identify feelings. The dramatist, on the other
hand, not only deals with particularized events but, characteristically, reveals character, thought, and feeling through externalizations, through verbal acts. The dramatist must rely on the
audience's ability to infer character, thought, feeling, and unity
of action from their external signs; the narrator's summaries
leave these externalizations to the reader's imagination. The narrator draws inferences from unspecified signs, leaving it to the
reader to imagine what the signs must have been; the dramatist
presents the signs and leaves it to the audience to draw the
inferences.

This is the most important and definitive of all our distinctions between the two methods, since it concerns the manner in
which the reader apprehends the nature of the object represented. In this distinction one sees most clearly why the dramatic
method is more vivid and immediate than the narrative, and why
critics such as Percy Lubbock should feel that the narrative
method, uncontrolled, tends to make the reader doubt the verac-
ity of the picture presented. The degree of dependence placed
upon the reader's inferences is the most elementary measure of
an author's intervention or nonintervention into his story.

A narrative thus becomes dramatic in proportion to its use
of the kind of economy typical of drama — that is, as it leaves
things to inference instead of explaining them. The writers of
the twenties differ most generally from their forebears in their
much greater dependence upon such inferences. These "dramatic" inferences should, of course, be distinguished from the
"grammatical" inferences required of the reader in grasping the
full meaning of the words in any text.[1] A dramatic inference

---

[1] The inferences necessary to interpret metaphors, according to this distinction, would be grammatical rather than dramatic, since they too are concerned
only with the intended meaning of the verbal act in itself and not with that act
as a sign of something else.

goes beyond the mere grasping of the meaning of a speech (or any other sign) to an interpretation of it as an act indicating or belonging to a sequence of events or manifesting character or thought.

Some of the inferences that stories of the twenties may require of the reader have already been indicated. The device of the "fallible" narrator utilizes dramatic inferences that must be made if the reader is to recognize the fallibility. The increased particularity in narration implies a greater dependence on dramatic inference for comprehension of the particulars. The implicit chronology illustrated by Hemingway's "In Another Country" (pp. 318–19 and Appendix I) requires the reader to infer the transitions and successive stages. Most of the analytically ordered stories oblige us to make inferences in order to perceive the unfolding of character and situation. In the tightly chronological episodes by Hemingway, especially, inferences are necessary in order to perceive the static situation illustrated by the episode.

But the dependence on dramatic inference is evident in other ways as well. It may be observed with respect to the depiction of character, the presentation of thoughts and feelings, and the clarification of the structure and intent of the story as a whole.

INFERENCE IN CHARACTERIZATION

Character in a story or a play is indicated most significantly by what an agent chooses to do. In most cases, the skeleton of main choices itself does not provide a sufficient characterization; speeches and subordinated or contributing actions are thus invented for the primary purpose of characterization. In a story, such speeches appear in the dramatic scenes, and such subordinated actions are represented in narration, as for example in the passage from Mrs. Freeman's "A New England Nun," quoted on page 300. Here, as already remarked, the actions cited are "generalized" ("Louisa used china every day . . ."). But they are "particular" with respect to their primary function, which is to characterize Louisa. In this respect it makes little difference whether the particulars of characterization are recurring actions or single ones — in either case they characterize through action and require us to make dramatic inferences if we are to see the character as she is.

In stories of the early period such methods of characterization are rarely allowed to stand alone.[2] Dramatic characterization is supplemented in various ways by more or less direct and explicit indications — at least with respect to the significant traits of the more important characters. Often this is done by an explicit moral characterization or evaluation by the author himself in his capacity as narrator. He fills in all the essential moral inferences about a character that the reader might otherwise have to make. The following instances (some of which have already been cited in other connections) demonstrate the practice:

Serenity and placid narrowness had become to her as the birthright itself . . . . Louisa sat, prayerfully numbering her days, like an uncloistered nun. (Freeman, "A New England Nun")

This was Minty's true flower time. Everything worthy in her was awake and astir and glowing . . . . She . . . was as perfect a woman as she would ever be in this world. She seemed to rise triumphant by this noble abasement from any lower level where she might have been. (Freeman, "A Wayfaring Couple")

The kitchen colonel fought faithfully in his humble field, where maybe he would some day win a homely glory all his own. (Freeman, "A Kitchen Colonel")

Haskins worked like a fiend, and his wife, like the heroic woman that she was, bore also uncomplainingly the most terrible burdens . . . . (Garland, "Under the Lion's Paw")

His heroic soul did not quail. With the same courage with which he had faced his Southern march he entered upon a still more hazardous future.

Oh, that mystic hour! (Garland, "The Return of a Private")

[Scratchy Wilson was] no student of chivalry . . . [merely a] simple child of the earlier plains. (Crane, "The Bride Comes to Yellow Sky")

---

[2] Such methods of characterization in the early period usually stand alone only where the character is morally neutral, as in an episode of discovery, e.g., Crane's "Horses — One Dash!" and "Experiment in Misery."

[They] had turned for relief from pain to a perversity of pride. (James, "Broken Wings")

Almost as direct, although theoretically more dramatic, is the device of characterizing explicitly by means of an authoritative character whose voice is clearly that of the author. If some of the early writers are more hesitant than Mrs. Freeman and Garland to interpret in their own words, they tend to make up for it by this device. It is obvious in first-person narratives when the narrator's evaluations are essentially the same as the author's, as for example:

You are not to forget the nature of this man's act; it is not permitted to you to think of it as an instance of bravado, nor, on the other hand, a needless sacrifice of self . . . . "Let me pay all," says this gallant man—this military Christ! . . . That great soul whose beautiful body is lying over yonder, so conspicuous against the sere hillside—could it not have been spared the bitter consciousness of a vain devotion? Would one exception have marred too much the pitiless perfection of the divine, eternal plan? (Bierce, "A Son of the Gods")

"He was bitten by a snake," I replied. (Bierce, "Killed at Resaca." An authoritative judgment of what the hero's beloved has done to the hero.)

"It is you who would have to change—to die gradually, as I have died, till there is only one live point left in me." (Wharton, "The Quicksand." The heroine generalizes the present state of her character metaphorically but otherwise explicitly.)

"The world won't thank us," she went on. "What will, I wonder?" Not the deaf generations, she thought to herself, to which we all sacrifice.

"Not Geoffrey," she heard Glave saying. "He will never understand . . . . We haven't answered him. Life has answered him. Call it God, if you must." (Gerould, "The Bird in the Bush." Glave provides the authoritative evaluation of their sacrifice.)

"Every sin is the result of a collaboration. We, five of us, have collaborated in the murder of this Swede . . . you, I, Johnnie, old Scully; and that fool of an unfortunate gambler came merely as a culmination, the apex of a human movement, and gets all the punishment." (Crane, "The Blue Hotel." The Easterner allots the blame in a tragedy with a multiple protagonist.)

. . . she never saw; she had never seen anything, and she passed away with her fine blindness unimpaired. (James, "Greville Fane")

. . . the great and romantic fact was Brooksmith's final evasion of his fate . . . . now I trust that, with characteristic deliberation, he is changing the plates of the immortal gods . . . . But the dim ghost of poor Brooksmith is one of those that I see. He had indeed been spoiled. (James, "Brooksmith")

. . . a person whom vanity has had the odd effect of keeping positively safe and sound. This passion is supposed surely, for the most part, to be a principle of perversion and of injury, leading astray those who listen to it . . . but it has landed her ladyship nowhere whatever — it has kept her from the first moment of full consciousness, one feels, exactly in the same place. (James, "The Beldonald Holbein")

Even when such explicit means are avoided, an author may slant his narratives so strongly as to leave no doubt of his judgment of character. The following, for example, is not merely a statement of the plight of Haskins' son — it is almost as directly a sympathetic evaluation of Haskins, who is the more important character in the story:

An infinitely pathetic but common figure — this boy on the American farm, where there is no law against child labor. To see him in his coarse clothing, his huge boots, and his ragged cap, as he staggered with a pail of water from the well, or trudged in the cold and cheerless dawn out into the frosty field behind his team, gave the city-bred visitor a sharp pang of sympathetic pain. Yet Haskins loved his boy, and would have saved him from this if he could, but he could not. (Garland, "Under the Lion's Paw")[3]

The following is a critical judgment of society (a major "character" in the story) made by an authoritative character, and indirect only in that it is metaphorical:

"We're all imprisoned, of course — all of us middling people, who don't carry our freedom in our brains. But we've accommodated ourselves to our different cells, and if we're moved suddenly into new ones we're likely to find a stone wall where we thought there was

[3] In this passage one notes the author's deliberate attempts to universalize his picture. This is a characteristic device in the early period and is especially noteworthy in Garland. See also the passage from "Among the Corn Rows," quoted on p. 37.

thin air, and to knock ourselves senseless against it." (Wharton, "Autres Temps")

Though less broad as characterizations than those just quoted, the following are nearly as explicit as partial characterizations since they state or analyze explicitly a character's motivations or intentions in particular crucial situations. This is probably the most common of all kinds of explicit characterization in the early period, and can be noted especially in stories by James, who uses somewhat fewer of the more general characterizations than do other earlier writers:

> It was one of the secret opinions, such as we all have, of Peter Brench that his main success in life would have consisted in his never having committed himself about the work, as it was called, of his friend Morgan Mallow . . . . it was nowhere on record that he had, in the connexion, on any occasion and in any embarrassment, either lied or spoken the truth. Such a triumph had its honour even for a man of other triumphs — a man who had reached fifty, who had escaped marriage, who had lived within his means, who had been in love with Mrs. Mallow for years without breathing it, and who, last not least, had judged himself once for all. He had so judged himself in fact that he felt an extreme and general humility to be his proper portion. . . . (James, "The Tree of Knowledge")

This was the pang that had been sharpest during the last few years — the sense of ebbing time, of shrinking opportunity; and now he felt not so much that his last chance was going as that it was gone indeed. He had done all he should ever do, and yet hadn't done what he wanted. (James, "The Middle Years")

The dream was no blind chance; it was the expression of something she had kept so close a prisoner that she had never seen it herself; it was the wail from the donjon deeps when the watch slept. Only as the outcome of such a night of sorcery could the thing have been loosed. (Cather, "The Garden Lodge")

There was this to be said for him, that he wore his spoils with dignity and in no way made himself conspicuous. His chief greediness lay in his ears and eyes, and his excesses were not offensive ones. His dearest pleasures were the gray winter twilights in his sitting-room; his quiet enjoyment of his flowers, his clothes, his wide divan, his cigarette and his sense of power. He could not remember a time

when he had felt so at peace with himself. The mere release from
the necessity of petty lying, lying every day and every day, restored
his self-respect. He had never lied for pleasure, even at school; but to
make himself noticed and admired, to assert his difference from other
Cordelia Street boys . . . (Cather, "Paul's Case")

As a result of these methods, most of the early stories are
extremely lucid in their characterization; there is no question
where our sympathies are supposed to lie, nor of the kind of
sympathy we are supposed to feel. The characters themselves
however are not necessarily simple, although (as seen in chaps.
viii–x) they tend, except in James, to be simpler than those
in later stories. But where the moral quality of a character
is complex, as in Mrs. Gerould's "Pearls," Mrs. Freeman's "A
New England Nun," and James's "Greville Fane" and "Europe,"
special care is taken to show this explicitly in order to leave no
doubt that we evaluate it properly. Few stories by the early
writers leave the reader with any significant question about
moral character that he must resolve on the basis of dramatic
inference alone. As a result, despite the care taken to characterize *also* through speech and act, the explicit reiteration of such
characterization tends to give the story as a whole a narrative
rather than a dramatic quality.

There are, of course, a fair number of significant exceptions,
which tend to be more common in comic than in serious stories.
In the latter, important dramatic inferences as to character are
required only in some stories by Bierce and Crane and, to a lesser
extent, Mrs. Wharton. The most substantial inferences concerning character are called for in certain stories by James, despite
his explicit partial characterizations — especially such stories as
"The Lesson of the Master," "Paste," "Europe" (source of behavior, not evaluation), "Miss Gunton of Poughkeepsie," "Fordham Castle," "The Marriages," and "The Story In It." [4]

[4] The stories by Henry James, cited here, are comedies. Other early come-
dies requiring fairly important inferences: Wharton, "The Other Two"; Crane,
"Little Regiment"; Garland, "Mrs. Ripley," "Uncle Ethan"; Freeman, "Gala
Dress"; Cather, "Garden Lodge," "Flavia." Painful stories requiring important
inferences: Bierce, "Horseman in the Sky," "Affair at Coulter's Notch," "One
Kind of Officer," "Affair of Outposts"; Crane, "Monster," "Five White Mice";
Wharton, "Coming Home," "The Choice." The list does not include stories
which lack much explicit characterization because the protagonist is either
neutral or his character made self-evident in action (see p. 328).

In stories of the twenties a simple search for explicit evaluations and interpretations alone will reveal no contrast. Statements such as the following, some of which seem in their
directness like a conscious rejection of dramatic rigor, are frequent in all writers except Hemingway:

Louisa was from childhood a neurotic. (Anderson, "Surrender")

He was one of those rare, little-understood men who rule by a power
so gentle that it passes as a lovable weakness. In their feeling for the
boys under their charge such men are not unlike the finer sort of
women in their love of men. (Anderson, "Hands")

He, like most boys, was deeper than boys are given credit for being,
but he was not what the men of the town, and even his mother,
thought him to be. No great underlying purpose lay back of his
habitual silence, and he had no definite plan for his life. (Anderson,
"The Thinker")

He was forty years old, and by his nature very silent and reticent.
(Anderson, "The Strength of God")

Alone in the night in the winter streets she was lovely. . . . There
was something biting and forbidding in the character of Kate Swift.
. . . In reality she was the most eagerly passionate soul among them
. . . (Anderson, "The Teacher")

My father was, I am sure, intended by nature to be a cheerful, kindly
man . . . . Then an idea in regard to getting up in the world came
into his head. The American spirit took hold of him. He also became
ambitious. (Anderson, "The Egg")

[The very rich, of whom Anson Hunter is one] possess and enjoy
early, and it does something to them, makes them soft where we are
hard, and cynical where we are trustful . . . . They think, deep in
their hearts, that they are better than we are . . . (Fitzgerald, "The
Rich Boy")

Braggioni is cruel to everyone, with a kind of specialized insolence,
but he is so vain of his talents, and so sensitive to slights, it would
require a cruelty and vanity greater than his own to lay a finger on
the vast cureless wound of his self-esteem . . . . She has encased
herself in a set of principles derived from her early training, leaving
no detail of gesture or of personal taste untouched . . . . No dancer
dances more beautifully than Laura walks. (Porter, "Flowering
Judas")

Thus she passed from generation to generation — dear, inescapable, impervious, tranquil, and perverse. (Faulkner, "A Rose for Emily")

But after twelve years I think of us as bugs in the surface of the water isolant and aimless and unflagging . . . . Out of nothing we howled, unwitting the storm which we had escaped and the foreign strand which we could not escape; that in the interval between two surges of the swell we died who had been too young to have ever lived. (Faulkner, "Ad Astra")

But when these statements are considered in the total context of the stories from which they come, the reader perceives at once that most of them are not nearly as authoritative or complete as they seem. Although they tell us something important about a character, they also, like the statements of the fallible first-person narrator, previously noted, tend to omit something else of greater importance — something which usually can only be gathered through inference from the story as a whole. In "A Rose for Emily," for example, the adjectives "dear, inescapable, impervious, tranquil, and perverse" apply only to the judgment of the town upon her before the secrets of Emily's private life are exposed. The gentleness indicated in "Hands" is only part of what is important in Wing Biddlebaum; equally important are his exceptional naïveté, his fear of society, and his disastrous inability to understand the strain of homosexuality in himself. The characterization in "The Thinker" does not specify Seth's fundamental failure to understand himself, which, as noted elsewhere, is his most important characteristic, nor does the characterization of Louise, in "The Surrender," disclose her peculiar combination of innocence and cynical despair. The quotations from "The Teacher" and "The Strength of God" do not specify the sexual ambivalences that are the fundamental motives in both stories, nor do the statements in "The Egg" specify the gross misconception of the nature of humor at the heart of the father's trouble. Similar omissions can be cited for all the other characters, with the possible exception of Braggioni, who is, however, a secondary character, a foil to the heroine, and a good illustration of the way in which such explicit methods may be used in all but the most significant elements in the story. Yet, even with Braggioni, there is a dimension unsuggested by this or any other explicit characterization — the dimension suggested when he returns home to his wife and weeps with her: a significant, human warmth that even he possesses in contrast to Laura's **coldness.**

These examples suggest a tendency similar to that noticed in the particularizing of a story's events: in contrast to those of the early period, explicit statements of character are not summations of the same characterization that is presented dramatically; rather, they are, for the most part, contributing "particulars" in a larger characterization whose most essential elements are left to inference. By thus dramatizing what is most important and explaining the necessary but less crucial elements, these writers achieve a complex characterization both economically and dramatically.

Not all stories of the twenties show this, of course. But many of the most important kinds of character are represented in this manner. Perhaps the most common kind of character inference the reader has to make relates to the intended moral evaluation of a character, significant especially in those numerous stories, described in previous chapters, in which this evaluation is itself ambiguous, and in which petty or horrible elements are offset by romantic ones or a tension is set up between ridiculousness and seriousness in the character. We must make a moral inference in order to reconcile Wash Williams' ugly misogyny and his idealistic love, in Anderson's "Respectability," or Enoch Robinson's childish egotism and natural pathos, in "Loneliness." Such problems become more striking than ever later in the period in such stories as Miss Porter's "That Tree" and Faulkner's "A Rose for Emily," "Ad Astra," "Hair," "Victory," and "That Evening Sun."

Although the actual composition of a character's traits tends, in many cases, to be more immediately clear than the proper moral evaluation, the extent of inference required even to recognize these can be suggested by the large number of stories in which it is most difficult to summarize character without summarizing the character's acts. This is true, indeed, for almost all of Hemingway's stories as well as many other stories, of which Miss Porter's "The Cracked Looking-Glass," "Rope," and "The

Jilting of Granny Weatherall," Fitzgerald's "The Rough Crossing," "The Rich Boy," and "Absolution," and Faulkner's "A Rose
for Emily," "Divorce in Naples," "Red Leaves," "A Justice," and
"Hair" are striking examples.

We may pass quickly over the question of devices by which
the writer induces the reader to make the proper inferences concerning character. Although this question is of the utmost importance to the writer himself, there seems little evidence of
a general change in this regard between the two periods. When
character is not indicated explicitly, through general statements
or statements of particular motives, it tends to be inferred in
both periods primarily from the character's acts, thoughts, and
feelings, from which the reader develops an immediate sense of
what sort of person he is. Some of the celebrated devices of
drama and fiction are also used frequently in both periods, with
no striking difference in their use between the two periods: foil
or contrasting characters, fallible judgments by secondary characters (authoritative judgments have already been considered;
they are a kind of *explicit* treatment), and various universalizing
devices. The latter do show a possible development, but as this
change concerns other elements as well as characterization, it
will be considered in a later section.

INFERENCE CONCERNING THOUGHT AND FEELING
A generally similar contrast between the two periods prevails in
the treatment of a character's thought and feelings. In a play
these are learned indirectly from what a character does or from
indirect things he says, or directly, when he expresses them so,
the purest instance being the conventional soliloquy or aside.
According to the principles already indicated, the more purely
dramatic of these methods is the indirect.[5] But in the narratives
of the two periods several levels of directness may be noted.

"Explicit" as used here must be defined. A fully explicit element in a story or play is one whose nature is made fully comprehensible by a statement in words. This is why we say that
the most explicit statement of character is that which explains

[5] Soliloquies and asides are relatively undramatic. A play duplicates the
situation in life whereby we get to know people by watching them from outside
without the assistance of such aids.

the character's traits and motives and describes their moral quality. Similarly, the most explicit statement of action is an analytical summary of the change that takes place. The most explicit statement of thought is an analytical summary of the conceptions operating at the moment being described, and the most explicit statement of feeling is a definition of the feeling, either through appropriate terms such as "happy," "worried," "frightened," through summaries of the kinds of situations that give rise to such feelings (e.g., undeserved misfortune, as giving rise to pity), or through metaphors and analogies.

In the most fully dramatized parts of a play the only things that are fully explicit are the verbal acts of the characters — the particularized statements that compose the sequence of action. The sequence itself is not explicit, nor are the moral character and feelings "expressed" in these acts. Thought, indeed, is the only explicit element in them, and even thought is only partially so, since such acts leave to inference the thoughts that caused the agent to commit these acts or to choose which thoughts to express or withhold.

In stories of the early period the most explicit treatments of thought and feeling are summations and analyses of a character's state of mind made by a narrator who sees fully into that mind. Such treatment is characteristic of stories by Mrs. Wharton, Mrs. Gerould, and often James, perhaps because their subject matter requires them to deal with more complicated kinds of thinking than that of the other writers. A simple test for such explicitness is the extent to which it clearly appears that the author has reorganized or restated in his own words a character's thought. The following, from Mrs. Freeman's "A New England Nun," is an obvious simple example:

[Joe Dagget felt] much as an innocent and perfectly well-intentioned bear might after his exit from a china shop.

Louisa, on her part, felt much as the kind-hearted, long-suffering owner of the china shop might have done after the exit of the bear.

Here the presence of the interpreting author is evident because of her use of the same metaphor to describe the feelings of two different characters.

This passage illustrates a more extensive reorganization of a character's thoughts and feelings:

She was not unhappy during the intervening days. [A most direct summation of feeling; the following sentences explicitly divide this feeling into two parts in a balanced treatment that presents first the causes of her happiness and then the thing that qualifies it:] The sight of Leila's well-being, the sense of Leila's tenderness, were, after all, what she had come for; and of these she had had full measure. Leila had never been happier or more tender; and the contemplation of her bliss, and the enjoyment of her affection, were an absorbing occupation for her mother. But they were also a sharp strain on certain overtightened chords, and Mrs. Lidcote, when at last she found herself alone in the New York hotel to which she had returned the night before embarking, had the feeling that she had just escaped with her life from the clutch of a giant hand. (Wharton, "Autres Temps")

In the following passage, even though the suggestion is first made that Mrs. Lidcote's thoughts came to her at random and "without shrinking," the treatment exhibits, nevertheless, a characteristic reduction of thought to its logical composition:

She wanted no viaticum but that of her own thoughts; and she let these come to her without shrinking from them as she sat in the same high-hung sitting-room in which, just a week before, she and Franklin Ide had had their memorable talk.

She had promised her friend to let him hear from her, but she had not kept her promise. She knew that he had probably come back from Chicago, and that if he learned of her sudden decision to return to Italy it would be impossible for her not to see him before sailing; and as she wished above all things not to see him she had kept silent, intending to send him a letter from the steamer.

There was no reason why she should wait till then to write it. The actual moment was more favorable, and the task, though not agreeable, would at least bridge over an hour of her lonely evening.[6]

In the metaphors used to summarize feeling in typical passages the interpreting author is also evident:

They were not half as sad as they had thought they would be. Now

[6] Notice the cause-to-effect reasoning in the second paragraph; note how this reasoning is not specifically attributed to the present moment but is presented as a summation of thinking over a period of time. The decision in the third paragraph is more immediate — a specific thought of the actual moment — but even here the author's privilege to reorganize and summarize is exercised in the orderly presentation of reasons for the decision.

they were fairly on the mountain of their affliction, they found out there were flowers on it. (Freeman, "A Wayfaring Couple")

Rosina Sayle herself could hardly retrace her own winding path through the thicket of scruples that had intervened between her and happiness. She had not only the New England conscience, she had also the New England sense of humor — the distinctive characteristic of which is that neither grimness nor tragedy prevents its play . . . . The stepmother *motif* [her problem is that she is unable to love her stepson with as genuine a maternal feeling as she would like] had jigged across her romance as the Venusberg music jigs across the Pilgrim's Chorus. (Gerould, "The Miracle")

Somewhat more dramatic than these explicit summations are direct and indirect quotations of particular thoughts, also common in the early period. These correspond to the soliloquies and asides in a play, which, as has been noted, are the least dramatic devices a playwright may use in depicting thought:

Perchance they [the reflections of the men in the boat] might be formulated thus: "If I am going to be drowned — if I am going to be drowned — if I am going to be drowned, why, in the name of the seven mad gods who rule the sea, was I allowed to come thus far and contemplate sand and trees?" (Crane, "The Open Boat")

"What will Margery think?" she laughed to herself. "I wish I could have Margery with me, but I couldn't take her away from Monica. And would she have come? I'm afraid Margery will be disappointed in me. She belongs where she used to be when I was a child — in my mother's house, with all the Chippendale and the endless, torpid afternoons. I never can think of Margery in *my* house; but, then, I've never really had a house. Poor Margery! My nurse, and Monica's, and perhaps — oh, Monica! Monica! I hope you'll be happy, whoever he is." (Gerould, "The Great Tradition")

Even such passages, despite their presentation as direct quotations, clearly show an intervening author readjusting and reorganizing thought to make it presentable. Crane acknowledges as much by his phrase, "might be formulated thus"; in the dialogue of the story, the men never use such expressions as "the seven mad gods who rule the sea," "the sacred cheese of life," and "this old ninny-woman, Fate." The artificiality of the passage from "The Great Tradition" is especially evident when the heroine sums up information for the reader's benefit in a manner most unlike that of spontaneous thought.

Such marks of intervention by the author sometimes appear even when thought is presented in a literally dramatic way through dialogue and monologue. Garland himself admits the unusual eloquence that he has given to a simple farmer in the following piece of rhetoric from "A Branch Road:"

As we went on his argument rose to the level of Browning's philosophy.

"We can make this experience count for us yet. But we mustn't let a mistake ruin us — it should teach us. What right has any one to keep you in a hole? God don't expect a toad to stay in a stump and starve if it can get out. He don't ask the snakes to suffer as you do."

Especially extraordinary is the rhetoric of the heroine of Mrs. Wharton's "The Long Run" when she tries to persuade her lover to run away with her. Her argument, too long to be reproduced here, can be found in Appendix J.

Of course, as has been noted, many of the characters in earlier stories were rhetoricians; perhaps it is unfair to suggest that the author has revised the thought he has put into their mouths. Yet in truth this is a technical as well as conceptual matter; though the treatment is literally dramatic, the coherence, organization, and lucidity of the character's expression reduce the extent of inference that the reader must make. Thus the potentialities of the dramatic method are not exploited as fully as they might be. This does not mean that a dramatic depiction of thought must be inarticulate. It is not a question of improving or heightening a character's powers of language beyond a lifelike realism, but rather, of the completeness or fullness with which the character's most significant thought or feeling is summed up. The great Shakespearan soliloquies, for example, are as articulate and expressive as poetic speech can be; we feel this, however, not because they make fully explicit all that the character is thinking or feeling, but because they suggest so much thought and feeling beyond and beneath what is actually said.

The dramatic quality of dramatized speech seems to diminish

as the speech becomes more intellectual, more rational, unless
the act of reasoning is emotionally motivated. In Shakespeare, in
Jane Austen, in James, in the great "intellectual" novelists, it is
so motivated — intensely so. But the emotional motive must include not merely the desire to make the particular point being
argued, as with Mrs. Wharton's heroine; it must include a passion for reason, for intellect, for order as such, before we lose
the uncomfortable feeling that the author has injected his own
thinking into the speech of his character. This feeling is perhaps
most uncomfortable when a character begins to universalize his
thought in an unnatural manner. Of course, universal elements
must be present if the thought or speech is to be effective —
there must be some basis of common human experience whereby
the reader is enabled to understand what is happening to the
character and to appreciate the significance of the character as
a moral being. If, however, the character himself universalizes
his experience, we are likely to feel (unless the tendency to do
this is itself a significant feature of his moral character) that the
author is using him as a mouthpiece. This non-dramatic tendency is especially prominent in some of the early discovery
stories and stories of corrected attitude, in which the discovery or changed attitude is expressed in universal terms, as in the
following examples:

The knowledge now that it was not always exact justice that was
meted out to all and that it was not so much the business of the
writer to indict as to interpret was borne in on him with distinctness
by the cruel sorrow of the mother, whose blame, if any, was infinitesi-
mal. (Dreiser, "Nigger Jeff")

Long before Bert Chadwick returned from his laboratory, Sadie
slept, from utter weariness. She had discovered that sometimes the
intolerable must be borne. (Gerould, "Wesendonck")

We recognize the author at work here revising or reformulating
the thoughts of his characters, since it would be unnatural and
implausible for either of these characters, as we have known
them hitherto, not to be thinking and feeling about the intense
personal experiences that they have been through. This is not
to say that the discoveries made here are implausible, but only

that the statement of the discovery glosses over and suppresses the inevitable state of agitation which the character must feel and sums up its outcome from a detached point of view.

In James's stories a somewhat more dramatic way of treating thought and feeling is often seen — despite the intricacy and elaborateness of his analyses — in his use of a rudimentary stream-of-consciousness technique. Instead of following the principles of logic, the organization attempts to imitate the associational flow of thought. This method, which appears occasionally though not commonly in other early writers (chiefly Mrs. Wharton and Miss Cather, sometimes Mrs. Gerould and Crane), can be illustrated in its most usual form in the following passage from "The Middle Years":

> The idea of the help he needed was very present to him that night, which he spent in a lucid stillness, an intensity of thought that constituted a reaction from his hours of stupor. He was lost, he was lost — he was lost if he couldn't be saved. He wasn't afraid of suffering, of death, wasn't even in love with life; but he had had a deep demonstration of desire. It came over him in the long quiet hours that only with "The Middle Years" had he taken his flight; only on that day, visited by soundless processions, had he recognised his kingdom. He had had a revelation of his range. What he dreaded was the idea that his reputation should stand on the unfinished. It wasn't with his past but with his future that it should properly be concerned. Illness and age rose before him like spectres with pitiless eyes: how was he to bribe such fates to give him a second chance? He had had the one chance that all men have — he had had the chance of life. He went to sleep again very late, and when he awoke Doctor Hugh was sitting at hand.

The primary dramatic advantage in this passage is the suggestion of a chronology and of external circumstances ("that night," "a lucid stillness," "long quiet hours") affecting his feelings, so that his thinking and feeling themselves have the effect of an action. The order of the passage, pivoted on the clause, "It came over him," suggests that his feeling precedes the clarification of his thought — a natural order — and the absence of transition between thought and action ("he had had the chance of life. He went to sleep again . . ."), typical of James's habit of interweaving action and thought in a single narrative context, also suggests that the thoughts and feelings are part of a forward moving action.

Even so, the passage does not leave much thought or feeling to inference. The narrative treatment is largely explicit. The chief inferences demanded are of a fairly complex "gramatical" kind — inferences necessary to interpret the abundant metaphors. Feeling is defined directly ("desire"), through negatives ("he wasn't afraid of death"), and through typifying or analogical situations ("he was lost"). The reiteration of the latter phrase, it is true, is dramatic, for it suggests through dramatic inference an intensity not directly expressed. But even the general organization, despite the chronology, on close examination turns out to be a reorganization of his thought; the paragraph is essentially a definition, involving a narrowing-down of terms and an elimination of alternatives. The past-perfect flashbacks, especially, manifest the rearranging author at work.

The limits beyond which the associational technique was rarely if ever attempted in the early period may be fairly demonstrated by the following example from Mrs. Wharton's "The Reckoning":

Her first conscious thought was that she had not broken her word, that she had fulfilled the very letter of their bargain. There had been no crying out, no vain appeal to the past, no attempt at temporizing or evasion. She had marched straight up to the guns.

Now that it was over, she sickened to find herself alive. She looked about her, trying to recover her hold on reality. Her identity seemed to be slipping from her, as it disappears in a physical swoon. "This is my room — this is my house," she heard herself saying. Her room? Her house? She could almost hear the walls laugh back at her.

She stood up, weariness in every bone. The silence of the room frightened her. She remembered, now, having heard the front door close a long time ago: the sound suddenly re-echoed through her brain. Her husband must have left the house, then — her *husband?* She no longer knew in what terms to think: the simplest phrases had a poisoned edge. She sank back into her chair, overcome by a strange weakness. The clock struck ten — it was only ten o'clock! Suddenly she remembered that she had not ordered dinner . . . or were they dining out that evening? *Dinner — dining out —* the old meaningless phraseology pursued her! She must try to think of herself as she would think of some one else, a some one dissociated from all the familiar routine of the past, whose wants and habits must gradually be learned, as one might spy out the ways of a strange animal . . . (Wharton, "The Reckoning")

Here, too, despite the suggestion of chronology and the additional associational technique in which the words of one thought suggest another ("Her husband must have . . . — her *husband?*"), the only inference needed is an interpretation of the metaphor, "the simplest phrases had a poisoned edge." The character is stunned because her husband has announced his intention to divorce her. The passage is essentially a generalization of an idea with particular illustrations, and the principles of a logical summary of thought are close to the surface.

As with characterization, the result of these methods is intellectual clarity in the exposition of most thoughts and feelings. Few stories demand more extensive inference of these elements than that demanded by the illustrations cited. It is noteworthy that, among those that do, there is little attempt to narrate thought directly. The methods used in such cases are the traditional dramatic ones: the treatment is strictly external and the inferred thought or feeling usually has an ambiguous quality. The reader is not intended to make a clear and definite inference; he is faced rather with a choice of inferences impossible to resolve — a mystery of feeling whose remoteness from our understanding is meant to astonish him with shock, awe, or amusement. Such ambiguity marks a comedy such as James's "Miss Gunton of Poughkeepsie" and such horror stories as Bierce's "A Horseman in the Sky" and "The Affair at Coulter's Notch"; in other stories of astonishing choice such as Bierce's "One Kind of Officer," Mrs. Gerould's "Pearls," or James's "Europe," the motive is clear, the mystery residing in the power of the unexpressed passion that invests such a motive.

Otherwise, in stories of the early period, inferences concerning thought and feeling tend either to be extremely simple — as, for example, our inference in Mrs. Wharton's "The Other Two" that the hero at the end has acknowledged the error in his expectations (the evidence is the laugh with which he joins his wife and her former husbands whom he has previously tried to keep apart) — or to concern only some special, limited and precise process of reasoning, as when we infer, in Mrs. Freeman's "Life-Everlasting," what reasoning has persuaded the heroine to become a Christian, following an experience she has had with a criminal. The latter kind of inference is essentially grammatical or rhetorical rather than dramatic, requiring a determination not of feeling or of the way thought follows from character but only of the assumptions or premises that underlie the character's own direct explanation of her thought. More significant inferences concerning thought and feeling — thought and feeling that is neither explicitly described nor immediately obvious in the action itself — are rare and are important, for the most part, only in a few stories by Crane, James, and Dreiser.[7]

In stories of the twenties, the explicit methods of treating thought and feeling are still much in evidence, especially in stories by Anderson and Fitzgerald. At the same time, new methods are being developed whereby thought and feeling, often quite complex, are presented with more dramatic effect — chiefly as a result of the writer's greater sureness in the use of dramatic inference. Three methods are noteworthy, the first involving the use of dialogue, the second the use of summaries of thought, and the third the use of details of sensations experienced by characters. The first, of which Hemingway is the master, is simply a tightening of dramatic technique in the literal sense so that dialogue contains stronger implications of unspoken thought and feelings. This can be illustrated by a contrast between scenes of painful and embarrassing revelation in the two periods. The following passage from Mrs. Wharton's "Autres Temps" is a typical embarrassing confrontation in the early period:

"I believe — I remember now — Charlotte's young man was suggesting that they should all go out — to a music-hall or something of the sort. I'm sure — I'm positively sure that you won't find them."

Her hand dropped from the door, his dropped from her arm, and

---

[7] Appendix M lists the stories of the canon which leave to inference major questions of thought or feeling.

as they drew back and faced each other she saw the blood rise slowly through his sallow skin, redden his neck and ears, encroach upon the edges of his beard, and settle in dull patches under his kind troubled eyes. She had seen the same blush on another face, and the same impulse of compassion she had then felt made her turn her gaze away again.

Another, by the same author, is more strictly dramatic; nevertheless, the characters bring forth their painful and embarrassing feelings fully and explicitly:

"Good God! How can I go and leave you here with him?"

"You've done it often."

"Yes; but each time it's more damnable. And then I've always had a hope ———"

She rose also. "Give it up! Give it up!"

"You've none, then, yourself?"

She was silent, drawing the folds of her cloak about her.

"None — none?" he insisted.

He had to bend his head to hear her answer. "Only one!"

"What, my dearest? What?"

"Don't touch me! That he may die!"

They drew apart again, hearing each other's quick breathing through the darkness.

"You wish that too?" he said.

"I wish it always — every day, every hour, every moment!" She paused, and then let the words break from her. "You'd better know it; you'd better know the worst of me. I'm not the saint you suppose; the duty I do is poisoned by the thoughts I think. Day by day, hour by hour, I wish him dead . . ."

She broke off with a sob, and the loud lapping of the water under the floor was like the beat of a rebellious heart.

"There, you know the truth!" she said. (Wharton, "The Choice")

Contrast these with the following exchange, by Hemingway, in which Nick's embarrassment and Marge's disappointment are left almost entirely to inference:

"Go on and say it."

Nick looked on at the moon, coming up over the hills.

"It isn't fun any more."

He was afraid to look at Marjorie. Then he looked at her. She sat there with her back toward him. He looked at her back. "It isn't fun any more. Not any of it."

She didn't say anything. He went on. "I feel as though everything was gone to hell inside of me. I don't know, Marge. I don't know what to say."

He looked on at her back.

"Isn't love any fun?" Marjorie said.

"No," Nick said. Marjorie stood up. Nick sat there, his head in his hands.

"I'm going to take the boat," Marjorie called to him. "You can walk back around the point."

"All right," Nick said. "I'll push the boat off for you."

"You don't need to," she said. (Hemingway, "The End of Something")

Yet more suggestive is the brief exchange from Hemingway's "Hills Like White Elephants," quoted at the beginning of Part Three, in which the man betrays his insincerity and the girl her bitter disappointment:

"You've got to realize," he said, "that I don't want you to do it if you don't want to. I'm perfectly willing to go through with it if it means anything to you."

"Doesn't it mean anything to you? We could get along."

"Of course it does. But I don't want anybody but you. I don't want any one else. And I know it's perfectly simple.

"Yes, you know it's perfectly simple." [8]

The second noteworthy method of dramatizing thought in stories of the twenties is like the characteristic method of dramatizing character; it makes use of explicit summaries and direct statements as well as direct and indirect quotations, but subordinates them to a larger state of mind whose precise nature is left to inference. In stories of the early period, similar inferences might be drawn from particular passages, but usually these are ultimately made explicit, as in the scene that follows the passage from "The Reckoning" (quoted above, pp. 343–44). The heroine eventually states explicitly the import of her thoughts and feelings — her recognition, with regret, that she has made a great mistake. The writer of the twenties would be more likely to let the reader infer such a conclusion.

Such a technique in stories of the twenties tends to carry fur-

[8] See also the quarrels in Hemingway's "Soldier's Home," "Cat in the Rain," and "Doctor and the Doctor's Wife."

ther the kind of stream-of-consciousness that was suggested in the passage from "The Reckoning," although it still does not approach the extremes of free association developed by Joyce.[9] It can be illustrated by reproducing the conclusion of Anderson's "Nobody Knows":

When George Willard [after his rather unfriendly sexual initiation by Louise] got back into Main Street it was past ten o'clock and had begun to rain. Three times he walked up and down the length of Main Street. Sylvester West's Drug Store was still open and he went in and bought a cigar. When Shorty Crandall the clerk came out at the door with him he was pleased. For five minutes the two stood in the shelter of the store awning and talked. George Willard felt satisfied. He had wanted more than anything else to talk to some man. Around the corner toward the New Willard House he went whistling softly.

On the sidewalk at the side of Winny's Dry Goods Store where there was a high board fence covered with circus pictures, he stopped whistling and stood perfectly still in the darkness, attentive, listening as though for a voice calling his name. Then again he laughed nervously. "She hasn't got anything on me. Nobody knows," he muttered doggedly and went on his way.

This passage is notable for combining many signs of feeling in a chronological narrative: acts showing feeling ("Three times he walked up and down the length of Main Street"); directly quoted thoughts ("'She hasn't got anything on me'"); and explicit summaries of feeling ("George Willard felt satisfied. He had wanted more than anything else to talk to some man"). As in "The Reckoning," the chronology gives dramatic quality to this passage. More significant is the fact that George's state of mind is not directly indicated — not even by the explicit summaries or the direct quotations. He is far from "fully satisfied," nor is he confident that "she hasn't got anything on" him. The most explicit statements are actually the most ironic in their implications. The true state of his mind, which is left to inference, is a delicate mixture of feelings. George's triumph is mixed with

[9] In the twenties the extremes in chronological free-association and stream of thought are reached in Porter's "Jilting of Granny Weatherall" and Faulkner's "Carcassonne."

doubts, and he is trying "doggedly," for the sake of self-respect, to deny that he has such doubts.

The same technique, is a somewhat more complicated form, is illustrated by a scene from Anderson's "An Awakening," reproduced at length in Appendix K. The scene attempts to depict by dramatic narrative the burgeoning of egotistical, romantic thoughts in George Willard's mind as he walks at night. A basic irony underlies this. For though George conceives of this moment as an "awakening" of his spirit, a discovery that he is "too big to be used," the real awakening does not come until later when he discovers that he is indeed being used, that he is not too big to be thrust aside like a child by Ed Handby, and that the same neighborhood that had before seemed so romantic now "seemed to him utterly squalid and commonplace." His romantic view in the scene quoted is a kind of self-love, easy to deflate. Since the narrator does not tell us this explicitly, the inference gives it a dramatic quality.

More important dramatically is the fact that the described and quoted thought does not begin to cover what is really on George's mind, but descends through steps to a mere gibberish of disconnected words. His mind is divided: "It seemed to him that some voice outside of himself had been talking as he walked." He is watching himself think and is puzzled as to "where . . . [his thoughts] had come from." In presenting these details the author uses a point of view internal to one part of George's mind to give a dramatic, externalized picture of another part. Mental division as a device for dramatizing the deeper levels of feeling, evident, to some extent, in all stories that deal with eruptions from the unconscious, is one of the most distinctive new devices of the period.

The thought of this passage, furthermore, is only a sign of the state of emotion that is here the author's primary object of depiction. At first glance this emotion seems to be summed up quite explicitly and non-dramatically; "Hypnotized . . . fervor . . . excited his already aroused fancy . . . something heady in his brain . . . oddly detached . . . excited . . . felt unutterably big and remade." What is not specified is the cause of this seemingly spontaneous eruption of exaltation. Only when the story is finished does it become clear that it was a typically adolescent upwelling of sexual anticipation and vanity, stimulated in part by thoughts of Belle Carpenter and in part (perhaps) by biological growth, typically camouflaged by a pompous and largely meaningless idealism.[10]

The third noteworthy method of dramatizing thought and feeling in the twenties is a major extension of methods scarcely realized by any of the early writers except occasionally by Crane. Instead of using external signs to suggest a character's feeling or thought, the author presents certain causes or stimuli and allows us to infer the feeling or thought that would result when a character experiences them. In itself this is not new. In any story or play, when a character's thought and feeling are not specified, we infer that certain things will be felt as a result of what happens: for instance, "Mother's" satisfaction in her husband's capitulation in Mrs. Freeman's "The Revolt of 'Mother,'" or the heroine's horror, in Mrs. Wharton's "The Choice," when her lover dies. The novelty lies in the application of this sort of inference to major revelations and in the extensive development of certain kinds of stimuli used to suggest such inferences. The most frequent stimuli so exploited are what may be broadly called "sensations" — experiences gathered by a character through the senses and recorded by the narrator *before* the character has assessed them in relation to the total situation. This accounts, in large part, for the marked increase in the use of physical details of setting in stories of the twenties.

Physical details of setting, the stimuli and sensations provided by a character's immediate surroundings, have always been a potent means of evoking a mood or enhancing the emotion of a character. But the use of such detail as both the cause and sign of a character's particular state of mind, without the

[10] Other stories showing a similar technique include Anderson's "Loneliness," "Man Who Became a Woman," "New Englander," "Respectability," "Strength of God," "Teacher," "Thinker"; Fitzgerald's "Absolution," "Benediction," "Rough Crossing," "Winter Dreams"; Hemingway's "In Another Country," "Alpine Idyll," "Soldier's Home," "Simple Enquiry," "Now I Lay Me"; Miss Porter's "Cracked Looking-Glass," "Flowering Judas," "Jilting of Granny Weatherall," "That Tree," "Theft."

assistance of the narrator's interpretation, was only incompletely realized by earlier writers. The following passage from Garland's "A Branch Road" is typical of the earlier use of setting to suggest a state of mind:

Above the level belt of timber to the east a vast dome of pale undazzling gold was rising, silently and swiftly. Jays called in the thickets where the maples flamed amid the green oaks, with irregular splashes of red and orange. The grass was crisp with frost under the feet, the road smooth and gray-white in color, the air was indescribably pure, resonant, and stimulating. No wonder the man sang!

The last sentence states a conclusion that later writers leave to the reader: the setting is a cause for the man's joy. But even if the sentence about his singing were left out, the reader would still recognize, from the language and the orderly presentation, the interpreting hand of the narrator. The scene is being witnessed separately and simultaneously by both the narrator and the man, rather than by the narrator through the man's eyes.[11]

Mrs. Wharton's "The Triumph of Night" (not included in the canon) shows a similar bypassing of the immediate stimuli, despite the vivid evocation of pain. The analogy and the imaginings in the passage are thoughts by the character in *response* to the actual sensations, which are left to our imagination. They are signs but not causes of the character's feelings:

The blast that swept him came off New Hampshire snow-fields and ice-hung forests. It seemed to have traversed interminable leagues of frozen silence, filling them with the same cold roar and sharpening its edge against the same bitter black-and-white landscape. Dark, searching and sword-like, it alternately muffled and harried its victim, like a bull-fighter now whirling his cloak and now planting his darts.[12]

[11] This point is bolstered, immediately following, by the revelation that the man's joy has as much to do with his love as with the setting.

[12] Other uses of setting are, of course, frequent in the early period. In the passage from Bierce's "Horseman in the Sky," quoted on p. 314, a description of setting is necessary to account for the action; note that the hero himself is asleep at the moment described. The following, from Mrs. Whartan's "Bunner Sisters," illustrates the use of setting to enhance a characterization, essentially a kind of indirect interpretive commentary by the narrator: "The sole refuge offered from the contemplation of this depressing waste was the sight of the

In the twenties the use of sensations on a clear and simple level is seen in many stories by Hemingway. The following passage from "Big Two-Hearted River" or the passage from "Cross-Country Snow," reproduced in Appendix L, are illustrations:

Nick climbed out onto the meadow and stood, water running down his trousers and out of his shoes, his shoes squlchy. He went over and sat on the logs. He did not want to rush his sensations any.

He wriggled his toes in the water, in his shoes, and got out a cigarette from his breast pocket. He lit it and tossed the match into the fast water below the logs. A tiny trout rose at the match, as it swung around in the fast current. Nick laughed. He would finish the cigarette.

He sat on the logs, smoking, drying in the sun, the sun warm on his back, the river shallow ahead entering the woods, curving into the woods, shallows, light glittering, big water-smooth rocks, cedars along the bank and white birches, the logs warm in the sun, smooth to sit on, without bark, gray to the touch; slowly the feeling of disappointment [for failing to land a big trout] left him. It went away slowly, the feeling of disappointment that came sharply after the thrill that made his shoulders ache. It was all right now. His rod lying out on the logs, Nick tied a new hook on the leader, pulling the gut tight until it grimped into itself in a hard knot.

The description evokes Nick's pleasure — his satisfaction in resting after fishing. The details are given not for the direct pleasure of the reader but as a means of delineating Nick's state of mind. The description is not devoted simply to details of setting; it is a chronological record of perceptions. Many of these perceptions are simply things seen (sometimes looked at twice, with new perceptiveness the second time: "The river shallow ahead entering the woods, curving into the woods . . ."). Some are actual acts by the protagonist — acts that are not signs of feeling but are themselves virtual sensations like the other perceptions

Bunner sisters' window. Its panes were always well-washed, and though their display of artifical flowers, bands of scalloped flannel . . . [etc.] had the undefinable greyish tinge of objects long preserved in the showcase of a museum, the window revealed a background of orderly counters and white-washed walls in pleasant contrast to the adjoining dinginess."

Only Crane in the early period anticipates the practice of the later writers in his use of setting.

("He wriggled his toes in the water . . .").[13] A few details are statements of emotions, but even these are treated on the level of sensations. (". . . slowly the feeling of disappointment left him"). The end of disappointment is one of a multitude of sensations that produce in Nick a consciousness of deep and restful satisfaction.

The feeling so delineated is of the utmost importance to the story as a whole. Here, as in "Cross-Country Snow," the pictured satisfaction is urgently sought by Nick, as relief or protection from evils that threaten him (though the specific nature of these evils is not given). This too we know largely by inference.

In many stories of the twenties the sensations or perceptions so used are somewhat more complicated, being embodied in metaphors or symbols perceived by the character. This can be seen in a passage from Miss Porter's "Flowering Judas":

Braggioni catches her glance solidly as if he had been waiting for it, leans forward, balancing his paunch between his spread knees, and sings with tremendous emphasis, weighing his words . . . . His mouth opens round and yearns sideways, his balloon cheeks grow oily with the labor of song. He bulges marvelously in his expensive garments. Over his lavender collar, crushed upon a purple necktie, held by a diamond hoop: over his ammunition belt of tooled leather worked in silver, buckled cruelly around his gasping middle: over the tops of his glossy yellow shoes Braggioni swells with ominous ripeness, his mauve silk hose stretched taut, his ankles bound with the stout leather throngs of his shoes.

The primary inference to be drawn from this passage is the revulsion, disgust, and fear that Laura feels in Braggioni's presence, and it depends to a large extent on the metaphors used in presenting many of the details. But, unlike those noted in "The Triumph of Night" (p. 351), these metaphors are a part of Laura's perception, not a response to her perception; she actually feels as a sensation how he "catches her glance," and sees him "swelling with ominous ripeness." The reader infers the revulsion and fear not from what the metaphors describe but from the perception of the metaphors themselves.

[13] In this passage there is a single instance of an act that is a sign rather than a stimulus of feeling: "Nick laughed."

The difference between this and the more conventional use of metaphor to depict feeling can be stated as follows: Whereas the conventional metaphor is merely a device of expression, used by the narrator to describe a feeling already felt,[14] here the metaphor is an actual part of the experience of the character, who finds in it some relevance or pertinence to his case. The observed parallelism or symbolism here does not merely express, but rather forms feeling, as do the sensations recorded in "Big Two-Hearted River." The dramatic element here is twofold: we must infer both the metaphorical or symbolical significance that the character has perceived, and the feeling or thought that this perception evokes.

The device is less prominent in passages such as that quoted than in the large-scale use to which it is put in many stories. "Flowering Judas" itself furnishes an example in Laura's dream, which concludes the story. Here again Laura sees her situation in a metaphor — the images of a dream. The reader must infer not only what the dream expresses but also what it means to Laura. Usually, the perceived metaphor is an actual event that the protagonist witnesses or participates in and its perception is an essential part of the action itself, as in generalized discovery stories such as Hemingway's "In Another Country" and "An Alpine Idyll." The manner in which inferences are drawn in such stories has been described in a previous chapter. In "An Alpine Idyll" (see p. 255 ff.), the reader has to infer whatever connections may exist between the two parts of the story, each of which describes an experience without any direct causal relation to the other. This has been called a "thematic" relationship; more specifically, we infer that the two experiences must be analogues, meaningful to the hero because he sees in the peasant's experience a parallel to his own actual or potential case. This parallel is not actually described by the narrator or by anyone in the story. The reader must conclude (as with Laura's dream) both what the parallel is and what it means

---

[14] See for example the metaphorical description of a blush in "Autres Temps," quoted, p. 104. The blush is what counts; we know that Mrs. Lidcote will react to it with certain feelings. The metaphor merely describes it vividly; it contains nothing in itself to influence her reaction. Laura, on the other hand, actually sees details of Braggioni's person as cruel, gasping, ominously ripe, and so on.

to the narrator. Thus both the discovery and the narrator's feeling about it are presented in a fully dramatic way that depends wholly on the inferences that can be drawn from stimuli to, rather than from signs of, thought and feeling in the given character.

In Hemingway's "In Another Country," the episode of the major's bereavement functions in the same way; so, in Miss Porter's "Theft," does the episode with the janitress, and, in Fitzgerald's "The Ice Palace," the episode in the ice palace. Similar methods, less fully developed, are employed in several other stories by Hemingway — in the "old ruin" in "The End of Something," the cat in the rain or the hills like white elephants in the stories so titled, in the drunken Indians in "Ten Indians," and — in certain stories by Anderson — the naked women in "The Strength of God" and "Respectability" or the horse's skull at the end of "The Man Who Became a Woman."

These techniques for delineating thought and feeling contrast sharply with the general explicitness of stories of the early period. No matter how explicit the writer of the twenties may be concerning secondary thoughts and feelings, if thought and feeling are central to the action he is more than likely to leave to inference their most essential elements. The technique is well adapted to the peculiar mental states in which writers of the twenties were most interested. If the knowledge acquired in a discovery remains on the intuitive level in the character's mind, it is natural for the writer to leave it on this level when describing it, thus achieving the effect of dramatic inference. Likewise, if the problems have to do with unconscious feelings, and the interest of the story is directed less to the analysis of these feelings than to their effect on the character's behavior and happiness, it is natural for the writer to present these things from the viewpoint of the character's consciousness, which is itself blocked off from full understanding, thereby achieving a dramatic quality. Well over a third of the stories in the canon deal with such problems and require major inferences as to thought and feeling. The most striking of these inferences, along with those in stories of the early period that may require similar inference, are summed up briefly in Appendix M.

The opposite to this kind of treatment can be illustrated by many passages from James, of which the following, from "Flickerbridge," is a good example. It describes Frank Granger's first feelings upon his discovery of Flickerbridge, a beautiful old English place untouched and unspoiled by the modern age:

He was indeed to learn on arrival to what he had been committed; but that was for a while so much a part of his first general impression that the particular truth took time to detach itself, the first general impression demanding verily all his faculties of response. . . . He had presented himself with the moderate amount of flutter involved in a sense of due preparation; but he had then found that, however primed with prefaces and prompted with hints, he hadn't been prepared at all. How *could* he be, he asked himself, for anything so foreign to his experience, so alien to his proper world, so little to be preconceived in the sharp north light of the newest impressionism, and yet so recognised after all in the event, so noted and tasted and assimilated? It was a case he would scarce have known how to describe — could doubtless have described best with a full clean brush, supplemented by a play of gesture; for it was always his habit to see an occasion, of whatever kind, primarily as a picture, so that he might get it, as he was wont to say, so that he might keep it, well together. He had been treated of a sudden, in this adventure, to one of the sweetest fairest coolest impressions of his life — one moreover visibly complete and homogeneous from the start. Oh it was there, if that was all one wanted of a thing! It was so 'there' that . . . he had held his breath for fear of breaking the spell . . . Supreme beauty suddenly revealed is apt to strike us as a possible illusion playing with our desire — instant freedom with it to strike us as a possible rashness.

The reader is struck by the scarcity of specific details, in this and subsequent passages, suggesting why Granger's impression is "one of the sweetest fairest coolest" of his life; the passage tells us how astonished he is to have such an impression but it does not represent the actual feeling at all. The technique here, of course, accords with a famous Jamesian principle enunciated in the preface to "The Turn of the Screw": the reader's sense of evil will be greater if the evil itself is not specified. In the case of "Flickerbridge" (as, on a larger scale, in the case of

The Spoils of Poynton), a suggestion of indescribable beauty
is attempted by the avoidance of any description of it. This is a
narrative rather than a dramatic device. The actual perception
of beauty, or the actual apprehension of evil, is not "rendered"
but summed up. What James's theory involves is a careful dis-
crimination between that which, in such a story, *can* be effectively dramatized and that which cannot. He suppresses the
hero's actual perception of the beauty of Flickerbridge because
this feeling is less important to the story as a whole than its
consequences, the choices he must make once he becomes aware
of the feeling.

INFERENCE CONCERNING FORM

Relatively few stories of the twenties attempt dramatization on
all of the levels that have been discussed. The diversity of techniques itself offers a contrast to the stereotyped balance between dramatization and narrative that prevailed in most earlier
stories. Yet certain constant principles underlying this diversity
have emerged. The general effort is to obtain at least an equally
dramatic effect with more economical means. The achievement
of such an end is promoted by a heightened recognition of dramatic inference as the most powerful means of producing such
an effect. The gain in economy is made possible by exploitation
of the principle that success of the dramatic illusion depends
far more upon the treatment of the major elements in a story
than upon that of the secondary elements. The full potentialities of this principle were scarcely grasped by the early writers,
even though they saved their big moments for dramatic scenes
and used their narratives to bridge the secondary gaps. But
they did not trust purely dramatic methods alone to carry the
biggest moments. If the big scenes are dramatized, if scenic
methods are used to recall the past, provide characterizations,
to indicate thoughts and feelings, the final and most important
points in a story, nevertheless, are usually treated non-dramatically. The author or an authoritative character explains or sums
up the course of action when it is not obvious. Discoveries are
spelled out, and the proper judgments of character are made
explicit. Instances of these practices have been indicated in the

foregoing pages. The best evidence is the scarcity of early stories requiring the reader to make any crucial inferences in order to understand the story as a whole.

The earlier writers most likely to use this device are, as in so many other things, "forerunners" — Crane and Bierce — and also James. In most cases, even the inferences required by these writers are, in contrast to those in the twenties, fairly simple, nor are they, except in James, used consistently or in a way that suggests that they were "normal technique" for the time. As for James, here again is evidence of his greater mastery. Not only his statements of theory but his practice in these stories show clearly that James was more aware of the value of dramatizing economically than were other earlier writers; modern writers and critics alike are indebted to him for explaining and demonstrating the fundamental distinction between "rendering" and "stating" that underlies the most significant modern advances in technique. By far the most conscientious dramatist in the early period, he probably deserves more credit as a forerunner in this regard than do the others whom we have so labeled. Yet even James did not anticipate the peculiar sort of dramatic economy that was to become characteristic in the stories of the twenties. Though he speaks frequently in his prefaces of the difficulties encountered in condensing his large conceptions into the small compass of the short story, the fact remains that by later standards his stories are developed explicitly and elaborated to a great degree. They are "full," and this fulness means a considerable explicitness concerning essentials, supplementing his conscientiously dramatic representation.

The inferences demanded by James pertain, for the most part, to the proper final moral judgment of the character's situation and hence to the appropriate effect. They are, in other words, inferences as to "form." "The Lesson of the Master" and "Paste" are good examples — two stories that well exemplify the ambiguity that critics find in the works of James. The reader teeters between the judgment that the duping of the characters makes them ridiculous and the judgment that they have at least achieved a satisfying moral triumph or have admirably affirmed their moral integrity. Is the story comic, or is it a romance?

This study has shown with fair certainty that most such stories are ultimately comic and that the very effect of ambiguity is a part of the comedy, a complexity in the comic effect caused by the author's refusal to make explicit his evaluation of the situation.

In this respect the writers of the twenties go further than James does. Where their stories seem less "ambiguous," it is not because they leave less to inference or because the stories are less complex, emotionally and morally, but rather because they leave somewhat *more* to inference, making less effort to explain on the intellectual level what the issues are. The Jamesian ambiguity is an intellectual problem, a difficulty faced by the reader's reasoning powers when confronted with an exposition of a complex emotional and moral situation. A story such as Hemingway's "The Doctor and the Doctor's Wife," on the other hand, is no less complex emotionally, but since there is no intellectualizing of the issues, the reader responds to this complexity on the intuitive and emotional level and is less aware of the necessity of "resolving," or explaining, its ambiguity.

A majority of stories in the twenties require basic inference as to their forms. The reader must infer not merely the proper moral evaluation of character, as in the Jamesian examples, but, in many cases, what has actually happened in the story, or to put it more accurately, what principle governs the sequence of parts. He must infer what has changed, if the story depends upon change, or what is the nature of the constant element, if an episode. Usually such inferences are necessitated because significant elements of character, thought, or feeling are left to inference, or because action is particularized whose sequential principle is neither summed up nor self-evident.

In stories of the early period, except as already noted, the form of a story is usually perfectly clear. Even when other inferences are required, no exceptional inference as to what the main action is, or how to judge it, is needed. The fundamental horror of such stories as "A Horseman in the Sky" or "The Affair at Coulter's Notch," for example, is self-evident in the action, even though the precise feeling of the hero in performing each horrible act is, in each case, left to inference.

In stories of the twenties certain important kinds of forms are left to inference more regularly than others. This is true of most episodes of discovery, of suffering, or of choice. The reader must infer the discovery, or the causes of the change in suffering (if not always its nature), or the general motive of the choice. Inferences must often be made in order to understand the growth of feeling in the new romances, and in comedies (especially the caustic) in order to understand the absurdity of the protagonist's unrecognized misfortune or error. The determination of effects of both pathos and horror regularly depends on inferences not merely as to the moral evaluation of the situation but as to what it actually consists of.[15]

How the reader is led to make the desired inferences is apt to vary. In general, beyond such specific methods as have been indicated, the writers of the twenties appear to rely on two sources of comprehension. First, obviously, they expect their readers to be moderately (but only moderately) familiar with the kinds of moral and psychological ideas that were popular in America in their time. We should "know enough" not to take literally George's assertion, in "Nobody Knows," that he is satisfied by his sexual initiation; we must understand just enough about the force of unconscious motivation to make the behavior of the heroine of Anderson's "Adventure" comprehensible, and we must know enough elementary psychology to recognize that the symbols in Laura's dream, in "Flowering Judas," or the memories recalled by Granny Weatherall are the expressions of feelings. We must be enough aware of the disrepute of Vic-

[15] The demand upon the reader's powers of inference is especially great in such discovery stories of modified horror as "In Another Country" and "Theft." It will be noted that the most characteristic romances in the twenties depend on the inference of admiration in a manner not characteristic of the earlier stories (where admiration is much more obvious). This is notable in such stories as Hemingway's "Undefeated" and Faulkner's story "Hair," wherein the hero's admirable behavior is complicated by less creditable elements which are left to the reader to resolve.

In general, it appears that when a judgment is made clear to the reader, as it is in Hemingway's "Killers" (in the comments by the boys at the end of the story), either the nature of the action is left to inference (the inference here as to the nature of the episode as unifying principle) or, as in "Hands," the nature of significant character motivation or thought is left to inference. When these things are clear, as in "Undefeated," then judgment is left to inference. The stories of the twenties that leave least to inference are, for the most part, those comedies and romances by Fitzgerald that have been described as "light."

torianism among intellectuals of the twenties to recognize that Mr. and Mrs. Elliot are presented as prigs, that the boy in "I Want to Know Why" is not the repository of all truth, virtue, and purity, and that the heroine in "Hills Like White Elephants" is to be blamed less for consenting to an abortion than for doing so with such reasons and with such feelings.

Secondly, these writers expect their readers to be familiar enough with literary techniques to draw the appropriate conclusions when they encounter omissions of material in a story. The reader makes his inference because things are left out. In general, the writers of the twenties employ two devices which enable the reader to determine what the significant omissions are. One is the device of juxtaposition of related elements without an explicit indication of the relationship. This has been demonstrated elsewhere in this study by reference to "An Alpine Idyll," typical of the generalized discoveries, where this device is used most strikingly. The other, more important, is the device of truncating lines of potential development. This is the basis for our understanding of all the episodes of the twenties. In such stories our inference as to the nature of the static situation depends largely on the fact that the episode will remain trivial and meaningless *until* such inference is made. More specifically, each if these stories builds up certain probabilities or expectations that certain things will take place. These things do not take place within the compass of the story, but neither are counter-probabilities established to nullify them. The story thus ends with an apparent failure to "resolve" the tendencies implicit within it. Faced with such an ending, the reader has to infer the resolution for himself. Most commonly, he is convinced by the unresolved ending that resolution is impossible, at least for a time; hence the situation is static.

"The Doctor and the Doctor's Wife" (pp. 206–7) can be cited again to show how this works. The juxtaposition of the scene with the wife and the scene with the Indian not only makes clear the nature of the doctor's anger, as described above, but also raises an expectation that this anger will erupt in some kind of violence. This does not occur, but neither is any other satisfactory resolution of his emotions suggested. Thus we infer that in this particular situation no relief for his feelings will occur. His failure to assert himself against his wife's rebuff establishes a further probability: he is afraid of her. Since no counter-probability to this is established, we infer that she is the primary reason for his inability to relieve his feelings. We infer also, from the same evidence, as well as his immediate decision to go for a walk, that this conflict is no new thing in his life. Since no counter-probability is established to suggest possible relief from this conflict, the reader's attention is inevitably turned from the particular frustration to the more general one. The real story resides in the facts that the doctor's feelings are constantly frustrated by his wife, who has no understanding of either his sensitivity or his pretensions, and that this frustration depends upon both his fear and her blindness.

Almost two-third of the stories of the canon of the twenties require similar major inferences as to form. There seems little doubt that the skilful use of inference is the most general and distinctive technical development displayed by the short stories of the twenties.

XXII: THE DRAMATIC PRINCIPLE

The foregoing study of technique has been confined only to such aspects of the American short story as seem to have undergone significant change between the two periods, and these only as they pertain to the essential distinction between the narrative and the dramatic methods of treatment. Other technical problems have been by-passed: for example, that of symbolism — a matter that many modern critics have stressed. Symbolism as a technique, as a universalizing device, has been touched on in the treatment of metaphor as a source of inference, but it is felt that the problem of symbolism as such applies more to the didactic than to the artistic nature of a story. Most stories, of course, may be interpreted didactically — their characters and action viewed as exempla or symbols of general truths. A separate treatment of symbolism would refer to this didactic ele-

363

ment,[1] which can be regarded in the stories of the canon as secondary and external to their nature as artistic representations of particular actions.

The technical changes that have been observed show a consistent tendency toward a more economical dramatic treatment rather than toward one that is more dramatic in an absolute sense. Though this tendency is sometimes manifested in nearly perfect dramas such as Hemingway's "The Killers," the most significant manifestations are seen in the refinement of the techniques of narration to give the story more of the quality of drama freed of the bulkiness of the typical, old-fashioned dramatic scenes. To this end, dramatic attributes other than dialogue have been utilized extensively; the use of the first-person, of dramatic order, of dramatic particularity, and of dramatic inference, has been developed, and dramatic economy has been enhanced by a scupulous effort to apply these principles to the most important elements in the stories.

However one may judge the changes noted in Parts One and Two, this technical development can only be regarded as an improvement over the early period. The great advantage of the dramatic method, as has been said, is the vividness of the illusion it creates. The audience witnesses directly the thing being depicted. Such vividness is especially appropriate if one accepts the Aristotelian concept of art as "imitation"; the writer who dramatizes is imitating more directly than the one who narrates or sums up.[2] The technical experiments of the twenties have enlarged the range of what the writers can treat vividly. As Levin writes in describing the Joycean epiphany, the writer "is anxious to discover the most economical way of exposing the

---

[1] Symbolism within the story — symbolism intended to illuminate the action and symbols as seen by the characters themselves — has been touched on in the discussion of methods used for inferences and also suggested in the discussion of the intuitive psychology of the characters in stories of the twenties, although no attempt has been made to analyze the kinds of symbols used for these purposes.

[2] This statement assumes, of course, that all other elements are held constant. See the following statement by Elder Olson: "Representation . . . is a question of manner of limitation . . . Representation, whether narrative or dramatic, always makes things more vivid, and the latter is more vivid than the former." (*Critics and Criticism*, ed. R. S. Crane [Chicago: University of Chicoga Press, 1952], pp. 562–63.)

more evil or horror in a situation than first had met the eye — it is intensified in any story that makes exceptional use of such inferences.

The technical advances may perhaps also assist the writers of the twenties in their desire, noted in Chapter I, to depict "truth." For though a dramatic treatment by no means insures a "truthful" invention by the author, the objectivity of manner that it imposes at least forbids the writer from attempting in his own person to veil any falsehood in his invention. By not telling us whether the doctor in "The Doctor and the Doctor's Wife" should be regarded as laughable or pitiable — by letting his portrayal speak for itself — Hemingway avoids an otherwise almost inescapable esthetic falsehood: that of either trying to make us judge too narrowly the moral complexity of the action or of upsetting the delicate balance in the story by introducing the kind of detailed analysis that would be needed to formulate this complexity on the intellectual level.

Yet it would seem incorrect to characterize this development in the twenties as (in O'Brien's words) a "technical revolt."[5] The quest for more economically dramatic methods is a feature of the entire history of the modern short story. In stories of the early period the careful preparation for and handling of dramatic scenes is evidence of great concern with technical development — as is also the proliferation of studies and textbooks of the art of the short story. Though the writers of the twenties rejected certain stereotyped practices, both technical and formal, their motive was clearly not so much to reject as to carry further the earlier writers' search for dramatic economy.

[5] O'Brien, *Advance*, p. 247.

most considerable amount of that material." [3] T
be subtler than was possible before; characters a
of minds can be more complex; so, too, can be t
emotional issues underlying the story — even if, as]
gested, the intellectual issues of stories in the tv
to be less complex than in the work of some of the e
Subtle and mixed emotional qualities can now be a]
dramatically in situations less overtly dramatic. Wl
can concentrate on the evocation of delicate shades
that had previously been restricted characteristica
domain of lyric poetry.

A further advantage of the dramatic methods of the
is that they give pleasure by putting the reader to w
only must he exercise his intellectual faculties to gra:
ences, but he must exercise his intuitive faculties, his
to respond to suggestions of emotion, as well, for he is
to feel or understand the story intuitively before he can d
abstractly what it is actually about. He may, indeed, ne
able to tell all the story contains, and yet he may still resp
it as a moving story. This is appropriate to the subject n
of the twenties with its emphasis on felt or intuited experie
and also insures an emotional participation such as the re
might lose if the issues were immediately clear to him on
intellectual level. [4] It is especially appropriate in a story wl
dominant effect includes a caustic or a horrible quality, as
most stories of the twenties. The effectiveness of such stor
depends to a great extent on the shock that the reader is ma
to feel. Since shock, in life as in art, always involves the makir
of inferences — a delayed reaction, an astonished perception (

[3] Levin, p. 31.
[4] This point is based on my observation of the effect of these stories. It car
be explained by what appears to be a psychological truth, namely, that the intellectualizing of an emotion tends to dissipate (when it does not conceal) the
emotion. Stories that are too readily grasped intellectually tend to by-pass the
reader's emotions; by leaving essentials to inference, the stories of the twenties
force the reader to participate emotionally if he is to understand at all.

This does not mean, of course, that when the reader has finally made the
necessary inference the power of the story disappears. As noted elsewhere,
the intellectualizing process contributes to the catharsis. It remains a part of the
story's effect in the same sense that fear and hope are evoked by tragedies like
"Othello" on the tenth reading as on first.

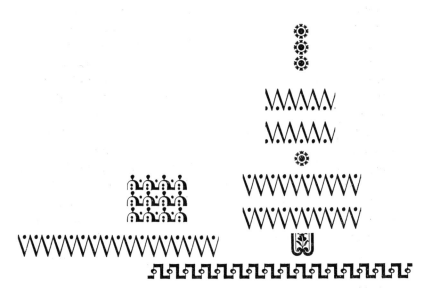

XXIII: CONTEXT AND SEQUEL

The "new look" of the short stories of the twenties is the result of changes in at least three different variables of artistic composition — subject matter, formal principles, and techniques. Problems concerning a practical morality in a faulty but perfectible society are replaced by problems concerning an intuitive morality in an emotionally distintegrated society. Rational people governed by reasoned principles of conduct are replaced by people strongly influenced by compulsive motivations that they scarcely understand. An "affirmative" attitude, reflected in the writers' selection of problems capable of solution (even if not always actually solved in time), is replaced by an attitude that leads writers to choose problems that resist solution. Romantic or idealistic forms (reflecting, of course, the early affirmative attitude) give way to forms of horror, pathos, and caustic

367

comedy. The magnitude of action is reduced, and forms such as the revealing episode and the nearly static revelation are developed — forms designed to evoke the new effects in delicately balanced combinations. In the treatment of these patterns more economical methods of dramatization are worked out — methods distinctive for their much enlarged dependence on inference concerning the most crucial matters in the story.

It is beyond the scope of this study to decide exactly why these changes took place. The knowing reader may recognize in them the consequences of many important intellectual, moral, and aesthetic influences upon the writers and the age. Insofar as the stories display a negative attitude, refusing to affirm the earlier morality, they suggest the temper of moral revolt that was strong in the intellectual life of the time, the temper of Mencken, the expatriates, the rebels against Victorian morality — which Frederick J. Hoffman called the "attitude of refusal." Insofar as they stress intuitive morality they remind us of another quality of the twenties noted by Hoffman — "the emphasis, the *insistence*, upon the value of personal vision" — even though we recognize similar values in major earlier novelists such as Conrad, Forster, and James in his novels (although the outcome of a Jamesian character's intuited morality is an affirmation of the kind of social morality revealed in the short stories of the early period). The intuitive morality is, furthermore, intimately related to the "pessimism" that West regards as the "major American tradition," as opposed to the equally American but deceptively optimistic tradition. Insofar as intuitive morality stresses inner conscience and individual determinism, it may even be compared to the oldest of all American traditions — that of Puritanism, which the writers of the twenties believed that they opposed. It also is closely related, in the particular forms displayed in our stories of the twenties, to anti-Puritan attitudes that have become increasingly popular in mid-twentieth century: the attitudes of existentialism.

Apart from such influences as these, the influence of the Freudian movement is perhaps most obvious.[1] Whether this

---

[1] It would be proper to describe this as the influence of the psychiatric and philosophical movement in which Freud was the chief figure and which has come to be identified with Freud. Freud's influence on writers has been studied

reached these writers directly or indirectly, it is manifest in the strikingly changed conception of character and society — in the problems of the emotionally disintegrated society, of internal ambivalence, and of compulsive and other kinds of unconscious or semiconscious behavior. To be sure, this is not allowed to distort the artistic purposes of these stories, which are neither expositions nor arguments in behalf of Freudian theory. Only the most elementary principles of Freudianism are exhibited; they are used only to furnish problems, and no clinical dissection of these problems is attempted. One story in the canon, Anderson's "Seeds," involves a psychoanalyst; and he is attacked for treating ailments that the narrator regards as incurable, and is himself overwhelmed by such difficulties.[2] Although several *Winesburg* stories treat abnormal phenomena familiar to anyone with a slight knowledge of modern psychology, and though several stories by Miss Porter display a distinctive modern interest in masculine and feminine kinds of rationalizations and inhibitions, only Anderson's "A Chicago Hamlet" probes more specifically Freudian problems such as the Oedipus complex — and there is no indication that Anderson needed Freud to supplement the inspiration received from Shakespeare.[3]

Aesthetically, too, one may recognize parellels between the developments in the short story and in other arts. Much that has

at length by Hoffman in *Freudianism and the Literary Mind*, who devotes a chapter to Freud and Sherwood Anderson, but does not treat the other writers in the canon. According to Hoffman: "Since the turn of the century at least, literary men have concerned themselves with the problem of 'the irrational.' So far as the philosophers of the nineteenth century have directed the interest in this problem . . . four men have been responsible — Schopenhauer, Nietzsche, Bergson, and Freud." (Pp. 1–2).

[2] The narrator says: "The illness you pretend to cure is the universal illness . . . . Fool — do you expect love to be understood?" The analyst says: "I am an amateur venturing timidly into lives . . . . I am weary and want to be made clean, I am covered by creeping crawling things."

[3] Hoffman insists that Anderson's psychological insights were developed independently of Freud: "Undoubtedly *Winesburg is* a contribution to psychoanalysis; it is more doubtful, however, that psychoanalysis has contributed anything to it." (Hoffman, p. 241). He criticizes those critics "who confuse a parallel interest with a direct interchange of disciplines" and argues that "We may therefore say that Anderson developed his themes quite independently of Freudian influence, but with such a startling likeness of approach that critics fell into the most excusable error of their times; it *seemed* an absolute certainty that Anderson should have been influenced by Freud." (P. 244).

been discussed in this study resembles tendencies seen in the novel — formal, technical, material — that were manifest — in a writer such as Conrad, for example — before the twenties. The technical developments have much in common with technical developments in modern poetry, which in the work of Yeats, Eliot, Pound, and their followers show analogues to the use of dramatic inference in the short story. It is more difficult to relate developments in the short story with those in other arts such as music and painting, where the formal and technical problems are utterly different. The developments in these arts were baffling to many because of the violence of their attack upon convention: it was thought that they deliberately sought obscurity, and were even trying, in a sense, to "destroy art." The short stories of the period never approached such obscurity (if indeed any comparison is possible), and to the modern reader they present no problems of comprehension. True, to readers accustomed only to the earlier kinds of stories, they too may well have seemed baffling at first because of what they left to inference. On the whole, however, one is chiefly impressed today with the unbroken development of the short story. We have seen how sharp the difference was between the stories of the twenties and those of the early period; yet, aesthetically if not materially, the latter stories were essentially an extension of developments already under way — developments antic- ipated abroad by Chekhov and Joyce and, in England, in a different way, by James. One feels that there was no sharp or radical break as in other arts, partly perhaps because the short story as a genre is younger than the other arts.

Obviously the changes noted in this study cannot be related to any one unifying motive, one ultimate source. Nevertheless, there is, as has been suggested, consistency in the more impor- tant developments. This can be graphically demonstrated by a brief re-examination of Hemingway's "Hills Like White Ele- phants," which exemplifies the most characteristic tendencies of the twenties. A hypothetical consideration of what the typi- cal earlier writer, with his typical preoccupations and artistic habits, might have done with the same materials illuminates the way in which all the various noted tendencies support each other.

In "Hills Like White Elephants" the specific problem — abortion — is an issue of a sort that is not dealt with in the early period. One can infer how it would have been regarded by considering other earlier stories that involve less drastic violations of social mores. Crane's "Maggie," for example, deals with prostitution, and several stories by Mrs. Wharton, Mrs. Gerould, and James deal with extramarital love. It is probable, from all that has been said about stories of the early period, that an unwanted pregnancy would be regarded as a "social problem," and the most significant consequence pointed to by it would almost certainly have been either social disgrace or fear of disgrace, to illustrate either the practical consequences of ignoring society's taboos or (possibly) the desirability of a more liberal attitude in society toward such mistakes (just as Mrs. Wharton's "Autres Temps" exposes the injustice of self-perpetuating ostracism). The early writer, if he were typical, would have used this material to affirm early values; he would perhaps have constructed some sort of romance or romantic tragedy, in which the heroine would discover the error she has made, as in Mrs. Gerould's "Wesendonck," or would display in the face of social rejection an admirable attitude of unselfish acceptance like that of the heroes of Garland's "A Day's Pleasure" or Mrs. Freeman's "Kitchen Colonel."

For Hemingway, however, the primary interest is masochism in his heroine, who accepts her lover's demand that she have an abortion. He wants neither to affirm the values of prudence or chastity nor to criticize the malfunctioning of society. He conceives it as a story of horror and pathos. This represents a striking departure from the early period, although many early characters are, like Hemingway's heroine, dependent and weak; a psychiatrically minded reader might find instances of masochism among them — Garland's lonely farm wife, who is so deeply grateful for a minor act of generosity (in "A Day's Pleasure"), Mrs. Freeman's ineffectual, henpecked husband, who wins a homely glory by sacrificing his vacation (in "A

Kitchen Colonel"), or many a Jamesian hero bent on renunciation. But whereas these writers scrupulously subordinate the protagonist's paralysis of will to his display of virtues and scrupulously avoid anything that might hint at self-pity or self-martyrdom, Hemingway, with equal scrupulousness, avoids anything which might distract attention from the horror of the heroine's neurotic enslavement. Thus he refuses to prepare the big dramatic scenes that the situation might allow, refuses to write a social tragedy or romance: the moment, for example, of the discovery of the pregnancy, or the moment when the lover first suggests the abortion, or moments in the hospital, or any number of possible incidents dramatizing social disgrace. To have included any of these seemingly dramatic events, all of which are implicit in the situation, would have weakened Hemingway's specific purpose, since all such scenes, by stressing error or social injustice, would have tended to affirm the very social values that Hemingway does not want to affirm. Instead, he takes only a piece of the situation — a non-decisive episode in which, more or less accidentally, the heroine reiterates the choice she has made. By focusing upon her choice, the episode emphasizes her masochism. By stressing the repetition of this choice rather than the original decision, the story dramatizes her failure to believe in this choice, thus emphasizing her suffering, the futility of her desires, and her weakness. The reduced magnitude of action is carefully adapted to the author's special emotional intention; intensity is provided by the dramatic technique of inference. By his omissions the author forces the reader to infer practically everything upon which the horror and pathos depend: the reasons for the heroine's choice, her inner conflict, her frustration and suffering. The reader becomes aware of these things upon reflection: whereas the earlier writer would present the issues of a romance explicitly so as to assure the reader that the virtues involved were indeed admirable, the reader of "Hills Like White Elephants" is shocked to realize that there is more pain and ugliness in the situation than meets the eye. If such a shock is necessary in a horror story, it is especially appropriate in a story such as this which tries to expose, in the lives of ordinary people, a kind of horror normally overlooked. In life the

horror and pathos of people like Hemingway's heroine are ordinarily obscured from public view; if such people are to remain
natural in a story this horror should emerge only in an indirect
manner. The "epiphany" here is in the reader's discovery of the
situation in all its horror, and the story illustrates how the action
and the technique of the epiphany are adapted to evoke such
effects from the lives of small people in a state of emotional paralysis, whether they be Dubliners, Winesburgers, expatriates,
or others.

That the major changes noted in the twenties reflect a new
interest in emotion, as such, and a distrust, or despair, of intellec-
tuality is one of the most curious seeming paradoxes in the movement of the twenties. Ordinarily stress on feeling rather than
intellect would appear to be a romantic attribute. Yet the writers of the twenties were formally less romantic, and they held
in great contempt the sentimentality of their elders. To an extent, perhaps, the paradox is an illusion, the result of an ambiguous interpretation of the word "romance." It can be partially
resolved by theoretical arguments concerning the implicit inter-
dependence of those opposites, romance and horror — or, at any
rate, romance and the mixture of horror and pathos. It could be
argued, for example, that both the purely romantic effect and
the effects of horror and pathos are, in contrast to the effects of
comedy and tragedy, sentimental in that they involve emotion
that has not been fully "tested" morally.[4] Such reasoning suggests that both periods are essentially romantic, the specific
difference being only that the romanticism of the twenties is
more complex and perhaps more serious than that of the early
period.

Whether or not this is so, the paradox accounts for what is
probably the most telling criticism that later critics have directed

[4] The term "sentimentality" is usually applied to excessive or unjustified
emotion. Romance as defined in Part Two depends on the exaltation of the good
(or of virtue) by subordinating evil. In simple romance, appreciation of the
good has not been subjected (as it would be in tragedy) to the test of all the
possible evil that might be measured against such a good; the merit of the good
element we are asked to admire has not, in a sense, been fully demonstrated.
Similarly, though the modified horror and caustic pathetic horror stories of the
twenties depict evil, they usually elevate the ugly character (make him important) by the display of virtues of a kind similarly untested.

against the writers of the twenties: the charge, by now common-place, that such seemingly tough-minded, honest writers as Hemingway and Anderson were as sentimental in their desire to avoid sentimentality as were their more frankly sentimental fore-bears. Hemingway himself was one of the first to make the charge of sentimentality against others in the movement when he attacked Anderson and Fitzgerald, and in recent years the charge has often been directed at Hemingway himself. The sub-stance of such attacks is suggested in the following summary by a modern critic of what was supposedly wrong with the writers of the twenties: "The naïve success dreams of a Fitzgerald; the burly-boy antics of a Hemingway; the sentimental cult of ex-perience which drove so many good writers into European exile . . . or which paralyzed them in infantile attitudes of defiance and rebellion, the old postures for killing the father." [5]

If the reputations of such writers as Anderson, Fitzgerald, and Hemingway are less impressive than they used to be, the weaknesses that have been discovered in Anderson and Hem-ingway are, however, more marked in their novels and later stories than in the stories written in the twenties. When the movement was fresh, they wrote many durable stories that even today seem much less dated than does, for example, much of the proletarian literature of later years. Although one cannot, by any means, define the nature of the modern short story by describing only the stories of our writers of the twenties, their work shows clearly, and with the freshness of discovery and the zest and en-thusiasm of originality, the distinctive and universal qualities that have dominated and given a modern character to the art of most major short-story writers in English in the past forty years.

In the short stories of today one sees, it is true, efforts by many writers to depart from the modern pattern that the writers of the twenties did so much to fix. Yet it is difficult to discern any consistent direction for these departures or any real agreement as to what needs to be done.

For most contemporary short-story writers of established reputation the chief area of experimentation is in subject matter

[5] Aldridge, *In Search of Heresy*, pp. 39–40, summarizing Leslie Fiedler's objections to fiction of the twenties. Aldridge himself is more sympathetic.

rather than in form or technique. The art of Hemingway or Miss Porter or Faulkner is applied to new groups of characters and to new kinds of problems and issues. Even these generally differ from those of the twenties less radically than the subject matter of the twenties differed from that of the early period: in suburbia, in the south, on the streets of New York, in the world of the juvenile delinquent or the disenchanted artist of jazz or the budding adolescent girl or the university professor or the rejected grandmother, the issues are still emotional problems in a disintegrating society, and the prevalent morality, though sometimes more subtle, is still a morality of feeling.

Some writers have experimented with new kinds of formal principles; writers such as Paul Bowles and Flannery O'Connor have reacted against the episode of discovery, the Joycean epiphany, the episode of exposure, by constructing plots of violent action — kinds of plots that were already making their appearance at the end of the twenties in some of the stories of Faulkner and that are closer in effect to the modern episodes than to old-fashioned kinds of plots. For the most part, however, the episode story remains the most usual kind of construction, despite the protests of critics who have grown thoroughly tired of it:

There consequently grew up [in the fifties] a special avant-garde etiquette of subject selection which became as restrictive in its effects on the quarterlies as the clichés and stereotypes imposed by the mass audience on the commercial magazines . . . . [The situations in the short stories] tended to turn on the mechanism of the muffled psycho-religious epiphany — the canonical equivalent of Aristotle's recognition-reversal sequence — and to have to do with adolescent hayloft intrigues, the death of small pet animals on Montana ranches, [etc.] . . . [6]

The distinctive objectivity of treatment displayed by writers of the twenties has been carried to such extremes by such writers as James T. Farrell and John O'Hara that some later writers such as John Cheever, Peter Taylor, J. D. Salinger, and Herbert Gold have reacted with a bold effort to reinstate the narrator's "personality" in their stories. Even these writers, however, have not abandoned the techniques of dramatic inference, which in

[6] Aldridge, *In Search of Heresy*, p. 20.

the past decade have been applied by many to subject matter of increasing psychological complexity. The best writers of recent years have tended not to abandon but to refine and extend the developments noted in this study. The refinement and subtlety of comic effects, complicated with caustic and pathetic elements, is well typified by the work of such differing writers as Gold and J. F. Powers, while the stories of Eudora Welty and Carson McCullers, as well as those of Bowles and Miss O'Connor, carry the Faulknerian patterns of the grotesque to new extremes of bizarre horror and of caustic comedy and pathos.

One dares not predict how much more wealth can be produced by the art of the modern short story as presently constituted, nor how much longer the modern short story will continue to satisfy. One feels even more danger in attempting to forecast what directions the short story of the future may take — whether striking new developments of techniques and forms are in store and, if so, what they will be like. For new forms and new techniques are inventions, and it is the writers, not the critics, who invent them. Just as the writers of the twenties shaped the short story of their time through experimentation and genius, so today only the experimentation and genius of writers can determine what the art of the future short story will be.

APPENDIX A THE CANON OF STORIES

◇◇

In this appendix are listed by author the stories constituting the canon upon which most of the specific contrasts and conclusions in this study are based. Dates given are those when the story first appeared in collected form.

A brief discussion of the principles by which this canon was selected follows the list of stories, p. 382.

Early Period

Ambrose Bierce (1842–1914?)

All of these stories appeared in *In the Midst of Life: Tales of Soldiers and Civilians* (New York: Albert & Charles Boni, 1924), first published in 1891:

"A Horseman in the Sky"

"An Occurrence at Owl Creek
  Bridge"

"Chickamauga"

"A Son of the Gods"

"One of the Missing"

"Killed at Resaca"

"The Affair at Coulter's Notch"

"Parker Adderson, Philosopher"

"An Affair of Outposts"

"The Story of a Conscience"

"One Kind of Officer"

"One Officer, One Man"

"George Thurston"

"The Mocking-Bird"

HENRY JAMES (1843–1916)

The following stories appeared in *The Novels and Tales of Henry James*, New York Edition, Vol. XV: *The Lesson of the Master, The Death of the Lion, The Next Time, and Other Tales* (New York: Charles Scribner's Sons, 1909). Original dates of publication (source: Matthiessen, F. O., and Murdock, Kenneth B., *The Notebooks of Henry James* (New York: Oxford University Press, 1947), pp. xxv–xxvii, are listed in parentheses following the titles:

"The Lesson of the Master" (1892)   "The Figure in the Carpet" (1896)
"The Death of the Lion" (1895)   "The Coxon Fund" (1895)
"The Next Time" (1896)

The following stories appeared in the New York Edition, Vol. XVI:
"The Middle Years" (1895)   "Paste" (1900)
"Greville Fane" (1893)   "Europe" (1900)
"Broken Wings" (1903)   "Miss Gunton of Poughkeepsie"
"The Tree of Knowledge" (1900)   (1900)
"The Abasement of the   "Fordham Castle" (completed
Northmores" (1900)   1904)

The following stories appeared in the New York Edition, Vol. XVIII:
"The Marriages" (1892)   "The Story In It" (1903)
"The Real Thing" (1890)   "Flickerbridge" (1902)
"Brooksmith" (1892)   "Mrs. Medwin" (1902)
"The Beldonald Holbein" (1901)

MARY E. WILKINS FREEMAN (1852–1930)

All of the following stories are from *A New England Nun and Other Stories* (New York: Harper & Bros., 1891):
"A New England Nun"   "A Gentle Ghost"
"A Village Singer"   "A Discovered Pearl"
"A Gala Dress"   "A Village Lear"
"The Twelfth Guest"   "Amanda and Love"
"Sister Liddy"   "Up Primrose Hill"
"Calla-lilies and Hannah"   "A Stolen Christmas"
"A Wayfaring Couple"   "Life-Everlasting"
"A Poetess"   "An Innocent Gamester"
"Christmas Jenny"   "Louisa"
"A Pot of Gold" [1]   "A Church Mouse"
"The Scent of the Roses"   "A Kitchen Colonel"
"A Solitary"   "The Revolt of 'Mother'"

HAMLIN GARLAND (1860–1940)

The following stories appeared in the first edition of *Main-Travelled Roads*, published by the Arena Publishing Company in 1891:
"A Branch Road"   "The Return of a Private"
"Up the Coolly" (originally "Up the   "Under the Lion's Paw"
Coulé")   "Mrs. Ripley's Trip"
"Among the Corn Rows"

[1] "A Pot of Gold," listed here, is not to be confused with the title story in a later volume of stories by Mrs. Freeman.

The above stories were reprinted, and the following were added, in the Border Edition of *Main-Travelled Roads* (New York: Harper & Bros., 1899):

"The Creamery Man"   "God's Ravens"
"A Day's Pleasure"   "A 'Good Fellow's' Wife"
"Uncle Ethan Ripley"

EDITH WHARTON (1862–1937)

The following stories are selected from *The Descent of Man and Other Stories* (New York: Charles Scribner's Sons, 1904):

"The Other Two"   "The Dilettante"
"The Quicksand"   "The Reckoning"

The following are selected from *Xingu and Other Stories* (New York: Charles Scribner's Sons, 1916):

"Coming Home"   "The Choice"
"Autres Temps"   "Bunner Sisters"
"The Long Run"

STEPHEN CRANE (1871–1900)

The following stories are from *Twenty Stories*, selected with an introduction by Carl Van Doren (New York: Alfred A. Knopf, 1940). Dates of original publication are given as listed in Amos W. Williams and Vincent Starrett, *Stephen Crane: A Bibliography* (Glendale, Calif: John Valentine, Publisher, 1948):

"Maggie: A Girl of the Streets"   "The Monster" (1898)
   (1893)   "Death and the Child" (1898)
"An Experiment in Misery" (1894)   "Horses – One Dash!" (1896)
"A Mystery of Heroism" (1895)   "The Five White Mice" (1898)
"The Little Regiment" (1896)   "The Bride Comes to Yellow Sky"
"Three Miraculous Soldiers" (1896)   (1898)
"A Gray Sleeve" (1895)   "The Blue Hotel" (1898)
"The Open Boat" (1897)   "An Episode of War" (1902)

THEODORE DREISER (1878–1945)

The following stories are selected from *Free and Other Stories* (New York: Boni & Liveright, 1918):

"Free"   "Old Rogaum and His Theresa"
"Nigger Jeff"   "The Cruise of the 'Idlewild' "
"The Lost Phoebe"   "Married"
"The Second Choice"

WILLA CATHER (1875–1947)

The following stories appeared in *The Troll Garden* (New York: McClure, Phillips & Co., 1905):

"Flavia and Her Artists"   "A Death in the Desert"
"The Sculptor's Funeral"   "The Marriage of Phaedra"
"The Garden Lodge"   "A Wagner Matinee"
                                      "Paul's Case"

KATHARINE FULLERTON GEROULD (1879–1944)

The following stories appeared in *The Great Tradition and Other Stories* (New York: Charles Scribner's Sons, 1915):

"The Great Tradition"   "The Miracle"
"Pearls"   "Wesendonck"
"The Dominant Strain"   "Leda and the Swan"
"The Bird in the Bush"   "The Weaker Vessel"

The Twenties

SHERWOOD ANDERSON (1876–1941)

The following stories are selected from *Winesburg, Ohio: A Group of Tales of Ohio Small Town Life* (New York: Modern Library, 1919):

"Hands"   "Tandy"
"Paper Pills"   "The Strength of God"
"Mother"   "The Teacher"
"The Philosopher"   "Loneliness"
"Nobody Knows"   "An Awakening"
"Surrender"   "'Queer'"
"A Man of Ideas"   "The Untold Lie"
"Adventure"   "Drink"
"Respectability"   "Death"
"The Thinker"   "Sophistication"

The following stories are selected from *The Triumph of the Egg: A Book of Impressions of American Life in Tales and Poems* (New York: B. W. Huebsch, Inc., 1921):

"I Want to Know Why"   "Unlighted Lamps"
"Seeds"   "The Door of the Trap"
"The Other Woman"   "The New Englander"
"The Egg"   "Out of Nowhere into Nothing"

The following are selected from *Horses and Men: Tales, Long and Short, from our American Life* (New York: B. W. Huebsch, Inc., 1923):

"I'm a Fool"   "The Man Who Became a Woman"
"'Unused'"   "The Man's Story"
"A Chicago Hamlet"   "An Ohio Papan"

The following stories are selected from *Death in the Woods and Other Stories* (New York: Liveright, Inc., 1933):

"Death in the Woods" (also in *O. Henry Prize Stories of 1926*)   "The Return" (also in O'Brien, *Best Stories of 1925*)

F. SCOTT FITZGERALD (1896–1940)

The following stories are selected from *Flappers and Philosophers* (New York: Charles Scribner's Sons, 1920).

Stories indicated with an asterisk are also to be found in *The Stories of F. Scott Fitzgerald: A Selection of 28 Stories with an Introduction by Malcolm Cowley* (New York: Charles Scribner's Sons, 1953):

"The Offshore Pirate"   "Bernice Bobs Her Hair" *
"The Ice Palace" *   "Benediction"
"Head and Shoulders"   "Dalyrimple Goes Wrong"
"The Cut-Glass Bowl"   "The Four Fists"

The following appeared in *Tales of the Jazz Age* (New York: Charles Scribner's Sons, 1922):
"May Day" *
The following are selected from *All the Sad Young Men* (New York: Charles Scribner's Sons, 1926):

"The Rich Boy" *
"Winter Dreams" *
"The Baby Party" *
"Absolution" *
"Rags Martin-Jones and the Pr–nce of W–les"

"The Adjuster"
"Hot and Cold Blood"
" 'The Sensible Thing' " *
"Gretchen's Forty Winks"

The following stories were uncollected until the Cowley edition of 1953:

"Magnetism" (1928)   "The Rough Crossing" (1929)

ERNEST HEMINGWAY (1892–   )

All the following stories appear in *The Short Stories of Ernest Hemingway: The First Forty-Nine Stories and the Play* The Fifth Column (New York: Modern Library, 1938). They were collected originally in the following volumes of Hemingway's stories:
In *Three Stories and Ten Poems* (limited edition; Paris, 1923):
"Up in Michigan"   "My Old Man"
"Out of Season"
In *In Our Time* (New York: Boni & Liveright, 1925):

"Indian Camp"
"The Doctor and the Doctor's Wife"
"The End of Something"
"The Three-Day Blow"
"The Battler"
"A Very Short Story"
"Soldier's Home"

"The Revolutionist"
"Mr. and Mrs. Elliot"
"Cat in the Rain"
"Cross-Country Snow"
"Big Two-Hearted River" (Parts One and Two)

In *Men Without Women* (New York: Charles Scribner's Sons, 1927):

"The Undefeated"
"In Another Country"
"Hills Like White Elephants"
"The Killers"
"Che ti Dice la Patria?"
"Fifty Grand"

"A Simple Enquiry"
"Ten Indians"
"A Canary for One"
"An Alpine Idyll"
"A Pursuit Race"
"Now I Lay Me"

KATHERINE ANNE PORTER (1894–   )

The following stories form the contents of *Flowering Judas and Other Stories* (New York: Modern Library, 1935), except for "Hacienda," which has been omitted. Stories marked with an asterisk also appeared in the original limited edition of *Flowering Judas* in 1930:

"Maria Concepcion" *
"Magic" *
"Rope" *
"He" *
"Theft"

"That Tree"
"The Jilting of Granny Weather-all" *
"Flowering Judas" *
"The Cracked Looking-Glass"

WILLIAM FAULKNER (1897–   )

The following stories form the contents of *These 13: Stories by William Faulkner* (New York: Jonathan Cape & Harrison Smith, 1931). All are also reprinted in *Collected Stories of William Faulkner* (New York: Random House, 1950):

"Victory"   "Hair"
"Ad Astra"   "That Evening Sun"
"All the Dead Pilots"   "Dry September"
"Crevasse"   "Mistral"
"Red Leaves"   "Divorce in Naples"
"A Rose for Emily"   "Carcassonne"
"A Justice"

THE SELECTION OF THE CANON

In addition to the principles enumerated in the Introduction the following considerations were significant. First, the "early period" was extended to 1890, partly because of the "drought" in good short-story production that has been noted in the first two decades of this century, partly because some of the earlier writers were at their best in the 1890's (e.g., Mrs. Freeman and Garland), and partly because significant forerunners (e.g., Crane and, before him, Bierce) wrote their stories in the nineties. It was not deemed necessary or desirable to go back before the nineties since one might expect differences from the stories of the twenties to be even more marked in such a case and hence more likely to obscure what was distinctive about the art of the new movement.

The limitation to stories in the so-called realistic tradition (conceived fairly broadly) and to stories whose emotional tone or effect is moderately serious meant that although comedy was not banished, the lighter farces, as well as all "trick" stories, fantasies, ghost stories, didactic tracts, and prose poems, were excluded. Such stories, it is true, loom large in the over-all history of the short story, including the history of the short story of the twenties. It was deemed best, however, to confine the study to the "main line" of development in the modern short story, which is realistic, even though this meant ignoring such an exotic writer as James Branch Cabell and such entertaining fantasies as Fitzgerald's "The Diamond as Big as the Ritz."

Another early decision concerned the question of whether the stories should be chosen from an unlimited number of writers or a few selected ones. Choice by the former method could hardly avoid being subjective; even if one relied almost entirely on the judgments of critics in selecting stories, it would have been difficult to resist the temptation to pick stories that supported one's prior assumptions as to what was to be found. It was hoped that a large, and within the given limits, non-discriminating sample from each of a number of generally accepted representative writers would provide greater objectivity.

In selecting the writers themselves one had to decide what to do with writers (e.g., Miss Cather, Mrs. Wharton, Mrs. Gerould) whose activity spanned both periods. It was decided that a writer's "period" could be best identified with the time in which he came into maturity as a writer or in which his works won recognition. Since older writers such as Miss Cather and Mrs. Wharton had formed their styles and established themselves much earlier, it was clear that they belonged to the earlier period. The same reasoning permitted us to place such an "older" writer as Sherwood Anderson with those of the twenties by virtue of his late start and his close association with the younger group.

Following these considerations the choice of actual writers for the twenties was determined largely on the basis of enduring reputation among responsible critics. It was not deemed necessary to confine the study to the work of some particular "group" who were closely associated with each other or who have been so associated with each other by critics; it was sufficient that the writers chosen be those who, getting their start in the period, acquired and maintained reputations as the most significant new short-story writers in the period. Such considerations made the choice of the particular five who represent the twenties almost inevitable. Despite the large number of other excellent writers in the period (see p. 5), the only one among them who has maintained a reputation as "major" to a degree comparable to those chosen is Ring Lardner. The exclusion of him and the inclusion of Fitzgerald is, admittedly, a bit arbitrary, although Fitzgerald has received a good bit more publicity lately and is more intimately associated with the twenties in the popular mind.

Anderson was an inevitable choice because he is so generally considered to have propelled forward the new movement at the beginning of the decade and because of his great influence on the younger writers of the period including Hemingway and Faulkner. The latter two were inevitable, also, because of their generally conceded pre-eminence as America's two greatest writers of short stories in this century. Miss Porter's reputation is also great, despite the relative slightness of her output. It is true that, although Anderson, Hemingway, and Fitzgerald were celebrated during the decade itself, Faulkner and Miss Porter did not win much recognition as short-story writers until somewhat later, their first collections not appearing until the decade was over. They are included as the most significant representatives of what was happening at the end of the decade, just as Anderson is more illuminating of the beginning and Fitzgerald and Hemingway of the middle of the period.

The earlier writers were chosen to represent all the major traditions that were dominant at the time and that resembled in the pertinent respects the new tradition of the twenties. It has been customary to divide these earlier writers into such groups as the regionalists, the followers of Henry James, and the writers of surprise-ending stories.[2] West, writing with more perspective in 1952, finds two main strands, the "naturalists," including such writers as Garland, Crane, Dreiser, and (in the twenties) Anderson, and what he reluctantly calls the "symbolists," including such writers as Hawthorne, Melville, James, and later, Hemingway and Miss Porter.[3]

[2] See the distinctions, for example, in O'Brien, *Advance*.

[3] Ray B. West, Jr., *The Short Story in America: 1900–1950* ("Twentieth Century Literature in America"; Chicago: Henry Regnery Co., 1952), pp. 13–14, 60–61.

He sees a third, illegitimate category of what he calls "trick" stories, descending from the ratiocinative tales of Poe and including the stories of such writers as O. Henry, Jack London, and Steele.[4]

The major short-story writer of the early period was James. The selection of the others in this study attempts to represent the major crisscrossing categories which historians have regarded as important, except for those of the "trick" stories and such other deviants from "realism" as have been previously eliminated. Garland is chosen as a leader of what West calls "naturalism" and as the leading exponent of what O'Brien calls "regionalism," and Mrs. Freeman has been added to enlarge the representation of regionalists. Mrs. Wharton, classified by O'Brien as a member of the "school of Henry James," cannot be omitted from any listing of major writers of the time, and Mrs. Gerould has been included as a second member of this school, highly regarded at the end of the period although apparently almost forgotten today. The other writers were included partly on the basis of their enduring reputation as good short-story writers (although this perhaps cannot be said of Dreiser) and partly because they have been regarded as significant forerunners of later developments. Bierce has been called "the connecting link between Poe and the American short story of today,"[5] and Crane's connection with later writers has been even more generally acknowledged. Dreiser's influence on Anderson is well known, and there is a tendency to treat Miss Cather as a writer of the twenties, although the stories used here were written almost twenty years before. These forerunners are especially important as a check on the contrasts noted between the two periods. Actually, of these eight, the writer whose appearance on the scene was the closest to the twenties was Mrs. Gerould, whose first significant volume (*Vain Oblations*) appeared in 1914. She too has been called a writer of the twenties;[6] the fact that she emerges in this study as one of the most conservative of the earlier writers lends a special interest to her inclusion.

If this list is compared with West's list of important writers from the period,[7] it will be seen that the only writers mentioned by West who are omitted from our early canon are O. Henry and Jack London. The omission of O. Henry — regarded by O'Brien as "the most representative short story writer of the period"[8] — can be defended on the grounds that he was primarily a "popular" or "commercial" writer, a master of the trick story, rejected in the twenties. Since the contrasts between O. Henry and the later writers are so very marked and obvious, his inclusion would only

[4] *Ibid.*, pp. 12, 81.

[5] H. E. Bates, *The Modern Short Story: A Critical Survey* (London: Thomas Nelson & Sons, 1941), p. 56.

[6] Robert E. Spiller, Willard Thorp, Thomas H. Johnson, and Henry Seidel Canby (eds.), *Literary History of the United States: Bibliography* (New York: Macmillan Co., 1953), p. 150.

[7] West, p. 10, lists Crane, Garland, James, Wharton, London, and O. Henry for this period. Miss Cather, Mrs. Freeman, and Mrs. Gerould are not included here. Dreiser is placed in the twenties. Bierce is placed earlier than Dreiser, although West admits that "we have . . . little reason for including Ambrose Bierce in the second category."

[8] O'Brien, *Advance*, p. 194.

magnify disproportionately the differences between the two periods. Similar reasoning will explain the omission of Jack London, whose achievement is widely believed to have fallen short of his potentialities and who is lumped by West with O. Henry and regarded as inferior to him.[9]

Two additional restrictions have been set up in selecting the stories from these writers: the stories must have been collected and published in book form, and they must have been written during the period they are meant to represent. The first restriction is useful in winnowing out a writer's second-rate work; the second is intended to eliminate distortions resulting from the external influences upon a writer's habits as he moves into another period. But even after these restrictions have been made, not all the stories of each writer are used. For the twenties, every collection available to me has been examined, and only those stories which do not fall within the prescribed limits or which are obviously inferior work have been eliminated (the latter decision was necessary only for some stories by Anderson and Fitzgerald). The "rules" were relaxed a little in the case of Faulkner and Miss Porter, in that a few stories written after 1929 were included so that their representation might be large enough to be significant. Thus Faulkner's *These 13* dates from 1931, and a few characteristic stories which did not appear in the original 1930 edition of Miss Porter's *Flowering Judas* but did appear in the 1935 edition have been included.

For the early period, a published collection of the writer at his representative best has been used wherever possible, although in a few cases stories have been drawn from several collections. In the case of James, three volumes of the New York Edition which contained the largest number of stories originally published after 1890 were used; stories in those volumes which appeared before 1890 were omitted as were a few — fantasies or ghost stories — which did not meet other specifications.

APPENDIX B   CLASSIFICATION BY FORMS

◇◇◇

The following classification of the stories in the canon by forms should not be taken too seriously. The reasons are obvious. In the first place, it seems to deny the very things that make these stories significant works of art, on the one hand by ignoring the obvious truth that each story is a unique construction with its own individual life and character and on the other hand by ignoring everything but the dominant effect, by ignoring all the emotional shadings, all the ambiguous colorations and overtones of opposite effects that distinguish the great stories in these categories from the second-rate ones. In the second place, such a classification gives a false impression of both ease and finality in the analysis of any story. It suggests that the form of any story can be identified as positively as fingerprints

[9] West, pp. 12, 81.

under a microscope. I grant these difficulties, but I cannot accept the conclusion that formal classifications cannot or should not be attempted. If stories differ from each other, and if analysis of stories is possible, then classification is possible and legitimate, provided its purposes and limitations are clearly understood.

The purpose of this classification is simply to summarize in the most concise manner possible the general *kind* of interpretation I have accepted for each story, so that the reader may have more concrete evidence (and perhaps clarification) for some of the important points made in Chapters XII–XV.

Page numbers refer to the discussion in the text. Symbols in parentheses are those used in the index of stories to indicate how each story has been classified.

I. PAINLESS FORMS

SIMPLE ROMANCE (R) Pages 174–85

Plots of Deserved Good Fortune (pf) (asterisk indicates story lacks character or attitude change)
Freeman, "Amanda and Love," "Calla-lilies and Hannah," * "A Discovered Pearl," "Louisa," * "A Wayfaring Couple"; Garland, "A Branch Road," "A 'Good Fellow's' Wife"; Fitzgerald, "The Four Fists"; Porter, "Maria Concepcion."

Plots of Choice (pc)
Correction: Freeman, "Sister Liddy," "A Solitary," "Up Primrose Hill"; Garland, "God's Ravens"; Wharton, "The Dilettante," "The Quicksand," "The Reckoning"; James, "The Middle Years"; Gerould, "The Miracle," "Wesendonck"; Fitzgerald, "The Adjuster," "The Ice Palace."
Renunciation: Bierce, "A Son of the Gods"; Gerould, "The Bird in the Bush," "The Great Tradition," "Leda and the Swan."
Reiteration: Hemingway, "The Undefeated."

Episodes of Choice (ec)
Freeman, "A Kitchen Colonel," "The Scent of Roses"; Garland, "A Day's Pleasure," "The Return of a Private"; Hemingway, "Cross-Country Snow," "The Revolutionist."

Episodes of Discovery (ed)
Anderson, "The Return," "Sophistication," "The Untold Lie"; Hemingway, "Big Two-Hearted River"; Faulkner, "Carcassonne."

Exposed Situation (s)
Anderson, "Death in the Woods."

ROMANTIC COMEDY (RC) Pages 193–202

Plots of Deserved Good Fortune, with change in character-attitude (pf)
Freeman, "A Gala Dress," "A Stolen Christmas"; Garland, "The Creamery Man"; James, "Broken Wings"; Fitzgerald, "The Offshore Pirate."

Plots of Deserved Good Fortune, without character change (pf)
Freeman, "A Gentle Ghost," "Christmas Jenny," "An Innocent Game-

ster," "A Church Mouse," "The Revolt of 'Mother' "; Garland, "Among
the Corn Rows"; Fitzgerald, "Gretchen's Forty Winks," "Rags Martin-
Jones and the Pr–nce of W–les."

Plots of Choice (pc)

> *Correction*: Freeman, "Life-Everlasting," "A Poetess," "A Village
> Singer"; Fitzgerald, "Hot and Cold Blood"; Anderson, "I'm a
> Fool"; Faulkner, "Divorce in Naples."
>
> *Dilemma*: Freeman, "A New England Nun"; Gerould, "Pearls."
>
> *Reiteration*: Bierce, "George Thurston"; James, "Brooksmith," "Miss
> Gunton of Poughkeepsie"; Faulkner, "Hair," "All the Dead Pilots."

Plots of Discovery (pd)

> Freeman, "A Pot of Gold"; James, "The Abasement of the North-
> mores," "The Tree of Knowledge"; Crane, "A Gray Sleeve"; Cather,
> "Flavia and Her Artists"; Dreiser, "Married"; Fitzgerald, "Head and
> Shoulders."

Episodes of Choice (ec)

> Garland, "Mrs. Ripley's Trip," "Uncle Ethan Ripley"; Crane, "The
> Little Regiment," "A Mystery of Heroism," "Three Miraculous Sol-
> diers"; James, "Fordham Castle," "The Story In It"; Dreiser, "The
> Cruise of the 'Idlewild' "; Hemingway, "The Three-Day Blow," "Ten
> Indians"; Faulkner, "Ad Astra."

Episodes of Discovery (ed)

> Crane, "The Bride Comes to Yellow Sky," "The Five White Mice,"
> "Horses — One Dash!"

OBJECTIVE COMEDY (C) Pages 186–90

Plots of Choice (Comeuppance and Reiterated Absurdity) (pc)

> James, "The Beldonald Holbein," "The Coxon Fund," "Europe,"
> "The Real Thing," "The Lesson of the Master"; Gerould, "The Domi-
> nant Strain," "The Weaker Vessel"; Anderson, "The Egg"; Fitzger-
> ald, "Magnetism."

Plots of Discovery (Comeuppance) (pd)

> James, "The Marriages," "Paste"; Wharton, "The Other Two," "The
> Long Run"; Cather, "The Marriage of Phaedra"; Fitzgerald, "Bernice
> Bobs Her Hair."

Episode of Discovery (Comeuppance) (ed)

> Hemingway, "Cat in the Rain."

Exposed Situation (s)

> James, "Greville Fane."

SYMPATHETIC COMEDY (SC) Pages 190–93

Plots of Good Fortune (pf)

> James, "Mrs. Medwin"; Anderson, "A Man of Ideas."

Plot of Lost Fortune (pf)

> James, "The Death of the Lion."

Plots of Choice (pc)

> James, "The Figure in the Carpet," "The Next Time," "Flicker-
> bridge."

Plots of Discovery (pd)

> Wharton, "Autres Temps"; Hemingway, "Che ti Dice la Patria?"

CAUSTIC COMEDY (XC) Pages 212–15

Plots of Undeserved Good Fortune (pf)
  Fitzgerald, "Dalyrimple Goes Wrong"; Hemingway, "Fifty Grand";
  Faulkner, "A Justice."
Plots of Choice (pc)
  Dilemma: Anderson, "Out of Nowhere Into Nothing"; Fitzgerald,
    "Benediction."
  Reiteration: Fitzgerald, "The Rich Boy"; Porter, "That Tree."
Episodes of Choice (ec)
  Anderson, "The Man Who Became a Woman," "Nobody Knows";
  Fitzgerald, "The Baby Party," "The Rough Crossing"; Porter, "Rope."
Episode of Exposure (ee)
  Hemingway, "A Canary for One."

CAUSTIC ROMANCE (XR) Page 211.

Plots of Choice (Reiteration) (pc)
  Faulkner, "Red Leaves," "Victory."
Episodes of Choice (Refused Discovery) (ec)
  Anderson, "An Awakening," "I Want to Know Why"; Hemingway,
  "The End of Something."

SIMPLE CAUSTIC (X) Pages 205–10.

Plot of Choice (Reiteration) (pc)
  Hemingway, "Mr. and Mrs. Elliot."
Episodes of Choice (ec)
  Hemingway, "The Doctor and the Doctor's Wife," "Out of Season,"
  "A Simple Enquiry," "A Very Short Story."

II. PAINFUL FORMS

TRAGEDY (T) Pages 223–24.

Plots of Misfortune, with Discovery (pf)
  Bierce, "One Kind of Officer"; Wharton, "The Choice."

ROMANTIC PATHOS (RP) Pages 225–29.

Plots of Misfortune (pf) (asterisk indicates story contains discovery)
  Freeman, "A Village Lear"; Garland, "Under the Lion's Paw" *;
  Wharton, "Bunner Sisters" *; Dreiser, "The Lost Phoebe"; Crane,
  "Maggie: A Girl of the Streets"; Anderson, "Unused."
Episodes of Discovery (ed)
  Garland, "Up the Coolly"; Cather, "A Death in the Desert," "A Wag-
  ner Matinee"; Crane, "An Experiment in Misery."
Exposed Situation (s)
  Anderson, "Paper Pills."

CAUSTIC PATHOS (XP) Pages 229–37.

Plot of Choice (pc)
  Anderson, "Death."
Plots of Discovery (pd)
  Crane, "Death and the Child"; Dreiser, "Free"; Anderson, "Unlighted
  Lamps."

Episodes of Suffering (es)
Anderson, "Adventure," "Drink," "The Door of the Trap," "Mother,"
"The New Englander," "The Other Woman," "The Philosopher,"
"'Queer,'" "The Strength of God," "The Teacher"; Hemingway,
"Soldier's Home," "Up in Michigan"; Porter, "He," "The Cracked
Looking-Glass."

Episodes of Exposure (ee)
Anderson, "Loneliness," "Seeds," "Tandy," "Respectability."

Exposed Situation (s)
Anderson, "Hands."

SIMPLE HORROR (H) Pages 239–44.

Moral Horror (Hm)
  Plot of Misfortune (pf)
  Bierce, "One of the Missing."

  Plots of Choice (pc)
  Bierce, "The Affair at Coulter's Notch," "A Horseman in the Sky,"
  "Killed at Resaca," "One Officer, One Man," "Parker Adderson";
  Wharton, "Coming Home."

  Episodes of Choice (ec)
  Porter, "Magic"; Faulkner, "Dry September."

  Exposed Situation (s)
  Faulkner, "A Rose for Emily."

Sympathetic Horror (Hs)
  Plot of Misfortune (pf)
  Bierce, "The Mocking-Bird."

  Plot of Discovery (pd)
  Bierce, "Chickamauga."

  Exposed Situation (s)
  Bierce, "An Occurrence at Owl Creek Bridge."

HORROR MODIFIED (M) Pages 244–58.

Moral Horror (Mm)
  Plot of Misfortune (pf)
  Cather, "Paul's Case."

  Plots of Choice (pc)
  Bierce, "An Affair of Outposts," "The Story of a Conscience";
  Crane, "The Monster"; Dreiser, "The Second Choice"; Ander-
  son, "Surrender"; Faulkner, "That Evening Sun."

  Episodes of Choice (ec)
  Cather, "The Garden Lodge"; Dreiser, "Old Rogaum and His
  Theresa"; Anderson, "The Thinker"; Hemingway, "Hills Like
  White Elephants," "A Pursuit Race."

  Episodes of Exposure (ee)
  Cather, "The Sculptor's Funeral"; Hemingway, "The Killers";
  Faulkner, "Mistral."

Sympathetic Horror (Ms)
  Plots of Discovery (Personal) (pd)
  Crane, "The Blue Hotel"; Fitzgerald, "The 'Sensible Thing,'"
  "Winter Dreams"; Hemingway, "My Old Man."

Episodes of Discovery (Personal) (ed)
> Crane, "An Episode of War"; Hemingway, "Now I Lay Me"; Porter, "Flowering Judas," "The Jilting of Granny Weatherall," "Theft."

Plots of Discovery (Generalized) (pd)
> Dreiser, "Nigger Jeff."

Episodes of Discovery (Generalized) (ed)
> Crane, "The Open Boat"; Fitzgerald, "Absolution"; Hemingway, "An Alpine Idyll," "The Battler," "In Another Country," "Indian Camp"; Faulkner, "Crevasse."

UNCLASSIFIED STORIES
> Freeman, "The Twelfth Guest"; Anderson, "The Man's Story," "A Chicago Hamlet," "An Ohio Pagan"; Fitzgerald, "The Cut-Glass Bowl," "May Day."

DISTRIBUTION OF PATTERNS OF ACTION

The figures below are based on the foregoing classification. Like the classification itself, these figures must not be taken too seriously. See Chapter XVI.

	Early Period	*Twenties*
PLOTS		
Misfortune with Discovery	5	0
Misfortune without Discovery	6	1
Good Fortune with Discovery	9	3
Good Fortune without Discovery	9	6
Choice (Reversed)*	28	8
Choice (Reiterated)	14	12
Discovery	17	7
Total Plots	88	37
EPISODES		
Choice	14	22
Discovery	9	16
Suffering	0	14
Exposure	1	7
Exposed Situation	2	4
Total Episodes	26	63

* Includes renunciation, dilemma, and all correction and attitude-change plots.

APPENDIX C   THE IDENTITY OF
THE PROTAGONIST

◇◇

The "protagonist" is defined in this study as the character (or figure) whose action or activity provides the unifying principle of the story — the person whom the story is "about," the center of interest. In most cases the identity of the protagonist is perfectly obvious. A few exceptions in the foregoing classification should, however, be noted.

For some of the stories in the canon it is assumed that the protagonist is not a single individual but a pair of characters or a group. Since it is difficult to conceive a unified story having more than one protagonist, this pair or this group should be regarded itself as a single "figure," existing through more than one individual. The attributes of a "multiple protagonist" must be these: the characters taken together must, in some sense, all undergo the same experience, or the variety of things that happen to them must all partake of some common action or kind of activity. The action of the story is this common experience or action. Similarly, the action must emanate from the "character" of the group as a whole rather than of its members as diverse individuals. If they do differ as individuals, this diversity itself, of course, may be a part of their character as a group.

Stories in the foregoing classification which are here regarded as having multiple protagonists are: James, "The Coxon Fund," "Broken Wings," "The Real Thing"; Freeman, "A Gala Dress," "The Scent of Roses"; Garland, "Uncle Ethan Ripley"; Crane, "The Little Regiment," "The Blue Hotel"; Cather, "The Sculptor's Funeral"; Anderson, "Unlighted Lamps"; Fitzgerald, "Head and Shoulders," "May Day," "The Rough Crossing."

APPENDIX D   THE USE OF THE FIRST PERSON

◇◇

The principles by which a writer chooses between a first-person and a restricted third-person point of view depend ultimately upon the very particular effect which the writer wants the story to produce. See page 288, note 9. Some of the kinds of principles which may determine such a choice may be suggested by a contrast between two stories by Hemingway, "Cross-Country Snow" and "An Alpine Idyll."

Both stories deal with Nick Adams; in both cases he is skiing in Europe. But "Cross-Country Snow" is in the third person, "An Alpine Idyll" in the first person. (It may be noticed, incidentally, that all the stories in the canon dealing with Nick as a boy are in the third person, probably for the reasons suggested on page 287, whereas a majority, but not all, of those dealing with Nick as an adult are in the first person.)

Both stories deal with the end of a skiing vacation for Nick; in each he is with a friend; in each he comes to an inn and orders a drink. The mood of the two stories differs. In "Cross-Country Snow," which begins with a fairly detailed account of skiing, such as to suggest his pleasure, he feels a certain melancholy because this is his last chance to ski here with his friend George. In the inn his casual conversation with George is suggested: they tell each other how much they enjoy skiing. It is revealed that the reason they must part is that Nick's wife is pregnant and Nick must return to the States. George suggests to Nick that it must be "hell" to do this, but Nick denies it. Whatever reversal the story contains is probably in this answer. George tries to get Nick to promise that they will ski together again sometime, but although he agrees that they ought to ski together again, he says "There isn't any good in promising." The story has been classified in this study as a simple romance, a nearly static episode designed to suggest the somewhat sentimental kind of pleasure tinged with sadness which Nick feels on this trip. The episode is actually a little more than this; as it develops it becomes apparent, especially in the "reversal" cited above, that Nick is somewhat more mature, somewhat more able to "take it," than is his friend. We see that his attitude is calm. This calm is crucial in enhancing the pleasurable emotion which the story produces.

The advantage of the third person can be suggested by considering what would happen if the story were told in the first person. (1) It would weaken the effect of the description of Nick's pleasure in skiing. In the following passage, the word *I* has been substituted wherever Hemingway uses *he*. "I held to my left and at the end, as I rushed toward the fence, keeping my knees locked tight together and turning my body like tightening a screw brought my skis sharply around to the right in a smother of snow and slowed into a loss of speed parallel to the hillside and the wire fence." A component in the intended effect is a certain admiration for Nick's skill as a skier; the first person turns this into bragging, which would be detrimental to our admiration. Another element is the intensity of Nick's pleasure in the activity. Yet it is an inarticulate pleasure; to express this intensity (which is what the transposed passage above would involve) would be to violate his more essential calm. (2) It would make the "reversal" less logical: much of the effect of the revelation of Nick's relative maturity depends upon the withholding of the evidence for this until near the end of the story. The evidence is in Nick's thoughts. For him to withhold these to show his maturity (rather than to emphasize his criticism of another character, as he does in the quite different story, "A Canary for One") would also suggest a kind of braggadocio that would be quite out of keeping with his character. (3) The dramatic scene with George, which most shows Nick's maturity, would, if Nick told it himself, also suggest pride, which would be out of keeping with his depicted state of mind.

Nick in this story is at peace. At the moment, he is not worried about himself. He is happy because he is preoccupied with externals, with completely unselfconscious absorption in the world outside him. The first person would lead the reader to a different conclusion, which would be damaging to the effect.

In "An Alpine Idyll," however, Nick's feeling after skiing is quite different. He feels that he has been skiing too long; his description of the heat of the sun and of his tired feeling has an almost ominous quality in its imagery, and indeed he describes spring in the high mountains as "unnatural." As he approaches the inn he observes a burial. Then in the inn he hears about the peasant whose wife is being buried. She had died in midwinter, but because of the snow the husband was unable to bring her for burial. Her corpse had frozen in the shed. Noticing a deformity of the woman's mouth, the priest had questioned the peasant and discovered that the latter had fallen into the habit, whenever he went out into the woodshed, of hanging his lantern in the mouth of the propped-up corpse. Although the priest questions and reproaches the peasant, he is unable to get any further explanation: Olz cannot explain why he did it, although he loved her "fine." Nick's reaction to this tale is not specified beyond a brief indication of curiosity, "Do you think it's true?" to which his friend replies, "Sure it's true . . . . These peasants are beasts." One feels that Nick does not share the latter judgment.

The story has been described elsewhere in this study as a generalized discovery by a neutral protagonist. We infer that the horrible comedy of the peasant's perversity, coupled with Nick's own perception of the unnaturalness of skiing too long, has suggested to him some sense of his own vulnerability to madness, given the right conditions. The story is calculated to evoke Nick's feeling in this discovery, just as "Cross-Country Snow" was calculated to evoke Nick's feeling, but in this case the feeling is very different: a queasy feeling bordering on terror. Such a feeling does not require us to admire Nick in any way, nor does it imply any special calm or maturity or self-detachment in him. Hence objections to the first person do not apply.

The advantage of the first person lies in the dramatic immediacy it provides. This comes from Nick's "fallibility" as a narrator; he is unable to be explicit about the subtle emotion he is describing; we have to infer it from the objective details which he presents. This enhances the vividness of the depiction, as is explained more fully in Chapter XVIII. Yet to translate this story into the third person would probably be less damaging than to change the point of view of "Cross-Country Snow." The alteration in quality would probably be most marked in a passage such as the following, in which the third person has been substituted for Hemingway's *we* and *I*: "They had been skiing in the Silvretta for a month, and it was good to be down in the valley. In the Silvretta the skiing had been all right, but it was spring skiing, the snow was good only in the early morning and again in the evening. The rest of the time it was spoiled by the sun. They were both tired of the sun . . . . They had stayed too long. Nick could taste the snow water they had been drinking melted off the tin roof of the hut. The taste was a part of the way he felt about skiing. He was glad there were other things besides skiing, and he was glad to be down . . ." Although it is a very delicate difference, the third person seems in this passage to give it a suggestion of an author's rearrangement of a character's thoughts, a non-dramatic quality which the first-person treatment here seems to lack.

APPENDIX E NARRATIVE AND SCENES IN "THE MIDDLE YEARS" AND "CALLA-LILIES AND HANNAH"

◇◇

The following is a sketch of the division into dramatic scenes and narrative portions of James's "The Middle Years" (see p. 291). (The edition used is that of the anthology by Robert Gorham Davis, *Ten Modern Masters; An Anthology of the Short Story*, 2d ed. [New York: Harcourt, Brace & Co., 1959].) The major scenes are 4–5 (mostly in narrative), 8, 10, and 13–15.

1. Narrator's description (Dencombe alone): 5 paragraphs, 145 lines, includes about 30 lines of flashback recapitulation; the whole narration is centered upon Dencombe sitting on a bench, and relates his thoughts to the activity of watching Doctor Hugh and his group approach.

2. Scene: Doctor Hugh and companions, 14 speeches, the last 5 interrupted by about 15 lines of narrative comment in 2 paragraphs.

3. Narrative: transition (preparing scene between Dencombe and Hugh), 1½ paragraphs, 25 lines.

4. Scene: Hugh and Dencombe, 3 speeches, with 5 lines of narrative.

5. Narrative: summary of the continuing scene between Dencombe and Hugh, 3 paragraphs, 114 lines, with 3 speeches recorded.

6. Narrative: summary of Dencombe's fainting, terminating previous scene (told retrospectively) and transition to next scene, 1 paragraph, 20 lines.

7. Transitional scene: Hugh and Dencombe, 1 speech of 8 lines in narrative paragraph of 14 lines, followed by transitional narrative paragraph (Dencombe thinking alone at night, 17 lines).

8. Scene: Dencombe and Hugh, 38 speeches, interrupted by two narrative paragraphs totaling 16 lines.

9. Transitional narrative: summarizing events leading to forthcoming scene with Miss Vernham, 2 paragraphs, 82 lines.

10. Scene: Dencombe and Miss Vernham, 9 speeches.

11. Narrative: summary of Dencombe's reaction to scene, his relapse, Hugh's departure and return, 3 paragraphs, 68 lines, followed by three short dramatic speeches.

12. Narrative: summary of Dencombe's decline, preparing for scene between Dencombe and Hugh, 3 paragraphs, 20 lines, with 2 dramatic speeches included.

13. Scene: Hugh and Dencombe, 7 speeches.

14. Narrative: transition, 1 paragraph, 10 lines. This passage covers "many days," but joins two scenes which are otherwise almost intimately related as one.

15. Scene: Dencombe and Hugh, 12 speeches.

The following is a sketch of the division of Mrs. Freeman's "Calla-lilies and Hannah" into dramatic scenes and narrative portions. The four major scenes are 1, 3, 5–7, and 15.

1. Dramatic scene: Martha and Mrs. Newhall, 29 speeches, approximately 16 lines of interposed narrator's explanations and "stage directions."

2. Narrator's transition: 2 paragraphs, 9 lines.

3. Dramatic scene: Hannah and Martha, 26 speeches, 29 lines of narrator's description. Twelve lines of description compose a single paragraph which interrupts the scene after the second speech and may be regarded as a part of transition 2, above.

4. Narrator's transition: 2 paragraphs, 9 lines.

5. Dramatic scene: Hannah, Mrs. Ward, 5 speeches.

6. Transition: 2 paragraphs, 12 lines (includes 1 short incorporated dramatic speech of 1 line).

7. Dramatic scene: Hannah, Mrs. Ward, the Mellens, 25 speeches (2 speeches are 10 lines long), 10 lines of narrator's description.

8. Narrator's transition (summation of Hannah's situation and feelings): 2 paragraphs, 12 lines.

9. Scene: Martha and Hannah, 3 speeches, 4 narrator's lines.

10. Narrator's description (Hannah at church): 8 paragraphs, 49 lines. This section incorporates 2 short anonymous dramatic speeches.

11. Scene: Martha and Hannah, 6 speeches, 2 explanatory lines.

12. Narrator's transition (covers a month): 4 paragraphs, 19 lines, 2 incorporated speeches.

13. Rapid sequence of short scenes: Hannah, employers, jeweler, 16 speeches, 5 paragraphs of narrative, 36 lines of narrative.

14. Narrator's transition (events leading to her theft of bread): 10 paragraphs, 64 lines. This description contains a two-speech scene between second and third paragraphs, and a four-speech scene at the end. It also incorporates 11 lines of Hannah's quoted thoughts.

15. Dramatic scene: Hannah and George, 50 speeches, totaling 117 lines. The scene contains in addition 6 explanatory narrator's paragraphs, totaling 29 lines. There is a short break in the chronology near the end of the scene when George goes out for a few minutes; this is covered by a three-line paragraph.

16. Narrator's conclusion: 5 paragraphs, 37 lines (includes 2 dramatic speeches totaling 12 lines). This is followed by a three-line speech by Hannah which concludes the story.

This story varies from the typical in the early period chiefly in the number of short transitional scenes; "The Middle Years" varies from the typical in the more than usual dependence upon narrative to sum up scenes.

APPENDIX F A DRAMATIC SCENE FROM "UNDER THE LION'S PAW"

◇◇

The following scene from Garland's "Under the Lion's Paw" is typical of the fullness and elaborateness of early dramatic scenes. (See p. 293.)

"Mother," [Council] shouted, as he neared the fragrant and warmly lighted kitchen, "here are some wayfarers an' folks who need sumpthin' t' eat an' a place t' snooze." He ended by pushing them all in.

Mrs. Council, a large, jolly, rather coarse-looking woman, took the children in her arms. "Come right in, you little rabbits. 'Most asleep, hey? Now here's a drink o' milk f'r each o' ye. I'll have s'm tea in a minute. Take off y'r things and set up t' the fire."

While she set the children to drinking milk, Council got out his lantern and went out to the barn to help the stranger about his team, where his loud, hearty voice could be heard as it came and went between the hay-mow and the stalls.

The woman came to light as a small, timid, and discouraged-looking woman, but still pretty, in a thin and sorrowful way.

"Land sakes! An' you've traveled all the way from Clear Lake t'-day in this mud! Waal! waal! No wonder you're all tired out. Don't wait f'r the men, Mis' ——" She hesitated, waiting for the name.

"Haskins."

"Mis' Haskins, set right up to the table an' take a good swig o' tea whilst I make y' s'm toast. It's green tea, an' it's good. I tell Council as I git older I don't seem to enjoy Young Hyson n'r Gunpowder. I want the reel green tea, jest as it comes off'n the vines. Seems t'have more heart in it, some way. Don't s'pose it has. Council says it's all in m' eye." Going on in this easy way, she soon had the children filled with bread and milk and the woman thoroughly at home, eating some toast and sweet-melon pickles, and sipping the tea.

"See the little rats!" she laughed at the children. "They're full as they can stick now, and they want to go to bed. Now, don't git up, Mis' Haskins; set right where you are an' let me look after 'em. I know all about young ones, though I'm all alone now. Jane went an' married last fall. But, as I tell Council, it's lucky we keep our health, Set right there, Mis' Haskins; I won't have you stir a finger."

It was an unmeasured pleasure to sit there in the warm homely kitchen, the jovial chatter of the housewife driving out and holding at bay the growl of the impotent, cheated wind.

The little woman's eyes filled with tears which fell down upon the sleeping baby in her arms. The world was not so desolate and cold and hopeless, after all.

"Now I hope Council won't stop out there and talk politics all night. He's the greatest man to talk politics an' read the *Tribune* — How old is it?"

She broke off and peered down at the face of the babe.

"Two months 'n' five days," said the mother, with a mother's exactness.

"Ye don't say! I want 'o know! The dear little pudzy-wudzy!" she went on, stirring it up in the neighborhood of the ribs with her fat fore-finger. "Pooty tough on 'oo to go galivant'n 'cross lots this way——"

"Yes, that's so; a man can't lift a mountain," said Council, entering the door. "Mother, this is Mr. Haskins, from Kansas. He's been eat up 'n' drove out by grasshoppers."

"Glad t' see yeh! —— Pa, empty that washbasin 'n' give him a chance t' wash."

Haskins was a tall man, with a thin, gloomy face . . . . You would have felt that he had suffered much by the line of his mouth showing under his thin, yellow mustache.

"Hain't Ike got home yet, Sairy?"

"Haint seen 'im."

"W-a-a-l, set right up, Mr. Haskins; wade right into what we've got; 'tain't much, but we manage to live on it — she gits fat on it," laughed Council, pointing his thumb at his wife.

After supper, while the women put the children to bed, Haskins and Council talked on . . . by and by the story of Haskins' struggles and defeat came out. The story was a terrible one, but he told it quietly, seated with his elbows on his knees, gazing most of the time at the hearth.

"I didn't like the looks of the country, anyhow," Haskins said, partly rising and glancing at his wife. "I was ust t' northern Ingyannie, where we have lots o' timber 'n' lots o' rain, 'n' I didn't like the looks o' that dry prairie. What galled me the worst was goin' s' far away acrosst so much fine land layin' all through here vacant."

"And the 'hoppers eat ye four years, hand runnin', did they?"

"Eat! They wiped us out. They chawed everything that was green. They jest set around waitin' f'r us t' die t' eat us, too. My God! I ust t'dream of 'em sittin' 'round on the bed post, six feet long, workin' their jaws. They eet the forkhandles. They got worse 'n' worse till they just rolled on one another, piled up like snow in winter. Well, it ain't no use. If I was t' talk all winter I couldn't tell nawthin'. But all the while I couldn't help thinkin' of all that land back here that nobuddy was usin' that I ought 'o had 'stead o' bein' out there in that cussed country."

"Waal, why didn't ye stop an' settle here?" asked Ike, who had come in and was eating his supper.

"Fer the simple reason that you fellers wantid ten 'r fifteen dollars an acre for the bare land, and I hadn't no money fer that kind o' thing."

"Yes, I do my own work," Mrs. Council was heard to say in the pause which followed. "I'm a-gettin' purty heavy t' be on m' laigs all day, but we can't afford t' hire, so I keep rackin' around somehow, like a foundered horse. S' lame — I tell Council he can't tell how lame I am, f'r I'm just as lame in one laig as t' other." And the good soul laughed at the joke on herself as she took a handful of flour and dusted the biscuit-board to keep the dough from sticking.

"Well, I hain't *never* been very strong," said Mrs. Haskins. "Our folks was Canadians an' small-boned, and then since my last child I hain't got up again fairly. I don't like t' complain. Tim has about all he can bear now — but they was days this week when I jes wanted to lay right down an' die."

"Waal, now, I'll tell ye," said Council, from his side of the stove, silencing everybody with his good-natured roar, "I'd go down and *see* Butler, *anyway*, if I was you. I guess he'd let you have his place purty cheap; the farm's all run down. He's ben anxious t' let t' somebuddy next year. It 'ud be a good chance fer you. Anyhow, you go to bed and sleep like a babe. I've got some plowin' t' do, anyhow, an' we'll see if somethin' can't be done about your case. Ike, you go out an' see if the horses is all right, an' I'll show the folks t' bed."

When the tired husband and wife were lying under the generous quilts of the spare bed, Haskins listened a moment to the wind in the eaves, and then said, with a slow and solemn tone, "There are people in this world who are good enough t' be angels, an' only haff t' die to *be* angels."

Since the primary action of the story concerns the exploitation of Haskins by Jim Butler, the only advance in the action in this scene comes in his last speech when Council first suggests that Haskins see Butler. Otherwise, and primarily, the scene is entirely expository in function, concerned with revealing, through dramatic flashback as well as dramatic manifestation, the initial situation from which the action is to develop. The essential points in this exposition are (1) the unfortunate situation of Haskins and his family, revealed partly by their demonstrated dependence at the moment, but mainly by the incorporated narrative (flashback) of their recent trials, (2) the kindness of the Councils, which is not merely reiterated by dramatic demonstrations but is stressed explicitly by both the narrator and by Haskins himself, as in his last speech, and (3) the busy garrulousness of the Councils. The second point is ultimately secondary in importance; the Councils are minor characters in the plot, useful, along with other neighbors, chiefly as foils to set off the villainy of the usurer, Jim Butler. The third point is irrelevant, except as a "life-like" detail to give the Councils and their kindness additional vividness.

This does not mean that the scene is not well-integrated or that it fails to function effectively. It serves to focus a strong suspense on behalf of Haskins: will he be able to justify the kindness that is shown to him here? How he meets this challenge in following scenes is crucial in magnifying the bitterness of his ultimate betrayal by Jim Butler. Yet, by later standards, the evocation of suspense is slow and laborious, requiring further development in subsequent scenes. It is only a contributing element in the more fundamental suspense as to whether Haskins will get on his feet; it could presumably be developed much more swiftly and economically than it is here.

APPENDIX G   A SCENE FROM "THE TEACHER"

◇◇

The climactic scene from Anderson's "The Teacher" is reproduced in full to show how a scenic quality is retained in narrative through the use of particular incidents, although only the climactic verbal acts are actually quoted. (See p. 297.)

On the night of the storm and while the minister sat in the church waiting for her, Kate Smith went to the office of the *Winesburg Eagle,* intending to have another talk with the boy. After the long walk in the snow she was cold, lonely, and tired. As she came through Main Street she saw the light from the print shop window shining on the snow and on an impulse opened the door and went in. For an hour she sat by the stove in the office talking of life. She talked with passionate earnestness. The impulse that had driven her out into the snow poured itself out into talk. She became inspired as she sometimes did in the presence of the children in school. A great eagerness to open the door of life to the boy, who had been her pupil and whom she thought might possess a talent for the understanding of life, had possession of her. So strong was her passion that it became something physical. Again her hands took hold of his shoulders and she turned him about. In the dim light her eyes blazed. She arose and laughed, not sharply as was customary with her, but in a queer, hesitating way. "I must be going," she said. "In a moment, if I stay, I'll be wanting to kiss you."

In the newspaper office a confusion arose. Kate Swift turned and walked to the door. She was a teacher but she was also a woman. As she looked at George Willard, the passionate desire to be loved by a man, that had a thousand times before swept like a storm over her body, took possession of her. In the lamplight George Willard looked no longer a boy, but a man ready to play the part of a man.

The school teacher let George Willard take her into his arms. In the warm little office the air became suddenly heavy and the strength went out of her body. Leaning against a low counter by the door she waited. When he came and put a hand on her shoulder she turned and let her body fall heavily against him. For George Willard the confusion was immediately increased. For a moment he held the body of the woman tightly against his body and then it stiffened. Two sharp little fists began to beat on his face. When the school teacher had run away and left him alone, he walked up and down in the office swearing furiously.

APPENDIX H A SCENE FROM "THE DOCTOR AND THE DOCTOR'S WIFE"

The climactic scene from Hemingway's "The Doctor and the Doctor's Wife" is reproduced to illustrate how coherence is retained in a fully dramatized scene in which, nevertheless, every speech not only reveals but increases the tension between the characters.

In the cottage the doctor, sitting on the bed in his room, saw a pile of medical journals on the floor by the bureau. They were still in their wrappers unopened. It irritated him.

"Aren't you going back to work, dear?" asked the doctor's wife from the room where she was lying with the blinds drawn.

"No!"

"Was anything the matter?"

"I had a row with Dick Boulton."

"Oh," said his wife. "I hope you didn't lose your temper, Henry."

"No," said the doctor.

"Remember, that he who ruleth his spirit is greater than he that taketh a city, said his wife. She was a Christian Scientist. Her Bible, her copy of *Science and Health* and her *Quarterly* were on a table beside her bed in the darkened room.

Her husband did not answer. He was sitting on his bed now, cleaning a shotgun. He pushed the magazine full of the heavy yellow shells and pumped them out again. They were scattered on the bed.

"Henry," his wife called. Then paused a moment. "Henry!"

"Yes," the doctor said.

"You didn't say anything to Boulton to anger him, did you?"

"No," said the doctor.

"What was the trouble about, dear?"

"Nothing much."

"Tell me, Henry. Please don't try and keep anything from me. What was the trouble about?

"Well, Dick owes me a lot of money for pulling his squaw through pneumonia and I guess he wanted a row so he wouldn't have to take it out in work."

His wife was silent. The doctor wiped his gun carefully with a rag. He pushed the shells back in against the spring of the magazine. He sat with the gun on his knees. He was very fond of it. Then he heard his wife's voice from the darkened room.

"'Dear, I don't think, I really don't think that any one would really do a thing like that."

"No?" the doctor said.

"No. I can't really believe that any one would do a thing of that sort intentionally."

The doctor stood up and put the shotgun in the corner behind the dresser.

"Are you going out, dear?" his wife said.

"I think I'll go for a walk," the doctor said.

"If you see Nick, dear, will you tell him his mother wants to see him?" his wife said.

The doctor went out on the porch. The screen door slammed behind him. He heard his wife catch her breath when the door slammed.

"Sorry," he said, outside her window with the blinds drawn.

"It's all right, dear," she said.

In this scene even the reference to Nick is more than a merely "lifelike" detail. It is significant because, just a few lines later, the doctor allows Nick to come squirrel hunting with him instead of going to his mother as requested. It prepares, thus, for the doctor's one act of defiance of his wife.

APPENDIX I THE CHRONOLOGY OF "IN ANOTHER COUNTRY"

◇◇

The chronology of Hemingway's "In Another Country" can be traced as follows (see comment, p. 318):

In the first two paragraphs the narrator is interested only in how it feels to go to the hospital with his friends in the fall when they are no longer going to the war. At this point his relations with them are merely cordial: "there we met every afternoon and were all very polite and interested in what was the matter, and sat in the machines that were to make so much difference." He is interested in the machines, but doubtful of their efficacy, as indicated in the scene with the doctor which follows, after which he realizes that the major in the next machine is even more doubtful. In the following account of his walks back from the hospital with the others, there is no specific indication that this is a later period of time, but we see that he knows the others better than before. More important, he is becoming aware that he and his friends are cut off from people in the town because they are officers; this emerges casually in the course of what looks like an account of routine everyday action: "We walked the short way through the communist quarter because we were four together. The people hated us because we were officers, and from a wineshop some one called out, 'A basso gli ufficiali!' as we passed. Another boy who walked with us sometimes and made us five wore a black silk handkerchief across his face because he had no nose then and his face was to be rebuilt."

The next "event" in the sequence is his growing awareness of his separation from the other officers as well: "The boys at first were very polite about my medals . . . [but after they learned] that I had been given the medals because I was an American . . . their manner changed a little toward me, although I was their friend against outsiders." This culminates in his discovery that he is no "hunting hawk," whereupon he turns back to the major who does not "believe in bravery," with whom he has the bond of lessons in Italian grammar. The major, we realize indirectly, is more sophisticated about life than the "hunting hawks," and for a brief interval the hero seems to derive comfort from him. Then comes the crucial incident where he makes the final discovery. The chronology of the incident itself is very clear, but it is introduced in a very casual way: "There was a time when none of us believed in the machines, and one day the major said it was all nonsense. The machines were new then and it was we who were to prove them. It was an idiotic idea, he said 'a theory, like another.' I had not learned my grammar, and he said I was a stupid impossible disgrace, and he was a fool to have bothered with me. He was a small man and he sat straight up in his chair with his right hand thrust into the machine and looked straight ahead at the wall while the straps thumped up and down with his fingers in them. 'What will you do when the war is over if it is over?' he asked me. 'Speak gramatically!' "

This is the beginning of a scene in which the major breaks into an angry harangue and warning against marriage because if a man " 'is to lose everything, he should not place himself in a position to lose that.' " The major's distress is rendered dramatically, followed by his apology and explanation (the death of his wife, and his outcry, " 'I cannot resign myself.' "). The final description suggests indirectly the final stage of the hero's discovery — his realization of the inevitability (or incurability?) of loss and pain even for those who have outgrown a belief in bravery, with a sense of his own total inexperience of such rigors: "The major did not come back to the hospital for three days. Then he came at the usual hour, wearing a black band on the sleeve of his uniform. When he came back, there were large framed photographs around the wall, of all sorts of wounds before and after they had been cured by the machines. In front of the machine the major used were three photographs of hands like his that were completely restored. I do not know where the doctor got them. I always understood we were the first to use the machines. The photographs did not make much difference to the major because he only looked out of the window."

APPENDIX J   AN ARGUMENT FROM "THE LONG RUN"

◇◇

Some of the arguments used by Paulina Trant, in Mrs. Wharton's "The Long Run," in trying to persuade Merrick to elope with her are here quoted from the crucial scene between the two, as narrated by Merrick to the narrator (see p. 340):

" 'You think I'm beside myself — raving? (You're not thinking of your-self, I know.) I'm not: I never was saner. Since I've known you I've often thought this might happen. This thing between us isn't an ordinary thing. If it had been we shouldn't, all these month, have drifted. We should have wanted to skip to the last page — and then throw down the book. We shouldn't have felt we could *trust* the future as we did. We were in no hurry because we knew we shouldn't get tired; and when two people feel that about each other they must live together — or part. I don't see what else they can do. A little trip along the coast won't answer. It's the high seas — or else being tied up to Lethe wharf. And I'm for the high seas, my dear!'

" . . . 'I'm not talking, dear ——' I see her now, leaning toward me with shining eyes: 'I'm not talking of the people who haven't enough to fill their days, and to whom a little mystery, a little manoeuvring, gives an illusion of importance that they can't afford to miss; I'm talking of you and me, with all our tastes and curiosities and activities; and I ask you what our love would become if we had to keep it apart from our lives, like a pretty useless animal that we went to peep at and feed with sweet-meats through its cage?'

" . . . 'Remember, I'm not attempting to lay down any general rule,' she insisted; 'I'm not theorizing about Man and Woman, I'm talking about you and me. How do I know what's best for the woman in the next house? Very likely she'll bolt when it would have been better for her to stay at home. And it's the same with the man: he'll probably do the wrong thing. It's generally the weak heads that commit follies, when it's the strong ones that ought to: and my point is that you and I are both strong enough to behave like fools if we want to . . . .'

" 'Take your own case first — because, in spite of the sentimentalists, it's the man who stands to lose most. You'll have to give up the Iron Works: which you don't much care about — because it won't be particularly agree-able for us to live in New York: which you don't care much about either. But you won't be sacrificing what is called "a career." You made up your mind long ago that your best chance of self-development, and con-sequently of general usefulness, lay in thinking rather than doing; and, when we first met, you were already planning to sell out your business, and travel and write. Well! Those ambitions are of a kind that won't be harmed by your dropping out of your social setting. On the contrary, such work as you want to do ought to gain by it, because you'll be brought nearer to life-as-it-is, in contrast to life-as-a-visiting-list . . . .'

"She threw back her head with a sudden laugh. 'And the joy of not having any more visits to make! I wonder if you've ever thought of *that*? Just at first, I mean; for society's getting so deplorably lax that, little by litte, it will edge up to us — you'll see! I don't want to idealize the situ-ation, dearest, and I won't conceal from you that in time we shall be called on. But, oh, the fun we shall have had in the interval! And then, for the first time we shall be able to dictate our own terms, one of which will be that no bores need apply. Think of being cured of all one's chronic bores! We shall feel as jolly as people do after a successful operation.' "

APPENDIX K   A SCENE FROM
"AN AWAKENING"

◇◇

The following scene from Anderson's "An Awakening" typifies the technique of dramatizing thought by use of explicit summaries and direct and indirect quotations, all of which are particulars in a larger state of mind whose precise nature is left to inference (see p. 349). Omitted are some physical descriptions of the changing Winesburg scene through which George walks. These descriptions should of course be calculated among the things which produce the total picture of George's state of mind, but they can be omitted here for the sake of brevity:

Hypnotized by his own words, the young man stumbled along the board sidewalk saying more words. "There is a law for armies and for men too," he muttered, lost in reflection. "The law begins with little things and spreads out until it covers everything. In every little thing there must be order, in the place where men work, in their clothes, in their thoughts. I myself must be orderly. I must learn that law. I must get myself into touch with something orderly and big that swings through the night like a star. In my little way I must begin to learn something, to give and swing and work with life, with the law."

George Willard stopped by a picket fence near a street lamp and his body began to tremble. He had never before thought such thoughts as had just come into his head and he wondered where they had come from. For the moment it seemed to him that some voice outside of himself had been talking as he walked. He was amazed and delighted with his own mind and when he walked on again spoke of the matter with fervor. "To come out of Ransom Surbeck's pool room and think things like that," he whispered. "It is better to be alone. If I talked like Art Wilson the boys would understand me but they wouldn't understand what I've been thinking down here."

. . . In the scene that lay about him there was something that excited his already aroused fancy. For a year he had been devoting all of his odd moments to the reading of books and now some tale he had read concerning life in old world towns of the middle ages came sharply back to his mind so that he stumbled forward with the curious feeling of one revisiting a place that had been a part of some former existence . . . .

For a half hour he stayed in the alleyway, smelling the strong smell of animals too closely housed and letting his mind play with the strange new thoughts that came to him. The very rankness of the smell of manure in the clear sweet air awoke something heady in his brain. The poor little houses lighted by kerosene lamps, the smoke from the chimneys . . . all of these things made him seem, as he lurked in the darkness, oddly detached and apart from all life.

The excited young man, unable to bear the weight of his own thoughts, began to move cautiously along the alleyway . . . . George went into a vacant lot and throwing back his head looked up at the sky. He felt unutterably big and remade by the simple experience through which he had been passing and in a kind of fervor of emotion put up his hands, thrusting them into the darkness above his head and muttering words. The desire to say words overcame him and he said words without meaning, rolling them over on his tongue and saying them because they were brave words, full of meaning. "Death," he muttered, "night, the sea, fear, loveliness."

George Willard came out of the vacant lot and stood again on the sidewalk facing the houses. He felt that all of the people in the little street must be brothers and sisters to him and he wished he had the courage to call them out of their houses and to shake their hands. "If there were only a woman here I would take hold of her hand and we would run until we were both tired out," he thought. "That would make me feel better." With the thought of a woman in his mind he walked out of the street and went toward the house where Belle Carpenter lived. He thought she would understand his mood and that he could achieve in her presence a position he had long been wanting to achieve. In the past when he had been with her and had kissed her lips he had come away filled with anger at himself. He had felt like one being used for some obscure purpose and had not enjoyed the feeling. Now he thought he had suddenly become too big to be used.

The scene is not complete without pointing out the change in the words George mutters in the air when he has gone to Belle Carpenter and has taken her out to walk: "Lust," he whispered, "lust and night and women."

APPENDIX L   THE USE OF SENSATIONS

◇◇◇

The following passages, like that by Hemingway quoted on page 352, illustrate the characteristic use of sensations, visual and otherwise, as stimuli to emotions which the reader must infer (see p. 350). The first is from Hemingway's "Cross-Country Snow":

He climbed the steep road with the skis on his shoulder, kicking his heel nails into the icy footing. He heard George breathing and kicking in his heels just behind him. They stacked the skis against the side of the inn and slapped the snow off each other's trousers, stamped their boots clean, and went in.

Inside it was quite dark. A big porcelain stove shone in the corner of the room. There was a low ceiling. Smooth benches back of dark, wine-stained tables were along each side of the rooms. Two Swiss sat over their pipes and two decies of cloudy new wine next to the stove. The boys took off their jackets and sat against the wall on the other side of the stove. A voice in the next room stopped singing and a girl in a blue apron came in through the door to see what they wanted to drink.

"A bottle of Sion," Nick said. "Is that all right, Gidge?"

"Sure," said George. "You know more about wine than I do. I like any of it."

The girl went out.

"There's nothing really can touch skiing, is there?" Nick said. "The way it feels when you first drop off on a long run."

"Huh," said George. "It's too swell to talk about."

Though the last two speeches are not part of the delineation through sensation, they help to emphasize, now by an external *sign*, Nick's feeling of pleasure *after* skiing, which involves the conscious recollection of the skiing itself. George's comment, incidentally, is illuminating as to Hemingway's method.

The following two passages, by Stephen Crane, typify the limit which was reached in the early period in anticipating such a use of sensations in the twenties. One is the famous beginning of "The Open Boat":

None of them knew the colour of the sky. Their eyes glanced level, and were fastened upon the waves that swept toward them. These waves were of a hue of slate, save for the tops, which were of foaming white, and all of the men knew the colours of the sea. The horizon narrowed and widened, and dipped and rose, and at all times its edge was jagged with waves that seemed thrust up in points like rocks.

The following is from "An Experiment in Misery." The effect of these perceptions upon the hero is left almost entirely to inference:

And all through the room could be seen the tawny hues of naked flesh, limbs thrust into the darkness, projecting beyond the cots; upreared knees, arms hanging long and thin over the cot-edges. For the most part they were statuesque, carven, dead. With the curious lockers standing all about like tombstones, there was a strange effect of a graveyard where bodies were merely flung.

Yet occasionally could be seen limbs wildly tossing in fatalistic nightmare gestures, accompanied by guttural cries, grunts, oaths. And there was one fellow off in a gloomy corner, who in his dreams was oppressed by some frightful calamity, for of a sudden he began to utter long wails that went almost like yells from a hound, echoing wailfully and weird through this chill place of tombstones where man lay like the dead.

The resemblance of the room to a graveyard is a perception by the hero like his other perceptions. What it means to his state of mind is not made explicit.

APPENDIX M   INFERENCES CONCERNING THOUGHT AND FEELING

◇◇

Some major inferences as to thought or feeling are required in the stories listed below. The nature of the inference can be suggested by a question which the story's treatment raises and which is not answered in explicit terms (see p. 355).

In the early period:

Bierce — "Affair at Coulter's Notch," "A Horseman in the Sky," "One Kind of Officer": In each case, how much horror does the hero feel in the act which he commits?

Freeman — "Live-Everlasting": What process of reasoning leads the heroine from John Gleason to Jesus Christ? (See p. 194. A purely intellectual inference is required here.) "A Poetess": How does the heroine's deathbed experience satisfy her frustrated artistic ego?

Garland — "Mrs. Ripley's Trip" and "Uncle Ethan Ripley": Does not Mrs. Ripley love her husband more than she admits?

Crane — "An Episode of War": What are the hero's unexpressed feelings about his injury? "An Experiment in Misery": What does the hero's experience with the bums of the Bowery mean to him? "Five White Mice": What does the hero's unexpectedly easy escape from death mean to him? "The Little Regiment": Do not the brothers really love each other? "A Mystery of Heroism": Whence comes the hero's irrational bravado?

Wharton — "The Other Two": What does the hero's laugh at the end signify? What does he feel in giving up his struggle?

Dreiser — "Married": What feeling, tender or otherwise, accompanies the hero's discovery that he must always be reassuring his wife of his love? "Old Rogaum": What unconscious feeling accounts for Theresa's restlessness?

Gerould — "The Miracle": Whence comes the heroine's burgeoning of maternal feeling for her stepson? (Note: in Mrs. Gerould's "Pearls" and "The Dominant Strain," similar questions are explicitly raised by the narrator. How great was the man's passion in each case? They are a way of making virtually explicit the fact that the passion depicted was astonishingly obsessive, a point fully implicit in the action itself.)

James — "Europe": What is the explanation of the old lady's inconsistent attitude towards her daughters' traveling? "Miss Gunton of Poughkeepsie": How much of the heroine's inconsistent attitudes are sincere, how much are sham? "The Marriages": What does the heroine discover as a result of the other woman's revelation?

In the twenties: Anderson — "Adventure": What is the cause of the heroine's unconscious eruption? "An Awakening": See Appendix K and pp. 349 ff. "The Door of the Trap": What feeling causes the hero's decision? "Drink": What is the source of fantasy? "I Want to Know Why": Why is the boy so extremely disturbed? "The Man Who Became a Woman": What is the source of the hero's fear? What is its true nature? "The

New Englander": What causes the eruption in the corn field? "Nobody
Knows": see p. 348. "Paper Pills": How deep was Reefy's grief? "The
Philosopher": What feeling causes the hero's final remarks? "Respectability": What is the source of the hero's rage? "Sophistication": What is
the "thing" that George and Helen, like "mature people," have discovered? "The Strength of God": What is the source of the initial impulse?
What is the cause of its dissipation? "The Teacher": What is the nature
of Kate Swift's repression? "The Thinker": What is the emotion felt in
the scene with Helen?

Fitzgerald — "Absolution": What is the source of the priest's madness?
"The Rough Crossing": What is the unconscious feeling shared by the
couple?

Hemingway — "An Alpine Idyll": What is discovered? "The Battler":
What is discovered? "Big Two-Hearted River": See p. 353. What is being
evaded? "Cat in the Rain": What is the source of the heroine's restlessness? "Cross-Country Snow": See Appendix D. "The Doctor and the Doctor's Wife": What is the nature of the doctor's anger? What is his feeling
toward his wife? "The End of Something": What is the reason for Nick's
decision? "Hills Like White Elephants": What is the feeling of the heroine at the end of the story? "In Another Country": What is the nature of
the discovery? "Indian Camp": What is the nature of the discovery? "My
Old Man": What is the boy's reaction to the discovery? "Now I Lay Me":
What is the source of the illness? "Out of Season": What is the reason
for the decision? What is the feeling toward the wife? "A Pursuit Race":
What feeling is the hero concealing? "The Revolutionist": What feelings
are concealed? "Soldier's Home": What is the source of the soldier's
apathy? "Ten Indians": What is the boy's true attitude toward the jilting?
"Three-Day Blow": What are Nick's real feelings about Marge? "Up in
Michigan": What are the heroine's real feelings about Joe? "A Very Short
Story": What are the hero's real feelings about being jilted?

Porter — "The Cracked Looking-Glass": What are the heroine's real
feelings about her husband and the possibility of a younger lover? "Flowering Judas": What does the dream mean, in itself, and to the heroine?
"He": What are the mother's real feelings toward her son? "The Jilting
of Granny Weatherall": What unconscious feelings account for Granny's
distress? "Maria Concepcion": What is the nature of the heroine's discovery? "Rope": What is the source of the eruption between the couple?
"That Tree": What are the hero's real feelings at the close? "Theft": What
reasons determine the heroine's final thought?

Faulkner — "All The Dead Pilots": What is the specific cause of Sartoris' frenzy? "Dry September": What are McLendon's unconscious
feelings? How do they account for his actions? "Hair": What are Hawkshaw's true feelings about his wife-to-be? "Mistral": What is the hikers'
discovery? "A Rose for Emily": What is the nature of Emily's passion?

BIBLIOGRAPHY

◇◇

I. The following titles include the volumes from which the canon of short stories were selected, plus a few of the better recent anthologies and a few of the most interesting older anthologies.

ANDERSON, SHERWOOD. *Death in the Woods and Other Stories.* New York: Liveright, 1933.

———. *Horses and Men: Tales, Long and Short, from Our American Life.* New York: B. W. Huebsch, 1923.

———. *The Triumph of the Egg: A Book of Impressions of American Life in Tales and Poems.* New York: B. W. Huebsch, 1921.

———. *Winesburg, Ohio: A Group of Tales of Ohio Small Town Life.* Introduction by Ernest Boyd. New York: The Modern Library, 1919.

BIERCE, AMBROSE. *In the Midst of Life: Tales of Soldiers and Civilians.* New York: Albert & Charles Boni, 1924 (First published, 1891.)

BREWSTER, DOROTHY (ed.). *A Book of Modern Short Stories.* New York: Macmillan Co., 1928.

CARTMELL, VAN H., AND GRAYSON, CHARLES (eds.). *The Golden Argosy: A Collection of the Most Celebrated Stories in the English Language.* Revised edition. New York: Dial Press, 1955.

CATHER, WILLA. *The Troll Garden.* New York: McClure, Phillips & Co., 1905.

———. *Youth and the Bright Medusa.* New York: Alfred A. Knopf, 1920.

CERF, BENNETT (ed.). *Great Modern Short Stories.* New York: Modern Library, 1942.

CRANE, MILTON (ed.). *50 Great Short Stories.* New York: Bantam Books, 1952.

CRANE, STEPHEN. *Twenty Stories.* Selected with an introduction by Carl Van Doren. New York: Alfred A. Knopf, 1940.

———: *An Omnibus.* Edited by Robert W. Stallman. New York: Alfred A. Knopf, 1952.

DAVIS, ROBERT GORHAM (ed.). *Ten Modern Masters: An Anthology of the Short Story.* Second edition. New York: Harcourt, Brace & Co., 1959.

DREISER, THEODORE. *Free and Other Stories.* New York: Boni & Liveright, 1918.

FAULKNER, WILLIAM. *Collected Stories of William Faulkner.* New York: Random House, 1950.

———. *These 13.* New York: Jonathan Cape & Harrison Smith, 1931.

FITZGERALD, F. SCOTT. *All the Sad Young Men.* New York: Charles Scribner's Sons, 1926.

———. *Flappers and Philosophers.* New York: Charles Scribner's Sons, 1920.

———. *The Stories of F. Scott Fitzgerald: A Selection of 28 Stories.* Introduction by Malcolm Cowley. New York: Charles Scribner's Sons, 1953.

———. *Tales of the Jazz Age.* New York: Charles Scribner's Sons, 1922.

[FREEMAN], MARY E. WILKINS. *A New England Nun and Other Stories.* New York: Harper & Bros., 1891.

GARLAND, HAMLIN. *Main-Travelled Roads.* Border Edition. New York: Harper & Bros., 1899. (Enlarged from first edition, published 1891 by the Arena Publishing Co.)

GEROULD, KATHARINE FULLERTON. *The Great Tradition and Other Stories.* New York: Charles Scribner's Sons, 1915.

HEMINGWAY, ERNEST. *Hemingway.* ("The Viking Portable Library.") Edited by Malcolm Cowley. New York: Viking Press, 1944.

———. *In Our Time.* Introduction by Edmund Wilson. New York: Charles Scribner's Sons, 1930. (First published 1925; New York: Boni & Liveright.)

———. *Men Without Women.* New York: Charles Scribner's Sons, 1927.

————. *The Short Stories of Ernest Hemingway: The First Forty-Nine Stories and the Play* The Fifth Column. New York: The Modern Library, 1938.

JAFFE, ADRIAN H., AND SCOTT, VIRGIL (eds.). *Studies in the Short Story.* New York: William Sloane Associates, 1949.

JOYCE, JAMES. *The Portable James Joyce.* Introduction and notes by Harry Levin. New York: Viking Press, 1947. (Reprints *Dubliners*, first published, 1914.)

LUDWIG, JACK BARRY, AND POIRIER, W. RICHARD (eds.). *Stories: British and American.* Boston: Houghton Mifflin Co., 1953.

MANSFIELD, KATHERINE. *The Garden Party and Other Stories.* New York: Alfred A. Knopf, 1922.

McCLENNEN, JOSHUA (ed.). *Masters and Masterpieces of the Short Story.* New York: Henry Holt & Co., 1957.

O'BRIEN, EDWARD J. (ed.) *The Best Short Stories of 1915 and the Yearbook of the American Short Story.* Boston: Small, Maynard & Co., 1916. (A continuing annual anthology, which after 1926 was published in New York by Dodd, Mead & Company. The series has continued to the present day. Since 1933 it has been published in Boston by Houghton Mifflin Company, and since 1942 it has been edited by Martha Foley.)

PORTER, KATHERINE ANNE. *Flowering Judas and Other Stories.* New York: Harcourt, Brace & Co., 1935.

SHORT, RAYMOND W., AND SEWALL, RICHARD B. (eds.) *Short Stories for Study: An Anthology.* Revised edition. New York: Henry Holt & Co., 1950.

STEGNER, WALLACE AND MARY (eds.). *Great American Short Stories.* Laurel edition. New York: Dell Books, 1957.

WARREN, ROBERT PENN, AND ERSKINE, ALBERT (eds.). *Short Story Masterpieces.* New York: Dell Books, 1954.

WHARTON, EDITH. *The Descent of Man and Other Stories.* New York: Charles Scribner's Sons, 1904.

————. *Xingu and Other Stories.* New York: Charles Scribner's Sons, 1916.

SOCIETY OF ARTS AND SCIENCES [New York]. *O. Henry Memorial Award Prize Stories: 1919.* Introduction by Blanche Colton Williams. Garden City, N.Y.: Doubleday, Page & Co., 1920. (A continuing annual anthology. Beginning with the volume for 1927 the publisher was Doubleday, Doran & Co., and beginning with the volume for 1929 the editorship and selection were attributed to Miss Williams, who remained editor through 1932.)

II. The following volumes deal with the period in a general way or with individual writers, without special emphasis upon the art of the short story. (Works dealing with individual writers in which the short stories are considered in some detail are indicated with an asterisk.) Also included are general histories of the short story.

ALDRIDGE, JOHN W. *After the Lost Generation: A Critical Study of the Writers of Two Wars.* New York: McGraw-Hill Book Co., 1951.

————. *In Search of Heresy: American Literature in an Age of Conformity.* New York: McGraw-Hill Book Co., 1956.

ALLEN, FREDERICK LEWIS. *Only Yesterday.* New York: Harper & Bros., 1931.

BAKER, CARLOS. *Hemingway: The Writer as Artist.* Princeton: Princeton University Press, 1956.

BLAIR, WALTER. "U.S.A.: 1914 to Present," *The Literature of the United States: An Anthology and a History.* Vol. II: *From the Civil War to the Present.* Edited by Walter Blair, Theodore Hornberger, and Randall Stewart. Chicago: Scott, Foresman & Co., 1947, pp. 826–77.

BROOKS, VAN WYCK. *Days of the Phoenix: The Nineteen-Twenties I Remember.* New York: E. P. Dutton & Co., 1957.

BROWN, EDWARD KILLORAN. *Willa Cather: A Critical Biography.*° Completed by Leon Edel. New York: Knopf, 1953.

CANBY, HENRY SEIDEL. *The Short Story in English*. New York: Henry Holt & Co., 1909.

COWLEY, MALCOM. *Exile's Return: A Literary Odyssey of the 1920's*. Revised ed. New York: Viking Press, 1951. (Compass Books edition, 1956. First published, 1934.)

FOSTER, EDWARD. *Mary E. Wilkins Freeman*. New York: Hendricks House, 1956.

GEISMAR, MAXWELL. *The Last of the Provincials: The American Novel, 1915–1925*. Boston: Houghton Mifflin Co., 1947.

——. *Writers in Crisis: The American Novel: 1925–1940*. Boston: Houghton Mifflin Co., 1942.

HOFFMAN, FREDERICK J. *Freudianism and the Literary Mind*. Baton Rouge: Louisiana State University Press, 1945.

——. *The Twenties: American Writing in the Postwar Decade*. New York: Viking Press, 1955.

HOLLOWAY, JEAN. *Hamlin Garland: A Biography*. Austin: University of Texas Press, 1960.

HOWE, IRVING. *Sherwood Anderson.*° ("The American Men of Letters Series.") New York: William Sloane Associates, 1951.

KAZIN, ALFRED. *On Native Grounds: An Interpretation of Modern American Prose Literature*. New York: Reynal & Hitchcock, 1942.

LEVIN, HARRY. *James Joyce: A Critical Introduction*. ("The Makers of Modern Literature.") Norfolk, Conn.: New Directions, 1941.

MIZENER, ARTHUR. *The Far Side of Paradise: A Biography of F. Scott Fitzgerald*. Boston: Houghton Mifflin Co., 1951.

MOONEY, HARRY JOHN. *The Fiction and Criticism of Katherine Anne Porter.*° Pittsburgh: University of Pittsburgh Press, 1957.

O'BRIEN, EDWARD J. *The Advance of the American Short Story*. New York: Dodd, Mead & Co., 1923.

SPILLER, ROBERT E., THORP, WILLARD, JOHNSON, THOMAS H., AND CANBY, HENRY SEIDEL (eds.). *Literary History of the United States*. Revised ed. New York: Macmillan Co., 1953.

TRILLING, LIONEL. *The Liberal Imagination: Essays on Literature and Society*. New York: Viking Press, 1950.

WEST, RAY B., JR. *The Short Story in America: 1900–1950*. ("Twentieth-Century Literature in America.") Chicago: Henry Regnery Co., 1952.

WILSON, EDMUND. *The Shores of Light: A Literary Chronicle of the Twenties and Thirties*. New York: Farrar, Straus & Young, Inc., 1952.

YOUNG, PHILIP. *Ernest Hemingway.*° ("Rinehart Critical Studies.") New York: Rinehart & Co., 1952.

III. The following list includes both significant and characteristic studies of short-story technique in the early period.

ALBRIGHT, EVELYN MAY. *The Short Story: Its Principles and Structure*. New York: Macmillan Co., 1931. (First published, 1907.)

CANBY, HENRY SEIDEL. *The Short Story*. ("Yale Studies in English," Vol. XII.) New York: Henry Holt & Co., 1902.

CROSS, ETHAN ALLEN. *A Book of the Short Story: Selected and Edited, With the History and Technique of the Short Story, Notes and Bibliographies*. New York: American Book Co., 1934.

——. *The Short Story: A Technical and Literary Study*. Chicago. A. C. McClurg & Co., 1914.

GRABO, CARL H. *The Art of the Short Story*. New York: Charles Scribner's Sons, 1913.

MATTHEWS, BRANDER. *The Philosophy of the Short-Story*. New York: Longmans, Green & Co., 1901.

NOTESTEIN, LUCY LILIAN, AND DUNN, WALDO HILARY. *The Modern Short-Story: A Study of the Form: Its Plot, Structure, Development and Other Requirements*. New York: A. S. Barnes Co., 1914.

POE, EDGAR ALLAN. "Hawthorne's 'Tales.'" *The Works of Edgar Allan Poe*. Collected and edited, with a memoir, critical introductions, and notes, by Edmund Clarence Stedman and George Edward Woodbery. Vol. VII, pp. 19–38. Chicago: Stone & Kimball, 1895.

SMITH, C. ALPHONSO. *The American Short Story*. Boston: Ginn & Co., 1912.

IV. The following list includes works celebrated for their examination of short-story techniques from a more modern viewpoint (most of these also include stories for analysis), a few titles that deal with critical methodology from a viewpoint somewhat related to that used in this study, and a few significant titles by the writers in the canon that are illuminating, directly or indirectly, of their techniques.

BATES, H. E. *The Modern Short Story: A Critical Survey*. London: Thomas Nelson & Sons, 1941.

BROOKS, CLEANTH JR., AND WARREN, ROBERT PENN (eds.) *Understanding Fiction*. New York: Appleton-Century-Crofts, 1943. (Second edition, 1959.)

CRANE, R. S., KEAST, W. R., McKEON, RICHARD, MACLEAN, NORMAN, OLSON, ELDER, AND WEINBERG, BERNARD. *Critics and Criticism: Ancient and Modern*. Edited with an introduction by R. S. Crane. Chicago: University of Chicago Press, 1952.

CRANE, R. S. *The Languages of Criticism and the Structure of Poetry*. ("The Alexander Lectures.") Toronto: University of Toronto Press, 1953.

GOODMAN, PAUL. *The Structure of Literature*. Chicago: University of Chicago Press, 1954.

JAMES, HENRY. *The Art of the Novel: Critical Prefaces*. Introduction by Richard P. Blackmur. New York: Charles Scribner's Sons, 1947.

O'FAOLÁIN, SÉAN. *The Short Story*. London: Collins, 1948.

PORTER, KATHERINE ANNE. *The Days Before*. New York: Harcourt, Brace & Co., 1952.

WEST, RAY B., JR., AND STALLMAN, ROBERT WOOSTER. *The Art of Modern Fiction*. New York: Rinehart & Co., 1949.

V. The following bibliographical works are particularly useful to students of the short story.

COOK, DOROTHY E., AND MONRO, ISABEL S. *Short Story Index: An Index to 60,000 Stories in 4,320 Collections*. New York: H. W. Wilson Co., 1953.

MERIWEATHER, JAMES B. *William Faulkner: A Check List*. Princeton: Princeton University Library, 1957.

SAMUELS, LEE. *A Hemingway Check List*. New York: Scribner's, 1951.

SCHWARTZ, EDWARD. *Katherine Anne Porter: A Critical Bibliography*, with an introduction by Robert Penn Warren. New York: New York Public Library, 1953.

THURSTON, JARVIS A., and others. *Short Fiction Criticism: A Checklist of Interpretations Since 1925 of Stories and Novelettes (American, British, Continental) 1800–1958*. Denver: Alan Swallow, 1960.

WILLIAMS, AMOS W., AND STARRETT, VINCENT. *Stephen Crane: A Bibliography*. Glendale, Calif.: John Valentine, Publisher, 1948.

INDEX

◇◇◇

Letters in parentheses following the names of stories in the canon refer to the formal classification provided in Appendix B, pp. 385–90. The symbols used are given below:

C–Objective comedy
Hm–Simple horror, moral
Hs–Simple horror, sympathetic
Mm–Horror modified, moral
Ms–Horror modified, sympathetic
R–Simple romance
RC–Romantic comedy

RP–Romantic pathos
SC–Sympathetic comedy
T–Tragedy
X–Simple caustic
XC–Caustic comedy
XP–Caustic pathos
XR–Caustic romance

ec–episode of choice
ed–episode of discovery
ee–episode of exposure
es–episode of suffering

pc–plot of choice
pd–plot of discovery
pf–plot of changing fortune
s–exposed situation

386; form, 181; listed, 381; subjects, 57, 82, 88, 98, 140
"Adventure" (XP es), analyzed, 231–32; classified, 389; form, 265; listed, 380; subjects, 49, 58, 71, 86, 113, 121, 128, 138, 407; quoted, 113· techniques, 292–93, 325, 360, 407
"Affair at Coulter's Notch, The" (Hm pc), classified, 389; form, 240–41, 244–45, 266; listed, 377; subjects, 35, 45, 59, 116, 407; techniques, 293, 312, 315, 332, 344, 359, 407
"Affair of Outposts, An" (Mm pc), classified, 398; form, 247; listed, 377; subjects, 35, 45, 97; techniques, 332
"After the Race," 272
Aiken, Conrad, 5
Albright, Evelyn May, 20–22, 155
Aldridge, John W., 374–75
"All the Dead Pilots" (RC pc), analyzed, 200–201; classified, 387; form, 200–201, 204, 211–12, 267; listed, 382; quoted, 122; subjects, 35, 38, 47, 49, 57, 71, 88–89, 121–23, 408; techniques, 282, 284, 298, 308, 408
All the Sad Young Men, 5, 381
"Alpine Idyll, An" (Ms ed), analysis of form, 254–56; analysis of narration, 391–93; classified, 390; form, 254–56, 264; listed, 381; quoted, 391–93; subjects, 30, 49, 58, 129, 134–35, 408; techniques, 281, 288, 293, 350, 354, 361, 391–93, 408
"Amanda and Love" (R pf), classified, 386; form, 175; listed, 378; subjects, 31, 61, 67, 81, 108; summarized, 67
Ambassadors, The, 117, 124, 148, 282
"Among the Corn Rows" (RC pf), classified, 387; form, 195; listed, 378; quoted, 37, 314; subjects, 36–37, 52, 68, 71, 82, 98, 103, 107, 109, 147; techniques, 312, 314, 330
ANDERSON, SHERWOOD: choice for canon, 383, 385; forms and effects, 155, 170, 218, 224–25, 239, 263, 267, 269–70; purpose, 15–16, 21, 150; mentioned, 11, 157; reputation, 2–3, 374, 383; stories listed, 380; subjects, 14–16, 18, 26, 28, 30, 39, 52, 63, 88, 134, 140, 142, 151–52, 369; techniques, 297, 304, 306–8, 320, 324, 345. *See also* individual titles
"Araby," 272
Aristotle, 9, 159, 165–66, 219, 226, 260–61, 364, 375

Art of the Novel, The, 19, 22, 282
Austen, Jane, 341
"Autres Temps" (SC pd), classified, 387; form, 190–91, 209; listed, 379; quoted, 104, 300–301, 312, 330–31, 338, 345–46; subjects, 39–40, 51, 56, 59, 104, 111–12, 371; techniques, 300–302, 312, 330–31, 338, 345–46, 354
"Awakening, An" (XR ec), analyzed, 349–50; classified, 388; form, 205, 211; listed, 380; scene quoted, 404–5; subjects, 31, 57, 71, 85, 88–89, 121, 134, 407; techniques, 293, 349–50, 407

"Baby Party, The" (XC ec), classified, 388; form, 214; listed, 381; techniques, 293
Balzac, Honoré de, 15
Bates, H. E., 384
"Battler, The" (Ms ed), classified, 390; form, 250, 254–56; listed, 381; protagonist, 250, 255; subjects, 30–31, 48–49, 99, 109, 121, 129, 134, 408; techniques, 286, 292–93, 408
"Beldonald Holbein, The" (C pc), classified, 387; form, 189–90; listed, 378; quoted, 330; subjects, 51, 53, 106, 144–45; techniques, 330
"Benediction" (XC pc), classified, 388; form, 214, 265; listed, 380; subjects, 49, 57, 78, 85–86, 88–89, 98, 128, 143, 151; techniques, 293, 350
Bergson, Henri, 369
"Bernice Bobs Her Hair" (C pd), classified, 387; form, 192; listed, 380; subjects, 31
Best Short Stories of 1915, The, 4
Best Short Stories of 1925, The, 380
BIERCE, AMBROSE: choice for canon, 11, 382, 384; forms and effects, 170, 193, 218–19, 224, 238–44, 248, 262, 267–68; stories listed, 377; subjects, 14, 26, 35, 39, 45, 62, 97, 112, 114–15, 118; techniques, 276, 291, 300, 307, 312, 315, 332, 358. *See also* individual titles
"Big Two-Hearted River" (R ed), analysis of form, 184–85, 263; analysis of techniques, 352–54; classified, 386; interpretations of, 38, 126; listed, 381; quoted, 352; subjects, 38, 49–50, 123, 126, 144, 408; tech-

most considerable amount of that material."[3] The action can
be subtler than was possible before; characters and their states
of minds can be more complex; so, too, can be the moral and
emotional issues underlying the story — even if, as has been suggested, the intellectual issues of stories in the twenties tend
to be less complex than in the work of some of the early writers.
Subtle and mixed emotional qualities can now be apprehended
dramatically in situations less overtly dramatic. Whole stories
can concentrate on the evocation of delicate shades of feeling
that had previously been restricted characteristically to the
domain of lyric poetry.

A further advantage of the dramatic methods of the twenties
is that they give pleasure by putting the reader to work. Not
only must he exercise his intellectual faculties to grasp inferences, but he must exercise his intuitive faculties, his ability
to respond to suggestions of emotion, as well, for he is obliged
to feel or understand the story intuitively before he can describe
abstractly what it is actually about. He may, indeed, never be
able to tell all the story contains, and yet he may still respond to
it as a moving story. This is appropriate to the subject matter
of the twenties with its emphasis on felt or intuited experiences,
and also insures an emotional participation such as the reader
might lose if the issues were immediately clear to him on the
intellectual level.[4] It is especially appropriate in a story whose
dominant effect includes a caustic or a horrible quality, as in
most stories of the twenties. The effectiveness of such stories
depends to a great extent on the shock that the reader is made
to feel. Since shock, in life as in art, always involves the making
of inferences — a delayed reaction, an astonished perception of

[3] Levin, p. 31.

[4] This point is based on my observation of the effect of these stories. It can
be explained by what appears to be a psychological truth, namely, that the intellectualizing of an emotion tends to dissipate (when it does not conceal) the
emotion. Stories that are too readily grasped intellectually tend to by-pass the
reader's emotions; by leaving essentials to inference, the stories of the twenties
force the reader to participate emotionally if he is to understand at all.

This does not mean, of course, that when the reader has finally made the
necessary inference the power of the story disappears. As noted elsewhere,
the intellectualizing process contributes to the catharsis. It remains a part of the
story's effect in the same sense that fear and hope are evoked by tragedies like
"Othello" on the tenth reading as on first.

more evil or horror in a situation than first had met the eye — it is intensified in any story that makes exceptional use of such inferences.

The technical advances may perhaps also assist the writers of the twenties in their desire, noted in Chapter I, to depict "truth." For though a dramatic treatment by no means insures a "truthful" invention by the author, the objectivity of manner that it imposes at least forbids the writer from attempting in his own person to veil any falsehood in his invention. By not telling us whether the doctor in "The Doctor and the Doctor's Wife" should be regarded as laughable or pitiable — by letting his portrayal speak for itself — Hemingway avoids an otherwise almost inescapable esthetic falsehood: that of either trying to make us judge too narrowly the moral complexity of the action or of upsetting the delicate balance in the story by introducing the kind of detailed analysis that would be needed to formulate this complexity on the intellectual level.

Yet it would seem incorrect to characterize this development in the twenties as (in O'Brien's words) a "technical revolt." [5] The quest for more economically dramatic methods is a feature of the entire history of the modern short story. In stories of the early period the careful preparation for and handling of dramatic scenes is evidence of great concern with technical development — as is also the proliferation of studies and textbooks of the art of the short story. Though the writers of the twenties rejected certain stereotyped practices, both technical and formal, their motive was clearly not so much to reject as to carry further the earlier writers' search for dramatic economy.

[5] O'Brien, *Advance*, p. 247.